Offshoring and Working Conditions in Remote Work

The International Labour Organization

The International Labour Organization was founded in 1919 to promote social justice and, thereby, to contribute to universal and lasting peace. Its tripartite structure is unique among agencies affiliated to the United Nations; the ILO's Governing Body includes representatives of government, and of employers' and workers' organizations. These three constituencies are active participants in regional and other meetings sponsored by the ILO, as well as in the International Labour Conference – a world forum which meets annually to discuss social and labour questions.

Over the years the ILO has issued for adoption by member States a widely respected code of international labour Conventions and Recommendations on freedom of association, employment, social policy, conditions of work, social security, industrial relations and labour administration, among others.

The ILO provides expert advice and technical assistance to member States through a network of offices and multidisciplinary teams in over 40 countries. This assistance takes the form of labour rights and industrial relations counselling, employment promotion, training in small business development, project management, advice on social security, workplace safety and working conditions, the compiling and dissemination of labour statistics, and workers' education.

Other recent publications by ILO and Palgrave Macmillan:

BLUNTING NEOLIBERALISM: TRIPARTISM AND ECONOMIC REFORMS IN THE DEVELOPING WORLD (*edited by Lydia Fraile*)

BUILDING DECENT SOCIETIES: RETHINKING THE ROLE OF SOCIAL SECURITY IN DEVELOPMENT (*edited by Peter Townsend*)

INTERNATIONAL AND COMPARATIVE LABOUR LAW (*by Arturo Bronstein*)

IN DEFENCE OF LABOUR MARKET INSTITUTIONS: CULTIVATING JUSTICE IN THE DEVELOPING WORLD (*edited by Janine Berg and David Kucera*)

MICROFINANCE AND PUBLIC POLICY: OUTREACH, PERFORMANCE AND EFFICIENCY (*edited by Bernd Balkenhol*)

GLOBALIZATION, EMPLOYMENT AND INCOME DISTRIBUTION IN DEVELOPING COUNTRIES (*edited by Eddy Lee and Marco Vivarelli*)

UNDERSTANDING GLOBALIZATION, EMPLOYMENT AND POVERTY REDUCTION (*edited by Eddy Lee and Marco Vivarelli*)

Offshoring and Working Conditions in Remote Work

Edited by

Jon C. Messenger
Senior Research Officer, International Labour Office

and

Naj Ghosheh
Research Officer, International Labour Office

© International Labour Organization 2010

The designations employed in ILO publications, which are in conformity with United Nations practice, and the presentation of material therein do not imply the expression of any opinion whatsoever on the part of the International Labour Office concerning the legal status of any country, area or territory or of its authorities, or concerning the delimitation of its frontiers.

The responsibility for opinions expressed in signed articles, studies and other contributions rests solely with their authors, and publication does not constitute an endorsement by the International Labour Office of the opinions expressed in them.

Reference to names of firms and commercial products and processes does not imply their endorsement by the International Labour Office, and any failure to mention a particular firm, commercial product or process is not a sign of disapproval.

First published 2010 by
PALGRAVE MACMILLAN

Palgrave Macmillan in the UK is an imprint of Macmillan Publishers Limited, registered in England, company number 785998, of Houndmills, Basingstoke, Hampshire RG21 6XS.

Palgrave Macmillan in the US is a division of St Martin's Press LLC, 175 Fifth Avenue, New York, NY 10010.

Palgrave Macmillan is the global academic imprint of the above companies and has companies and representatives throughout the world.

Palgrave® and Macmillan® are registered trademarks in the United States, the United Kingdom, Europe and other countries.

ISBN-13: 978–0–230–24886–1 hardback
ILO ISBN: 978–92–2–123001–4

This book is printed on paper suitable for recycling and made from fully managed and sustained forest sources. Logging, pulping and manufacturing processes are expected to conform to the environmental regulations of the country of origin.

A catalogue record for this book is available from the British Library.

A catalog record for this book is available from the Library of Congress.

10   9   8   7   6   5   4   3   2   1
19 18 17 16 15 14 13 12 11 10

Printed and bound in Great Britain by
CPI Antony Rowe, Chippenham and Eastbourne

Contents

List of Tables, Charts and Boxes   viii

Preface   xii

Acknowledgements   xvi

Notes on Contributors   xviii

List of Abbreviations   xx

1 Introduction   1
Jon C. Messenger and Naj Ghosheh

  1.1 Rationales for outsourcing and offshoring business
      services   3
  1.2 Potential impacts of offshoring and outsourcing
      on working and employment conditions   8
  1.3 Origins of outsourcing and offshoring in the services
      sector   9
  1.4 Business start-up and government follow-up:
      The emergence of ITES–BPO in developing countries   12
  1.5 The focus of the book   14

**2 Remote Work from the Perspective of Developed Economies:
A Multicountry Synthesis**   17
Philip Taylor

  2.1 Introduction   17
  2.2 Global Service Delivery   18
  2.3 Multinational Service Companies   19
  2.4 Global 'Captive' Companies   20
  2.5 Indian Companies   21
  2.6 Unevenness of Global Sourcing   22
  2.7 Linguistic Capability and Cultural Compatibility   23
  2.8 Underlying Economic, Geographical
      and Locational Dynamics   25
  2.9 'Taylorism' Through Relocation and 'Rising
      Up the Value Chain'   26
  2.10 Political Economy, Global Regulation and Governance   27
  2.11 Labour   29
  2.12 Offshoring, Nearshoring and Onshoring   30

2.13 United States   32
2.14 United Kingdom   41
2.15 Canada   51
2.16 Conclusions   56

3 Employee Dilemmas in the Indian ITES–BPO Sector   60
Premilla D'Cruz and Ernesto Noronha

3.1   Introduction   60
3.2   Research Methodology   61
3.3   The Indian ITES–BPO Sector   63
3.4   Profiling the Indian ITES–BPO Workforce   71
3.5   Recruitment and Training   75
3.6   Work Systems   79
3.7   Work–Life Balance   89
3.8   Human Resources Practices   91
3.9   Attrition   94
3.10 Collectivization and Union Formation   95
3.11 Conclusions   99
3.12 Recommendations   99

4 Offshored Work in Philippine BPOs   101
Maragtas S.V. Amante

4.1   Introduction and Objectives   101
4.2   Business Environment in the BPO Industry   102
4.3   Research Methodology   103
4.4   Overview of the Labour Market   104
4.5   The BPO Employers   105
4.6   Employee Characteristics   106
4.7   Education   107
4.8   Work Experience   108
4.9   Recruitment and Training   109
4.10 Legal and Regulatory Framework   109
4.11 Working and Employment Conditions   112
4.12 Conclusions   130

5 Remote Work in Brazil   135
Selma Venco

5.1   Introduction and Objectives   135
5.2   Research Methodology   135
5.3   The Business Environment for Outsourcing and
      Offshoring ITES Functions   137
5.4   The Labour Market in Brazil   140

5.5   The Labour Law in Brazil   143
5.6   The BPO Industry in Brazil   145
5.7   Working and Employment Conditions in the BPO
       Industry in Brazil   147
5.8   The Financial Services Industry in Brazil   148
5.9   The Telecommunications Industry   149
5.10   Call Centres and Customer Service Centres in Brazil   150
5.11   Conclusions   159

6   **Remote Work and Global Sourcing in Argentina**   **162**
    Andrés López, Daniela Ramos and Iván Torre

6.1   Methodology Used for This Study   164
6.2   Recent Trends in Trade in Services in Argentina   165
6.3   Working Conditions and Employment in Light of the
       New Trends in Services Exports in Argentina   174
6.4   Conclusions   191
       Annex: Interviews Conducted for This Chapter   193

7   **A Comparative Analysis of the Business Environment, Job**
    Quality and Work Organization in Offshored Business
    Services   **196**
    Jon C. Messenger and Naj Ghosheh

7.1   Introduction   196
7.2   Global, National and Organizational Environments of
       BPO Companies   197
7.3   An Analysis of Job Quality in RWAs   209
7.4   Conclusion: Summary of Job Quality in the BPO Industry   233

8   **Conclusion: Implications for Government Policies**
    and Company Practices   **236**
    Jon C. Messenger and Naj Ghosheh

8.1   Introduction   236
8.2   Key Factors Affecting Employment Conditions and
       Possible Responses   238
8.3   Concluding Remarks   244

Bibliography   246

Index   260

List of Tables, Charts and Boxes

Tables

1.1 The Outsourcing and Offshoring Decision: Organizational Results   5

2.1 Numbers of US Agent Positions, Agents and Contact Centres (2004–2006)   33

2.2 The UK Contact Centre Industry – Agent Positions and Employment (1995–2004)   43

2.3 Canadian Contact Centre Agent Positions/Agent Numbers (2004–2010)   52

3.1 Indian ITES–BPO Export Revenues   63

3.2 Indian ITES–BPO Employment Levels   67

3.3 Age of ITES–BPO Employees   71

3.4 Total Work Experience in any Sector/Organization, in the ITES–BPO Sector and in their Current Organization   72

3.5 Education Level of ITES–BPO Employees and Their Parents   73

3.6 Monthly Salary of ITES–BPO Employees   74

3.7 Perspectives of Managers on Sources of ITES–BPO Sector Recruitment ($n = 171$)   76

3.8 Perspectives of Managers on Criteria for ITES–BPO Employee Selection   77

3.9 Perspectives of Managers on Employee Selection Tools for the ITES–BPO Sector ($n = 169$)   78

3.10 Types of Training Given to ITES–BPO Employees   79

3.11 Overtime Rates Paid to ITES–BPO Employees   81

3.12 Perspectives of Employees and Managers on ITES–BPO Employees' Job-Related Discretion   83

3.13 Various Methods of Monitoring and Surveillance Used in ITES–BPO Employer Organizations According to Employees and Managers   85

3.14 Perspectives of Managers on Factors Influencing ITES–BPO Employees' Career Advancement ($n = 195$)   86

3.15 Perspectives of Managers on Performance Incentives Used in Indian ITES–BPO Employer Organizations ($n = 194$)   87

3.16 Types of Disciplinary Actions Used by ITES–BPO Managers and Employer Organizations According to Managers   88

3.17 Degree of Work-Related Pressure Faced by ITES-BPO
      Employees   89
3.18 ITES-BPO Employees Who Never Experienced Disruption of
      Nonwork Due to Work   90
3.19 Health Problems Faced By ITES–BPO Employees ($n = 249$)   91
3.20 Facilities Provided by ITES–BPO Employer Organizations to
      Their Employees   92
3.21 Satisfaction of ITES–BPO Employees with Working
      Conditions ($n = 725$)   93
3.22 Satisfaction of ITES–BPO Employees with Various Aspects of
      Work Life   93
3.23 Avenues for Grievance Redressal for ITES–BPO Employees
      ($n = 726$)   94
3.24 ITES–BPO Employees' Descriptions of the HR Department
      within Their Employer Organization ($n = 725$)   94
3.25 Perspectives of Employees and Managers on Reasons Behind
      ITES–BPO Employees' Desire to Quit Their Current Employer
      Organization   96
3.26 Perspectives of Managers on the Desirability of Unions in
      the Indian ITES–BPO Sector ($n = 37$)   97
3.27 Reasons for ITES–BPO Employees Wanting Unions   97
3.28 Reasons for ITES–BPO Employees Not Joining a Union   98
4.1   Growth of Philippine BPO Firms (2000–2009)   105
4.2   Philippine BPO Firms in the Survey Sample   106
4.3   Average Age of Employee Respondents (years)   107
4.4   How Long Do You Plan to Continue Work in BPO?
      (by work shift)   108
4.5   Average Monthly Pay of BPO Employees   112
4.6   Typical Monthly Pay of BPO Employees and Managers   113
4.7   A College Degree Matters for Pay of BPO Employees   114
4.8   Average Pay: Work in BPO Is First Job or Not   115
4.9   Simple Regression Analysis of BPO Employees' Pay   115
4.10 Operational Performance in Sample BPO Firms   121
5.1   Simulation of Operational Costs per Year (in US $)   139
5.2   Workers in Telecommunications (in thousands)   149
6.1   Argentina Services Exports (2000–2007)   166
6.2   Other Business Services Exports by Destination
      (2000–2007)   167
6.3   Computer and Information Services Exports by Destination
      (2000–2007)   167
6.4   Global Service Location Index (2007) (in index numbers)   169
6.5   SIS Sector Statistics in 'Late'-Entry Countries (2006) (or last
      available year)   171
6.6   Employment Structure in Argentina (2nd Quarter 2006)   177

6.7   Salaries and Employment in the Services Export Sector
      (sample of representative large firms)   181
6.8   Average Workforce in the Services Export Sector (2005 and
      2007) (sample of representative large firms)   182
7.1   Characteristics of the Global BPO Workforce (by country)   200
7.2   Job Quality Elements for the Call Centre Context   212
7.3   Comparison of Average Annual Wages per Agent Among
      BPO and ITO Destinations (US $) (2005)   214
7.4   Comparison of Annual Wages Among BPO and ITO
      Destination Countries, Selected Positions (2007)   216
7.5   Average Salaries in the BPO Industry by Country and RWA
      (2007)   217
7.6   Employee Benefits in the BPO Industry by Country and RWA
      (2007) (percent of employees receiving benefits)   217
7.7   Weekly Hours in the BPO Industry by Gender and Type of
      RWA (2007)   220
7.8   Work Schedules in the BPO Industry by Gender and Type of
      RWA (2007) (in percentages)   221
7.9   Irregular Work Schedules in the BPO Industry by Type of
      RWA (2007) (in percentages)   222
7.10 Job Discretion (5-point Likert Scale: 1 = not at all, 5 = a great
      deal) (Mean scores for BPO employees surveyed)   228
7.11 Stress from Interpersonal Relations (percentage of employees
      affected)   230
7.12 Stress from Specific Working Conditions (percentage of
      employees affected)   231
7.13 Stress from the Organizational Environment (percentage of
      employees affected)   231
7.14 Stress from Workplace Changes (percentage of employees
      affected)   232
7.15 Stress from Specific Working Conditions and Gender
      (percentage of employees)   233
8.1   Share of Total Employment in the Service Sector in Selected
      Countries (in percentages) (1980, 1990 and 2000)   237

Charts

4.1   Most Common Incentives Given to BPO Employees   116
4.2   How Often Does Your Work Schedule Change? (percentage)   118
4.3   Philippine BPO Services   120
4.4   Measures of Performance Outcomes in BPO Firms   120
4.5   Causes of Stress: Working Conditions   123
4.6   Psychosocial Symptoms of Stress in BPO Firms   123
4.7   Health Problems of BPO Employees   124

4.8 Reasons for Leaving Previous BPO 127
4.9 Sources of Worry for BPO Employees 128
5.1 Distribution of Occupations by Gender, Segments of Activity
or Primary Work (1995–2006) 141
5.2 Distribution of Employment by Gender and Category of
Employment (1995–2006) (percentage) 141

Boxes

1.1 Key Definitions Related to Remote Work and Global Sourcing 2
2.1 Principal Factors Driving and Inhibiting Offshore Relocation 31
4.1 Stress, Gender, Disobedience and Punishment 125

Preface

Changes in the nature of work that have been sweeping the globe offer both new opportunities and new challenges and risks for countries, employers, workers and governments. Just as the temporal patterns of paid work have been diversifying, so too have its *spatial* patterns. The globalization of markets, allied with dramatic advances in information and telecommunications technologies (ICTs) such as broad-banding, now make it increasingly possible to disaggregate a whole range of services into multiple, successive upstream–downstream stages. The rise of ICTs during the last decade has made it possible for businesses to implement a broad transformation in the geographic distribution of a wide variety of work activities and functions across the world, and, for the first time, to locate the processing of services not requiring direct physical customer interface at a distance from their consumption. Entire services, functions and tasks can now be distributed and carried out concurrently or sequentially in separate locations in different countries where the requisite skills and expertise are available, either through the company's own subsidiaries or purchased from independent ('third-party') service providers. These business services can then be delivered electronically from remote locations, where they are processed through the client company or by the third-party service provider and sent directly to the ultimate consumer.

This 'global sourcing' phenomenon can broadly be defined in terms of two components: (1) remote working and (2) the use of ICTs as the essential enabler. Information technology-enabled services (ITES), whether intermediate or entire service processes, can now be sourced remotely from a wide range of locations around the world for delivery to corporate clients or consumers in other parts of the world. This definition not only covers 'offshoring' and 'outsourcing' but also extends to the entire range of choices for sourcing services on a global basis, whether internally or from independent third-party service providers.[1] This trend includes the relocation of service work from higher-cost developed countries to lower-cost developing ones.

Global sourcing of services, however, has been expanding beyond being purely cost-driven. The delivery of business process services (BPs) from a wide range of locations around the world is increasingly seen as a strategic component of service delivery, not only to facilitate cost reductions, but also to enable enterprise transformation and support access to new markets. Business process outsourcing and offshoring, or BPO, is beginning to be treated as an industry unto itself. However, from a value-chain perspective, it is more plausible to understand this phenomenon as a spatial reorganization of the location of service activities within a wide variety of value chains (Dossani and Kenney, 2005).

These developments have opened up new opportunities for developing countries around the world to compete in the global marketplace for the provision of tradable services. Not surprisingly, this phenomenon has also emerged as a major concern in the popular media in many industrialized countries, particularly with regard to the transfer of work to so-called offshore call centres in countries such as Argentina, Brazil, Chile, India, Mexico, the Philippines, South Africa and many of the transition economies of Central and Eastern Europe. Among the most important studies that have explored this phenomenon was the Asian EMERGENCE project, which conducted a detailed analysis of 59 case studies of collective relocation of 'telemediated work,' defined as information processing work with a clear role of ICTs (Huws and Flecker, 2004). This study concludes that the global relocation of such work is moving from an experimental to a consolidation phase, in which the use of remote service suppliers via ICTs has moved from an initial experimental phase to become a normal, routine part of daily business activity (Huws and Flecker, 2004).

While the literature on global sourcing has tended to dwell primarily on the relocation of call centre operations, the fastest-growing segment in services relocation has actually been in more complex, higher-value business processes that typically require advanced qualifications and skills. These include such domain expertise-intensive functions as tax accounting, equity research, cash flow forecasting, fixed-income-asset pricing research, transaction processing, supply chain coordination, and increasingly, even R&D. In India, for example, call/contact centres have been becoming a relatively less important feature of the business landscape: in 2000, they represented 85 percent of the total ITES business, but because of the phenomenal growth in back-office services, by mid-2006 this figure was down to approximately 35 percent, according to NASSCOM.[2] Among the more notable types of business functions that can now be sourced globally and performed remotely are

- 'voice' services, such as call/contact centres and customer interaction services; translation and transcription services and
- 'nonvoice' or back-office and transaction processing services, including data search, integration and management; tax processing; business consulting; market and financial research; human resources management; and finance and accounting. These functions and business processes can be disaggregated further, for example, into credit card processing; loan processing and approval; credit checks and debt collection; payroll services and benefits administration; training, recruitment and staffing; and personnel administration and other HR functions.

The broad array of remote work arrangements that have been emerging has important but potentially very different implications for the working and employment conditions of those workers in these arrangements. For example, some recent studies of call centres – perhaps the best-known type of remote work arrangements – have found that in-house call centres, including those with subsidiaries (so-called 'captive' units) located in other countries, (i.e., those owned and operated by the firm for its own account, including at remote locations) tend to offer jobs with better working conditions, and higher pay, than firms that outsource this work (Batt et al., 2005a).

There is also some evidence that these in-house call centres have substantially lower levels of staff turnover than outsourced centres, which is important because turnover is associated with lower service quality and lower productivity (see, e.g. Weinkopf, 2002). In addition, at least one recent study indicates that working and employment conditions are generally better, and staff turnover lower, in those firms in the nonvoice or back-office segment of this industry, compared to the voice sector segment, that is, call/contact centres (Ofreneo et al., 2007). Nonetheless, the very limited research conducted to date means that these early findings remain highly inconclusive.

To respond to the need for a better understanding of the emerging trends in the spatial relocation of services, the International Labour Organization (ILO) initiated the Remote Work and Global Sourcing Project in 2007. A series of country case studies formed the foundation of this research project by providing the basic information necessary for a comparative analysis of trends in emerging remote work and global sourcing across selected countries and their implications for job quality in service sector employment. These country studies were carried out primarily in developing countries, in order to address the gaps in the knowledge of emerging trends in these countries, particularly those with substantial BPO 'industries.' The focus of these studies was the services sector, and in particular, the financial and professional services and the telecommunications industries.

The aim of these country case studies, and of this project, was twofold: (1) to build the ILO's knowledge base regarding the various types of remote work enabled by ICTs or ITES that currently exist, particularly regarding the working and employment conditions in these remote work arrangements and (2) to offer some suggestions for government policies and company practices designed to simultaneously improve both working and employment conditions and business outcomes for companies using these arrangements.

The analysis in each country study report was designed to identify trends in ITES, including the size, scope and characteristics of both firms using remote work enabled by ICTs and workers engaged in such remote work; the working and employment conditions in these remote work arrangements; and the key factors in companies that are associated with better working conditions. An understanding of these key factors was designed to permit the project to offer some suggestions for government policies and company practices to improve the conditions for workers in such arrangements. Improved conditions can, in turn, also benefit enterprises by, for example, reducing staff turnover, and thus lead to reduced costs and enhancements in service quality and firm productivity.

Service sector work is undoubtedly the wave of the future in most developing countries. One of the most dramatic changes in the structure of the world's economy over the last 30 years has been the profound 'tertiarization' in the nature of economic activity – that is, the substantial increase in the size of the service sector, particularly in terms of employment. This broad historical trend towards an increasing share of employment in services also applies in a wide array of developing countries as well. The growing share of service sector employment in developing countries makes developments in the BPO industry a potential forerunner of future developments in service sector employment in these countries. Thus, government policies and company practices designed to address these factors hold the potential not only to improve working and employment conditions in the BPO industry, but also to serve more broadly as models of good practice for the service sector in developing countries.

Jon C. Messenger
Naj Ghosheh

Notes

1. Definitions of key terms related to remote work and global sourcing are provided in the Introduction to this volume (see Box 1.1).
2. The National Association of Software and Services Companies (NASSCOM), India's trade association body for both the Indian software industry and Indian information technology-enabled services – business processing outsourcing (ITES–BPO) industry.

Acknowledgements

This report is the product of a 4-year effort that received invaluable contributions and support from numerous people around the world. First and foremost, this report benefited considerably from a series of country studies, and we are very grateful to the authors of these studies for their high-quality research and comprehensive country reports: Dr. Premilla D'Cruz and Dr. Ernesto Noronha, Associate Professors of Organizational Behaviour at the Indian Institute of Management in Ahmedabad, India; Dr. Maragtas S.V. Amante, Professor, College of Economics and Business Administration, Hanyang University, Ansan Campus, Republic of Korea (the research for this volume was completed when he was with the University of the Philippines, Diliman); Dr. Selma Venco, Researcher, Instituto de Filosofia e Ciências Humanas (IFCH) of Universidade Estadual de Campinas/UNICAMP in Campinas, Brazil; and Drs. Andrés López, Daniela Ramos and Iván Torre of the Centro de Investigaciones para la Transformación (CENIT) in Buenos Aires, Argentina. We are also grateful to Professor Phil Taylor of the University of Strathclyde Business School in Glasgow, Scotland, UK, who prepared for this volume the multicountry synthesis reviewing the BPO experience in selected developed countries.

We also appreciate the considerable support, both financial and technical, in initiating the country studies provided by our colleagues in the International Labour Office's (ILO) Sectoral Activities Programme (SECTOR), John Myers and John Sendanyoye, as well as the assistance of several ILO field offices. Our sincere thanks also go out to those business process outsourcing (BPO) managers and employees who kindly participated in the enterprise surveys conducted in India and the Philippines.

This report was immeasurably improved by the guidance of our three anonymous peer reviewers. We would like to thank these peer reviewers for their thoughtful and instructive comments.

We would also like to express our appreciation to several other individuals from the International Labour Office. First, we would like to thank the Chief of the Conditions of Work and Employment Programme (TRAVAIL), Manuela Tomei, for her support and encouragement throughout the years of research and writing for this book. We are also grateful to Ariel Golan and his team, Hiep Nguyen, Richelle Van Snellenberg and their colleagues in the ILO Bureau of Library and Information Services for both their invaluable contributions to this report and their continuing support for ILO research.

We are particularly grateful to two interns who worked closely with us on different components of the study. First, we would like to thank Carolina Dominguez Torres, who prepared a literature review covering those developing countries that are not explicitly analysed in the country studies. Second, we would like to offer our special thanks to Maartje Schouten, who performed additional statistical analyses on the survey interview data from the country studies in India and the Philippines, a number of which were incorporated into the comparative analysis chapter.

We would like to thank our colleagues in the ILO's Bureau of Publications, Charlotte Beauchamp and Helen Swain, for all of their assistance in the preparation of the manuscript, as well as for compiling a comprehensive set of references.

Finally, we would like to thank our wives, Drs. Laura Messenger and Esther Peeren, for their patience, understanding and support throughout the long and often difficult process of preparing this volume.

Jon C. Messenger
Naj Ghosheh

Notes on Contributors

Maragtas S.V. Amante is Professor at the College of Economics and Business Administration, Hanyang University, in the Republic of Korea. His research interests include outsourcing, industrial relations and management. The study conducted for this book was finished when he was with the University of the Philippines, Diliman.

Premilla D'Cruz is Associate Professor of Organizational Behaviour at the Indian Institute of Management in Ahmedabad. Her research interests include emotions in organizations, self and identity, organizational control and ICTs and organizations.

Naj Ghosheh is Research Officer at the International Labour Office, Conditions of Work and Employment Programme, Geneva. He holds a PhD from the University of Cambridge and law degrees from the University of Oxford. His research interests include offshoring and outsourcing, management and working conditions, the employment relationship and the sociology of labour and business law.

Andrés López holds a PhD in Economics from the University of Buenos Aires and is Director of the Centro de Investigaciones para la Transformación (CENIT). He is Full Professor of Development Economics at the University of Buenos Aires (UBA). He has been a consultant for different international organizations such as UNCTAD, ECLAC, WIPO, UNDP, IADB and others. He is the author of several studies on foreign investment, innovation and industrial economics.

Jon C. Messenger is Senior Research Officer at the International Labour Office, Conditions of Work and Employment Programme, Geneva. He specializes in policy-focused research on working time and work organization, with a special interest in issues relating to temporal and spatial flexibility (e.g., service sector telework), work sharing and gender equality.

Ernesto Noronha is Associate Professor of Organizational Behaviour at the Indian Institute of Management in Ahmedabad. His research interests include diversity at work, industrial relations, organizational change, organizational control and ICTs and organizations.

Daniela Ramos has a masters in Economics from the Instituto Torcuato Di Tella (UTDT) and a degree in Economics from the Universidad de Buenos

Aires (UBA). She is principal researcher at the Centro de Investigaciones para la Transformación (CENIT) and Professor of Argentine Economic Structure at the University of Buenos Aires (UBA). She specializes in trade and industrial economics and has authored several studies on foreign trade and investment as well as on the software and services sector.

Philip Taylor is Professor at the Business School of the University of Strathclyde in Glasgow, Scotland. His research interests include HR/OB in call centres, offshoring of business services, occupational safety and health and information and consultation in the workplace.

Iván Torre has a BA in Economics from Buenos Aires University and is an MA candidate at San Andrés University, Argentina. He has worked on services exports in Latin America, the development of agricultural technologies in Argentina and some aspects of Argentina's economic history.

Selma Venco is a researcher at the Instituto de Filosofia e Ciências Humanas (IFCH) of Universidade Estadual de Campinas/UNICAMP in Brazil. Her research interests include the sociology of work, technological change and social relations in the workplace and industrial relations.

List of Abbreviations

ABRAREC	Brazilian Association for Corporate and Customer Relations
AHT	average handling time per call
AICTE	All India Council for Technical Education
APEC	Asia-Pacific Economic Cooperation
BFSI	banking, financial services and insurance
BLES	Bureau of Labour and Employment Statistics
BOSS	burnout stress syndrome
BPAP	Business Processing Association of the Philippines
BPO	business process outsourcing
BPS	business process services
BRASSCOM	Brazilian Association of Software and Service Export Companies
CA	Court of Appeals
CBO	Brazilian Classification of Professions [Classificação Brasileira de Ocupações]
CCTVs	closed-circuit televisions
CLT	Consolidated Labour Law
CMM	capability maturity model
CMMI	capability maturity model integration
CSR	customer service representatives
DOLE	Department of Labour and Employment
DTA	domestic tariff area
DTI	Department of Trade and Industry
EHTP	electronic hardware technology park
EMEA	Europe, the Middle East and Africa
EOU	export-oriented units
FDI	foreign direct investment
FGDs	focus group discussions
GDP	gross domestic product
GSN	global services network
HCM	high-commitment management
HSBC	Hongkong and Shanghai Banking Corporation
IBGE	Brazilian Institute of Geography and Statistics
ICTs	information and communications technologies
IDA	Industrial Disputes Act
ILO	International Labour Organization
INPC	National Consumer Price Index [Indice Nacional de Precios al Consumidor]
ITES	information technology-enabled services

KPO	knowledge process outsourcing
MNCs	multinational corporations
MoU	memorandum of understanding
MSDs	musculoskeletal disorders
NAC	National Assessment of Competence
NASSCOM	National Association of Software and Service Companies
NCR	National Capital Region
NEDA	National Economic Development Authority
NLRC	National Labour Relations Commission
OBC	other backward castes
O2P	Outsource2Philippines
OFW	overseas Filipino workers
OSH	Occupational safety and health
RAIS	Annual Social Information Report
RBI	Reserve Bank of India
RBV	resource-based view
RWAs	remote work arrangements
SC	scheduled castes
SEZ	special economic zones
SMCs	service management centres
SPSS	Statistical Package for the Social Sciences
STP	software technology parks
SVP	senior vice-president
TCE	transaction cost economics
TL	team leader
TSE	technical support engineer
TSR or eREP	technical support eRepresentative
UBA	University of Buenos Aires
UGC	University Grants Commission
UNCTAD	United Nations Conference on Trade and Development
VDM	video display monitor
VDU	visual display unit
VOIP	voice-over-internet protocol
WBITSA	West Bengal Information Technology Services Association
WHO	World Health Organization
YPC	Young Professionals Collective

1
Introduction

Jon C. Messenger and Naj Ghosheh

The potential market for global outsourcing of business services is extraordinarily large: it has been estimated to be valued at up to US $386 billion (Tagliabue, 2007). According to a 2005 United Nations Conference on Trade and Development (UNCTAD) report (based on an estimate by the management consultancy McKinsey and Company), the business process outsourcing (BPO) 'industry' was worth only US $32–35 billion globally in the year 2002. By 2009, a recent UNCTAD report placed the estimate for 2008 at $80 billion (UNCTAD, 2009). Regardless of which estimate one chooses to believe, the total global value of this 'industry' is clearly substantial.

The BPO industry and the information technology-enabled services (ITES) that it provides at a distance from locations around the world have their own unique vocabulary; see Box 1 for a summary of key definitions related to remote work and the global outsourcing of business services. No matter how they are defined, however, these services have been expanding dramatically. According to Minevich and Richter (2005), the industry was expected to continue growing due to the expansion of services provided via technology and the emergence of a multitude of remote work arrangements (RWAs) in the BPO industry – the best known being call centres – which has translated into different, yet similar forms in various parts of the world, such as India, the Philippines, Central Europe, the Russian Federation and Latin America. A range of other BPO industry studies have made similarly optimistic forecasts for future growth (e.g., Kearney, 2007a). Even allowing for a certain amount of marketing hyperbole, the reality is that BPO has been growing at extremely rapid, and in some cases even exponential, rates.

Box 1.1 Key Definitions Related to Remote Work and Global Sourcing

Business Process Services (BPS): Services that involve the processing of business transactions, such as insurance, credit card claims and pay-roll. There is nothing particularly new about these business functions; the 'new' aspect is that many of these services are now *IT-enabled* (see the definition below), which means that they can now be 'out-sourced' or even 'offshored' (see the definitions below) with relative ease via ICTs.

Information Technology-Enabled Services (ITES): a form of BPS made possible by the use of advanced information and communications technologies (ICTs). ICTs are the *essential enabler* of the remote delivery of BPS. ITES is used in various industries, such as finance, insurance, telecommunications and so on. Examples are legal and medical transcription, accounting, insurance claim handling, credit card processing, and so on.

Remote Work: A more common name for business services provided at a distance using ICTs. Essentially, remote work is a synonym for ITES, although in this volume, we use the term mainly to describe those jobs that involve providing ITES to customers across the world.

Business Process Outsourcing (BPO): The name of the 'industry' that provides ITES functions and processes, along with the associated operational activities and tasks. The use of quotation marks around the term 'industry' is meant to signify that BPO actually consists of the ITES segments of *other* industries, such as finance and telecommunications.

Outsourcing: the subcontracting of a process, such as product design or manufacturing, to another company – called a third-party provider. Outsourcing may occur within a country or outside of the country; in the latter case, it is termed *offshoring*, or if a nearby country, *nearshoring*.

Offshoring: The phenomenon of locating IT-services and BPS in locations outside of the source country, largely enabled through recent advances in ICTs, to leverage differences in wage levels and the availability of skilled labour across borders.

Nearshoring: This term refers to sourcing ITES to a country that is relatively close to the source country in terms of geographic distance, time zone, or both (also called *nearsourcing* and *nearshore outsourcing*).

The dramatic expansion of the BPO industry up until recently – and its potential for future growth as well – is highly dependent on the diffusion, and the cost, of ICTs – that is, the level of development of the information society in a particular country. ICTs are the essential enablers for the remote delivery of BPS: this is the reason that we refer to such services as information technology-enabled services, or ITES – with the implicit understanding that we are referring to business services that are delivered to customers from distant locations by means of ICTs.

ICT diffusion in a particular country, in turn, can be measured by components such as: (i) the number of telephone lines, (ii) the number of personal computers and (iii) the number of internet users (Kearney, 2007a). Most of the countries analysed in this book have been modernizing their telecommunications infrastructure; deregulating their telecommunications sectors, largely in an attempt to lower costs; constructing networked facilities in free zones and expanding access to the Internet. Consequently, the level of development of the information society has been growing substantially.

The global economic crisis, which began in the financial industry in 2007, has spread into other sectors of the economy and has become a deep global recession as this book was being finalized in late 2009. This global economic downturn has had a profound negative impact on some BPO 'players,' particularly those in banking and insurance (e.g., the global insurance giant AIG) and appears likely to signal a reduction in the fortunes of the broader BPO industry – but only in the short term. For example, interviews in four call centres in India in early 2009 conducted by one of the contributors to this volume, Prof. Phil Taylor, found a substantial decline in the IT outsourcing (ITO) activities in those companies; however, despite the global recession, there has been only a modest decline in BPO activities. In fact, the fundamental factors that have driven the expansion of the global BPO industry – such as the continuous search for cost savings in the delivery of business services and increasingly sophisticated, inexpensive ICTs – appear unlikely to diminish; if anything, they will probably accelerate in the medium to long term.

1.1   Rationales for outsourcing and offshoring business services

The goal of most organizations that engage in outsourcing and offshoring is to enhance competitiveness by achieving a higher return on assets through less capital commitment and the increasing ability to adjust quickly to a changing environment – or in the vernacular, to 'do more, with less' (Insigna and Werle, 2000, p. 58). This *modus operandi* has forced many organizations (even public sector agencies) to continually examine all their functions, including basic functions, to see where costs can be minimized, and to consider whether the functions might be done just as effectively – and at less cost – if performed outside of the organization or at an offshore location.

However, companies and other organizations must be certain that they protect their core functions – those functions which, if lost, could compromise the viability of the organization as a whole. If core competence is about harmonizing streams of technology, it is also about the organization of work and the delivery of value (Prahalad and Hamel, 1990). In practical terms, this choice also involves greater specialization, as firms switch from producing goods and services internally to sourcing them from an external supplier (Sako, 2006). Thus, organizations need a strategy that defines the core functions that it must perform itself, and separates them from other functions that can be done at less cost and more efficiently by other organizations – by outsourcing to a contractor or an offshore service provider, preferably one specializing in the function in question.

However, the seductive qualities of outsourcing and offshoring for management, namely cost savings and improved efficiency, can be lost if firms are not cautious in their approach. The difference between success and failure in outsourcing/offshoring of services can depend on the approach taken by senior managers in the organization, namely whether the decisions to outsource/offshore are carried out in a systematic manner. The difficulties can begin when the strategy moves down through different operational levels (Insigna and Werle, 2000).

Aron and Singh (2005, p. 136) point out that if organizations are not systematic in their decision-making with regard to offshoring in particular, three fundamental mistakes can take place. The first mistake is focusing on location and price, rather than on evaluation of the processes that will be outsourced/offshored. The second mistake is management's use of cost/benefit analysis to make decisions rather than considering the risks that can result from offshoring a process (e.g., the possibility that the vendor will use their special position to hold the organization for 'ransom'), especially if the function is outsourced offshore. Finally, organizations can make the third mistake of viewing outsourcing/offshoring as an all-or-nothing proposition rather than as a choice with a range of options. The extent to which managers take these variables into account will have an impact not only on the success or failure of their outsourcing/offshoring decisions but also on the working conditions in these workplaces.

Therefore, a critical step to successively engage in outsourcing/offshoring is to develop a framework that will help determine core and noncore functions in the organization. Two theories have developed to help frame how such assessments can be made: (i) transaction cost and (ii) the resource-based view of the firm frameworks. The first framework is based on transaction cost economics (TCE), primarily the work of Oliver Williamson, who built on the earlier work of Ronald Coase (Williamson, 1975; Coase, 1937). According to this framework, those functions in a company or other organization that tend to be very specific, very uncertain, or frequently take place should be managed internally by an organization, but those not meeting these criteria can be more effectively outsourced and, by extension, offshored if feasible (Willcocks and Lacity, 2006).

The other theory that has been used as a framework for making outsourcing and offshoring decisions is the resource-based view (RBV) of the firm, initially developed by Edith Penrose (1959). This framework emphasizes that nonsubstitutable strategic functions should be retained within the organization, while other functions can be considered for outsourcing (and again, by extension, offshoring) (Willcocks and Lacity, 2006). The RBV framework, by contrast to the TCE framework, extends to the concept of learning and innovation and the development of capabilities that can benefit those organizations that take on the outsourced function, which can then, in turn, be transmitted back to the organization making the decisions upstream.

These two frameworks can provide at least some insight into how companies reach the decision to outsource and/or offshore ITES functions – a decision that is portrayed visually in Table 1.1. These two frameworks can provide at least some insight into how organizations generally make their decisions regarding outsourcing and/or offshoring ITES functions. For example, the call centre function is one of the first types of work that organizations determine they can outsource and/or offshore. For example, as the TCE and parts of the RBV framework would predict, the call centre function does not inherently require domain-specific knowledge, and it is often converted into a routine process to facilitate its outsourcing, particularly when such a function is offshored. Yet, the RBV framework may even influence companies to develop mechanisms for knowledge process outsourcing or offshoring, by establishing a relationship that ensures better communication and the development of capabilities, so that those providing the function downstream can better meet the needs of the organization upstream.

In principle, either of these frameworks might influence an organization's view that the call centre function can be outsourced or offshored easily, whereas the frameworks might suggest that more caution is needed with regard to back-office work and particularly knowledge processing functions.

Table 1.1   The Outsourcing and Offshoring Decision: Organizational Results

	Offshore the function? NO	Offshore the function? YES
Outsource the function? NO	In-house operation	'Captive' unit (subsidiary)
Outsource the function? YES	Third-party provider	Third-party offshore provider

The application of these two frameworks may also, in turn, explain some of the reasons why the employment conditions can vary so much between call centres and back-office positions, and much less among similar types of positions across different countries – a critical distinction that will be explored further in this volume.

However, while TCE and RBV are instructive theoretical research frameworks for examining the importance of organizational functions and what should and should not be outsourced/offshored, managers in practice may need to rely on more straightforward and swift methods to make these critical decisions. This is an important consideration, and the success or failure of the outsouring/offshoring process may hinge on it.

Aron and Singh (2005) identify a number of practical factors and issues that management may need to consider before engaging in offshoring functions, which are similar to TCE and RBV frameworks but are more practical for managers. First, when considering offshoring, companies need to rank their processes in hierarchical form to determine what can be offshored. They then need to identify and manage two forms of risk – operational and structural. Operational risk consists of two components: first, acknowledging that service providers initially will not be as quick as in-house staff upstream, and second, recognition that the metrics they may use to measure the offshore/outsource process are not all the same.

These operational risk metrics fall into four categories that include transparent processes (i.e., measurable processes), codifiable processes (i.e., processes are measurable, but barriers such as skill sets needed or time frames for work to be done can raise risks), opaque processes (i.e., companies can codify work, but not measure outputs) and noncodifiable processes (i.e., no precise method exists to codify the nature of the work, or the number of ways to respond to the work is so vast that no standard response can be developed and codified). On the other hand, structural risks occur when companies rely on vendors to act in certain prescribed ways. This is perhaps most problematic as the relationship in real terms can be altered by unrealistic expectations upstream (e.g., not fully accounting for the organizational risks), changes in the upstream demands that create downstream problems (e.g., not recognizing the organizational and structural risks this can pose to the vendor), or unrealistic promises by the vendor.

These considerations illustrate the fact that a company's decision to outsource and/or offshore ITES functions is not an end in itself as much as it is a beginning, creating new and different organizational imperatives. The challenge for an organization is to develop practices for managing the transfer of information across spatial and organizational boundaries, which on occasion requires some face-to-face meetings between the upstream firm and the 'captive' unit or third-party offshore provider (Manning et al., 2008; Willcocks and Lacity, 2006). However, those mechanisms needed to manage the function and the staff handling that function offshore, but within

the organization (e.g., the 'captive' unit or subsidiary), and those mechanisms necessary for managing outsourced offshore functions, are different.
In-house offshoring of business service functions requires mechanisms to
manage and transfer information within the organization, which if not
done properly can diminish the effectiveness and efficiency of the offshoring
operation. This mainly requires good communication: reliable channels to
communicate between managers sending work tasks and those receiving
them, as well as among the managers and workers performing the work in
the subsidiary's office.

If a company chooses to outsource *and* offshore its business functions,
then a different matrix of decision-making comes into play. Outsourcing
involves substantial risks for organizations, because they often have very
little control over operations in the outsourced firm. This problem can be
compounded by distance if the firm is offshore – particularly if the offshore
firm is too far away for regular onsite visits. If the organization engaging in outsourcing fails to consider or anticipate the potential issues in its
relationship with the third-party offshore provider, this situation can, at a
minimum, cause difficulties in the effective and efficient delivery of services
by the provider's managers and workforce. In the worst-case scenario, it may
even lead to a relationship so dysfunctional that the ITES function has to be
brought back in-house (Aron and Singh, 2005).

Ideally, organizations looking to outsource a function offshore would go
beyond a strict cost and functional analysis, to develop some criteria for
engagement with a third-party offshore provider. Such criteria might include
the following: investigating the market; planning the contract, including
how to assess the contractual relationship; understanding how to fit the
offshored, outsourced function into the core business strategy and work-
plan; motivating the third-party offshore provider and its staff, including
how they can develop and retain expertise; and evaluating the potential
impacts on customers (Willcocks and Lacity, 2006; Tate and van der Walk,
2008; Valverde et al., 2007).

Often, in order to achieve these aims, companies negotiate contracts with
third-party providers (whether in the same country or offshore), which are
sometimes called 'vendor agreements' (Holman et al., 2007). Such contracts
come in four general types: (1) a standard form in which the client signs a
standard agreement created by the firm that is sourcing the functions; (2) a
detailed contract that establishes a number of specific guidelines and rules;
(3) loose or task-based contracts in which the third-party provider agrees to
meet or complete a function done by the organization looking to outsource
and (4) mixed contracts that include both detailed and loose provisions
(Willcocks and Lacity, 2006, p. 20). Contractual issues are very important,
but they also are not an endpoint – although organizations looking to outsource functions may see it that way. Once a contract is signed, it is critically
important for the sourcing organization to assign a manager from its side to

oversee the contract and monitor performance, and also to identify a contact at the third-party provider (the owner or a designated manager) to address the administration of the contract and handle any issues that develop on either side regarding the delivery of the function(s) specified in the contract.

1.2   Potential impacts of offshoring and outsourcing on working and employment conditions

Managing the relationship between company headquarters and the offshored unit or offshored/outsourced function is critically important, and can have a profound effect on the working and employment conditions of those performing the downstream function in the 'captive' unit (subsidiary) or the third-party offshore provider. For example, if the targets or deadlines in the contract or agreements between the organization and offshore provider are not clear (which happens more often than might be expected), managers in the offshore facility may require their workers to work longer hours to meet or exceed what they believe the target is, rather than losing the work from the upstream organization.

Offshoring business functions requires managers from both the sourcing organization upstream and its downstream subsidiary or third-party offshore provider to communicate regularly regarding the work performed, how it is delivered and also to sort out any problems encountered. This often means going beyond a number of social and organizational boundaries, often simultaneously (Espinosa et al., 2003). Such boundaries can include national culture, organizational culture and various operational boundaries (e.g., different locations, different time zones, etc.). Managers in the sourcing organization need to bear in mind that managers downstream play a key role, not only in the delivery of the service function, but also in managing the workforce to deliver upstream. Unclear communication, a lack of technical expertise and being unrealistic in terms of task delivery can often be stumbling blocks that are compounded by the boundary issues. If the relationships are managed positively and with constant and effective communication, this can bring benefits for all the parties involved – including better working conditions for workers in offshore operations.

However, if the managers for the parties involved do not develop a good working relationship, a number of problems can result. With regard to those functions that are merely offshored to a 'captive' unit, rather than also outsourced to another firm offshore, the problems are likely to be primarily in reconciling the relationships and developing mechanisms to overcome boundaries in geography and culture. Research has indicated that if the organization upstream treats the workers in the offshore part of the organization as 'second rate,' this can stifle the relationship in a way that no manager can overcome (Levina, 2008).

Once again, the complexities multiply if the relationship is both offshored and outsourced. Due to the competitive pressures in certain parts of the BPO industry, particularly call centres, owners of third-party offshore providers may promise more than their company can deliver. Problems may also occur if there is any misunderstanding regarding the requirements of the vendor agreement or contract that is signed between the parties, and thus expectations for delivery are in a constant state of flux. This situation can complicate the delivery of the service function and create a lot of pressure on managers to resolve the resulting problems. In such circumstances, the so-called rule of organizational gravity applies: any problems that affect managers will soon become issues for workers as well.

The problems that arise during the ongoing relationship between the organization and its offshore subsidiary or third-party provider can have significant consequences for the working and employment conditions in these organizations. For example, if the offshore managers do not have a clear understanding of what business functions are to be delivered, and how, the manager may be inclined to ask for greater efforts from the workforce to compensate for the lack of clarity. However, this situation can create role ambiguity for workers in these 'captive' units or third-party offshore providers. Role ambiguity for workers takes place when they struggle to provide effective responses to unpredictable circumstances or lack certainty regarding the consequences of the performance of their work tasks (Pearce, 1981). Under these circumstances, managers might also increase workloads or increase the monitoring of workers to attempt to achieve unrealistic or fluctuating targets that are not adequately explained to the workers – which can, in turn, raise the stress levels of the workforce.

1.3   Origins of outsourcing and offshoring in the services sector

Outsourcing is not a new concept and has been a staple in the manufacturing sector for many years (Gereffi, 2005). It is not even particularly new in the services sector. Some dimensions of services sector outsourcing, such as call centres, were developed and have been an industry staple for over 20 years in some industrialized countries, primarily the United States, but also in the United Kingdom, Australia, Canada and, more recently, Spain (see Chapter 2 in this volume).

The transformation in the configuration and location of service delivery in the US originated with call centres in the telecommunications industry (Batt and Monihan, 2002). Telephone operator call centres were viewed by managers in the telecommunications industry as a model of efficiency, which they hoped to reproduce for other types of service delivery. According to a study by Batt, the growth of call centres in the US varied by industry, with the longest-established centres in the telecommunications industry (starting about 20 years ago); by way of contrast, call centres in the finance and IT industries were developed comparatively more recently (about 10 years ago) (Batt et al., 2005a).

In the early stages of their development, call centres were located regionally and often in suburban or more rural locations to keep labour costs down (see Chapter 2 in this volume). These early incarnations did not address national markets, although as time passed the typical call centre began serving national markets on a more frequent basis (Bain and Taylor, 2002). However, as Dossani and Kenney (2007) have noted, while there was considerable cost savings in these locations, one of the main factors limiting the scale of operations, and their potential growth, was the lack of highly educated employees in these locations.

In addition to concerns about the scarcity of qualified labour, other developments during the 1990s also began to impact the existing call centre model. The saturation in the markets for such centres, competitive pressures and the dot.com collapse in 2000–2001 all compelled companies to search more intensively for ways to reduce costs, especially the costs of labour. In this context, companies began to experiment with what is called *nearshoring*, wherein call or customer service centres were still relocated outside of the US, but in countries that were geographically closer, such as Canada and Mexico. Such efforts did lower costs to some degree, but other developments in business management that were also occurring during this period would eventually lead to an even greater expansion of these activities into what has now become the global BPO industry.

One important development that helped to drive this expansion was the process reengineering movement in management and business in the 1990s, which focused on the cost savings that could be achieved through reorganization and restructuring of business processes. This involved the standardization of activities to complete a process, and by means of this standardization, the creation of *pinch points* through which handoffs would allow the separation of work either geographically, organizationally, or both. This process included the digitization of work tasks or entire processes through which managers could calculate the most cost-effective way to complete an activity. It should be noted that at this point in time, there was little or no precedent for offshoring business services, with only limited activity in software development in India, Ireland and Israel, and in call centres and data processing facilities for credit cards (with workers performing low-skilled data entry work) in Latin America and the island countries of the Caribbean (Dossani and Kenney, 2007).

Another important factor driving the expansion of the BPO 'industry' has been advances in ICTs, such as voice-over-internet protocol (VOIP) and automated call distribution systems. The ability to reengineer processes that essentially erased organizational and especially geographic boundaries, combined with new and increasingly inexpensive ICTs, opened up a whole new dimension in the ability to offshore service sector work. These factors unleashed the potential for the development of the BPO industry in developing countries.

Nonetheless, as Dossani and Kenney (2007) saliently point out, techno-logical advances (and also process reengineering) were a necessary, but not sufficient, condition for firms to move their services sector activities offshore. According to these authors, however, it was equally important that the decision-makers in companies based in industrialized countries be persuaded that offshoring was acceptable, or in their words a 'legitimate strategy'.

While the experiences described here are in reference to India, similar concerns can be voiced by companies with regard to offshoring to any coun-try in the developing world, including all of the countries reviewed in this book. As business pressures never cease and the need to cut costs always exists, companies worldwide will continue to look offshore for a least some of their ITES functions. Also, in the same way that providers of offshored functions in India have provided assurances of business continuity and secu-rity to their clients (Dossani and Kenney, 2007), providers in other countries looking to attract ITES will no doubt seek to emulate the Indian experience.

Companies consider many different variables in making offshoring deci-sions. Much depends on the ITES function that is chosen for offshoring and what that function is meant to achieve. Perhaps the most important vari-able is cost, which can include labour costs, infrastructure costs and tax costs (among others). Another important variable is sufficient availability of skilled or trained labour, which, as noted above, can be difficult to find in typical BPO locations, and which, in numerical terms, may influence whether the activities to be performed are relatively simple or more complex in nature. The geographic location of the offshored and/or outsourced func-tion can also play an important role in this choice, depending on the market to be served and the importance placed on communication with the source organization (i.e., the company that is offshoring the service function).

Because of the uncertainty surrounding how offshoring might be accom-plished in countries in which firms have limited or no experience, the location decision can certainly be a challenging one. However, a number of organizations have developed advisory services for companies with limited offshoring experience regarding where they should consider locating their offshore business service operations. For example, private companies such as neoIT, A.T. Kearney and McKinsey regularly offer advice based on inter-nally developed matrices about countries that are, or should be, of interest when offshoring ITES functions. Some academics have also developed matri-ces that suggest why there may be a preference for certain countries over others for specific functions. While such sources of information have their merits and have likely influenced some organizational decision-making, it is likely that the variables highlighted earlier – that is, cost savings, the avail-ability of skilled labour and access to target markets – together play a decisive role in establishing the criteria for company decision-making concerning offshoring.

1.4   Business start-up and government follow-up: The emergence of ITES–BPO in developing countries

ITES offshoring developed in many countries either organically or through organizations, usually multinational corporations, that established subsidiaries in those countries. The countries that are the focus of this volume are notable because they have developed varieties of ITES, as well as satisfied the criteria influencing organizational decision-makers to locate offshore services functions in other countries. For example, in India, while some computer programming was being done there as far back as the 1980s, it was not until 1993 that a number of multinational firms actually located operations there (Dossani and Kenney, 2007; Noronha and D'Cruz, 2008a). From that time on, local ITES began to develop, and the pace has accelerated in recent years. Argentina, Brazil and the Philippines have all experienced similar developments, though in the Latin American countries the growth of third-party service providers is not as far advanced as in India or the Philippines (Lopez *et al.* 2008; Venco, 2008; Amante, 2008; D'Cruz and Noronha, 2008a).

The initial location that many North American and European companies look to when they are considering offshoring ITES functions is Asia. This in part relates to the fact that countries such as India and the Philippines have established themselves as cost-effective locations for the provision of ITES. Perhaps owing to this fact, the time zone issue is less of a factor, although as will be detailed later in this chapter, this is only because firms in Asia have made the hours adjustment in their workplaces via the extensive use of night work (in voice services), in order to meet client needs in North America and Europe – which also has negative implications for working conditions.

In this context, India has a long-established reputation in the BPO industry, which can be traced back to the 1970s, when software development established the precedent for offshoring services to that country (Arora and Athreye, 2002). Since that time, India has continued to develop its position in ITES and has aggressively sought to move up the 'value chain' towards the provision of more complex services (Taylor and Bain, 2006; Chapters 2 and 3 in this volume). Due to the evolving reputation of ITES–BPO in India, clients can be found in many parts of the world, including the US, Canada and Europe, as well as in countries more proximate to India's time zones in the Middle East, Australia and Asia, and internally within India itself (Noronha and D'Cruz, 2008a).

The historical development of the BPO industry in the Philippines is similar to that of India. However, whereas in India the provision of computer programming services for international companies helped to stimulate the industry, in the Philippines the domestically grown IT firm SPi helped initially established a presence for the BPO industry there, in addition to multinationals that also placed functions of back offices in that country (Engman, 2007). Moreover, due to labour and infrastructure costs, coupled with the fact that English is widely spoken due to the country's historical ties with the US, the Philippines has become a destination of choice for many US-based multinational enterprises, particularly call centres, and is seen as a strong competitor to India in providing voice services in English (Magitbay-Ramos et al., 2008; Amante, 2008; Engman, 2007).

With regard to offshoring destinations closer to companies in North America and western Europe, Latin America has been receiving increasing attention with regard to offshoring ITES functions to this part of the world. The growth of the Hispanic population in the US, the emergence of Spain as a major source country for BPO and the desire to access the ready markets in Central and South America have all led companies to explore establishing operations in Latin America. In addition, Latin American countries are attractive to North American and European companies due to the workforce's language skills (notably in Spanish and English), low labour and infrastructure costs and the availability of a qualified workforce (Venco, 2008). An additional advantage of offshoring business services to Latin America is that the time differences are not a factor between North and South America. Interest in Argentina as a BPO destination has grown because of the availability of skilled labour, an educated workforce with good language skills (mainly Spanish but also English), low costs when measured in US dollars and a time zone that allows it to serve markets in both the Americas and Europe, without the need to resort to night work (Lopez et al., 2008).

The Brazilian BPO industry, on the other hand, has developed quite differently from the one in Argentina. While having many of the same positive qualities as Argentina, the immense size of Brazil, coupled with the fact that it is the largest Portuguese-speaking country in the world, has meant that Brazilian BPO companies do not have any large external markets that they can readily serve. As a result, the development of BPO in Brazil has been largely focused internally, and to some degree linked with that of other Portuguese-speaking nations (Venco, 2008).

While different countries have taken different policy and legal actions to promote the development of the BPO industry, there are two phenomena that appear to be similar with regard to government influences on the BPO industry and its workforce. First, while government policies and legal activity in major BPO destination countries have taken different forms in order to stimulate the development of a BPO industry, there have been some common features in the policy/legal actions of these governments. One important legal action taken by these governments has been to deregulate the telecommunications industry, and this form of deregulation has played an important role in the development of the BPO industry in all of these countries, because it has helped to open up new possibilities for telecom-munications activities and has generally lowered infrastructure costs and charges for line use in the industry. Without greater ICT access and lower ICT costs, it would have been extremely difficult for BPO to grow as an off-shore industry, as it is the central cost component and a vital link in the delivery of this type of service. For example, in Brazil, the General Telecom-munications Law of 1997 (Federal Law No. 9742/97) had at its core the right of access to communication services for the entire population at 'reasonable prices' (Venco, 2008, p. 43).

A second common factor in promoting the development of the BPO industry is the locations where such an industry has developed in these destination countries. Due to the fact that multinational enterprises have historically planted the 'industrial seeds' in such countries through their subsidiaries, it should not be surprising that major cities or locations near those cities have been the main location for these facilities.

In recent years, however, there have been growing efforts by national gov-ernments, as well as by provincial, state and local governments, to offer incentives for BPO companies to locate in a particular region of a country. Companies, both foreign and domestic, have pursued these incentives to the regions in question. What is striking about this development, however, is that the result is a clustering of the BPO industry in certain 'hubs' within each country. Cities such as Cordoba and Rosario in Argentina, the Rio de Janeiro–São Paulo corridor in Brazil, Hyderabad and Bangalore in India and metro Manila in the Philippines – all these cities tend to have the highest concentrations of BPO industries in their respective countries (Lopez et al. 2008; Venco, 2008; D'Cruz and Noronha, 2008a; Amante, 2008).

While such a pattern of industry concentration is logical for offshore outsourcing in manufacturing, it is curious that an industry in which the provision of services from a distance is a hallmark – and hence could in theory locate its operations almost anywhere – would have such a geo-graphic clustering of facilities. One of the logical consequences of this clustering of BPO companies is that the labour market for the BPO indus-try also has become concentrated in particular locations, which may in part explain some of the similarities in the working and employment conditions experienced by workers in similar parts of this industry across different coun-tries. It may also help to explain why the labour market in the BPO industry is so fluid, a topic that will be further discussed throughout this volume.

1.5   The focus of the book

The current volume attempts to build on what we know about the BPO industry and ITES functions and activities around the world and, more espe-cially, the jobs that it provides. The discussion draws from the extensive existing literature regarding call centres – particularly in developed countries – expanding this literature to the developing world and also to other types of ITES. In that effort, we are aided by research teams from four different countries: Argentina, Brazil, India and the Philippines – all of them major 'players' in the global BPO industry. Each of these research teams conducted a comprehensive study of the BPO industry in their respective countries, with a particular focus on the quality of the working and employment conditions in the ITES or remote work positions that have been created. Two of these country studies – those in the India and the Philippines, with the largest BPO 'industries' in the developing world – went even further: they conducted surveys of BPO employers and employees, in an attempt to zero in more closely on the day-to-day realities of working life in remote work positions in the BPO industry. These realities not only include basic working conditions, such as wages, benefits and working hours, but also consider crucial issues for the industry such as work organization, stress and staff turnover – which, as we shall see, is almost universally high in this industry.

The order of our investigation proceeds as follows. Following this Introduction, Chapter 2 provides a broad overview of the ITES offshoring phenomenon by Dr. Phil Taylor of the University of Strathclyde, including a detailed discussion of the key factors that have been driving it. This chapter also describes the evolution of ITES, first within the main source countries – the United States, the United Kingdom and Canada – and then follows its logical evolution to offshore destinations. Chapters 3–6 cover in depth four major destination countries for global sourcing: India, the Philippines, Brazil and Argentina. Each of these chapters examines both the key characteristics of the BPO industry and its component firms in their respective countries, as well as analysing the quality of those remote work jobs in the industry – with a particular focus on those aspects that are related to working and employment conditions in different types of positions. Specifically, the analysis in each country chapter identifies trends in ITES, including the size, scope and characteristics of firms using remote work enabled by ICTs; the characteristics of workers engaged in such RWAs; the organization of work and employment conditions in these companies; and some key BPO business indicators, particularly the number one business issue in the global BPO industry: staff turnover.

Following this country-by-country analysis, in Chapter 7 the authors synthesize the material from the various studies of individual countries and integrate it with the (very limited) existing literature on the labour market and working conditions in the BPO industry. The aim is to identify some common patterns and important differences among those developing countries with substantial BPO 'industries,' with a particular emphasis on the four BPO destination countries that are the main focus of this volume. In this chapter we also develop a basic categorization of the major types of

RWAs that exist in BPO companies, and focus on some key indicators of the quality of jobs in the BPO industry (e.g., wages, working hours), and to the extent possible, given data limitations, within different RWA categories.

This analysis leads to a better understanding of the quality of employment in RWAs, and assists in the identification of some key factors associated with better employment conditions – and hence better job quality – in such positions. Based upon this understanding, the final chapter of the book, Chapter 8, offers some suggestions for government policies and company practices that hold the potential to improve the quality of these jobs. Such improvements can, in turn, also benefit BPO companies by, for example, reducing staff turnover, and leading to enhancements in service quality, productivity and, ultimately, the competitiveness of these companies.

2
Remote Work from the Perspective of Developed Economies
A Multicountry Synthesis

Philip Taylor

2.1 Introduction

The overall purpose of this chapter is to examine the dynamics under-pinning the global relocation of business services from the perspective of developed countries, and to consider the consequences for work, employment and employee relations that prevail in these countries. Since the offshoring of call centre and diverse back-office activities has been largely an anglophone phenomenon, the three countries selected for study – the US, the UK and Canada – are those from which the overwhelming volume of business services has been migrated.

Evidence for this dominance is not hard to find. For example, the employers' organization for the Indian software and business process outsourcing (BPO) industry, NASSCOM,[1] estimates that 60 percent of the value of BPO services delivered by India are from the US and a further 22 percent from the UK (NASSCOM, 2009, p. 64). These statistics have significance because India remains the single-most important destination for remotely located business services. Thus, the US and the UK are the most pronounced instances of developed countries that have experienced the outward migration of business services to remote locations, while Canada represents a somewhat different case because, although it too has had processes offshored to low-cost destinations, it simultaneously is a destination country as a *nearshore* location for services delivered to US customers.

We apply the same data template to each of these geographies in turn, beginning with an evaluation of the scale and nature of business service provision at the national level. In this undertaking, we note the greater ease of identifying call centres at the aggregate level, acknowledging that diverse back-office or business processes are often deeply embedded within organizations, notwithstanding varying degrees of domestic subcontracting. Often the latter only become manifest when externalized and relocated. Mindful of this limitation, we then construct an employment profile for each geography, with disaggregation by region, industrial sector and workforce demography, before evaluating the nature, scale and impact of offshoring. We then summarize the characteristics of working conditions and employment relations before providing concluding comments for each country. Data have been gathered from diverse sources, from industry and consultants' reports, government studies and from a range of academic studies and articles. Foregrounding the three developed country studies that form the bulk of this chapter is some necessary contextualization, aimed at situating the remote location of business services within the unfolding global landscape.

2.2   Global Service Delivery

A point of departure for this multicountry synthesis is the acknowledgement that the geographical relocation of business services from so-called developed countries to 'developing' countries now extends far beyond earlier experimental phases (Huws and Flecker, 2004). Indeed, the remote delivery of services to low-(or lower-)cost destinations has become a core element in corporate restructuring and process reengineering programmes. Many companies have shifted from tactical to strategic offshoring and in some cases to what is known as transformational offshoring. The latter implies not only a thorough alteration of the processes relocated, but also a concomitant transformation in the operational structure.

As the scale, diversity and complexity of information technology-enabled services (ITES)[2] subject to migration have grown, so too has the breadth of geographical reach. The increasing use of the term *global service delivery* by the multinational corporations (MNCs) providing business services is not mere rhetoric, but reflects an evolving material change in the geography of sourcing and service supply chains. Thus, we should alter the prism through which offshoring is viewed. Until recently, the relocation of business services was comprised principally of one-to-one migratory flows between an organization in a developed country and a remote operation in a particular developing country. Admittedly, offshoring companies often had more than one supplier, but the discussion was almost exclusively framed in terms of offshoring to specific *individual* geographies, notably India.

What have been emerging are multilocational, multisite strategies from both the demand and the supply sides, which have sought to capitalize on differing combinations of available skills and resources accessible in diverse locations, and which also serve different geographical markets or customer segments (Taylor and Bain, 2006). For example, a firm seeking lower-cost solutions may simultaneously outsource English-speaking voice services from India or the Philippines; Spanish-language services from Mexico or elsewhere in Latin America; various IT, technical and multilingual requirements from Eastern Europe; data processing from China and so on.

Consultants' reports articulate what global service delivery entails. For example, Kearney (2007, pp. 12–13) recommends that larger companies should develop 'cluster' footprints where the aim is to have one primary location supported by one or more secondary locations. The rationale is as follows:

> By staggering functions in multiple locations, companies can make cost–benefit trade-offs and adjust the functional mix over time as costs and availability of people vary....

Kearney further advises that in conditions where 'low-end' business transactions are involved, leveraging low costs is the dominant and perhaps even the sole driver, but where 'higher-end' activities are concerned, accessing deeper skills may be the most important criterion. In addition, if avoidance of disruption to services is an imperative, then care should be taken not to source from high-risk areas. Decisions should be influenced by additional factors such as language needs, time zones, cultures and regional coverage:

> [L]ocations should realise the best economies of scale. [...] [T]his model is flexible so tasks and functions can flow between centres over time as cost and talent situations change. (Kearney, 2007, pp. 13–4)

Scale and volume are salient aspects because, from the perspective of client demand, only the largest companies can pursue these strategies. For companies seeking modest offshoring a single-country strategy may be all that is needed. Notwithstanding the need to keep a sense of perspective, in that the overwhelming majority of business services are still delivered within the developed countries, a key starting point for considering global service delivery is the transformative role played by multinational companies. This is not to deny the importance of geography and place, whether at the national, regional or local scales (Dicken, 2007), nor is it to support the perspective of the 'hyperglobalists' (Ohmae, 1995) that national borders have become irrelevant as information and capital now flow across the world without inhibition. The world is not 'flat' Friedman (2005) contends. Indeed, one of the report's themes is that *globalization* actually heightens the importance of the characteristics of those specific places in which companies choose to situate facilities (Harvey, 1989, p. 294). Nevertheless, the transformation wrought on the supply side by multinational service companies has contributed greatly to a rapidly evolving global service landscape.

2.3 Multinational Service Companies

The role played by multinational service companies such as IBM Global Services, Accenture, Convergys, Sykes, Teleperformance and Hewitt Associates should not be underestimated. Most are MNCs with home bases in the US. Some are generalist providers of diverse services, from IT/software, to data management and customer relationship management (such as IBM). Others provide specialist services. In the expanding human resources outsourcing market, Hewitt Associates and now employs 24,000 'associates' in 34 countries (http://www.hewittassociates.com). Others specialize in the similarly expanding horizontal area of finance and administration. While Accenture is a multifaceted consultant and business service provider, its portfolio includes specialization in finance and administration processes.

A cluster of MNCs focus specifically on providing customer contact services. Teleperformance (http://www.teleperformance.com) claims 'the largest global footprint in the industry' with 293 centres servicing over 75 markets from 13 nearshore and offshore locations. Another excellent example is Sykes. Its locational map indicates the current reality of global delivery: eight centres in the US, ten in Canada (850 agents), two in Argentina (2,600+ agents), one each in El Salvador (500+ agents) and Costa Rica (3,000+ agents), one in Brazil, two in China (1,000 agent positions), eight in the Philippines (9,000+ agents) and 18 in Europe, the Middle East and Africa (EMEA) (4000+ agents).

Specialist voice companies are simultaneously onshore, nearshore and offshore providers, delivering services in multiple languages according to the different customer bases served. What these different types of MNCs have in common is their transnational reach and their ability to utilize common technology platforms to 'leverage' global sourcing.

Allowing for promotional hyperbole, EDS provides a good example of the technological infrastructure underpinning global operations, claiming that 'seamless transition' happens in its global services network (GSN):

> The GSN connects EDS's service management centers (SMCs) and data centers around the world in order to deliver uninterrupted service to clients and, ultimately, enable virtualization of data. [...] The GSN creates a mesh of data centers making it possible to move a single application that EDS delivers for a client anywhere in the world while sitting at a computer screen. (http://www.eds.com/news/features/3931/)

The ability of MNCs to 'source' from different geographies is enhanced by acquisition. For example, both IBM and EDS acquired leading Indian BPO companies Daksh (2003) and Mphasis (2007), respectively, enabling them to expand capacity in a single stroke by buying local expertise.

2.4   Global 'Captive' Companies

The Hong Kong and Shanghai Banking Corporation (HSBC) is an excellent example of a company operating in a single distinct sector, or 'vertical' in the parlance of the BPO industry', which delivers services in-house from multiple global locations. Headquartered in the UK, HSBC operates at least 15 global service centres in eight countries, with 20,000+ employees in India serving US and UK customers. Indeed, HSBC illustrates how the tentacles of global sourcing are reaching previously untapped destinations in the search for accessible skills at costs lower than in 'home' geographies. By late 2007, HSBC employed 500 people in Malta providing voice services for UK credit card customers. Relocation was precipitated by concerns over the quality of service from India, with the higher costs in Malta offset by greater linguistic and cultural empathy.

2.5 Indian Companies

We will examine the strategies of Indian BPO companies because they provide additional insight into the emergence of global service delivery. Major Indian BPO companies have been influenced by the need to emulate and compete with US service providers such as IBM and Accenture, and have moved beyond single-shore offerings to become transnational in their scale of operations. The most notable case is GE, which metamorphosed from a 'captive' provider into Genpact, a third-party global BPO company providing 'end-to-end customer support' for processes such as finance, accounting and collections.

> For example, we process and scan documents in Mexico for a customer. These documents are then used by our teams in India, China and Hungary. [...] In addition, for the same customer we provide voice support for their global locations from all four of our regions, depending on the language needs. A caller requiring Spanish gets routed to Mexico, while the one in English gets routed to India, Japanese to China and French to Hungary. (Pramod Bhasin, Genpact CEO, in NASSCOM, 2005, p. 16)

The seamless service, which Bhasin claims is delivered by Genpact, means that customers remain unaware of the dispersed and networked routing of processes. Bhasin's corporate aspirations give an indication of the extent to which ambitious client demand has changed the paradigm of offshoring since the early 'substitutionable' models, when processes or parts of processes were simply replicated in a transfer dominated primarily by consideration of cost. Genpact has stimulated Indian suppliers to develop global footprints (e.g., Evalueserve in China, Infosys in the Czech Republic). Further evidence of global diversification can be seen in the fact that Indian BPO providers now own several UK facilities. Such reverse shoring includes HCL in Belfast, FirstSource with two facilities in Northern Ireland and Tata Consultancy Services in Peterborough. Hero-ITES recently purchased the Scotland-based outsourcer Telecom Service Centres (TSC). Significantly, many Indian companies have opened sizable operations in the Philippines.

2.6   Unevenness of Global Sourcing

The emergence of new countries as important centres for sourcing has not meant the end of India's dominance. Global sourcing does not mean a level global playing field. NASSCOM-McKinsey (2005, p. 55) estimated that India accounts for 46 percent of all offshored BPO. NASSCOM's (2009) most recent calculation is that 790,000 people are employed in the Indian BPO industry.

Second in the global field of offshore destinations is the Philippines, which by one recent calculation has a total of 376,000 people employed in BPO, with no fewer than 227,000 employed in call centre services (BPAP, 2009). The Philippines' recent growth is remarkable given that at most 30,000 were employed in BPO as recently as 2003. It is clear that the country's development of back-office, data transcription and other services is leading to greater diversification beyond its earlier overwhelming concentration in voice activities.

Another growing location in English-language services is South Africa. It had 1,342 contact centres in 2008 (Patel et al., 2009, p. 43–44), nearly double the number for 2003 (Kearney, 2007), although Datamonitor (2006a, p. 41) presents a more conservative estimate.

What is most striking here is the sheer range of locations that are now considered as destinations for offshoring. The relative attractiveness of the diverse locations on a range of criteria is provided by consultant A.T. Kearney's (2007) *Global Services Index*, which ranks the top 50 locations worldwide for 'IT services and support, contact centres and back-office support.' Care should be taken in ascribing literal meaning to Kearney's numeric rankings, which should be regarded as indicative measures of *relative* importance rather than as definitive rankings. Kearney's metrics include IT and software services alongside BPO. In addition, the rankings do not indicate a firm's importance in the scale of markets, workforce size and other factors. For example, BPO in Thailand (ranked 4th) is not more important than the Philippines (ranked 8th), nor will the former supersede the latter as a destination. Despite obvious limitations, Kearney's rankings do provide some insight into the changing trends in the global services market.

A notable conclusion of Kearney's 2007 report is how the relative cost advantage of leading destinations has declined 'almost universally,' while scores for people skills and business environment have risen. While India and China continue to lead the index by wide margins, Southeast Asian countries remain their primary alternatives. India 'still offers an unbeatable mix of low costs, deep technical and language skills, mature vendors and supportive government policies,' despite a 30 percent increase in compensation costs over the previous 12-month period (from 2006 to 2007).

The Philippines present an additional interesting case in that while remaining the second most important offshore location, rapid growth and currency appreciation have increased wages in US dollars by around

30 percent. The five main Latin American destinations have risen in the rankings. Stimulated by India's example, state policies have promoted service exports, both nearshore to North America and remotely to Spain. Brazil's development is notable in one survey (Datamonitor, 2006a), which estimates 153,000 agent positions in outsourced call centres, albeit largely for domestic markets. It is claimed that new Central and Eastern European locations (e.g., Bulgaria, Slovakia, the Baltic states) are 'outshining' more established countries (e.g., Czech Republic, Hungary). Both Bulgaria and Romania have sharply improved their business environment scores following reforms required for EU membership. However, evidence of the Baltic states' markets indicates small-scale operations.

Datamonitor (2006b) estimates agent position numbers for Estonia, Latvia and Lithuania in 2007 at only 9,000, 1,000 and 2,000, respectively. The case for these locations has not been proven and their capacity is infinitesimal when compared to India or the Philippines. The general point is that the *potential* of many countries should not be confused with their *actuality* and their ability to provide services at a certain scale. In sum, there is often a lot of noise about newer destinations – but much less substance.

A key theme of this chapter, and a conclusion drawn from the evidence of the selected country studies, is that, notwithstanding the increasing global reach of offshoring, the bulk of service provision remains in the onshore and nearshore locations of developed countries. To repeat, a sense of perspective is required when the scale of offshoring is considered in relation to the overwhelming bulk of business services delivered within the developed countries.

2.7 Linguistic Capability and Cultural Compatibility

When mapping global relocation to developing countries it is necessary to stress a vital point – that offshoring largely follows the contours of linguistic and cultural compatibility, which is often the legacy of colonialism. Thus, as indicated in the Introduction, the largest proportion of all relocated services is in the English language. Significantly, from the perspective of the US, UK and Canadian case studies, the English-speaking Indian BPO industry derives around 60 percent of its revenues from the US (NASSCOM, 2009), which represents a relative or proportionate decline from an estimated 85 percent in 2002 (NASSCOM, 2002), suggesting faster rates of relocation from other countries.

NASSCOM (2009) estimates that 22 percent of its revenues come from the UK, a relative increase from the 20 percent of Indian BPO revenues that were calculated as coming from western Europe in 2005 (NASSCOM, 2005), although other European states have been negligible in comparison to the contribution of the UK. Recent figures provided by the Business Process Association of the Philippines suggest that 90–95 percent of its industry 'faced' the US market. Thus, US companies are the most significant actors in shaping the relocation of business processes and in developing the BPO sectors in the two most important destinations.

The limited French offshoring has been to the francophone African countries – Morocco, Tunisia, Mauritius and Senegal (Datamonitor, 2006a, pp. 23–40). Services from Spain have migrated to Latin America, which also serves Spanish-speaking North American customers. According to Datamonitor (2006a), the Czech Republic, Hungary and Poland are the most important destinations for German-speaking services. Wherever language capability exists in developing countries, companies based in developed countries will attempt to leverage cost advantages through relocation. Even small pockets are sourced. Dalian, a city in northeast China, serves as a Japanese hub because it has approximately 100,000 Japanese speakers.

In contrast to 'globalized' manufacturing, the linguistic abilities of workers in relocated business services are key to successful delivery, particularly in the case of voice services. However, it is necessary to draw a distinction between call centres, which interact with customers in the 'home' geographies, and many back-office processes, which do not. Of course, linguistic competencies are important for the latter because they require employees to read, interpret and communicate in written English, but the importance of sophisticated language skills is far greater for voice services (Taylor and Bain, 2005).

The implication that ITES cannot be located just anywhere is truer for voice work than for back-office work. If finding the lowest costs was the *sole* criteria driving the global location of BPOs (and more specifically call centres), then China, Vietnam and states with costs lower than India would be the preferred destinations for English-language services. While China does deliver some data processing for overseas markets, the level of international call centre services hardly registers. Datamonitor (2006) estimates only 7600 outsourced agent positions, largely for Japanese clients. Despite rapidly expanding numbers of English-speakers, the relocation of voice services to China is not currently a viable proposition.

The specific case of multilingual contact centres further illustrates the sensitivity of voice services to the availability of advanced linguistic skills. These centres emerged in the mid-1990s and tended to be pan-European operations run directly by, or on behalf of, US multinationals. IBM's Greenock operation is a notable UK example. Ireland, in particular Dublin, and the Netherlands have been most prominent. Research by the author (Taylor, 2007) indicates that these countries remain the most important hubs despite the claimed promise of lower-cost multilinguistic capacity in Eastern Europe and undeniable growth in the Czech Republic, Poland and Hungary. The scarcity of European languages in India means that multilingual centres are not feasible, other than for delivering domestic services in the different Indian languages.

Arguably, the global relocation of business processes and particularly call centres may be regarded as a *qualified* 'race to the bottom.' It is a combination of factors (including infrastructure, connectivity, telecom costs, regulatory environment, skills, educational levels, managerial knowledge, linguistic capability and cultural empathy) *combined with* the lowest possible costs that provides the basis of comparison between places and informs locational decisions. According to this reasoning, BPO offshoring contradicts the received wisdom of the so-called hyperglobalizers that capital is *entirely* footloose and helps explain why it is that, notwithstanding the dramatic expansion in global sourcing, many business services will remain either in the 'home' developed countries or may be 'glocalized' to nearshore destinations.

Of course, the desire to leverage lower costs remains the principal economic driver behind relocation; however, many other factors (quality, temporal flexibility, etc.) are also an important part of the equation. Commensurate with this understanding, the distinction between call centres and non-customer-facing processes is important, because the latter appear less susceptible to linguistic sensitivities and arguably can be more readily relocated. In this rapidly changing global landscape, the emerging trend appears to be that non-voice processes and will continue to be offshored at a faster rate than voice services.

2.8 Underlying Economic, Geographical and Locational Dynamics

There always has been a geographical, or spatial, dimension to the location (and relocation) of business services *within* developed economies. Information and communication technologies (ICTs) have profoundly shaped the organization of work and facilitated geographical diffusion in the subsectors of 'information network services,' particularly finance and telecommunications (Miozzo and Soete, 2001).

The vital point is that distance-shrinking technologies have both enabled remote delivery *and* generated economies of scale through the centralization of previously dispersed facilities. The restructuring of work organization is inseparable from a thorough transformation of the spatial division of labour. The reconfiguration of the *processes* of service delivery is intimately connected with a transformation in their *loci*.

In the UK, distinctive clusters of call centre and back-office activity emerged in so-called peripheral regions as companies evaded high-cost metropolitan locations and capitalized on the availability of less expensive labour possessing the requisite skills, low property costs, advanced telecoms connectivity and regional incentives. From this perspective, the drive to relocate overseas should be regarded as an extension, albeit dramatically and at a *transnational* scale, of the same cost-saving, profit-enhancing, spatial dynamic that operated at the *national* scale. Evidence suggests similar patterns in the US.

Further, for some companies now engaged in offshoring, the experience of *domestic* outsourcing has proved a necessary transitional stage that has helped to instill confidence in the potential for later transnational migration. At the same time, for many companies the relocation of back-office and/or call centre services was legitimized by the earlier success of the remote outsourcing of IT/software development work, notably to India. Thus, growth in business services offshoring is intimately linked to the prior development of India's software sector and its favourable institutional environment (Dossani and Kenney, 2007).

2.9 'Taylorism' Through Relocation and 'Rising Up the Value Chain'

Prefiguring the studies of countries, it is helpful to provide insight into the actual migratory process from 'source' to 'destination.' Different approaches can be detected, which are often related to the contractual relationship between the company engaged in relocation and the service provider. At one pole there is the 'captive' model in which the firm owns and controls its remote operations (e.g., HSBC). At the other pole, there is the classic outsourced paradigm in which a third party undertakes to deliver services on behalf of the company that purchases its services. Between these poles lie diverse arrangements through which differing degrees of control and ownership are exercised. These include build–operate–transfer, by which a partner establishes the remote operation and agrees to transfer the process to the 'host' company after an agreed period, various types of co-sourcing, and joint ventures.

Despite contractual differentiation, certain common tendencies are detectable in the migratory process. A typical initial approach was 'lift and shift,' in which processes were transplanted without modification and tight service level agreements monitored remote delivery. Yet reengineering most often precedes, accompanies or follows migration and has tended to involve the disaggregation of processes into distinct constituent parts. Prior to migration, it is usually concerned with ensuring that the process is made as 'risk proof' as possible and can withstand transition without damage or error. During migration the process can be re-engineered, again to minimize risk, but also for leveraging cost advantages. Re-engineering following migration is mostly related to bringing cost and quality improvements. All this recalls the re-engineering revolution (Hammer and Champy, 1993) by which processes were decomposed and standardized with the focus on cost-effectiveness. The author's research (Taylor and Bain, 2006) evidences this re-engineering. For example, GE pioneered an approach that involved a 12-step methodology that, in one case, saw 46 diverse process components reduced to 7 standardized components.

What have been relocated the most have *tended* to be the most standardized and transactional voice and back-office processes, which are further segmented and standardized through migration. This 'Taylorism through export' should be seen as one of the main factors facilitating relocation. While the initial focus may be on ensuring that processes are delivered reliably, with minimal risk, at comparable levels of quality and at lower cost, following migration clients and suppliers seek to leverage improvements in speed, flexibility, innovation and productivity. The longer the processes have been migrated the more the emphasis shifts to continuous improvements rather than simple replication (Dossani and Kenny, 2006).

Synthesizing evidence from multiple sources, we conclude that global sourcing has been and will remain largely dominated by the relocation of standardized transactional flows, where scale economies prevail. However, two trends towards greater complexity can be detected: first, modest increases in complexity in a portion of services within this standardized provision, and second, the emergence of distinctively knowledgeable or professionally customized services of higher value, which are increasingly considered under the rubric of knowledge process outsourcing (KPO). Certain firms have emerged in the developing countries, such as Evalueserve in India, which are dedicated KPO providers (http://www.evalueserve.com/Home.aspx), while the larger MNC providers (e.g., IBM, Accenture) do provide services with this greater complexity. Thus, the answer to the perennial question of whether offshored BPO is rising up the value chain and is of greater complexity is a highly qualified affirmative.

2.10   Political Economy, Global Regulation and Governance

While there is no enough space in this book for detailed analysis of the global political–economic contexts, regulatory frameworks and their impact upon ITES location, certain observations are essential. The most obvious is to understand that what is driving global servicing is not just the revolution in ICTs, nor the transformative role played by transnational corporations, nor the sharply competitive markets and sectors in which companies operate, but broader underlying changes associated with liberalization, privatization and deregulation (Harvey, 2005).

The dissemination of ICTs that are integral to the relocation of business services has been hugely facilitated by profound changes in the structure and markets of the global telecommunications industry, which largely derive from deregulation. Since the mid-1980s governments have subjected state-controlled telecom monopolies to competition. Following the UK's Telecommunications Act (1984), the pace accelerated with similarly named US legislation (1996) and the EU's 1998 decision to liberalize the sector (Fransman, 2002). Deregulation has proceeded albeit unevenly across the globe. For example, in India the National Telecom Policy (1999) generated reductions in business rates and opened up national, long-distance and international connectivity to competition. This deregulation hugely facilitated the growth of ITES by reducing costs and making remote delivery attractive to North American and UK clients. In addition, the long-term deregulation of financial markets provided a complementary impetus, notwithstanding the fact that certain regulatory constraints have been put in place.

At the broadest environmental level, relocation has been encouraged by the promotion of free trade agendas through the World Trade Organization (since 1995), notably General Agreement of Trade in Services (GATS), and by other institutions of global governance. That these agendas are embraced to varying degrees in both developed and developing countries underscores the importance of the state's role in promoting business environments conducive to offshoring. The UK is a good example of a state committed to the globalizing and deregulatory agendas. The government's 'globalization' White Paper (DTI, 2004a) celebrated the virtues of trade liberalization, arguing that offshoring and the free trade in services are beneficial to the economies of both source and destination geographies through increased overall demand. While it is conceded that offshoring might pose certain 'challenges to which the government will respond' (DTI, 2004a, p. 40), such as the need to consult with workers, concerns over breaches of labour standards, redundancies and skill issues, the protectionist case is emphatically rejected.

> [T]here are often good business reasons for offshoring. If a company has concluded that moving one function overseas will increase its chances of growing and prospering in the longer term, then it would be wrong for Government to try to stand in its way. (DTI, 2004a, p. 41)

The UK government presumes that extensive (if not universal) benefits derive from business service relocation. In the US, similar corporate and political commitment to offshoring has been partially qualified by the opposition of several states to the relocation of public sector work as part of a general political rejection of offshoring. Much of this coincided with John Kerry's presidential candidacy in 2004 at the height of concerns over offshoring (Blinder, 2006). It remains to be seen what the outcome will be of President Obama's proposals aimed at preventing the tax benefits enjoyed by companies engaged in offshoring.

Meanwhile, states are compelled to address issues of data security and privacy, although with contrasting responses. The US acted independently and the EU collectively to revise existing laws. The EU Data Protection Act bars the transfer of personal information from EU countries to others 'unless that country's laws have been certified by the EU as providing "adequate" protection of the personal data.' In contrast, the US has passed laws (e.g., the

Health Insurance Portability and Accountability Act) that consolidate the 'mosaic' of state laws.

Acknowledging the dominance of neo-liberalism in the growth of global sourcing should not lead us to minimize the importance of the state as a proactive agent shaping the contours of business service relocation. Intervention occurs in order to ensure that, in competition with other states, their particular 'territories' are recipients of inward investment. This happens in both developed and developing countries, at both national and local/regional levels, and takes manifold forms including material benefits (e.g., tax credits, training grants, regional assistance, export zones), the promotion of favourable legislation, the deregulation of labour markets and so on.

While recognizing common trends in business process relocation that transcend differences between countries, it is necessary to acknowledge the strong institutional shaping of business practices at the national level. Hall and Soskice (2001), in challenging the perspective of globalization as generating an undifferentiated market model, emphasize the power of national institutions to shape particular forms of government in particular contexts. One acknowledges pertinent differences between liberal market economies (e.g., US and UK), characterized *inter alia* by labour market deregulation, and coordinated market economies (e.g., Germany) with greater regulation. Huws (2003) makes reference to the further distinction with Mediterranean economies, perhaps typified by networks of small firms.

2.11 Labour

The offshoring and indeed the nearshoring of business services have created a new international division (or divisions) of labour. The most common interpretation assumes that a fundamental dualism now prevails between labour in the global North and the global South. For labour in developed countries, the received wisdom is that workers have little choice but to resign themselves to wholesale redundancies in the face of global low-cost competition and a 'race to the bottom.'

In particular regions, the actual or potential threat to jobs is magnified by a recent dependence on call centre and business process employment in the context of deindustrialization. The UK's Department of Trade and Industry (now BERR) estimated in 2003 that 38 percent of new jobs were in call centres, a proportion greater in 'peripheral' regions. Similar concerns may be advanced in relation to Eastern Canada and parts of the US. In addition to profound job insecurity, other expected outcomes include an intensification of work, downward pressures on pay and conditions and 'concession bargaining.' To the extent that employees are collectively organized, relocation poses a major threat to trade unions and their ability to protect jobs and defend working conditions. Superficially, at least, it appears that unions and workers in developed countries are powerless to prevent or mitigate the consequences of service relocation.

Further, it is popularly supposed that it is almost impossible to make common cause with ITES 'professionals' in the global South, since they are presumed to see themselves as benefiting from the very job losses that afflict labour in the global North. As this dichotomy suggests, the effects of 'globalization' are experienced differentially by groups of workers in different places (Dicken, 2007, p. 489).

In the context of protecting jobs and defending labour standards, Union Network International's Call Centre Charter (http://www.union-network.org/UNIsite/Events/Campaigns/CallCenter/CallCentresCharter. html) might be seen as a limited starting point for a response, but the establishment of global framework agreements (GFAs), which might establish worldwide bargaining arrangements, remains an elusive objective. In the UK country study below, we refer to union attempts to resist job loss as a consequence of offshoring and indicate the range of responses that unions have adopted – from internationalistic and solidaristic to nationalistic and protectionist. Nevertheless, embryonic union organizing initiatives in developing countries, notably UNITES in India (http://www.unitespro.org/), indicate the additional potential for developing connections between labour in the source and destination geographies (Taylor and D'Cruz et al., 2009).[3]

2.12   Offshoring, Nearshoring and Onshoring

Any consideration of the actual and potential impacts of offshoring from the perspective of developed countries must take account of the dynamics of global sourcing. If the study of trends in developed countries can provide a valuable counterpoint to the developing country studies, then it is important that the former are embedded in this broader framework of global service flows. Consequently, from the perspective of the firms, sectors and labour in the developed countries selected for study (the US, the UK and Canada), it is necessary to acknowledge the combination of 'shores' that might be involved in the location and relocation of business services. Thus, this study is framed by an understanding of the possibilities, impacts and threats suggested by *offshore, onshore* and *nearshore* delivery.[4]

A key question driving this chapter follows from our understanding of these dynamics: to what extent have the advantages that were realized in the initial phases of internal relocation within developed countries been supplanted by greater advantages that can be realized by either nearshore or offshore relocation? What might helpfully frame our country studies is an evaluation of the principal factors driving and inhibiting offshore relocation as informed by this preliminary discussion. The following list in Box 2.1 is not definitive but indicative. It is not being suggested that each country study will be able to examine each factor in detail, but the framework can be used to guide the study.

Box 2.1 Principal Factors Driving and Inhibiting Offshore Relocation

Drivers

- Extent of realizable cost reduction, particularly labour cost drivers
- Labour market factors in developed countries – labour/skill shortages, attrition, recruitment difficulties
- Perception of advantages deriving from labour factors in offshored or nearshored destinations, language and cultural attributes, skills, availability
- Ability to migrate more complex processes
- Competitive pressures and vertical and sector-specific drivers
- Company restructuring, including mergers and acquisitions
- Shareholder pressures
- Ability to achieve labour flexibilities
- Avoidance of union recognition
- Regulatory frameworks in destination geographies, data security, etc.
- Governments (national and local) support/incentives
- The supportive role of industry bodies
- Perceived technological and infrastructural capabilities in destination geographies

Inhibitors

- Evidence and impact of rising costs/especially labour costs in destination geographies
- Difficulties in overcoming language, accent and cultural difference
- Doubts over ability to handle more complex work
- Difficulties in exercising managerial control over remote, distant operations
- Problems of scalability
- Technological difficulties and other infrastructural problems
- Security risks
- Attrition, recruitment, training and other HR problems
- Immaturity of ITES sector in destination geography
- Political backlash in home country

Box 2.1 (Continued)

- Lack of customer confidence/customer resistance
- Trade union campaigns and their effects
- Negative effects on domestic operations, e.g., poor morale, job insecurity
- Alternatives to offshoring, e.g., automation, increased flexibilities, intensification of effort.

In examining the impact of offshoring or nearshoring, call centres are more identifiable than back-office processes at aggregate levels. Non-customer-facing processes are often deeply embedded within organizations and become manifest only when relocated. Consequently, in the national studies, locational developments are easier to chart for voice services than for the back office. Nevertheless, we can employ approaches that enable us to make some sense of developments in nonvoice-ITES. We can 'track back' to the country of origin the processes relocated given our knowledge of ITES industries in developing countries. Also, the author's UK primary research delivers insights into the relocation of non-customer-facing processes.

2.13   United States

2.13.1   Introduction

The transformation of the configuration and loci of service delivery in the US originated with telecom call centres (Batt and Moynihan, 2002, p. 16). The centralization of customer contact eliminated jobs and reduced the variety and complexity of the remaining positions. Thus, telephone operator call centres provided the model of efficiency that was emulated throughout the economy in the 1990s. In those early days, call centres were more likely to be located in regional rather than national markets, but in the current decade, the typical call centre serves national, rather than local, regional or international markets. In the 1990s, annual growth rates were spectacular at 15–20 percent (Anton, 1999) so that, by 2000, nearly 3 percent of the US workforce was employed in call centres (Datamonitor, 1999). In the current decade, growth has slowed significantly as companies that could have benefited from call centres have already mostly done so. *Maturation* of the 'industry' coincided with the economic recession following the dot.com crash and widespread pressures in increasingly competitive markets to cut costs. Within these contexts, the options of outsourcing domestically, nearshoring to Canada (and Mexico) and offshoring to distant locations became attractive. Although new centres have opened and many

Table 2.1 Numbers of US Agent Positions, Agents and Contact Centres (2004–2006)

Year	No. of Contact Centres	Percent growth	Agent positions	Percent growth
2004	58,300	−1.0	3,115,000	−0.3
2005	57,600	−1.2	3,090,000	−0.8
2006	56,900	−1.2	3,070,000	−0.7

Source: Contact Babel, 2006, pp. 36–38.

existing ones have expanded, the combined effects of externalization and consolidation have produced a net employment decline (Table 2.1).

Business processes, the catch-all term for myriad white-collar processes that organizations undertake in servicing employees, vendors and customers (Dossani and Kenney (2003, p. 9), became one of the fastest growing job categories during the economic 'boom' of the 1990s (Goodman and Steadman, 2002). What occurred was the decomposition of these activities into their constituent elements and then, as part of re-engineering and digitization, the outsourcing of these activities to both generalist service providers such as EDS, IBM and Accenture, and to clusters of smaller third-party operators.

This involved the disaggregation of processes into 'core' and 'noncore' elements, whereby the latter – as the most standardized, and involving the least risk – could be externalized. The 'hollowing out' of firms occurred as the contracting out of services was expanded to encompass larger proportions of 'noncore' activities. Initial relocation of services was intranational. As call centres relocated from higher-cost cities to lower-cost towns, attempts to reduce wage costs for back-office work also saw firms move operations out of cities to the Midwest and elsewhere where accents of workers were neutral, educational levels were acceptable and labour costs were lower. The resulting cost savings could be up to 20–30 percent, but on the down side, shallow labour pools often limited scalability. In a pattern common to developed countries, factor costs and skills availability became the principal locational determinants as physical and technical constraints declined in importance. The transfer of processes to outsourcers *within* the US helped legitimize remote location at a later stage. In this sense, domestic outsourcing and offshoring should be seen as steps in a continuum of externalized arrangements that leads to offshoring rather than as discrete initiatives (USGAO, 2005, p. 10).

2.13.2 Employment Profile

Although precise data on contact centre employment levels do not exist, it is possible to make informed estimates based upon recent reports and academic studies. For the year 2006, Contact Babel (2006. p. 10) calculates that there were 56,900 centres and 3.1 million agent positions, which translates into roughly 5 million employees, or 3.7 percent of the employed population. There was a large number of small call centres. Contact Babel (2006, p. 12) calculates that 92 percent employed 100 or fewer employees, compared to 44 percent in Batt et al.'s (2005a) sample.

Conversely, disproportionately large employment has been found in the biggest centres, particularly in outsourcing and in the retail, financial services and telecommunications sectors. Given that the larger the call centre, the more standardized the processes and the greater the economies of scale, the conclusion has been that these sectors were the most vulnerable to offshoring.

One additional pertinent factor has been that financial services, outsourcing, telecommunications and retail also have had the highest proportions of outbound calling. Outbound voice services are an important element in the ITES industries of India and the Philippines. Finally, evidence from the available reports suggests that the US contact sector employment level is likely to remain stable or may only marginally decline. Expansion in the public sector workforce combined with some growth in the transport, travel, leisure and medical sectors will not offset contraction in the financial services, telecommunications, retail, utilities and IT industries. In its forecast for the future, Contact Babel (2006, p. 40) expected the contact centre sector to be 65,000 employees smaller by 2009.

2.13.3   Location by Region

Data on locational dynamics provide important insights. Contact Babel divided the call centre sector in 2006 into four regions – West, Northeast, Midwest and South – and found that although the South had the most agent positions, the industry was least vital to that region in the proportion of the employed population (3 percent). The Midwest and Northeast have the greatest share of the workforce in contact centres, at 4.1 and 5.2 percent, respectively. At the level of 'division' (groupings of similar states as employed by Contact Babel), New England (6.2 percent), Middle Atlantic (4.9 percent), West North Central (4.2 percent) and East North Central (4.1 percent) had the greatest concentrations of employment.

Batt et al. (2005a, p. 27) note that centres tend to cluster in certain locations. Despite the spatial flexibility offered by distance-shrinking technologies, and the fact that firms are opting for smaller nonmetropolitan or suburban areas, metropolitan areas still account for most new call centre investments. These patterns are influenced by incentives offered by local or state authorities. In the 1990s, many domestic outsourcers (e.g., Teleperformance, Teletech) and generalist providers pursued these advantages, capitalizing on labour flexibilities and lower union densities to site facilities in low-cost states.

2.13.4 Sectoral Breakdown

Three vertical sectors (finance, retail/distribution and telecommunications) and the domestic outsourced subsector (which is considered separately by consultants, industry bodies themselves and academics) are the most important sectors, accounting together for nearly 55 percent of employment (Contact Babel, 2006, p. 15). Financial services is the most significant sector, and it is amongst companies with the largest centres that the tendency towards offshoring appears most marked. The second most important sector is retail and distribution, which includes catalogue/direct mail retailers, package couriers, retail support for stores and niche retailers. Retail has grown quickly through telephone support for online shopping. The telecommunications sector, including fixed-line and mobile operators, accounts for one-in-eight of the workforce and, particularly where large standardized operations for the mass market are involved, has been susceptible to offshoring. Contact Babel (under)estimates the outsourced subsector at over 10 percent of the call centre workforce. Batt et al.'s (2005a) sample divided into 86 percent in-house and 14 percent outsourced operations.

2.13.5 Demographic Profile of the BPO Workforce

Acknowledging the difficulties in accessing comprehensive data for the diverse BPO employment category, it is nevertheless possible to draw upon data from call centres which might, despite all the evident qualifications, serve as a partially satisfactory proxy. In this respect, data from *The Global Call Center Industry Project* are a relatively recent and helpful source. A general point to note is variability according to diverse demographic characteristics.

Batt et al. (2005a, pp. 9–11) found that the mean age of a worker was 30 years old, with the average age in the newer outsourced subsector 27 years old, and in financial services 28 years old, which were lower than in the more established telecommunications (31 years old) and retail (30 years old) subsectors. In other words, the age distribution of the workforce was consistent with the relative age of the establishments.

In terms of gender distribution, women make up almost two-thirds and men slightly more than one-third of the US call centre workforce. Nevertheless, the difference is observable with greater proportions of males working in what might be considered higher-end centres in larger businesses and IT (59 percent and 56 percent, respectively), while women constitute between two-thirds and three-quarters of employees in lower-paying jobs and in outsourced centres. This pattern of intrasectoral differentiation extends to employees' educational level. The lowest levels are in the outsourced and retail subsectors, and the highest levels are in financial services, business and IT client centres.

High levels of attrition have long been recognized as a widespread feature of the contact centre sector. Batt et al. (2005a) found attrition rates to be the greatest amongst outsourcers (51 percent per annum) and in retail centres (47 percent), and lowest amongst large business centres (28 percent) and in telecoms (26 percent), in which case unionization exercises a positive influence, reducing workers' propensity to leave. By definition, attrition rates are directly related to tenure rates. For example, 40 percent of workers in retail and outsourced centres had less than a year's experience on the job (Batt et al., 2005a, p. 23). By contrast, centres in telecoms and those serving large business units had about 20 percent of employees with less than a year's tenure. We do not know the comparable figures for attrition rates in business services, but recognize that attrition rates are higher and tenure rates lower amongst employees engaged in the most standardized of processes.

2.13.6   Offshoring

Business service offshoring is not a new phenomenon. Credit card processing and some call centre work have been done in Latin America and the Caribbean for two decades. What is new is the pace and the scale of developments, driven by organizational and technological changes and economic pressures, and also by pioneering initiatives in India.

The impact of decisions taken by American Express and GE Capital to relocate facilities in India in the 1990s was huge. The motivating factor was the promise of substantial cost savings under the conditions of tightening domestic labour markets in the 1990s 'boom.' NASSCOM–McKinsey (2002) claimed that GE achieved annual savings of $340 million from its Indian operations. Thus, GE demonstrated that the global relocation of business services, firstly to India, was a viable proposition.

The earliest offshoring involved in-house operations, and early mover 'captives' included Dell and Hewlett-Packard. However, the complexion of the industry and the specific impetus for offshoring changed thereafter. Indian third parties such as EXL, Spectramind, 24/7, Mphasis and WNS increasingly attracted US work as the post-dot.com downturn intensified sectoral competition and focused boardrooms on the need to cut costs. Under these conditions the appeal of remote locations took off. Subsequently, multinational service providers (e.g., IBM, Convergys, Accenture) entered the Indian BPO space and significantly accelerated offshoring. As major domestic outsourcers, these firms possessed 'domain' knowledge and could now promise the same service quality at much lower cost. For clients, the leap into the global unknown was seen as less perilous if it was being undertaken by an IBM or Convergys rather than by a relatively unknown Indian company. Further, providing back-up in the US allowed for service-level guarantees that firms operating only in India could not deliver.

Beyond the two most significant destinations (India and the Philippines), consideration should be given to the relocation of Spanish-speaking services to Central and Latin America. It has been suggested that the preferred strategy of US outsourcers is to create or deepen a presence through partnerships with, or acquisitions of, local firms. For example, Sykes bought Apex, an Argentinean-based outsourcer, and Stream acquired the Supra Telecom contact centre in Costa Rica. Service delivery from Latin America can involve layers of subcontracting through local outsourcers. In Guatemala, the BPO company Cap Gemini hired Transcatel to answer calls for the utility company TXU Energy. Not all the services for the US are in Spanish; Ateneto, a call centre outsourcer owned by Spain's Telefónica, employs 125 agents in Guatemala serving US Airways' English-speaking customers.

The fact that the bulk of the processes offshored are at the low end of the value-added spectrum (Dossani and Kenney, 2003, p. 21) is confirmed by extensive primary research (Taylor and Bain, 2003, 2006). This generally low level of complexity has characterized both voice and nonvoice processes in the most important 'vertical,' financial services, and also in telecoms, retailing, utilities, IT, travel and hotels. Mention should be made of diverse, specialized, but also standardized ITES services that have been relocated, such as medical transcription. A partial qualification to this generic standardization is technical help-desk work. However, voice services still constitute around 50 percent of all the work transferred to India, and up to 90 percent to the Philippines.

In sum, the evidence from 'source' and 'destination' countries demonstrates that the bulk of back-office work that is offshored is routinized and transactional. Nevertheless, there is evidence of some moves up the value chain. For example, by 2005, GE reported that equity research for investment banking, analytical capabilities for price modelling, risk management and underwriting were all being offshored. Increasingly, US companies are relocating what has been termed KPO centred on professionals who possess appropriate skills and educational qualifications, such as engineers, accountants and lawyers. KPO delivered from India and Eastern Europe marks a significant development, enabling higher-quality jobs to be relocated. Clearly, the threat to professional occupations has grown, but a sense of proportion is required as these genuinely higher-skilled posts are only a small proportion of offshored activity.

It is impossible to calculate the precise numbers of jobs 'lost' to offshoring, a conclusion drawn by others (Dossani and Kenney, 2007). Although the Bureau of Labor Statistics (BLS) of the US Department of Labor began minimal reporting of offshored jobs in 2004, data gathering is quite incomplete. A USGAO study (2004, p. 3) admitted that federal statistics provide only limited information. Thus, the US government's analysis appears speculative and supported by little empirical evidence (USGAO, 2004, 2005). They concluded that offshoring was 'not likely to affect aggregate US employment in the long run, but acknowledge that in the short run, workers will lose their jobs when employers relocate production abroad' (2005, p. 25). The USGAO (2004, p. 34) based on Mass Layoff Survey data, showed that 'overseas relocation' was given as a reason for only a small fraction of workers laid off between 1996 and 2003. Of the 1.5 million layoffs reported in the 2003 Mass Layoff Survey, only 13,000 (0.9 percent) were due to overseas relocation, and 96 percent of those were in manufacturing. The USGAO concludes that industries associated with services offshoring had experienced growth in the previous decade and were expected to grow up to the year 2012.

Two approaches help in assessing the scale of offshoring. Firstly, from what we know of employment levels in the destination geographies and the share of services that are provided for US clients in the destination geographies, it is possible to make some estimate of the numbers of US 'facing' jobs. Since, as of 2008, there were approximately 790,000 employees in Indian BPO and we know from NASSCOM's figures that around 60 percent of the business volumes derive from the US, then we can adopt this proportion as a rough guide to employment levels. By this deductive method – which obviously produces indicative estimates rather than definitive findings – it is not unreasonable to suggest that approximately 470,000 Indian BPO employees 'face' the US. In the Philippines, around 90 percent of employees are engaged in US work (BPAP, 2009), which yields approximately 330,000 jobs, the overwhelming majority in call centres. Combining these two geographies, perhaps 800,000 jobs 'face' the US. The data on other locations are too sketchy for reasonable estimates.

Secondly, the data from individual companies that exclusively or largely provide services for the US provide insight. By late 2007, Citigroup had around 20,000 posts in India; JP Morgan 9,000; Genpact 20,000; Dell 15,000; IBM 23,000; Convergys 12,000; EDS 20,000; Sutherland 12,000 and Accenture 35,000. In the Philippines, Dell had 2,500; Teleperformace 3,500; Sykes 9,000+; Accenture 15,000; Stellar 3,500; Convergys 11,000 and Teletech 17,500.

However, within the conditions of overall business growth, employment growth in India and the Philippines does not mean the displacement of exactly the same numbers of US jobs. Nevertheless, significant job loss has occurred in specific sectors (e.g., financial services, telecoms, retail, outsourcing) and for particular occupations, mostly but not exclusively in contact centre roles. Given weaknesses in official data sources, research by the Communications Workers of America (CWA) and 'tracking' by Washtech (Washington Alliance of Technology Workers) provide some knowledge of the deleterious effects of offshoring on workers, challenging the USGAO's benign assessment.

Legislation aimed at preventing offshoring has focused on government procurement contracts, although if the restrictions were broadly construed they could inhibit offshoring generally (Schultz, 2007). As of 2004, 23 states and the US Congress had bills pending. A regulatory framework pertaining to specific 'verticals,' or offshoring in general, requires compliance with various laws, including the Sarbanes Oxley Act, the Gramm–Leach–Billey Act, HIPAA, the Fair Debt Collections Act and the US–EU Safe Harbour Act.

Speculation surrounds the possible return of call centre jobs. The much-publicized decision by Dell in 2003 to repatriate 150 jobs was seized upon by opponents of offshoring, although it was the outcome of a wider rationalization that ultimately boosted employment in India. Another example is AT&T's decision to return 3000 customer service posts previously offshored and outsourced to Accenture in 2004–2005. New centres in Texas, Indiana, Florida, Kentucky and Louisiana have opened, but only following concessions made by the CWA (2007) in respect of pay and conditions. To persuade AT&T to repatriate technical support posts, the CWA negotiated a separate a job title and pay scale, including a rate for labour productivity. In sum, the scattered instances do not constitute a general trend towards repatriation.

Detailed evidence about the implications for workers and unions comes from the CWA (2004, 2005a, 2005b). Their central argument is that the relentless search for lower labour costs, which drives both outsourcing and offshoring, is 'hollowing out' US companies. Concrete examples indicate the effects for workers. They cite the case of a major unionized telecom firm that has been squeezed by low-cost competition from new entrants. Consequently, 40 percent of 'consumer service' calls have been migrated to Convergys (India), VXI (Philippines) and ACS (Mexico). The CWA estimated 1500 jobs had been lost by 2005. In 'business services,' 1000+ jobs were lost to IBM and Accenture in India. Another unionized incumbent outsourced 3300 technical support roles to TeleTech, Televist and CallTech, with 2000 offshored.

Meaningful opposition to, or the ability to mitigate the effects of, offshoring has only occurred in firms where trade unions have an organized presence. Concretely, this has meant the CWA in telecoms as the most vigorous opponent of offshoring, although even when able to defend jobs, as at AT&T, it was at the cost of diluting conditions. A national officer explained: 'The most important protection against job loss through offshoring and the loss of jobs is the union contract and through it working together with employers' (Interview with a CWA national officer, August 11, 2007).

The paucity of collective agreements in financial services and elsewhere means that outsourcing and offshoring appear wholly uncontested. The fact that many multinational service providers are nonunion, if not antiunion, is additionally significant. If unionized workers are vulnerable, then the fears for job security and worsened conditions are magnified amongst the many millions who lack the organized protection of a union. It is principally for this reason that the CWA has argued that union organization is the most effective protection against offshoring (CWA, 2004, p. 7). Where the CWA is present, it has affected the course of outsourcing. Yet unions generally recognize that additional political and legislative action is required to dissuade companies from pursuing low-wage options. Initiatives include campaigns over 'right-to-know' legislation in which companies would need to inform

customers from where calls were being handled, restrictions on states contracting out to non-US call centres, educational campaigns highlighting
customer service and data security issues and the demand that offshored jobs
be tracked by government agencies including the Bureau of Labor Statistics.

2.13.7   Employment Relations

Batt et al. (2005a) explore deeply into the characteristics of work organization, working conditions and HRM practices. Essentially, they conclude that
the large nonunion component has become the dominant business model.
This is the 'low road' in which pay is often at a minimum, conditions are
inferior, work routines are intense, training and development are limited
and attrition levels are high. By contrast, unionized centres have better pay
(16 percent higher on average) and conditions, high performance work practices and a more committed and productive workforce with lower attrition.
However, in conditions of intense sectoral competition, even 'high road'
unionized companies are under pressure to cut costs through intensification,
outsourcing and ultimately offshoring.

Given that employment relations are strongly influenced by prevailing
institutional arrangements, the extent of collective bargaining coverage
is an important factor. The salient fact is that overall US union density is around 12 percent, although it is lower in the sectors in which
business services are embedded. The highest densities are in telecoms,
which were dominated until the early 1990s by public monopolies, and
which retain clusters of unionized centres. The unionized companies (e.g.,
AT&T, Qwest and Verizon) negotiate comprehensive collective agreements
with the CWA.

Deregulation of the industry threatens unionized centres directly with
new, nonunionized competitors, and indirectly with downward pressures on
pay and working conditions resulting from outsourcing. Union density has
declined markedly over the years so that less than one in three of Batt et al.'s
(2005a, p. 29) telecoms sample are unionized. There is also the virtually
union-free independent segment, including the 'bottom-feeders.'[5] The most
important wireless carriers (e.g., Verizon–Vodafone, Sprint PCS, T-Mobile,
Winstream) and cable companies (e.g., Comcast), similarly, are almost all
nonunion. Unionization in financial services is negligible, at less than 2 percent. Equally significant regarding the ability to challenge offshoring is the
absence of union representation in outsourcing and retail. In sum, there is
a gulf between the unionized pockets, notably in telecoms and what can be
described as organizational deserts.

2.13.8   Conclusion

In assessing the impact of offshoring, the US government (USGAO, 2004,
2005) has supported the view that free trade in services is beneficial and
has downplayed its negative effects. The USGAO (2005, p. 8) suggests
that US direct investment in developing countries (e.g., India, Philippines,

Malaysia, China) has been relatively small, about 1 percent or less of total US direct investment in each case. Furthermore, the USGAO (2005, p. 27) concludes that even estimates of domestic job loss represents 'a small enough fraction of the total number of jobs destroyed and created' so that the labour market is capable of absorbing the changes despite the possible longer-term structural effects of offshoring and job displacement. Others are more alarmist. Bardham and Kroll (2003) examined the BLS's occupational categories and found that up to 14 million service jobs, whose content could be easily routinized and exported, were vulnerable to offshoring. Kroll (2005) upgraded this to almost 15 million (12 percent of the labour force), although he qualified this by observing that not all are *likely* to be offshored.

Call centre employment seems set for marginal decline, and the finance, telecom and outsourcing sectors will continue to be hit most by offshoring. The largest centres, handling the most transactional calls, will be most affected. This may have particular geographical impact given the locational patterns that have been established over the past two decades.

While the majority of processes have been standardized in content, certain professional and higher-skilled positions are increasingly threatened by relocation. This is undoubtedly related to the fact that through global service delivery, US multinational providers now access diverse labour pools of higher skills. Despite legislative restrictions on government contracts and regulatory requirements, there appear few restraints on relocation. Where union organization is absent, the decision of organizations to relocate often goes uncontested. Despite the best efforts of the CWA, Washtech and others, workers are highly vulnerable to corporate decisions that are often presented as a *fait accompli*. There is a democratic deficit which only wider union organization can ultimately remedy. From the perspective of addressing this imbalance, the formulation of appropriate labour standards and codes of corporate conduct would be a meaningful exercise.

2.14 United Kingdom

2.14.1 Introduction

The proliferation of UK call centres in the mid-1990s was prefigured by the earlier establishment of data processing centres. Typically, these were new centralized operations, or expanded existing facilities, located at some distance from higher-cost metropolitan areas in which company headquarters or government departments were situated. However, it was in financial services that locational trends affecting the back-office and particularly voice services most profoundly influenced developments across the UK economy, driving firms towards relocation, domestic outsourcing and ultimately offshoring.

Several factors combined to revolutionize the sector's structure, operational methods, loci and employment relations. Regulatory reform through the Financial Services Act (1986) and the Building Society Act (1986) collapsed the distinctions between the banking, insurance and mortgage subsectors, intensified competition and ushered in an era of mergers and acquisitions. Back-office rationalization was soon accompanied by the transformation of interactive customer servicing, to produce the distinctive organizational form of the call centre.

The integration of telephonic and communication technologies was fundamental to this development (Taylor and Bain, 1999), in particular the introduction of Automatic Call Distribution (ACD) switches enabling calls to be routed to waiting operators within and, crucially for later offshoring, *between* centres. The centralization of previously dispersed – or newly created – interactive servicing and sales processes generated cost savings and significant scale economies, at the same time transforming the labour process and leveraging added value.

The question of scale is extremely important, as many centres developed as large-scale sites of mass service delivery. The DTI (2004, p. 29) estimated that 56 percent of centres employed 250 people or more. Scale was inextricably related to space and place as, crucially, it was no longer necessary to situate call centres in physical proximity to customers. 'Distance-shrinking' technologies simultaneously encouraged relocation to regions, cities and towns characterized by a supply of relatively inexpensive skilled labour, in addition to significant cost and infrastructural advantages (Richardson and Marshall, 1996). Thus, even before the advent of offshoring, there had always been this *spatial* dynamic inherent in call centres, that is, an underlying geographical imperative that was inseparable from corporate concerns over cost reductions and profit maximization.

The call centre became central to an organization's pursuit of competitive advantage. It was the lean, demonstrably efficient and profitable financial services call centre model that provided the template for telecoms, retailing, entertainment, travel, holidays, utilities and, later, public services. We note also the rapid growth of the outsourced sector and the growing presence of US third-party providers. Although overstated, the figures (Table 2.2) demonstrate the dramatic expansion in employment followed by a decline in the *rate* of growth from the late 1990s. Additional sources confirm these general trends (IDS, 1997–2005; Taylor and Bain, 2001, 2003).

The emerging paradigm was the mass production call centre (Batt and Moynihan, 2002), in which standardized call flows prevailed, call throughput was prioritized and ICTs were utilized to control employees and to measure productivity. This does not deny the existence of more complex forms of 'quality' customer interaction, particularly for higher-value customers. However, it helps explain that the technologically driven, low-cost, and lean-production organizational form had, by virtue of its *relative* spatial flexibility, the potential to be located overseas. What was true for voice services was also true for the back office.

Table 2.2 The UK Contact Centre Industry – Agent Positions and Employment (1995–2004)[6]

Year	Agent positions	Employment[6]	Growth rate (%)
1995	143,900	230,240	N/A
1996	169,800	271,680	18
1997	203,800	326,080	20
1998	264,800	423,680	30
1999	331,200	529,920	25
2000	387,500	620,000	17
2001	430,100	688,160	11
2002	460,200	736,320	7
2003	494,300	790,880	7
2004	538,700	861,920	9
2005	616,700	986,720	8

Source: DTI, 2004b, p. 26, from Gartner Dataquest, Datamonitor and Contact Babel.

2.14.2 Employment Profile

The UK government (DTI, 2004) memorably forecasts that the call centre workforce would surpass 1 million by 2007. Yet, official statistical sources are unable to provide exact figures since occupational classification does not adequately capture the full extent of call centre employment. Informed sources, such as the Contact Centre Association (Interview, Anne-Marie Forsyth, CEO, September 10, 2007), suggest current employment at over 800,000. Notably, the domestic industry is continuing to expand *at the same time* that overseas migration is growing. A majority of organizations in IDS's (2005) survey expected growth, while only 8 percent predicted contraction (largely through offshoring). Current growth is not confined to existing facilities, as UK and international companies are still setting up new operations; e.g., in the last 3 years, Barclays, Dell and O^2 have sited sizeable facilities in Glasgow.

2.14.3 Location by Region

Much discussion has centred on the concentration of activity in the 'peripheral' regions. Yorkshire, northeast England and Scotland all emerged as early call centre and business process clusters (Bristow et al., 2000). Just as national states compete for inward investment, so too can intranational competition be observed. In the mid-1990s, each of these regions claimed to be the UK's 'call centre capital.' Other regions – the Northwest, South Wales, the Midlands and later Northern Ireland – followed their example, promising lower costs (enhanced by incentives) and skills availability as labour markets tightened, costs rose marginally and attrition grew in 'first mover' locations.[7] Dispersion increased as facilities were situated in 'untapped' towns, and for some organizations, at least, this geographical shift represented an 'externalization' by which services were transferred to an outsourcer domestically that perhaps facilitated offshoring at a later stage. Confirmation that costs are related to region comes from evidence of salary variation, although sectoral effects and occupational differences are perhaps more important influences for the call centre and back office (IDS, 2005, pp. 29–31). West Midlands and the Northwest are the lowest cost regions, and London and the Eastern regions are the highest. Comprehensive regional data was provided by the DTI (2004b, pp. 37–42). The Southeast has the greatest number of agents, but the Northwest, Yorkshire and Scotland have the densest concentrations and the greatest numbers working in large centres.

2.14.4 Sectoral Breakdown

The largest numbers are employed in financial services. The DTI (2004b. p. 32) estimated that 25.5 percent of employees are in this 'vertical,' while Taylor and Bain (2003, p. 32) estimated 31.6 percent. In turn, the next most important sectors are telecoms, retail and distribution, utilities, transport/travel, IT, leisure, media and the public sector. Disagreement exists over the importance of outsourcing. The DTI's claim (2004b, p. 32) that 6 percent of agent positions are in third-party operations is an underestimate. With confidence it can be concluded that outsourcing employs at least 20 percent of the UK workforce and is continuing to expand. The most recent comprehensive audit of Scotland's contact centre sector found that 28.5 percent of employment was in the outsourced sub-sector (Taylor and Anderson, 2008, pp. 27–28)

2.14.5 Demographic Profile of the BPO Workforce

The overall youth of the call centre workforce is confirmed by many sources. The DTI (2004, p. 60) cited a national survey that estimated the average age of an agent at 28 years, and Taylor and Bain (1997, 2003) calculated that two-thirds of employees were aged 35 years or younger. Baldry et al. (2007, p. 239) found that 84 percent of employees were aged 40 years or younger. Similar to the US workforce profile, there is an obvious relationship between the age of the centre and the age of its workforce, with a younger profile in particular amongst newer entrants. While the presence of young people who leave school early and a transient student cohort act to reduce the mean age, the numbers of women 'returners' exercise an opposite effect.

In common with the US, women form the majority of the UK workforce. Estimates vary but most sources agree that they comprise around two-thirds of those employed (Belt et al., 2002; DTI, 2004, p. 61). Longitudinal data from Scotland's contact centre sector suggest, however, a discernible trend to a proportionate decrease of women and, conversely, a relative increase in the numbers of men employed. By 2008, females comprised 58 percent of employees and males 42 percent. Nevertheless, gender has an effect, with men tending to be concentrated in the IT/computer sector, in technical/help desk roles, and in certain higher-level financial services' activities. Higher proportions of women are employed in the travel/transport/holiday sector and in 'pure' customer service roles generally.

There are also similarities to the US with respect to the educational levels of workers, with higher skills found in particular sectors and roles. Almost two-thirds of the workforce have school certificates, Higher National Certificate (HNC), vocational or further education qualifications. Reflecting the student and ex-student segment, one study (Baldry et al., 2008, p. 239) found as much as many as 28 percent of employees had undergraduate or even post-graduate experience or qualifications. Given the latter, there was a proportion of the workforce might be seen to be underemployed.

Only limited data exist on marital status. In Baldry et al.'s study (2008, p. 240), 28 percent of the contact centre sample were married/living with a partner and had no children, a further 25 percent lived with a partner and children, 23 percent lived with parents and 19 percent lived on their own or with flatmates.

As in the US, attrition is seen as a particular problem, despite the tendency to underestimate rates of turnover. The annual rate of 13 percent as proposed by Holman and Wood (2002) is perhaps the most obvious example of inaccuracy and reveals the difficulty of trusting figures provided by management. More reliable and recent data come from Incomes Data Services (IDS), which calculated annual attrition from its most recent annual survey at 24 percent (IDS, 2008, pp. 15–16). Outsourcing reported the highest incidence of attrition at 39 percent, followed by retail at 31 percent and was lowest in the public sector at 17 percent. IDS also calculated the average tenure of contact centre agents at 34 months, but rates varied according to sector. Again, we note all the qualifications about transposing this contact centre specific data for business services.

2.14.6 Offshoring

During autumn 2002, two decisions changed the landscape of offshoring. Prudential announced the closing of its Reading call centre and the transfer of 850 jobs to Mumbai, and HSBC migrated 4,000 posts to India and Malaysia. While the overseas relocation of voice services had been presaged by the migration of IT/software and some processing, the offshoring of call centres and back-office operations to India grew rapidly thereafter. Just as financial services had been the principal sector involved in relocation within the UK, so too has it played a key role in overseas migration. Initiatives by UK and foreign-owned companies (with UK facilities) include Aviva, Lloyds/TSB, Barclays, Royal and Sun Alliance, Zurich and Axa.

Second in these terms is the telecoms sector. The key decision was British Telecommunications' 'remote sourcing' strategy (2003), in which 2200 posts were transferred to Indian third parties, which was followed by the off-shoring by mobile operators such as Vodafone, 3G and OneTel. In the travel/holidays sector, companies included British Airways, Virgin Atlantic, Thomas Cook and National Rail Enquiries Service. The point to empha-size is the sectoral diversity, which also includes utilities (e.g., Centrica), media/entertainment (e.g., BSykB) and motor services (e.g., Automobile Association).

Mention should also be made of UK domestic outsourcers (e.g., Vertex, Capita, Ventura, Xansa) who have built capacity in India, creating the pos-sibility of work being offshored via a common platform. The long-term impact on the public sector may be considerable. Despite political sensitiv-ities against offshoring government services, there is evidence of contracts being awarded that use offshored capacity. In February 2007, Xansa signed a £19 million, 6-year deal with the National Health Service to provide finance and payroll services from sites in Southampton and Pune.

Although early commentary on offshoring was dominated by discussion of call centres, it soon became clear that more than voice services were being migrated overseas; for example, in November 2003, when Aviva announced that 2300 posts were to be created in India, the majority were in the back office. The principal driving force has been the perception that relocation will deliver cost savings and increase profits. This is a reason overwhelm-ingly reported by firms (Taylor and Bain, 2003, p. 55; 2006, p. 149). Initial attempts at reducing costs *domestically* through technological innovation,[8] work intensification (Taylor et al., 2005) or domestic outsourcing could not generate savings on the scale promised by offshoring. The underlying impor-tance of sectoral competition was summarized by one operations manager of a major insurer:

> We took back-office work to India predominantly for reasons of cost. This was also true for the front office as well, but there are limitations in the front office. What lay behind the need to offshore was the competitive nature of the insurance industry and its regulations. The effect was to really squeeze the margins, which means that if you are going to exist and thrive in this sort of business the cost of your organization becomes abso-lutely key. And that is why you'll see a lot of financial services companies going to India. [...] (Taylor and Bain, 2006, p. 150)

This initial competitive cycle led to a 'herd' mentality as shareholder pres-sure profoundly influenced corporate decisions to offshore. Related to the fundamental cost-cutting and profit-maximizing imperatives are the closely related factors of accessing supplies of skilled labour. Other advantages cited by employers include the need to expand a company's global operations, to extend operational flexibility, and to do work that would be economi-cally prohibitive in the UK. Others report their desire to escape tight labour markets and overcome labour retention problems. While there is no evidence that union avoidance has been a *primary* motive driving relocation, the benefits of utilizing labour without being encumbered by the need to consult with workers is acknowledged.

Offshoring also provides the opportunity to undertaking process re-engineering. Relocation has rarely meant the wholesale substitution of services in India for those in the UK, but it has involved the slicing-off of the least risk-laden and most standardized processes. Following initial migration of the most transactional processes, further operational reviews might reveal additional activities that could be offshored. Offshoring has increasingly led to some dichotomization in call centres, whereby the most routinized services are offshored while value-adding, cross-selling and higher-end customer relationship management are retained onshore. Scale economies and business volumes are intimately related to offshoring. In 2003, the mean size of call centres operated by companies engaged in offshoring was more than twice the industry average (Taylor and Bain, 2003, p. 52). What is important is not size *per se,* but the fact that larger companies with larger facilities have higher volumes of standardized calls which lend themselves to relocation. Certain regions with higher proportions of large centres were more vulnerable to offshoring (DTI, 2004b, p. 41).

While several powerful forces drive offshoring, several factors inhibit migration. UK employers indicate that the most commonly reported disadvantages have been linguistic and cultural problems, which impact negatively on service quality. Inevitably, organizations are reluctant to admit to these problems, but occasionally revelations emerge that provide insight into the difficulties. The following is a selection from the minutes of an internal Q&A session on offshoring led by the CEO of a major insurance company (November 26, 2006):

> He also felt that regional accents within India proved an issue; the Pune accent was not as easily understandable as other sites. They have listened to feedback and household claims have returned from India to the UK. [...] [He] has also offered management the opportunity to bring the whole operation back to the UK provided it can be run for the same cost as in India, but this isn't financially possible. [...] [He] stated that off-shoring had a big image problem. He has banned outbound calling from India because customers don't like it and neither do the staff in India. There was 80 percent staff turnover in the outbound area. [...]

Breaches in data security and confidentiality have periodically surfaced, causing some to question relocation. Many companies also report problems in controlling operations remotely, a difficulty exacerbated when third parties are used. Increasingly, companies have become aware of labour market difficulties in India in relation to recruitment, training and retention associated with rising labour costs. Companies (2006, pp. 189–192) reported that labour shortages in overheated markets in India might restrain further offshoring.

For many firms, then, the advantages of offshoring have not always been seen to outweigh the disadvantages and, even when decisions to off-shore have been taken, there have been constraints on the types of services involved. Although cost differentials are fundamental to offshoring, it is a much more nuanced and complex process than commonly understood. We note the cluster of financial service companies to have publicly rejected call centre offshoring (e.g., Royal Bank of Scotland, Nationwide Building Society) and who used their decisions to lever competitive advantage.

Many organizations initially offshored only the most simplified and tightly scripted call flows, and it is clear that the bulk of those calls migrated thereafter remain standardized services. In banking, this means, as a senior manager put it, 'the full range of banking inbound inquiries,' and in insurance it typically means the first notification of claims, policy renewals, and so on. Yet, several organizations report some increase in complexity whether through help lines or cross-selling. Yet, this is a matter of *relative* complexity. Back-office offshoring also consists largely of routine processes.

Over time, a small amount of more complex work has followed, but some organizations regard specific types of work as unsuitable for migration, particularly where stringent regulatory compliance by the Financial Services Authority (FSA) is involved.[9] However, continued re-engineering might make hitherto complex processes amenable to offshoring by 'taking the complexity out,' as one manager has said. The evidence suggests that more complex work will be offshored in non-customer-facing roles than in call centres where the factors inhibiting offshoring apply to a greater extent. Contradictorily, call centres still form the largest part of services to have been migrated, although they are the most susceptible to customer dissatisfaction. Several organizations have announced the return of all or part of their voice services; these include Powergen (*Financial Times*, June 16, 2006), Lloyds/TSB, Abbey and Esure. Yet these decisions do not represent a general trend, nor are they paralleled by similar repatriation decisions in respect to back-office functions.

Closure and downsizing have led to compulsory redundancies even when firms have claimed that job loss could be accounted for by voluntary redundancies. Examples include the closure of Lloyds-TSB's Newcastle call centre (2004), Aviva's Newcastle facility (2004) and six HSBC data centres (2003–2005). Most often, redundancies are carried out across an organization's operations. Unionization appears to be a prerequisite for meaningful opposition to offshoring (Bain and Taylor, 2008; Taylor and Bain, 2008), and we can draw certain conclusions from the campaigns of UK unions. The threats to membership and influence are real, since many offshoring firms do recognize unions for collective bargaining, particularly in financial services. Often unions have only been able to achieve limited success in preventing the migration of work.

Two examples of relative effectiveness are Amicus at Prudential (2002), where the union secured a 3-year job security agreement,[10] and USDAW at the home-shopping company Reality (2004), where it was able to cap the posts offshored. In both cases members were mobilized in effective campaigns and strike actions were threatened. Unions have not striven to secure compulsory agreements as a minimum, but in practice this often has meant some involuntary job loss. Some union campaigns have been imbued with a tone of nationalist protectionism (e.g., Lloyds-TSB Union), while others have taken a more principled internationalist position. For example, Amicus reps at Prudential argued that Indian workers had the right to jobs and decent conditions, and their campaigning focus challenged corporate rationales of cost-cutting and profit-maximization.

No offshoring company that recognizes unions in the UK has extended collective bargaining overseas. Consequently, the aspiration for unions in transnational companies is to achieve GFAs, which can protect labour standards, secure rights and mitigate the effects of globalization. UK unions also work through international bodies such as Union Network International to share information and coordinate activities. In recent years, the finance sector of Unite has collaborated with UnitesPro in India, the union established in September 2005, with the aim of providing a voice for Indian BPO employees. Delegates from UnitesPro were invited to Unite's Finance Sector Conference in June 2008. Finally, unions are concerned with the indirect effects of offshoring, particularly a further intensification of work as call centres and the back office become ever more 'lean.' Several motions to Amicus' (now Unite's) 2006 Finance Sector conference opposed employers' use of benchmarking against overseas operations as a justification for raising performance targets. In sum, offshoring poses enormous challenges for unions by removing certain elements of the insulation they have always enjoyed by organizing at a national level.

2.14.7 Employment Relations

Issues of work organization and management practices in call centres have attracted considerable academic and popular attention. The most convincing analyses have demonstrated that, notwithstanding similarities in technological architecture, call centres are differentiated according to many variables including sector, functions undertaken, the customer segment served, the degree of simplicity/complexity, call times and the extent of managerial control (Deery and Kinnie, 2004). Nevertheless, most centres assume a mass-production type, producing a fairly distinctive call centre 'regime' in which employee discretion is circumscribed, manifold controls (technological, bureaucratic, cultural-normative) operate, and for many employees work is experienced as pressurized and often stressful (Taylor et al., 2003).

From what is known, much the same can be said of routine back-office tasks. However, business services are more variegated, ranging from basic processing to analytical and professional work involving high levels of discretion and autonomy. Trade unions have largely been successful in extending recognition from the organizations with which they have agreements to newly established call centres (Bain and Taylor, 2002; IDS, 2003). However, recognition remains uneven with most union members found in financial services, the public sector and utilities – where strong collective bargaining traditions exist – and with fewer clusters in telecommunications (outside BT), travel and retail.

2.14.8 Conclusions

The complexity, contradiction and nuance of developments must be emphasized. Certainly, powerful forces drive relocation (overwhelmingly to India,[11] with the principal driving force the perception of significant savings. Despite rising costs and the erosion of India's longstanding advantage, the differential with the UK is so great that India still remains attractive. Other factors act to inhibit migration, but these restraints apply more to customer-facing call centres than to the back office. There remain compelling reasons why organizations retain many facilities onshore. Contrary to the received wisdom of globalization, it is not the case that 'everything will go.' Cataclysmic predictions of mass offshoring have proved unfounded as the domestic call centre sector has grown *at the same time* as offshoring (ONS, 2005). Synthesizing extensive primary and secondary data, and calculating numbers from 'source' and 'destination,' we make the informed estimate of at most 80,000 agents in India, who either 'face' UK customers or undertake back-office work for the UK. A sense of scale is necessary because this equates to only around 10 percent of the UK's call centre workforce.

The decisions of firms to relocate services are shaped by the complex interplay of many factors. Larger firms are increasingly locating certain processes onshore and others offshore. Given cost differentials and regional incentives, locating within the UK often resembles *nearshoring*. Indeed, Scotland now promotes itself as a nearshore location offering *relatively* lower costs (compared to metropolitan London and the Southeast) combined with high-end skills.

Locational decisions are not based solely on cost criteria alone, so that proximity to the customer base, linguistic and cultural affinity and sensitivity to customer preferences might dispose organizations to choose more costly but less risky nearshore delivery over remote shoring for some business services. In addition, automated solutions, technological change, process re-engineering, raising the levels of productivity and intensification of effort and domestic outsourcing all remain alternatives or complements to offshoring. This does not deny the prospect of increased offshoring, nor does it negate the fact that many workers will face insecurity and job loss. The processes most vulnerable to offshoring in voice and nonvoice are among the most standardized.

The evidence suggests that we may be on the cusp of a new offshoring wave, which may hit the 'peripheral' regions with greater impact, but this is more likely to be in diverse back-office processes than in voice services. Existing trends do suggest that offshoring will encompass more complex and higher-skilled areas, particularly in finance and accounting, human resources, shared services and legal, but also in design, animation and architecture (*The Guardian*, November 24, 2007). Thus, the vulnerabilities that routine white-collar workers are experiencing will extend to higher-status occupations. Many professionals can no longer consider themselves immune from the effects of globalization.

2.15 Canada

2.15.1 Introduction

Canada is important not only as a developed country case study but also because it is a defined case of nearshoring. As a consultant's study of Canadian contact centres summarizes: 'American companies have utilized Canada as a natural place to outsource given the cost advantage, the cultural and technological similarities and the proximity to the US marketplace' (Mercer, 2006). Thus, this country study will provide insights into the extent to which Canada as a developed economy of the Global North has been able to present itself as a relatively lower-cost and 'safer' destination for US companies as they make location decisions in the context of the wider migratory flows to the Global South.

Huws (http://www.chs.ubc.ca/emergence/workshop.html) aptly describes Canada as having an *ambiguous* role in that it is simultaneously a source *and* a destination country. A crucial question is the extent to which remote delivery is eroding Canada as a nearshore location.

Canada's contact centres grew dramatically in the years after 1997. It is estimated that the sector's share of the labour force grew by 7 percent per annum throughout the 1990s, compared to less than 1 percent for the economy overall (Centre for Spatial Economics, 2004). The application of the call centre model promised cost savings in familiar sectors (telecoms, financial services, IT, media) and involved the re-engineering and reconfiguration of processes by the largest corporations, paralleling developments in the Anglo-Saxon economies.

There were two dimensions to location or relocation – firstly, the establishment of centres serving national or regional markets and, secondly, the emergence of Canada as a nearshore destination for US clients. The evidence suggests that although the sector is expanding in size, the *rate* of growth has declined. Nevertheless, the dispersion of the call centre market has continued and, with e-government public sector activity, has actually notably expanded. However, it appears that employment has now stabilized or even contracted in parts of Canada, such as Manitoba (MCCA, 2007). Although modestly growing demand from the US has been maintained until recently (Contact Babel, 2006), it has been suggested that nearshoring is being undermined by changes in the exchange rate, which reduce Canada's cost advantage.

2.15.2   Employment Profile

Statistics Canada, the federal government agency, does not collect data on contact centre employment. The method adopted is to select six proxy occupational groups, but these underestimate the overall workforce size. Nevertheless, figures from diverse sources enable us to provide a workable estimate of the numbers employed. At the high end are figures from a study conducted for the Canadian industry that calculated employment at 500,000, or 3.4 percent, of the working population (HRDC, 2002). At the low end is the Labour Force Survey figure of 112,000 (Statistics Canada, 2005). Datamonitor (2006a) and Contact Babel (2006) estimate the number of 'agent positions' at 248,000 (approximately 400,000 employees) and 298,500 agent positions (480,000 employees) in 2007, respectively (Table 2.3). These are consistent with the Centre for Spatial Economics' total of 370,000 for the year 2000. In sum, the current contact centre workforce is estimated to be between 450,000 and 500,000 employees.

2.15.3   Location by Province/Region

Studies disaggregate the sector by employment, nature of operations, sectoral composition and characteristics of work organization according to province or region. Van Jaarsweld et al. (2007, p. 9) found the greatest concentrations in the central provinces (Ontario, Québec) with 42 percent

Table 2.3   Canadian Contact Centre Agent Positions/Agent Numbers (2004–2010)

Year	Agent Positions	Agent Numbers	Percent growth
2004	274,600	439,360	n/a
2005	281,200	449,920	2.4
2006	290,500	464,800	3.3
2007	298,500	477,600	2.8
2008	305,000	488,000	2.2
2009	311,000	497,600	2.0
2010	315,500	504,800	1.4

Source: Contact Babel, 2006. *North American Contract Centres in 2006: The State of the Industry*, Contact Babel: Sedgefield, UK.

of total Canadian employment, followed by the western provinces (British Columbia, Alberta, Saskatchewan, Manitoba) with 32.9 percent and the eastern provinces (Nova Scotia, Newfoundland, New Brunswick, Prince Edward Island) with 25.1 percent. The most important area of activity is Ontario, with more than one-third of Canada's total workforce.

Developments beneath national or regional levels are important. In metropolitan areas a recognizable trend is many employers establishing operations in suburbs and adjacent smaller urban centres in order to access untapped labour pools escape labour market overheating and capitalize on lower cost infrastructure (Mercer, 2007). Further, there are disproportionate levels of employment in specific locales, notably the much-publicized case of New Brunswick. Comprising 2.3 percent of Canada's population, New Brunswick has an estimated 8.5 percent of Canada's workforce (van Jaarsveld et al., 2007). This is the legacy of successful attempts by its government to attract contact centre business from elsewhere in Canada and the US. By 2004, New Brunswick employed 18,000 people – 4.6 percent of its labour force (UNCTAD, 2004, p. 197) – in call centres. Current employment is 21,000. New Brunswick was a model for other provinces and development agencies as they competed to attract inward investment. The eastern provinces, particularly New Brunswick, have provided greater incentives than other provinces and have therefore been more successful as near-shoring destinations.

2.15.4 Sectoral Breakdown

The data on sectoral composition generally mirror the profile of other developed economies, in that financial services, telecoms and retail all have the densest concentrations of activity. Recent surveys differ in the specific weightings. While Contact Babel (2006) finds financial services to be the most significant 'vertical,' for van Jaarsveld et al. (2007) telecoms is the leading sector. Studies do agree on the salience of outsourcing. Van Jaarsveld et al. (2007, p. 11) found that outsourced centres comprise 37.7 percent of all centres, a finding consistent with Contact Centre Canada (2005) at 37 percent. Again the influence of region (or subregion) is important. According to van Jaarsveld et al., greater numbers of outsourced centres are found in the eastern provinces (50.8 percent) than in the central (43.8 percent) or western (25.8 percent) provinces. A recent study (CCA, 2007) concludes that smaller, lower-cost communities in the eastern provinces engaged disproportionately in lower-value activities such as telemarketing, market research and order taking.

2.15.5 Demographic Profile of BPO Workforce

Limited data exist on the demographic profile of the Canadian BPO workforce, even for the more researched and identifiable call centre segment. The average age of employees in the sector is estimated to be 32 years

(Skarlicki et al., 2007). Gender composition is similar to that in the US and the UK, with one calculation suggesting that 69 percent of the workforce is composed of women (Jaarsveld et al., 2007). Once again there is differentiation within the industry, with near-equivalence between males and females in IT and the subsector's help desks and a much larger proportion of women in the general areas of inbound customer service and collections. The lowest education levels in van Jaarsveld's study are found amongst agents in outbound centres, while the highest education levels are found in in-house centres.

2.15.6   Nearshoring

Studies reveal Canada's emergence as an important nearshore location for US companies. Van Jaarsveld et al. (2007) found that 30 percent of centres serve US customers. The CCA (2006) reported that US customers accounted for 20 percent of Canadian call volume and US work was significant for 30–35 percent of centres. Important differences between the regions can be discerned. Almost six in ten centres in Eastern Canada serve international markets compared to roughly a quarter in Central or Western Canada. 'International' services are provided by Canadian firms, by US companies and by global service providers such as Convergys, Teletech, Teleperformance and Sykes. Five of Sykes' ten Canadian centres are located on the eastern seaboard. An *ensemble* of cost, quality, labour supply, infrastructure and political factors has driven relocation from the US.

Never solely a question of cost arbitrage, there has always been a trade-off between cheaper labour costs *and* considerations of quality. Costs are approximately 20 percent lower in parts of Canada than in the 'source' geography. KPMG suggested labour costs to be as much as 37 percent lower in Canada's ICT sector (*The Economic Times*, November 5, 2005). Cost savings include those associated with Canada's national health care system which removes the necessity for employers to provide employee insurance, so cross-border relocation transfers part of the social costs from employer to the state.

Additional attractions of Canada as a nearshore location are its proximity to, and shared time zones with, the US. Canada's legal and governmental frameworks also matter for they reduce many of the risks and control problems associated with remote shoring. For US firms considering whether to locate overseas or nearshore to Canada, the understanding that it is not necessary to invest in language, accent and cultural training must weigh in the latter's favour.

Finally, we must emphasize the impact of low exchange rates between the US and Canada, which have provided additional impetus since the late-1990s. However, in the last 5 years the Canadian dollar has appreciated by roughly 55 percent against the US dollar. Stories are now emerging about the negative consequences of this appreciation. In August 2007, Connect North

America abruptly closed two 'outbound' centres in New Brunswick, causing 375 redundancies (*The Telegraph-Journal*, August 31, 2007). The nearshore *outsourced* model is likely to face the greatest threats from unfavourable exchange rates. The CCC study (2007, p. 3) concludes that 'the higher Canadian dollar has fundamentally altered the competitive environment [as] Canadian contact centres no longer enjoy a significant cost advantage over contact centres in the US., that are situated in population centres of comparable size.'

2.15.7 Offshoring

The limited data suggest a contradictory picture. There certainly is evidence of job loss as a consequence of offshoring to India and the Philippines. Newspaper reports are peppered with examples, including the relocation to India of an Air Canada passenger complaints call centre, although the company claimed no involuntary redundancies (*Montreal Gazette*, January 26, 2006). Dialogue Management Group laid off 170 call centre agents when it transferred work to Convergys centres in Salt Lake City and Pune (*Windsor Star*, August 21, 2007). Indian-based Sutherland Global Services has shifted work, including processes for Dell, from its Canadian locations to offshored sites. Telecoms have been particularly affected where the offshoring of services has followed the well-established trend to domestic outsourcing. (The only exception has been the publicly owned SaskTel of Saskatchewan.)

For example, in January 1999, during contract negotiations with 2400 operators represented by the Communications, Energy and Paperworkers' Union (CEP), Bell partnered with the Arizona-based outsourcing specialist Excell (now Stellar) to create a new company to provide services. Bell's employees were offered employment with inferior wages and conditions. The threat of offshoring became a reality in 2003, when according to Joe Hanafin, Communications Director of CEP, around 5000 jobs started to be lost (Telephone Interview, November 13, 2007).

All the Canadian telecoms companies, particularly the big two, Bell Canada and Telus, have offshored customer service roles. The highest-profile case has been at Telus, where the company threatened, and then used, offshoring to its global facilities to degrade working conditions. Ultimately, this became a key case when the employees' union (TWU) wished to draw a line in the sand over outsourcing and offshoring and its effects. However, some studies suggest that Canada might be less affected from global relocation than the US (CCC, 2007, p. 14). It does appear that the domestic contact sector demonstrates robustness and the indicators are that in the short term the loss of jobs overseas will be offset by continued growth. Yet, this does not deny the impact of the related processes of re-engineering and offshoring. Three sectors identified by Contact Babel as set to experience a net loss (2006–2009) are telecoms (−5 percent), utilities (−3.3 percent) and financial services (−2.4 percent).

2.15.8   Employment Relations

What emerges from Van Jaarsveld et al. (2007) and other sources is the correlation between location and pay levels. It is well established that in the eastern provinces where there is the greatest density of outsourced centres, compensation levels are lowest. Mercer (2006, p. 11) concludes that the west coast metropolitan areas are among the highest paid regions with base salaries in Greater Vancouver up to 18 percent higher than the national average. In contrast, cities in the Atlantic provinces pay below the national average, with the lowest being for Moncton, New Brunswick – 11 percent below the national average.

Relatedly, pay levels in outsourced operations are lower than for in-house centres and often significantly so. Thus, the eastern provinces have attracted a disproportionate volume of outsourced business. The interconnections between location, pay and the distinction between in-house and outsourced centres can be mapped onto trade union recognition. The bulk of Canada's sector is nonunionized, but density is even far lower in outsourced centres. Unlike the UK, recognition in financial services is negligible. Public company call centres tend to be unionized. Recognition does cover parts of the telecoms sector, but the number of employees organized is declining as workforces contract and unions face the twin threats of outsourcing and offshoring. There is no denying the general weakness of unions in the contact centres and, although organizing opportunities present themselves, unions have faced an uphill struggle to organize employees. Weaknesses in domestic organization exacerbate the difficulties faced by unions as they seek to extend union organization to offshored destinations.

2.16   Conclusions

Perhaps the most significant conclusion is that Canada's nearshoring advantage appears to have been undermined by changes in the exchange rate between Canada and the US. This may impact most upon the outsourced sector in those provinces and communities that have pursued low-cost locational strategies. The CCC predicts a 'curtailment or a flattening of contact centre growth in smaller communities in the near future' (2007, p. 4). At the same time, offshoring will continue to have an impact on jobs, particularly 'low-value interactions,' and induce downward pressures on pay and conditions similar to those in the US. Following the Telus case, telecoms may be particularly vulnerable. In addition, labour market shortages are exerting an influence, prompting firms to seek alternatives through automation as well as offshoring. Mercer (2006, p. 1) found that 34 percent of call centres reported difficulties in finding candidates with appropriate skills. Against this, there is some evidence of modest growth in the sector as a whole.

A major conclusion of this overview of remote work from the perspective of the three developed economies – the US, the UK and Canada – is that the extent of the offshoring of business services to date should not be exaggerated. Taking the most visible segment of business services to have been relocated – call or contact centres – it is evident that the overwhelming volume of services is still provided within these countries to customers at national, regional or even local scales (Holman et al., 2007). The same general conclusion applies to the diverse range of non-customer-facing business services that remain embedded within organizations or have been outsourced domestically to generic or specialized providers. Given the massive hype that has attended offshoring and has led to cataclysmic predictions regarding the future of service jobs, this more tempered conclusion provides an important sense of perspective. Until the financial sector crisis of September 2008 and the consequent global recession, the growth in remote sourcing had occurred at the same time as the continued expansion, albeit at slowing rates, of business services within these developed economies.

Nevertheless, the relocation of business services from the developed countries to developing countries, particularly India, over the past decade has been truly remarkable. The figures speak for themselves. According to NASSCOM, 102,000 people were employed in Indian BPO in 2002, a total that has risen to 790,000 in 2009. IBM now employs almost 60,000 people in business services in India, and Accenture has a larger workforce in India than in the US. Driven by systemic and sectoral pressures to reduce costs and to maximize profits, companies based in these liberal market economies (Hall and Soskice, 2001) sought to exploit the massive labour cost arbitrage that prevailed between developed and developing countries.

Yet, the locational strategies adopted were not random nor exclusively dictated by cost imperatives. As we have insisted throughout, the globalization of business services, and in particular interactive voice services, does not represent the eradication of the differences between places but rather a heightened appreciation of them. The availability of supplies of labour with the appropriate attributes – linguistic ability, cultural empathy, 'soft' skills and technical capability – in tandem with the presence of particular regulatory, institutional and infrastructural advantages – are locational prerequisites that restrict the choices available to companies.

It is necessary to appreciate also that a series of countervailing factors have served to inhibit the overseas migration. Problems with language and communication, difficulties in exercising control remotely, customer resistance in the home countries and, until recently, rising costs *inter alia* have all combined to restrain migratory flows. However, to the extent that these constraints apply and labour is not automatically substitutable between the different nodes of the global service supply chain, they do so to a greater extent to voice services than to the diverse range of back-office functions. It is in this light that the nearshoring phenomenon should be considered. Canada is the archtypical nearshoring location that has benefited from the desire of US companies to minimize risk and maintain closer cultural proximity to customers whilst still being able to leverage some cost advantage.

What of the future? It is too early to draw any definitive predictions regarding the impact of the recession, because its profound consequences may recast the structure and dynamics of the global servicing landscape. It is quite possible, though, that cost-cutting imperatives will provide renewed impetus to outsourcing and offshoring in and from the developed countries but, equally, alternative strategies such as automation and work intensification and companies' ability to exploit slacker labour markets and regional economies *within* the boundaries of the developed economies may prove influential. In other words, companies may vary the combination of 'shores' utilized as part of their locational strategies. On the basis of pre-recession trends it would not be unreasonable to expect the greater relocation of the back office vis-à-vis voice services and, as part of the former, the continued migration of higher-value and more complex business and professional services.

Some consideration, finally, must be given to the circumstances of labour in the economies of developed countries. Already facing distinct challenges from offshoring and outsourcing – representing a certain 'hollowing out' of their organizations – workers and their trade unions, to the extent that the latter have coverage, have borne the brunt of the recession. It is an unmistakable fact that financial services is the sector responsible for the greatest number of business service and call centre jobs and, of course, it has been most affected (along with manufacturing) in the developed countries. Job loss, intensification of work and profound employment insecurity are the dominant experiences – outcomes that place an even greater premium on the need for adequate labour standards and protection from unilateral management fiat. With fragmentary evidence of leaner and harsher workplace regimes in both India and the developed countries, the post-recession environment highlights the importance of monitoring working conditions and labour standards and underscores labour's common cause across the global servicing divide.

Notes

1. National Association of Software and Services Companies, which represents both constituent elements of the Indian offshored industry – software/IT services and BPO. The latter is the designation used by the Indian industry and is largely employed globally to encompass call centre (voice) services and business processes of various kinds.
2. It is important to distinguish between ITES (information technology-enabled services) and IT services.

3. A literature has emerged in recent times on the potential for union organizing in India (see Taylor et al., 2009).

4. Nearshoring involves relocation to lower-cost geographies adjacent to the higher-cost point of origin. The archetypal example cited is of Canada and the US.

5. This term was used by a CWA national official to describe outsourcers that offer employees inferior conditions. They may seek to locate in the low-tax states such as Mississippi, or in 'right-to-work' states.

6. Contact Babel and Datamonitor use agent positions as the basic metric. Converting these into employee numbers is not an exact science. Contact Babel's average of 1.6 employees per agent position is employed.

7. Even marginal differences in costs between locations (particularly in respect to labour costs) impact upon locational decisions, as long as labour with the requisite skills is available in sufficient quantities.

8. The late-1990s saw increases in efficiency-enhancing technologies aimed at 'pushing through as many calls as possible' (DTI, 2004b, p. 140).

9. Key to regulating offshoring are the Data Protection Act (1998) and, for financial services, the FSA. In 2005, the FSA reviewed UK operations in India. Critics believed this was a superficial exercise in self-regulation.

10. Even where unions have limited offshoring, agreements are typically partial and temporary. Following the ending of its agreement with Amicus, in 2005, Prudential embarked on a programme of renewed offshoring and outsourcing.

11. Other countries receiving UK work include Sri Lanka, South Africa, the Philippines and Eastern Europe.

3
Employee Dilemmas in the Indian ITES–BPO Sector

Premilla D'Cruz and Ernesto Noronha

3.1 Introduction

Offshoring and outsourcing are not recent by-products of the emergence of the new economy in services. The first wave of offshoring and outsourcing, encompassing the manufacturing sector, began in the mid-1980s, motivated by low costs, the availability of skilled labour, the promotion of a business-friendly environment and the existence of production and supply networks in places such as China, Republic of Korea, Malaysia and Taiwan (Bardhan and Kroll, 2003). At that time, it was predicted that developed nations, nurtured by giant multinational corporations (MNCs), would evolve into service-based economies (Dossani and Kenney, 2003), requiring buyers and sellers to be frequently available in the same geographic location (Henley, 2006). This implied that while manufacturing jobs would move to other areas of the globe, service jobs would remain in the West.

Today, however, the same cost-driven logic espoused earlier by the manufacturing sector is being applied to business services. Offshoring and outsourcing now include the relocation of interactive service work and an expanding range of back-office processes from developed countries to developing countries (Taylor and Noronha et al., 2009), covering business functions such as human resources, accounting, auditing, customer care, telemarketing, tax preparation, claims processing and document management, among others (Dossani and Kenney, 2003).

The liberalization of emerging markets in the 1990s and the simultaneous developments in information and communications technologies (ICTs) have boosted the growth of offshoring and outsourcing (Bardhan and Kroll, 2003; Henley, 2006). The 'push' factors for offshoring and outsourcing are similar to those for manufacturing and are largely cost-driven, while the 'pull' factors and attributes of countries and economies providing off-shored and outsourced services may be different. Nonetheless, the ongoing offshoring and outsourcing of business services jobs to countries such as India, the Philippines, Malaysia and South Africa are due to the widespread acceptance of English as a medium of education, business and communication in these countries; a common accounting and legal system (at least in some of the countries); general institutional compatibility and adaptability; the time-differential determined by geographical location leading to a 24/7 capability and overnight turnaround time; simpler logistics than in manufacturing and a steady and copious supply of technically savvy graduates (Bardhan and Kroll, 2003).

This chapter discusses the work experiences of employees engaged in offshoring and outsourcing in India's information technology enabled services–business process outsourcing (ITES–BPO) sector.

3.2   Research Methodology

The rapid growth of India's ITES–BPO sector has drawn the attention of a number of researchers whose work has spanned various aspects of the 'industry' such as cultural transformation and identity formation of employees (Cohen and El-Sawad, 2007; Cowie, 2007; D'Cruz and Noronha, 2006; McMillin, 2006; Mirchandani, 2004; Pal and Buzzanell, 2008; Poster, 2007; Ramesh, 2004); emotional labour (D'Cruz and Noronha, 2008); gender (Ng and Mitter, 2005; Patel, 2006); management practices (Batt et al., 2005b; Batt et al., 2005c; Budhwar et al., 2006; Mahesh and Kasturi, 2006; Mehta et al., 2006); organizational control (D'Cruz and Noronha, 2006) and union formation (Noronha and D'Cruz, 2006; Ramesh, 2004; Taylor and Bain, 2008; Taylor et al., 2008).

Though the ITES–BPO sector includes both call centres and back offices, most research examines call centres, greatly neglecting back offices [see, as an exception, Noronha and D'Cruz's (2007a, 2008b) studies focussing on teleworking among medical transcriptionists]. Furthermore, barring a few studies (see, e.g., Batt et al., 2005b, 2005c; Budhwar et al., 2006; Ramesh, 2004; Taylor et al., 2008), most research uses qualitative methods with small samples.

Addressing these shortcomings, we undertook a large survey of both call centre and back-office employees across five Indian cities. Employee data were supplemented with managerial perspectives from a multicity survey that included both call centres and back offices. Both surveys, conducted in New Delhi and NCR (National Capital Region), Bangalore, Mumbai, Chennai and Hyderabad (Tier 1 Indian cities that together contain 80 percent of India's ITES–BPO sector[1]), relied on structured interview schedules. As ITES–BPO organizations were not willing to permit us access to their employees or to the operations floor (this has been a common experience during the conduct of empirical research in Indian industry both within and beyond the ITES–BPO sector), we had to resort to snowball sampling for the entire study. We began our initial data collection by relying on informal contacts such as our former students and our social network as well as on UNITES's (Union for ITES Professionals) office-bearers. Through these people, we were put in touch with ITES–BPO employees and managers.

Seven-hundred-and-twenty-nine ITES–BPO employees (hereafter also referred to as agents or respondents – see Section 3.4 for a profile of survey respondents) participated in our survey. Their citywise distribution – in Bangalore (25.5 percent), Chennai (16.6 percent), New Delhi and NCR (18 percent), Hyderabad (17 percent) and Mumbai (18.8 percent) – more or less corresponded with the distribution figures given by National Association of Software and Service Companies (NASSCOM).[2,3] Of these, 450 (61.7 percent) were employed in call centres and 279 (38.3 percent) were employed in back offices. Though NASSCOM has not disaggregated call centre activity from the back office, these proportions are in line with Taylor and Bain's (2006) estimate that voice services account for 60–65 percent and various back-office activities for 35–40 percent of ITES–BPO employment.

One-hundred-and-ninety-five managers (35 women and 160 men), who were located in Mumbai (13 percent), Hyderabad (18 percent), New Delhi and NCR (27 percent), Bangalore (12 percent) and Chennai (29 percent), participated in the survey. Only five of this entire group were HR (human resources) managers; the rest were operations managers. HR managers refused to participate in the study without prior permission from their employer organizations, for which they required our proposal and interview schedule. Yet, despite forwarding these documents to them, they did not get back to us. This was not the case for operations managers who eagerly agreed to participate in the study. Of the five HR managers included in the sample, four were employed by back-office organizations while only one was employed by a call centre. Of the 190 operations managers in the study, 99 were employed by call centres and 91 by back-office organizations.

Data gathered from employees and managers were analysed statistically using Statistical Package for the Social Sciences (SPSS). These data provided insights into the profile of the workforce, recruitment and training, work systems, work–life balance, HR policies, attrition and collectivization and union formation in India's ITES–BPO sector.

Key informant interviews were conducted with trade unionists, with lawyers working in the ITES–BPO sector and with labour commissioners. These individuals were located in Mumbai, Chennai, Bangalore, Hyderabad, New Delhi and Kolkata. Data from these interviews, which were recorded and transcribed, deepened our understanding of the work experiences amongst India's ITES–BPO employees.

The presentation of study findings in this chapter is preceded by a description of the sector.

3.3   The Indian ITES–BPO Sector

3.3.1   Sectoral Overview

India's ITES–BPO sector encompasses the offshoring and outsourcing of processes that can be enabled by information technology (NASSCOM, 2003) including both call centres and back-office services. The figures provided by NASSCOM are undeniably impressive (Table 3.1). ITES–BPO exports were estimated to have grown from US (US dollar) $1.5 billion in 2001–2002 to US $6.3 billion in 2005–2006, while revenues in domestic ITES–BPO grew from US $0.6 billion to US $0.9 billion from 2004–2005 to 2005–2006 (NASSCOM, 2006a).

According to NASSCOM (2006a), the key catalyst of Indian ITES–BPO export has been globalization. The rapid spread of globalization has added competitive pressure across geographic markets, impacting both growth and profitability. This has pushed organizations towards cost-efficient business models resulting in global offshoring and outsourcing. Today, global offshoring and outsourcing are key elements in the business strategy of organizations and have moved beyond mere functional support.

India, because of its demonstrated superiority, sustained cost advantage and powered value propositions, has emerged as the global leader in this area. Offshoring and outsourcing to India have provided companies around the world with significant benefits in terms of labour arbitrage. Apart from providing organizations with annual cost savings of 40–50 percent as compared to the annual wage inflation of 10–15 percent, such operations also leverage declines in telecom costs and other overheads while at the same time enhancing productivity. The large English-speaking and technical talent pool available in India is the critical component in this process. NASSCOM (2006a) points out that India's numerous advantages have resulted in a steady increase in the scale and depth of existing service lines and in the addition of newer vertical-specific and emerging, niche business services, fuelling the growth of this sector. Indeed, the fact that, globally,

Table 3.1   Indian ITES–BPO Export Revenues

Financial year	US $ (billion)
1999–2000	0.6
2000–2001	0.9
2001–2002	1.5
2002–2003	2.5
2003–2004	3.1
2004–2005	4.6
2005–2006	6.3

Source: NASSCOM, 2006a, p. 262.

India is considered to be a competent and valued offshoring and outsourcing destination is borne out by the growing trend worldwide of locating higher-value knowledge-based processes there, in addition to the existing lower-end business processes (NASSCOM, 2006a).

Locating India within the global space, NASSCOM-McKinsey (2005) calculate that India accounts for 46 percent of all offshored and outsourced ITES–BPO – an increase from 39 percent in 2001. Thus, India has captured an increasing share of the expanding global ITES–BPO industry. Further, this report estimates that, going forward, India can continue to grow its offshored and outsourced IT (Information Technology) and ITES–BPO industries at an annual rate of 25 percent. By 2010, these industries combined could generate export revenues of about US \$60 billion.

The role of the Indian government in facilitating the growth and development of the country's ITES–BPO sector cannot be denied, with the liberalization of the Indian economy proving to be a critical turning point. According to NASSCOM (2006a), from 1991 onward, the Indian government has encouraged the in-flow of foreign capital not only as a source of finance but also as a facilitator of knowledge and technology transfer. Today, foreign direct investment (FDI) in most sectors is permitted under the automatic route[4] and only requires notification of India's central bank, the Reserve Bank of India (RBI). Procedures relating to the transfer of shares, repatriation and introduction of foreign technology have been made simple. In addition, the procedures governing approval are continuously reviewed and updated, to ensure continued ease of operation.

With specific reference to the ITES–BPO sector, support for growth and development has emerged from various Indian government ministries and departments, particularly the Ministry of Communication and Information Technology, which has formulated policy and legal frameworks to facilitate the process. The policies promoted by India's central and state governments have been critical in creating favourable environments for both foreign investors and domestic companies. The implementation of a series of incentives, concessions and subsidies and the simplification of procedural requirements, has served as an important catalyst (NASSCOM, 2006a). As NASSCOM (2006a, pp. 216–231) highlights, these include relaxation of policies relating to inbound and outbound investments; exchange control relaxations; incentives for units located in a domestic tariff area (DTA) or under export-oriented units (EOU), software technology parks (STP), special economic zones (SEZ) and electronic hardware technology park (EHTP) schemes; and state-level incentives, waivers and subsidies.

Most state governments in India have announced special promotional schemes for the ITES–BPO sector. These schemes focus on the key issues of infrastructure, electronic governance, IT education and providing a supportive environment for increasing IT proliferation in the respective states.

While these are state-specific initiatives, there is a fair degree of uniformity across states as newer locations have modelled their schemes on states that have already successfully nurtured a thriving ITES–BPO industry (NASSCOM, 2006a).

The Indian ITES–BPO industry has grown despite serious constraints imposed by the country's infrastructure including road systems, public transport, electrical power supply, telecommunications connectivity, and so on, across Tier 1, Tier 2 and Tier 3 cities. Taylor and Bain (2003) believe that India's huge advantage in the area of labour cost is offset by proportionally greater costs in relation to, amongst other things, equipment, telephony, telecommunications connectivity and power supply. In the case of the latter two components, the inescapable requirement to provide 'redundancy,' that is, alternative provision, adds significantly to the cost base of Indian suppliers. The authors go on to state that, although NASSCOM consistently estimates that overall cost savings of 40–50 percent can be realized by offshoring and outsourcing business processes to India (NASSCOM, 2006a), such a position represents optimism and oversimplification since a variety of factors including the nature of the process, the degree of complexity, the scale and volume of the activity, the nature and terms of the contract and the stage of the migratory cycle all impact on the level of achievable savings (Taylor and Bain, 2006).

The distinction within India's ITES–BPO industry in terms of types of organizations reveals its heterogeneous nature. 'Captives,' essentially in-house service providers for global companies (e.g., HSBC, Dell, Hewlett-Packard, Prudential), which directly own and control their own offshored and outsourced operations and who dominated the industry in its early years, remain pre-eminent according to NASSCOM (2005, p. 90). 'Third-party MNCs,' that is, multinational companies operating out of India that essentially act as third-party service providers with a broad portfolio of business processes delivering services for their clients, form yet another category. Both these types can be distinguished from 'Indian third-party' service providers that act as classic offshoring and outsourcing operations. This diverse category encompasses both what are known as 'pure plays' (Indian companies providing voice, nonvoice or both services to clients in multiple sectors and geographies overseas – e.g., Transworks or Firstsource) and the ITES–BPO arms of Indian IT companies such as Wipro or Infosys. Finally, it is important to take account of the more recent emergence and significant expansion of the domestic ITES–BPO subsector (NASSCOM, 2005).

While the principal location for the ITES–BPO industry remains Tier 1 cities, namely New Delhi and NCR, Mumbai, Bangalore, Chennai and Hyderabad, there has been considerable expansion of operations into Tier 2 and Tier 3 cities and towns (including Pune, Mangalore, Vishakhapatnam, Madurai, Chandigarh, Jaipur, Kochi and Thiruvananthapuram) in the last 3 years. Tier 2 and Tier 3 locations offer both talent pools as well as lower cost structures besides reducing organizational risk through geographical dispersion and enabling utilization of state government sponsored financial and other assistance schemes (NASSCOM, 2005, 2006a). Indeed, so rapid has been the growth of some Tier 2 locations that they have come to resemble Tier 1 cities in terms of overheated labour markets, rising costs and overstretched infrastructure, reinforcing the search for and development of new business districts beyond the boundaries unencumbered by these constraints (NASSCOM-McKinsey, 2005). In the midst of this development is a group of organizations that remain undecided whether the advantages of locating in Tier 2 or Tier 3 cities sufficiently outweigh the benefits of continuing to remain in their established places. The view here is that relocation to Tier 2 and 3 cities provides temporary relief, but does not address critical issues within the industry, particularly those relating to employee competence and retention and other HR difficulties (Taylor and Bain, 2006).

While NASSCOM has not disaggregated call centre activity from back-office activity in the Indian ITES–BPO sector, Taylor and Bain (2006) maintain that, based on a review of all available evidence, it is reasonable to conclude that voice services account for 60–65 percent of sectoral employment and the various back-office activities for 35–40 percent, although a proportion of employees are employed in both types of activity. Finance and accounting (F&A), customer interaction services (CIS) and human resource (HR) administration are key service categories accounting for 89 percent of industry revenues. Within these sectors, banking, financial services and insurance (BFSI) is among the most mature verticals estimated to account for approximately 35–45 percent of offshored and outsourced ITES–BPO and possessing the greatest service line depth (NASSCOM, 2006a). Emerging vertical-specific and niche business services are estimated to account for 11 percent of the total value of ITES–BPO activity undertaken in India (NASSCOM, 2006a).

Taylor and Bain (2006) maintain that services offshored and outsourced to India are essentially lower-end, encompassing basic voice services and simple transactional business processes that are highly standardized and routinized. In their view, it is limited facility with conversational English that inhibits participation in the provision of more complex services. Taylor and Bain (2006) assert that the claims that Indian ITES–BPO firms are moving up the value chain to more complex and higher-value services, while rooted in actual developments, are frequently exaggerated, and relatively routinized and standardized call centre services continue to dominate.

One exception remains the emerging knowledge process outsourcing (KPO), which entails genuine complexity and high-value services. KPO includes service providers with higher-end research and analysis-based services in both traditional service lines and new business areas. Unlike conventional back-office work where the focus is on process expertise and high volumes, thereby favouring standardization, in KPO the focus is on knowledge expertise and on advanced technical and analytical skills, emphasizing customization (Taylor and Bain, 2006).

In overall terms, then, the ITES–BPO industry in India still tends to provide largely standardized, routinized services of generally low complexity, despite limited moves up the value chain to KPO (Taylor and Bain, 2006). Accordingly, it has been demonstrated that the work system in Indian call centres largely approximates, and indeed may well constitute, an exaggerated form of the mass production model (Batt et al., 2005c; Taylor and Bain, 2005).

3.3.2 Labour Market

Direct employment in India's ITES–BPO sector (not including employment in the IT industry) was calculated at 553,000 for 2006–2007. Reviewing the figures in Table 3.2 as provided by NASSCOM, the rapid growth of the ITES–BPO industry in India is obvious (Taylor et al., 2007).

Offshoring and outsourcing to India are driven by labour cost arbitrage. It is believed that the ability to achieve such high levels of cost reduction by seeking services from India essentially emerges because of the availability of highly skilled talent at significantly lower wage costs and the resultant productivity gains derived from having a very competent employee base. The advantages of cheap labour primarily arise because of the ability of potential employees to speak English, an indispensable prerequisite for an industry serving English-speaking geographies. There is no question that facility with the English language distinguishes India from some alternative offshoring and outsourcing locations. Indeed, there is an ample supply of graduates of universities and colleges with at least 15 years of education in English (NASSCOM, 2006a).

Table 3.2 Indian ITES–BPO Employment Levels

Financial year	Employees (000s)	Yearly increase (%)
2001–2002	107	N/A
2002–2003	171	60
2003–2004[a]	216	26
2004–2005[a]	316	46
2005–2006	409	29
2006–2007[b]	553	35

Source: Taylor et al. (2007), based on data from NASSCOM (2007a; 2006a, p. 73; 2003, p. 59).
[a]The totals have been recalculated to exclude certain service lines.
[b]Figures presented at NASSCOM ITES–BPO Strategy Summit in Bangalore in August 2007 (NASSCOM, 2007a).

Indeed, NASSCOM flaunts India's ability to produce qualified 'manpower' as a source of competitiveness. According to the NASSCOM-McKinsey study (2005), India had around 347 institutes of higher education and 16,885 colleges with a total enrolment of over 9.9 million students. This produces about 495,000 technical graduates, nearly 2.3 million other graduates and over 300,000 postgraduates every year. Also, with English being widely accepted, a large proportion of the graduate pool is proficient in the language (NASSCOM, 2007b).

To further ensure the availability of qualified personnel for this sector. NASSCOM signed a Memorandum of Understanding (MoU) with the University Grants Commission (UGC) and the All India Council for Technical Education (AICTE) to strengthen professional education (through curricula, faculty, infrastructure and pedagogy improvements) in line with the ITES–BPO industry's demand for skilled professionals. NASSCOM's National Assessment of Competence (NAC) initiative, launched in 2006, operates as an industry standard assessment and certification programme to ensure the transformation of a 'trainable' workforce into an 'employable' workforce (NASSCOM, 2007b).

The industrial relations climate that characterizes the Indian ITES–BPO sector adds to its attractiveness in the labour market. It is widely believed across the country that the ITES–BPO sector does not fall within the purview of existing labour laws. As discussed below, this view is maintained and promoted by employers within the sector and supported by government apathy. Taylor and Bain (2003) assert that India is attractive to organizations that wish to capitalize on the possibilities for flexible labour utilization. They point out that given the absence of trade unions in the Indian ITES–BPO sector, offshoring and outsourcing offer an opportunity to deliver services in an industrial relations environment in which organizations are less constrained by the need to consult with workforce representatives (Taylor and Bain, 2003).

In assessing the labour-related advantages offered by India, Taylor and Bain (2003, 2006) caution that participation in 15 years of education in English does not automatically prepare the workforce to interact effectively with remote customers for whom English is their mother tongue. That is, while formal command of English among agents is largely satisfactory, they do not necessarily possess the depth of understanding and flexibility of expression to ensure that more than routine tasks can be performed. Furthermore, some commentators suggest that despite the efforts of Indian organizations, the deep-rooted cultural differences between India and the West might adversely affect interaction between agents and customers (Taylor and Bain, 2003).

Moreover, there is no doubt that the ITES–BPO workforce is covered under existing labour legislation. Under the Constitution of India, labour falls under the concurrent list which implies that both the central and the state governments are competent to enact related legislations, subject to certain matters being reserved for the centre's jurisdiction such that in cases of conflict, the provisions of the centre prevail.

In the context of ITES–BPO organizations, the relevant state legislation is the Shops and Commercial Establishments Act as promulgated in various Indian states, while the central legislations are the Workmen's Compensation Act (1923), the Payment of Wages Act (1936), the Industrial Disputes Act (1947), the Minimum Wages Act (1948), the Employees State Insurance Act (1948), the Maternity Benefit Act (1961), the Contract Labour (Regulation and Abolition) Act (1970), the Payment of Gratuity Act (1972) and the Equal Remuneration Act (1976).

As highlighted earlier, however, the popular notion held in Indian society is that the above-mentioned legislation and related institutional measures do not apply to this sector, and hence it is believed that ITES–BPO employees are not covered by the same labour laws applicable to blue-collar workers. That some scholars believe that the Shops and Commercial Establishments Act became a passive instrument once ITES–BPO organizations in most Indian states were granted the status of 'public utility service' providers under the 1947 Industrial Disputes Act, echoes the popular view (see, e.g., Banerjee, 2006.)

To clarify this misperception, India's labour minister has confirmed in Parliament that ITES–BPO organizations *are* covered under existing labour laws and that state governments *are* the 'appropriate government' legally vested with powers to deal with violations of these laws.

Our discussions with labour commissioners across five Indian states were in line with the Minister's position. In reality, then, none of the ITES–BPO organizations has been granted 'public utility service' status as per the 1947 Industrial Disputes Act. The only exemptions granted by various state governments pertains to their respective Shops and Commercial Establishments Acts, whereby ITES–BPO companies are permitted to run their operations around the clock, 7 days a week, 365 days of the year, employing women at all times of the day including night hours (provided that the requisite security and transport facilities are provided to such women by the employer organization).

Further, it is important to note that rising labour costs, conservatively estimated at the rate of 10–15 percent per annum for the last 3 years (NASSCOM 2006a), and emerging essentially due to wage inflation, are eating into cost savings. High and rising rates of attrition are significant here. Indian organizations appear to be paying higher salaries in order to retain existing staff or to recruit from a labour pool in which competitive pressures are intensifying. High attrition has the added effect of increasing recruitment and training budgets. The supply of experienced and competent Indian call centre agents, at unchanging cost levels, cannot therefore be regarded as inexhaustible (Taylor and Bain, 2003).

Taylor and Bain (2006) point out that these rising labour costs vary across the country and across processes while also being higher for management as compared to employees. There are additional aspects of the cost base in India that might not appear obvious at first glance. The expenses incurred in the complex and extensive logistical exercise of transporting agents to the call centre workplace and the provision of free or subsidized food, among other things, are significant additional costs that have to be borne by Indian employers. For all these reasons, the spectacular savings that *prima facie* appear to be offered in India, when labour costs are assessed in isolation, are qualified in practice (Taylor and Bain, 2003).

Nonetheless, NASSCOM (2006a) maintains that India remains the most cost-competitive sourcing base in the world for ITES–BPO offshoring and outsourcing. Despite these increasing labour costs, offsetting declines in telecom costs, lower depreciation and other infrastructure costs, improvements in productivity and utilization and scale economies have all allowed India to maintain its advantage. Indeed, attempts to sustain the long-term viability of India's cost advantage have led to the adoption of various tactics and strategies, including increased company size and increased facilities that can handle a higher volume of processes as well as the management of productivity through re-engineering and optimal use of equipment and labour such that efficiencies can be leveraged.

To help institutionalize the concept of process excellence in the industry, NASSCOM is, in association with several agencies, developing a benchmarking service to provide companies with a robust framework for self-assessment that may be administered at regular intervals so that benchmarks of industry performance for meaningful comparison and subsequent action may be obtained. Movement to Tier 2 and 3 cities is also seen as lowering the costs of labour, infrastructure and overheads (NASSCOM, 2006a). Beyond organization-level initiatives, government and industry are working towards increasing labour supply, improving infrastructure and providing an enabling environment. In addition, process superiority is also seen as driving significant savings from improvements in quality, speed and flexibility, productivity and delivery innovation (NASSCOM, 2006a).

Despite infrastructure problems and labour-related challenges, various studies (including the McKinsey Global Institute Survey and A.T. Kearney) maintain that India remains the offshoring and outsourcing destination of choice, delivering the best bundle of benefits globally. Yet, in the words of Taylor and Bain (2006, p. 47), '[T]he pressure on the cost base, particularly from rising labour costs, is set to continue, and is likely to prove more significant in its impact than the combined counter-effect of all the cost reduction measures, and the anticipated further decline in telecom costs. In other words, India will remain an attractive destination because of its low cost base, but in overall terms the slow erosion of the cost differential seems set to continue.'

3.4 Profiling the Indian ITES–BPO Workforce

3.4.1 Gender

Earlier researchers of India's ITES–BPO sector drew attention to the fact that the media representation of ITES–BPO employment in India as being primarily female is incorrect (Patel, 2006). Patel's estimate that 60 percent of Indian ITES–BPO employees are men coincides with the data of Poster (2007) and Mirchandani (2003), who each found that 50–70 percent of Indian call centre employees are men. Our sample of ITES–BPO employees, which included 176 women (24.1 percent) and 553 men (75.9 percent), is just short of these estimates. The gender-related distribution was 74 percent men and 26 percent women in call centres, and 79 percent men and 21 percent women in back offices. The under-representation of women in our study sample as compared to the estimates made by other scholars is probably because leads available about women to the researchers were fewer than those available for men. This was in spite of having recruited two men and four women to do the data collection.

3.4.2 Age

ITES–BPO employees in our sample had an average age of 24.5 years. Among call centre agents, the mean age was 24.3 years, whereas among back-office agents, the mean age was 24.8 years. Most of the agents fell into the 21–25 years age bracket (65 percent), and a substantial number also fell in the age bracket of 26–30 years (27 percent) (see Table 3.3). Clearly, ITES–BPO employees constitute a young workforce, most of whom are unmarried (85 percent). The findings concur with earlier studies of Indian call centre employees, which reported that the mean age of an employee was 25 years (Ramesh, 2004), with most employees falling in the age bracket of 21–25 years (McMillin, 2006).

3.4.3 Work Experience

This youthful profile of ITES–BPO employees does not imply that only fresh graduates join the industry. The mean total work experience of agents in any

Table 3.3 Age of ITES–BPO Employees

Age (years)	Frequency (%)
< 20	36 (4.9)
21–25	473 (65.1)
26–30	195 (26.8)
31–35	18 (2.5)
36–40	2 (0.3)
40+	3 (0.4)
Total	727 (100.0)

Table 3.4   Total Work Experience in any Sector/Organization, in the ITES–BPO Sector and in their Current Organization

Duration of work experience (in months)	Frequency (%)		
	Total work experience in any sector/organization	Total work experience in ITES–BPO sector	Total work experience in current organization
< 6	45 (6.2)	74 (10.2)	171 (23.5)
7–12	10 (13.9)	163 (22.4)	230 (31.6)
13–18	116 (15.9)	128 (17.6)	124 (17.0)
19–24	116 (15.9)	118 (16.2)	85 (11.7)
25–30	67 (9.2)	58 (8.0)	43 (5.9)
31–36	93 (12.8)	84 (11.6)	42 (5.8)
37–42	30 (4.1)	24 (3.3)	12 (1.6)
43–48	51 (7.0)	37 (5.1)	12 (1.6)
49–54	18 (2.5)	11 (1.5)	3 (0.4)
55–60	40 (5.5)	12 (1.7)	2(0.3)
61–66	4 (0.5)	2 (0.3)	2 (.3)
67+	48 (6.6)	16 (2.2)	2 (.3)
Total	729 (100.0)	727 (100.0)	728 (100.0)

industry was 31.46 months for the entire sample – 32.31 months for those from back offices and 30.92 months for those from call centres. Fifty-two percent of the sample had total work experience of 24 months or less, and 74 percent had experience of 36 months or less. The remainder had total work experience ranging from 37 to 85 months or more.

In terms of agents' total work experience in the ITES–BPO sector, 66 percent of the sample had 24 months or less experience, while 86 percent had 36 months or less work experience (Table 3.4). The mean total work experience in the ITES–BPO sector was only 23.75 months, being 24.75 months for back-office employees and 23.12 months for call centre employees. This implies that employees from other sectors had moved into the ITES–BPO sector.

Attrition becomes visible when we look at agents' mean total work experience in their current ITES–BPO organization which was 15.81 months, or 8 months less than the mean total work experience in this sector. Further, the mean total work experience in the current ITES–BPO organization was 16.96 months for back-office employees and 15.10 months for call centre employees, indicating that call centre agents had a tendency to quit their employer organization faster. About 84 percent of the respondents had worked for 24 months or less in their current ITES–BPO organization, while 96 percent had worked for 36 months or less in their current ITES–BPO organization.

3.4.4 Education

Seventy-five percent of the ITES–BPO employees in our sample were college graduates and 17 percent were postgraduates, reflecting the high university graduate population in India. Those who had studied below the graduate level (undergraduate and less than higher secondary/high school) constituted only 6 percent of the sample (Table 3.5). These findings are in line with those of other researchers such as Ramesh (2004), who indicates that 97 percent of Indian call centre agents are college graduates, and Batt et al. (2005c) and Budhwar et al. (2006) who report that Indian call centre agents, on an average, have completed about 14 or more years of formal education, or a basic undergraduate degree.

Further, the level of education of agents in India compares favourably with that of the agents in the US. The typical worker in an Indian call centre has 14 years of education (on average, 2 years of college) compared to 13.3 years among US in-house establishments and 12.6 years for US subcontractors, where the typical worker has an average education of a high school diploma only (Batt et al., 2005b).

However, if parental education is any indication of the education level attained by children, parents of ITES–BPO employees have reasonably good education levels. Ramesh (2004) states that 94 percent of the fathers and 63 percent of the mothers of call centre agents were college graduates. Our findings, although not that optimistic, reveal that 57 percent of the fathers of agents in the sample were graduates while around 23 percent had studied less than or up to the high/higher secondary school level, and nearly 5 percent were illiterate. Forty-three percent of the mothers in the sample

Table 3.5 Education Level of ITES–BPO Employees and Their Parents

Education level	Frequency (%)		
	Employees	Employees' mothers	Employees' fathers
Illiterate	—	63 (8.7)	33 (4.6)
High/higher secondary school and below	20 (2.7)	295 (40.6)	169 (23.5)
Undergraduate	23 (3.2)	—	—
Graduate	545 (74.9)	312 (42.9)	415 (57.7)
Postgraduate	121 (16.6)	26 (3.6)	62 (8.6)
Diploma	19 (2.6)	3 (0.4)	3 (0.4)
Not known	—	27 (3.7)	37 (5.1)
Total	728 (100.0)	727 (100)	719 (100)

were college graduates, while around 41 percent were at the high/higher secondary school level and about 9 percent were illiterate (Table 3.5). The difference in educational levels between agents and their parents appears to give the former a sense of being professionals, an orientation that has had important implications for collectivist endeavours in this sector (D'Cruz and Noronha, 2006; Noronha and D'Cruz, 2006).

3.4.5 Salary

Agents' sense of professionalism was further fuelled by the high salaries[5] they earned in this sector (D'Cruz and Noronha, 2006; Noronha and D'Cruz, 2006). Mitter et al. (2004) found the mean initial salary for call centre agents to be approximately 8000 Indian rupees (Rs) (US $174) per month, which increased to Rs 12,000 (US $261) per month within a year. Ramesh (2004) shows that 53 percent of call centre employees receive a monthly salary of Rs 10,000 (US $218) or more, while 19 percent receive Rs 8000–10,000 (US $174–218) per month. Further, McMillin's (2006) findings reveal that 66 percent of the employees at the agent level earned Rs 5000–10,000 (US $109–218) per month, though 20 percent of this group earned Rs 10,000–15,000 (US $218–326) per month. The above points were borne out by the mean take-home salary (inclusive of incentives) for respondents in our sample which was Rs 13,637.71 (US $296) per month. Most of the respondents (35 percent) were in the range of Rs 10,000–15,000 (US $218–326) per month. This was followed by two groups, namely, those who were in the range Rs 5000–10,000 (US $109–218) per month (24 percent) and those who were in the range Rs 15,000–20,000 (US $326–435) per month (24 percent) (Table 3.6).

It is important to note that variation in incentives can have a considerable impact on take-home salaries. Nonetheless, though these salaries may seem meagre by American or British standards, they provide a high quality of life to agents in India (Mitter et al., 2004). Materially, the Indian ITES–BPO sector allows agents to gain employment opportunities, upgraded salaries

Table 3.6 Monthly Salary of ITES–BPO Employees

Monthly salary (Indian Rupees/Rs)	Frequency (%)
Less than 5000 (less than $109)	2 (0.3)
5000–10,000 (US $109–218)	170 (23.9)
10,000–15,000 (US $218–326)	252 (35.4)
15,000–20,000 (US $326–435)	169 (23.7)
20,000–25,000 (US $435–543)	98 (13.8)
25,000–30,000 (US $543–652)	19 (2.7)
30,000–35,000 (US $652–761)	2 (0.3)
Total	712 (100.1)

and comfortable working conditions (Poster, 2007). A host of researchers have argued that Indian call centres pay competitive compensation packages as compared to the remuneration available in other sectors such as factory work, secretarial work and teaching, at times enabling agents to earn more than their parents (Budhwar et al., 2006; D'Cruz and Noronha, 2006; Poster, 2007).

Financial independence emerged as the most important reason for agents to join the ITES–BPO sector (35 percent), followed by financial difficulties of the family (20 percent), an economic downturn in other sectors (16 percent) and the need to finance one's further education (14 percent). Contrary to common perceptions, only 7 percent of agents saw their employment in this sector as a stop-gap arrangement.

3.4.6 Religion and Caste

Some researchers, like Ramesh (2004), suggest that caste-wise segregation of employees in the ITES–BPO sector confirms that only the so-called 'creamy layer' of the Indian population (96%)[6] is employed in this sector. Our findings suggest that while the 'creamy layer' does dominate, there are agents from the scheduled castes (SCs) and other backward castes (OBCs) who are employed in the ITES–BPO sector. With regard to religion, more than 79 percent of the agents in the sample were Hindus, while Christians and Muslims accounted for about 8 percent and 10 percent each, respectively. In terms of caste, 78 percent of the sample belonged to the general category, around 11 percent each belonged to the SC and OBC groups and less than 1 percent were from the scheduled tribes group. Eighty-three percent of the call centre sample came from the general category as compared to 70 percent of the back-office sample. Eighteen percent of the back-office group belonged to the category of other backward castes as compared to 6 percent of the call centre sample. There was not much difference between the representation of two groups where scheduled castes and scheduled tribes were concerned.[7]

3.5 Recruitment and Training

By and large, call centres in India employ full-time permanent employees, as compared with the part-time and temporary workers typical in many Western countries. In fact, part-time and temporary workers form only a very small employee group in call centre organizations in India (Budhwar et al., 2006). In our sample, all the employees had permanent jobs.

3.5.1 Recruitment

A typical recruitment process involves initial screening of resumes and final selection based on aptitude tests, group discussions and personal

Table 3.7   Perspectives of Managers on Sources of ITES–BPO Sector Recruitment ($n = 171$)

Sources of ITES–BPO sector recruitment	Frequency (%)
Referrals	132 (75.9)
Training institutes	54 (31.0)
NAC	34 (19.5)
Advertisements	84 (48.3)
Walk-in interviews	135 (77.6)
Campus placements	82 (47.1)
Consultants	144 (82.8)
Employment exchanges	16 (9.2)

interviews (Thite and Russell, 2009). Often, walk-in/telephonic interviews, placement agencies, call centre colleges and referrals are used for sourcing candidates, following which written tests, group discussions, aptitude tests and tests on communication skills and language ability are administered (McMillin, 2006; Ramesh, 2004). Managerial data in our study confirm that various avenues were relied upon for recruitment. These include referrals (76 percent), training institutes (31 percent), NAC (20 percent), advertisements (48 percent), walk-in interviews (78 percent), campus placements (47 percent), consultants (83 percent) and employment exchanges (9 percent) (see Table 3.7).

Displaying fluency with spoken and written English, being able to multitask, having computer skills, possessing a pleasant voice, being persuasive, having a positive approach, possessing good communication skills and a neutral accent, harbouring positive attitudes, having high energy levels and being a quick learner were all qualities that were valued by call centres while selecting employees (Batt et al., 2005c; McMillin, 2006; Ramesh, 2004). Employee-related factors considered by most managers in our sample to be very important during the process of recruitment included high energy levels (83 percent), good communication skills (81 percent), proficiency in English (81 percent), enthusiasm (80 percent) and obedience (77 percent). These findings were consistent with the mean scores for these factors, calculated on a scale of 1 to 5, where 1 was very important and 5 was not at all important. Call centres appeared to be more demanding than back offices in matters of selection, indicating lower mean scores on all parameters except knowledge of computers, technical knowledge, typing skills, prior work experience and affiliation to unions (Table 3.8).

Counterintuitively, customer orientation and related factors such as mother-tongue influence and tone of voice were not considered to be that important. This is in keeping with D'Cruz and Noronha's (2006) prediction

Table 3.8 Perspectives of Managers on Criteria for ITES–BPO Employee Selection

Criteria for ITES–BPO employee selection	Response of 'very important' for both call centres and back offices (%)	Mean score		
		Call centres and back offices	Call centres	Back offices
Proficiency in English	139 (80.8)*	1.28	1.08	1.54
Good communication skills	140 (81.4)*	1.26	1.09	1.47
Energy	143 (83.1)*	1.17	1.12	1.19
Enthusiasm	137 (79.7)*	1.23	1.14	1.29
Obedience	133 (77.3)*	1.24	1.21	1.28
Typing skills	100 (58.1)*	1.61	1.62	1.61
Tone of voice	54 (51.9)*	1.78	—	—
Previous work experience	64 (37.3)*	1.97	1.93	2.01
No mother-tongue influence	41 (39.4)**	1.76	—	—
Customer orientation	49 (28.5)*	1.94	1.80	2.16
Knowledge of computers	64 (37.2)*	2.01	2.07	1.91
Technical knowledge	61 (35.5)*	2.22	2.3	2.06
Prior work knowledge	7 (4.1)*	3.88	4.11	3.57
No affiliation to unions	4 (2.3)*	4.06	4.28	3.75

*$n = 172$.
**$n = 104$.

that emphasis on these criteria would decline over time. Nonetheless, it is important to note that customer orientation scores were marginally higher for call centres where the mean score was 1.80 as compared to the ITES–BPO sector as a whole where the mean score was 1.94.

Union affiliation was not considered to be a very relevant criterion for recruitment, ostensibly because union formation in this sector is still in a nascent phase and recruitment focuses more on fresh talent rather than on experienced people (who are more likely to be members of unions in other sectors), paralleling trends in Australia (Todd et al., 2003).

Managers indicate that interviews (98 percent) are the most important tool for agent selection, followed by group discussions (44 percent), psychometric tests (39 percent), tests of analytical abilities (29 percent), tests of verbal abilities (27 percent) and tests of numerical abilities (26 percent) (see Table 3.9).

Table 3.9   Perspectives of Managers on Employee Selection Tools for the ITES–BPO Sector ($n = 169$)

Employee selection tools	Frequency (%)
Psychometric tests	66 (38.8)
Verbal ability tests	46 (27.1)
Numerical ability tests	44 (25.9)
Analytical tests	50 (29.4)
Interviews	166 (97.6)
Group discussions	74 (43.5)

3.5.2   Training

Once recruited, training forms an important component of the call centre set-up and encompasses a 4–8 week period (Ramesh, 2004; Thite and Russell, 2009). Training activities receive at least 25 percent of the organization's budget (Budhwar et al., 2006) and include generic (such as cultural and linguistic training, communication skills and emotional labour skills) and process-specific modules. These modules could be conducted by in-house trainers and experienced agents or be subcontracted to adult education sites where individuals themselves pay for the training they receive (Budhwar et al., 2006; McMillin, 2006; Mirchandani, 2004; Ramesh, 2004). While making comparisons with the US, Batt et al. (2005b) state that the initial training in US subcontracted call centres is less than half of that found in Indian offshored call centres, but once cultural and linguistic training is accounted for, it appears that Indian call centres do not provide more initial training for other aspects of the job. Post-training employees in Indian offshored call centres take 13 weeks to become proficient on the job. Similarly, the amount of on-the-job training and the annual rates of ongoing training are not substantially different, with Indian offshored call centres providing 4.7 weeks on an average and in-house US call centres providing 3.9 weeks on an average.

Over 92 percent of the ITES–BPO employees included in our study indicated that they had undergone training at the time of joining the organization with which they were currently working. This figure (97 percent) was substantially higher for managers in the study who stated that the employer organization provided training to agents at the time of joining. This difference may reflect the fact that though training is emphasized, the recruitment of employees who require minimal training is stressed (Ramesh, 2004). Among our call centre respondents, 87 percent underwent process training, 58 percent underwent voice and accent training and 29 percent underwent cross-cultural training. Similar components were included for back-office employees, with 91 percent of the respondents reporting having

Table 3.10 Types of Training Given to ITES–BPO Employees

Types of training	Frequency (%)		
	Call centres ($n = 449$)	Back offices ($n = 279$)	Both call centres and back offices ($n = 728$)
Process	391 (87.1)	253 (90.7)	644 (88.5)
Voice and accent	259 (57.7)	—	259 (35.5)
Typing	—	45 (16.1)	45 (6.1)
Cross-cultural	12 (28.6)	58 (20.8)	186 (25.6)

gone through process training, 16 percent having undergone training in typing and 21 percent having completed cross-cultural training (Table 3.10).

Employees express high degrees of satisfaction with the training that they receive (see Table 3.22, p. 93), echoing the findings of Thite and Russell (2009). Following training, agents 'go live' and are on 3 months' probation. Their performance during probation determines decisions about their confirmation and/or retention with the company (McMillin, 2006).

3.6 Work Systems

In terms of organization type, client and customer location and nature of work, agent data illustrate what is already known about this sector. That is, 33 percent of the ITES–BPO employees in our sample works for 'captive' units, 41 percent works for MNC or Indian third-party providers and 25 percent works for domestic ITES–BPO firms (the small remainder did not wish to divulge the name of the organization they worked for). The organizations that respondents work for have clients located in various parts of the world, mostly in the US (58 percent), the UK (15 percent), Australia (6 percent), but also in a number of other locations such as Canada, Europe, the Middle East and East and Southeast Asia including India (20 percent).

Call centre agents in the study handle inbound customer service (40 percent); sales and customer service (15 percent); inbound technical support and customer service (25 percent); and outbound sales, telemarketing and collections (17 percent). Back-office employees in the study work in a variety of processes including legal assistance (9 percent), insurance claims (16 percent), travel planning and bookings (4 percent), equity research (4 percent), loans and mortgages (7 percent), medical transcription (6 percent), application processing (2 percent), billing and collections (10 percent), web design (4 percent), data entry (13 percent), preparation of invoices (2 percent), payments (9 percent), reconciliation of accounts

(3 percent) and other tasks such as business intelligence, mail support, procurement and so on (27 percent). Of the back-office respondents, 44 percent interacted with customers through email (38 percent), via web pages (4 percent) and over the phone (21 percent).

3.6.1   Working Time

Ninety-one percent of the agents included in our study work in shifts, while 9 percent stated they do not. Respondents' shifts vary around the clock. While 67 percent of the respondents have daily shifts of 9 hours and around 18 percent of the respondents have daily shifts of 8 hours (in keeping with the Shops and Establishments Act which provides for 9 hours of work inclusive of breaks), 11 percent of the sample report shifts of 9.5 hours or more.

Asking agents to come to the office early for briefings or to stay after their normal shift hours was not uncommon. This has been borne out with data that shows that while about 26 percent of the respondents are expected to arrive on time for their shift, 31 percent arrive about 30 minutes earlier and 31 percent arrive 10–15 minutes prior to the onset of the shift.

Seventeen percent of the respondents report that the length of their shifts have been extended due to work pressures. This has ranged from 30 minutes to beyond 90 minutes, and can vary in regularity from once in a while to every day. Where compensation for overtime is paid, the rates are not always in accordance with the various Shops and Establishments Acts, which require employers to pay employees working overtime at a rate of twice their normal wages. Interestingly, data from a few managers support this finding (Table 3.11).

Call centre employees work in shifts that are punctuated by three breaks (Ramesh, 2004). There are two tea and coffee breaks of 15 minutes each and a lunch/dinner break of 30 minutes (D'Cruz and Noronha, 2008). However, breaks are decided by team leaders on the basis of call levels or call queues. Unscheduled breaks during working hours are not permitted while scheduled breaks are tracked by specially designed software (McMillin, 2006; Noronha and D'Cruz, 2006).

Seventy-one percent of the ITES–BPO employees in the study also report having three breaks per shift while approximately 19 percent get two breaks per shift. Tea and coffee breaks are of 15 minutes each for almost 90 percent of the respondents, while lunch/dinner breaks are of 30 minutes each for 87 percent of the respondents. In any case, the total break time usually does not exceed 60 minutes. Only 7 percent of the respondents have their breaks reduced because they are asked to work extra hours (of these, a larger group are from call centres – 9 percent – as compared to a smaller group from back offices – 5 percent). Employees who are asked to work extra hours can lose up to 15 minutes of their break time in the process. Only

Table 3.11 Overtime Rates Paid to ITES–BPO Employees

Overtime rate (in Rs per hour)	Frequency (%)			
	Call centre and back-office employees	Call centre employees	Back-office employees	Managers
Normal rate of salary	64 (32.2)	49 (33.1)	15 (29.4)	4 (14.8)
One-and-a-half times salary	13 (6.5)	9 (6.1)	4 (7.8)	3 (11.1)
Twice the salary	78 (39.2)	55 (37.2)	23 (45.1)	18 (66.7)
Less than the normal rate of salary	8 (4.0)	6 (4.1)	2 (3.9)	2 (7.4)
Rs 333	1 (0.5)	1 (0.7)	0 (0)	—
Rs 250	2 (1.0)	2 (1.4)	0 (0)	—
Rs 150	1 (0.5)	0 (0)	1 (2.0)	—
Rs 100	20 (10.1)	14 (9.5)	6 (11.8)	—
Rs 125	4 (2.0)	4 (2.7)	0 (0)	—
Rs 120	1 (0.5)	1 (0.7)	0 (0)	—
Rs 90	1 (0.5)	1 (0.7)	0 (0)	—
Rs 50	1 (0.5)	1 (7.0)	0 (0)	—
Rs 30	2 (1.0)	2 (1.4)	0 (0)	—
Not known	3 (1.5)	3 (2.0)	0 (0)	—
Total	$n = 199$ (100.0)	$n = 140$ (100)	$n = 51$ (100)	$n = 27$ (100.0)

2 percent of the managers in our sample indicate that agents' breaks are reduced for the purpose of work, and when this happens, it does not exceed 10 minutes.

Employees' leave records are meticulously tracked. Availing of leave, including sick leave, requires prior request to and consent from management so that work is not interrupted (Noronha and D'Cruz, 2006). Some researchers have stated that agents are sometimes denied leave even in cases of serious ailments or problems, especially when call volumes are high (Noronha and D'Cruz, 2006). However, the majority of agents in our study state that it was somewhat easy (65 percent) to get leave sanctioned, with 23 percent finding it easy and 13 percent reporting difficulty in getting leave approved.

Nonetheless, based on the information available with agents, the average number of days of leave that agents are entitled to is 25.08 days per year, which was lower than that provided for in the Shops and Establishments Acts of various Indian states. Moreover, agents are neither able to provide this information with certainty nor are they able to give a breakdown of the various types of leave available to them. Thus, it is difficult to make a judgement about the extent to which the provisions of the Shops and Establishments Acts are being violated.

The number of work days in a week seems to be getting extended for some employees. Almost 74 percent of the respondents mention 5-day work weeks. This is higher for back-office employees (86 percent) compared to call centre employees (67 percent). Twenty-four percent indicate 6-day work weeks (with call centres being higher – 31 percent – than back offices – 12 percent), while 2 percent had 5.5-day work weeks. While 86 percent state that they have not been asked to work for more days in a week than stipulated in their contract (once again, the back-office group is higher – 91 percent – than the call centre group – 83 percent), 14 percent indicate that they have indeed been asked (17 percent from call centres and 8 percent from back offices). Employees who have been asked to work beyond their stipulated work week indicate that this happens about once or twice a month.

3.6.2 Job-Related Discretion

The majority of employees from both call centres and back offices indicate low levels of job-related discretion (on a scale of 1 to 5, with 1 for not at all and 5 for a large extent), with not much difference between the two groups (Table 3.12). Managers' ratings of the degree of discretion enjoyed by agents were even lower than those provided by the agents themselves (Table 3.12). This discrepancy between managers and employees may be related to the ability of agents to find their own spaces of discretion through various acts of resistance (Noronha and D'Cruz, 2006).

Most ITES–BPO employees in our sample work in contexts that resemble the mass service/engineering model (Holman, 2003), which emphasizes a factory-like division of labour (Taylor and Bain, 1999; van den Broek, 2004), with jobs being characterized as dead-end, with low complexity, low control, repetition and routineness (Knights and McCabe, 1998; Taylor and Bain, 1999). Batt et al. (2005b) conclude that despite relying on a more educated and full-time workforce, Indian call centres have work systems that are more tightly constrained and standardized than those found among US subcontracted or in-house call centres. With the exception of reliance on scripts, which is higher in the US subcontracted call centres, Indian call centre managers report substantially lower levels of job-related discretion given to agents over handling customer requests and use of problem-solving groups. Indeed, mechanisms that facilitate employee participation in management decisions and problem-solving groups, both of which improve employee morale and performance as well as knowledge sharing and reduce attrition, were found to be very low in Indian call centres. Low levels of discretion also apply to the pacing of work, the scheduling of rest breaks and the handling of unexpected

Table 3.12 Perspectives of Employees and Managers on ITES–BPO Employees' Job-Related Discretion

Areas of job-related discretion	Employees		Managers	
	Response of 'moderate discretion or less'		Response of 'moderate discretion or less'	
	Frequency (%)	Mean score	Frequency (%)	Mean score
Set own pace of work	419 (57.9)[a]	3.36	192 (98.5)[g]	2.16
Decide when to take a break	503 (69.5)[a]	2.60	186 (95.4)[g]	1.93
Plan how to carry out work	516 (71.6)[b]	2.89	178 (91.3)[g]	2.35
Set own work targets	541 (75.2)[c]	2.63	178 (91.3)[g]	2.19
Have to work overtime when do not want to	637 (88.6)[c]	1.93	164 (84.1)[g]	2.23
Handle unpredictable situations	601 (83.8)[d]	2.34	158 (80.9)[h]	2.29
Deal with problems that are difficult to solve	610 (84.4)[e]	2.43	159 (84.5)[g]	2.73
Repeat the same task over and over again	578 (79.9)[e]	2.61	163 (83.6)[g]	2.80
Use personal initiative and judgement	450 (62.3)[f]	3.15	171 (86.7)[g]	2.94

[a]$n = 724$; [b]$n = 721$; [c]$n = 719$; [d]$n = 717$; [e]$n = 723$; [f]$n = 722$; [g]$n = 195$; [h]$n = 194$.

customer requests/complaints (Batt et al., 2005b). It was, therefore, not entirely surprising when Indian call centres came to be called 'new-age sweatshops' (Budhwar et al., 2006), being characterized by an exaggerated form of the mass production model (Batt et al., 2005c; Taylor and Bain, 2005) with agents working there being called 'cybercoolies' (Ramesh, 2004).

3.6.3 Monitoring and Surveillance

In keeping with this mass production model, stringent controls form part and parcel of work life in the call centre. ICTs facilitate pacing of work, monitoring, surveillance and maintenance of archival records, which allows for the use of numerous quantitative and qualitative performance measures (Ramesh, 2004). Our data on monitoring and surveillance and on performance evaluation primarily highlight techno-bureaucratic controls.

Call centre agents participating in our study mentioned various means used for the purposes of monitoring and surveillance. These include automatic call dialling (39 percent), predictive dialling (22 percent), remote listening (45 percent), call recording (74 percent), call barging (82 percent), side-jacking (54 percent), quality checks (66 percent), archival storage and retrieval (39 percent), the master screen of the team leader and other superiors on the call floor[8] (49 percent), customer feedback (68 percent), the presence of the team leader and other superiors on the call floor (69%), security checks at entry points (65 percent) and surveillance cameras and closed-circuit televisions (CCTVs) (65 percent).

Back-office respondents reported the use of tracers (62 percent), archival storage and retrieval (39 percent), quality checks (79 percent), the master screen of the team leader and other superiors (47 percent), customer feedback (39 percent), the presence of the team leader and other superiors on the production floor (60 percent), security checks at entry points (60 percent) and surveillance cameras and CCTVs (52 percent) (Table 3.13).

While managers' data for call centres indicate that monitoring and surveillance is more pervasive than perceived by agents, it is possible that agents are unaware of the details of monitoring and surveillance. In back offices, the pervasiveness of monitoring and surveillance seems to be less pronounced as indicated by the smaller difference between managers' and employees' scores (Table 3.13).

Agents from both call centres and back offices harboured a variety of opinions about being monitored. While monitoring and surveillance were initially stressful, it soon became routine (22 percent), were seen as part of the job (51 percent), were viewed as useful for feedback and performance (57 percent) and were deemed useful for providing protection from clients and customers (11 percent). Only 3 percent of the sample considered monitoring and surveillance to be intrusive. Overall, agents are comfortable with monitoring and surveillance and other performance evaluation mechanisms and consider them to be fair as well as relevant for both the employee organization and for measurement of task performance. This finding hints perhaps at the presence of successful identity regulation and a socio-ideological control process (D'Cruz and Noronha, 2006; Noronha and D'Cruz, 2009a).

3.6.4   Performance

Indian ITES–BPO organizations generally conduct the employee performance appraisal process once or twice a year. Performance-related data (97 percent), commitment to work (95 percent) and relationships with team members (91 percent) were considered by managers to be the most important criteria for the performance appraisal and career advancement process. Other relevant factors were the agents' relationship with their immediate superior (77 percent) and the agents' visibility (66 percent), which was linked to the performance of extra work (42 percent) (Table 3.14). There appeared

14 Perspectives of Managers on Factors Influencing ITES–BPO Employees' Advancement ($n = 195$)

influencing career advancement	Response of 'very important'	
	Frequency (%)	Mean score
...ance-related data/statistics	190 (97.4)	1.03
...tment to work	186 (95.4)	1.05
professional relationship with team ...bers	177 (90.8)	1.10
' professional relationship with ...ediate superior	151 (77.4)	1.24
...ty of agent	128 (65.6)	1.35
...vork/tasks performed by agent	81 (41.5)	1.62
...ess to superiors	21 (10.8)	2.14
...' informal networks	5 (2.6)	2.47
...r of agent	1 (0.5)	2.94
...n of agent	1 (0.5)	2.98
...l status of agent	1 (0.5)	2.98
...of agent	2 (1.0)	2.97

a communication gap between managers and agents with regard to ...rmance evaluation parameters, although it is difficult to state this with ...ority as managers and agents in the sample were not matched as per ...employer organization. Nonetheless, almost half of the agents (51 per-...felt that the evaluation process was reasonably fair while 27 percent ...idered it to be very fair.

...rformance-based data (which may include the amount of leave an ...loyee has taken), besides being used to determine compensation, salary ...ments, promotions and training needs, were consolidated over time ...publicly displayed. Employees who topped performance charts were ...idered to be role models while those at the bottom were provided assis-...e by way of training and feedback (Budhwar et al, 2006; Ramesh, 2004). ...se failing to show marked improvement in performance faced dismissal.

. terms of performance-related rewards, managers highlighted that mon-...y incentives remained the most frequently used reward (87 percent), ...tered by incentives in kind such as gift vouchers, holiday vouchers and ...n (71 percent) that appealed to agents (Table 3.15). Training was used ...derately (60 percent) as a reward. Lateral and horizontal movements were ...om used (this situation was indicated by 88 percent of the managerial ...ple), implying limited opportunities for growth, a finding that runs con-...y to managerial claims made to agents at the time of recruitment (see ...onha and D'Cruz, 2009a).

...he mean scores here were 1.14, 1.31, 2.87 and 2.85, respectively, for ...netary incentives, incentives in kind, lateral movement and horizontal

Table 3.13 Various Methods of Monitoring and Surveillance Used in ITES-BPO Employer Organizations According to Employees and Managers

Monitoring and surveillance methods	Frequency (%)					
	Employees			Managers		
	Call centres (n = 449)	Back offices (n = 278)	Both call centres and back offices (n = 727)	Call centres (n = 99)	Back offices (n = 91)	Both call centres and back offices (n = 190)
Automatic call dialling	177 (39.4)			78 (78.8)		
Predictive dialling	97 (21.6)			67 (67.7)		
Remote listening	204 (45.4)			77 (77.8)		
Call recording	334 (74.4)			94 (94.9)		
Call barging	369 (82.2)			93 (93.9)		
Side-jacking	243 (54.1)			88 (88.9)		
Quality checks	298 (66.4)	218 (78.7)	516 (71.1)	82 (82.8)	62 (68.1)	144 (75.8)
Archival storage and retrieval	173 (38.5)	135 (38.9)	308 (42.5)	51 (51.5)	46 (50.5)	97 (51.1)
Master screen of team leader/other superiors	220 (49.0)	131 (47.1)	351 (48.3)	51 (51.5)	23 (25.3)	74 (38.9)
Customer feedback	304 (67.7)	109 (39.2)	413 (56.8)	54 (54.5)		
Presence of team leader/other superiors	308 (68.6)	167 (60.1)				

Table 3.15 Perspectives of Managers on Performance Incentives Used in Indian ITES–BPO Employer Organizations ($n = 194$)

Performance incentive	Response of 'most frequently used'	
	Frequency (%)	Mean score
Monetary incentives	169 (87.1)	1.14
Incentives in kind	136 (70.5)	1.31
Specialized training	4 (2.1)	2.35
Lateral movement	2 (1.0)	2.87
Vertical movement	2 (0.5)	2.85

movement, on a scale of 1 for most frequently used and 3 for seldom used. Not only do the findings emphasize lack of career growth opportunities, but also 53 percent of the managers indicated an increase in organization hierarchy over time in order to overcome the problem (see Noronha and D'Cruz, 2009a).

3.6.5 Discipline

The threat of agents being dismissed from their jobs remained omnipresent, heightening employment insecurities. According to managers in our sample, for various acts of indiscipline an official warning emerged as the most important form of disciplinary action used by employer organizations and managers. In cases of extending breaks, warnings were as high as 74 percent while in cases of transferring calls to the wrong department and noting false email addresses, warnings were used by 30 percent and 47 percent, respectively, of employer organizations and managers. Warnings and dismissals were resorted to by 30 percent of employer organizations and managers for call dropping cases and were relied upon by 17 percent of the employer organizations and managers in instances of extension of wrap-up time. Outright dismissal was used when calls were transferred to the wrong department (11 percent) or when false email addresses were noted (10 percent), though it was rarely used against agents for loitering. Managers stated that agents were sent for training for noting down false email addresses (17 percent), transferring calls to the wrong department (16 percent) or escalating calls to team leaders (19 percent), but this form of disciplinary action was rarely resorted to when breaks were extended beyond the authorized break periods. Similarly, salary deductions were also rarely relied upon as a disciplinary mechanism (Table 3.16).

Where dismissals are used as a mechanism for disciplinary action, doubts can be expressed about the procedures employed. For instance, a lawyer representing employee interests in this sector described a case where an ITES–BPO employee challenged her dismissal in court and the court

Table 3.16 Types of Disciplinary Actions Used by ITES–BPO Managers and Employer Organizations According to Managers

Types of disciplinary action	Frequency (%)								
	Dropping calls[a]	Not taking calls[b]	Extending breaks[c]	Loitering[d]	Customer abuse[e]	Extending wrap-up time[f]	Escalating call to team leader[g]	Transferring call to wrong department[h]	Noting down false email addresses[i]
Warning	33 (55.0)	40 (58.8)	84 (73.7)	69 (70.4)	34 (54.8)	60 (57.1)	48 (50.5)	21 (38.2)	41 (46.6)
Dismissal with warning	18 (30.0)	22 (32.4)	23 (20.2)	25 (25.5)	17 (27.4)	18 (17.1)	15 (15.8)	12 (21.8)	15 (17)
Outright dismissal	7 (11.7)	4 (5.9)	6 (5.3)	2 (2.0)	7 (11.3)	3 (2.9)	7 (7.4)	6 (10.9)	9 (10.2)
Sent for training	2 (3.3)	2 (2.9)	1 (0.9)	2 (2.0)	4 (6.5)	20 (19.0)	18 (18.9)	9 (16.4)	15 (17.0)
Warning and sent for training	—	—	—	—	—	4 (3.8)	7 (7.4)	7 (12.7)	7 (8.0)
Salary deduction	—	—	—	—	—	—	—	—	1 (1.1)

[a]n = 60; [b]n = 68; [c]n = 114; [d]n = 98; [e]n = 62; [f]n = 105; [g]n = 95; [h]n = 55; [i]n = 88.

Table 3.17 Degree of Work-Related Pressure Faced by ITES-BPO Employees

Degree of work-related pressure	Frequency (%)		
	Call centres[a]	Back offices[b]	Both call centres and back offices[c]
Not at all pressurized	69 (15.4)	48 (17.6)	117 (16.3)
Not very pressurized	196 (43.8)	140 (51.5)	336 (46.7)
Quite pressurized	161 (36.1)	80 (29.4)	241 (33.5)
Highly pressurized	21 (4.7)	4 (1.5)	25 (3.5)

[a]$n = 447$; [b]$n = 272$; [c]$n = 719$.

directed the employer organization to follow the appropriate disciplinary procedure [Vinod Shetty/Young Professionals Collective, personal communication]. However, instances of agents approaching the court for redressal in cases of dismissal are rare since it is far easier for them to find a new job than to get justice through the legal system (Penfold, 2008). Moreover, some researchers argue that protective labour laws are not effective in the case of call centre employees (Noronha and D' Cruz, 2006), who are seen as peripheral workers to be summarily replaced or dismissed (Ramesh, 2004).

Looking at the overall impact of work systems on ITES–BPO employees, about 41 percent of call centre respondents experience relatively high degrees of work-related pressure as compared to about 31 percent of back-office respondents (Table 3.17).

In terms of mean score, on a scale of 1 to 4, with 1 being not at all pressurized and 4 being highly pressurized, ITES–BPO employees in our study stood at 2.25.

3.7 Work–Life Balance

As mentioned earlier, call centres operate around the clock throughout the year, relying on night shifts to service overseas markets for which time zones are ahead or behind that of India (McMillin, 2006; Noronha and D'Cruz, 2006; Ramesh, 2004). This has been identified by many call centre agents as the most difficult part of their jobs, thus reflecting the fundamental immobility of time and their continued embeddedness within their local social contexts (Mirchandani, 2004). Odd working hours lead to disturbances in both their personal and social lives. There are problems related to maintaining friendships, keeping in touch with relatives, accomplishing household duties and finding time for sound family relations (McMillin, 2006; Mirchandani, 2004; Noronha and D'Cruz, 2006; Poster, 2007; Ramesh, 2004; Singh and Pandey, 2005).

In examining the work–life balance of the agents, we looked at various areas of interference of work into nonwork aspects of life. Looking at the combined data for back-office and call centre respondents, most ITES–BPO employees met expectations only on two indicators, that is, never taking work home (87 percent) and never having to work on holidays and weekends (78 percent). Except for this, 67 percent of ITES–BPO employees state that they think about work after they leave the office; 81 percent feel exhausted after work; 52 percent have their sleep disrupted on account of work; 61 percent are prevented from spending enough time with their family/partner due to work concerns; 66 percent are prevented from spending time with their friends due to work demands; 57 percent find it hard to get time to take care of personal/family matters; 54 percent find it hard to take holidays when they wished to do so; 57 percent indicate that their shift patterns affect their social life and 63 percent need to party with, or go on outings with, their office colleagues during nonwork hours (Table 3.18).

These responses indicate a poor work–life balance, a result that is not unexpected. Noronha and D'Cruz (2006) had earlier stated that ITES–BPO

Table 3.18   ITES-BPO Employees Who Never Experienced Disruption of Nonwork Due to Work

Experience of disruption of nonwork due to work	Frequency (%)		
	Call centres	Back offices	Both call centres and back offices
I never continue to think of work after office hours	165 (36.8)[a]	63 (25.3)[d]	234 (32.5)[g]
I never feel exhausted after work	87 (19.4)[a]	51 (18.6)[e]	138 (19.1)[h]
My sleep is never disrupted on account of work	202 (45.1)[a]	143 (52.4)[d]	345 (47.9)[i]
I spend enough time with parents	133 (29.7)[a]	145 (52.9)[e]	278 (38.5)[h]
I spend enough time with friends	123 (27.5)[b]	120 (43.6)[f]	243 (33.7)[h]
I never take work home	389 (87.0)[b]	247 (89.8)[f]	636 (88.1)[h]
I never find it hard to get time to take care of family	155 (34.6)[b]	157 (57.3)[f]	312 (43.2)[h]
I never find it hard to take holidays	173 (38.9)[c]	158 (57.5)[f]	331 (46.0)[i]
I am never affected by poor shift patterns	164 (36.6)[a]	144 (52.4)[f]	308 (42.6)[j]
I never have to go for official party during nonwork hours	146 (32.6)[a]	123 (44.7)[f]	269 (37.2)[j]
I never have to work on holidays or weekends	351 (78.3)[a]	215 (78.2)[f]	566 (78.3)[j]

[a]*n* = 448; [b]*n* = 447; [c]*n* = 445; [d]*n* = 273; [e]*n* = 274; [f]*n* = 275; [g]*n* = 721; [h]*n* = 722; [i]*n* = 720; [j]*n* = 723.

Table 3.19 Health Problems Faced By ITES–BPO Employees (*n* = 249)

Health problems faced by ITES–BPO employees	Frequency (%)
Voice problems	29 (15.9)
Eye strain	55 (22.1)
Hearing problems	23 (12.6)
Digestion	38 (15.3)
Physical strain	138 (55.4)
Sleep	83 (33.5)
Mental and psychological stress	32 (12.9)

managers expected employees to have foremost responsibility to their job rather than to their family. Therefore, skipping company outings to spend quality time with the family is often equated with a lack of commitment to the team and the employer organization.

This situation is exacerbated by constant changes in shifts, causing agents to continuously adjust to new work times, which has a significant impact on their health (Mirchandani, 2004), as manifested by several symptoms of mental and physical illness such as nervousness, chronic fatigue, stiff neck, sore eyes, backaches and headaches, impaired vision, numbness in fingers, body ache, fever, asthma, sore throats, nausea, dizziness, rashes, insomnia, anxiety, restlessness, irritability, depression, drowsiness, loss of appetite, changes in body weight, decreasing vigilance and gastrointestinal problems (McMillin, 2006; Noronha and D'Cruz, 2006; Poster, 2007; Ramesh, 2004). (See Table 3.19.) It is also noted that agents develop poor eating habits in addition to smoking, drinking excessive coffee and so on to cope with the psychological and physical strain engendered by their jobs (McMillin, 2006; Ramesh, 2004; Singh and Pandey, 2005).

Thirty-five percent of the ITES–BPO employees in our sample confirm that they have had illnesses they believe were related to their work. Of these, 55 percent have had physical strain such as back, neck or shoulder problems, and about 34 percent have spoken of sleep-related problems (Table 3.19). Comparing back-office and call centre respondents, we found that while 42 percent of the agents in call centres report health problems, 24 percent of the back-office agents mention health problems. As Poster (2007) maintains, call centre employees have much to lose in this scenario of transnational call centre work, standing to compromise their bodies, their mental stability, their family lives as well as their career trajectories.

3.8 Human Resources Practices

High-commitment management (HCM) practices are seen as a means of staving off the oppressive aspects of the call centre labour process (see

Hutchinson et al., 2000; Kinnie et al., 2000) and earlier research on the Indian ITES–BPO sector highlights the use of these practices in this sector. Not only do Indian ITES–BPO organizations offer various facilities such as reading rooms, Internet browsing centres, gymnasiums, free transportation after night shifts, free or subsidized meals, facilities for games and medical benefits, but there is also an effort to portray the workplace as a 'fun place' by organizing recreational and cultural activities such as get-togethers, outings, picnics and family days to break the routinization, monotony and pressures of the job (Budhwar et al., 2009; D'Cruz and Noronha, 2006; Ng and Mitter, 2005; Poster, 2007; Ramesh, 2004).

Moreover, international call centres in India are housed in clean, well-organized buildings that often have entrances decorated with glass and marble (Mirchandani, 2004), compelling some scholars to argue that the physical working conditions in Indian call centres resemble those in the West (see Budhwar et al., 2009; Carroll and Wagar, 2009; Russell and Thite, 2009; Thite and Russell, 2009) or are actually better than those of some call centres in the West (Poster, 2007).

Apart from highlighting the presence of HR departments in ITES–BPO organizations (as reported by 98 percent of our respondents), our data further reveal that only cafeterias (98 percent) seem to be common to all organizations, while substantially fewer organizations provide for gymnasiums and sports facilities (64 percent), recreation facilities (52 percent), de-stress rooms (54 percent), sleeping facilities (49 percent) and telephone/email/Internet facilities (58 percent) (Table 3.20).

With regard to the physical environment at work, including temperature, ventilation, noise levels, work space, health facilities, recreation facilities

Table 3.20 Facilities Provided by ITES–BPO Employer Organizations to Their Employees

Facilities	Frequency (%)		
	Call centres[a]	Back offices[b]	Both call centres and back offices[c]
Cafeteria	438 (97.8)	270 (98.9)	710 (98.2)
Gymnasiums and sports facilities	285 (63.6)	179 (65.1)	464 (64.2)
Recreation facilities	448 (52.2)	140 (50.9)	374 (51.7)
De-stress rooms	243 (54.2)	146 (53.1)	389 (53.8)
Sleeping facilities	221 (49.4)	130 (47.3)	351 (48.6)
Telephone, email and internet	271 (60.5)	145 (52.7)	416 (57.5)

[a]$n = 448$; [b]$n = 275$; [c]$n = 723$.

Table 3.21   Satisfaction of ITES–BPO Employees with Working Conditions ($n = 725$)

Working conditions	Response of 'most satisfied'	
	Frequency (%)	Mean score
Temperature	194 (26.8)	4.18
Ventilation	224 (30.9)	4.23
Work space	228 (31.4)	4.24
Health facilities	211 (29.1)	4.13
Recreation facilities	222 (30.7)	4.11
Toilet facilities	246 (33.9)	4.22
Facilities for employees with disabilities	222 (30.7)	4.06
Noise levels	189 (26.3)	4.13

and toilet facilities, agents rated them as satisfactory or very satisfactory on a 5-point scale that ranged from 1 for mostly dissatisfied to 5 for mostly satisfied (see Table 3.21).

ITES–BPO employees report fairly high levels of satisfaction with their working life. Mean scores for factors such as interaction with customers, interaction with colleagues, interaction with superiors, use of computer technology, training, working hours and shifts, workload, work environment, break time, health and safety and cafeteria menu were in the range of 3.79 to 4.15 on a 5-point scale, with 1 being mostly dissatisfied and 5 being mostly satisfied. Salary had the lowest level of satisfaction, with a mean score of 3.55 (Table 3.22).

Table 3.22   Satisfaction of ITES–BPO Employees with Various Aspects of Work Life

Aspects of work life	Response of 'most satisfied'	
	Frequency (%)	Mean score
Interaction with customers	93 (14.1)[a]	4.0
Interaction with colleagues	171 (23.6)[b]	4.12
Interaction with superiors	181 (25.0)[b]	4.07
Use of computer technology	203 (28.0)[b]	4.15
Training	164 (22.7)[c]	4.01
Salary	120 (16.6)[d]	3.55
Working hours and shifts	132 (18.2)[b]	3.79
Workload	133 (18.4)[e]	3.84
Work environment	152 (21.1)[f]	4.04
Break time	138 (19.0)[b]	3.94
Health and safety	157 (21.7)[e]	4.01
Cafeteria menu	139 (19.2)[c]	3.92

[a]$n = 658$; [b]$n = 725$; [c]$n = 723$; [d]$n = 722$; [e]$n = 724$; [f]$n = 721$.

Table 3.23   Avenues for Grievance Redressal for ITES–BPO Employees ($n = 726$)

Avenues for grievance redressal	Frequency (%)
Team leader	635 (87.5)
Project manager	82 (11.3)
Operations manager	27 (4.0)
HR manager/department	56 (8.0)
Assistant manager	4 (1.0)
Top management	2 (0.2)

Table 3.24   ITES–BPO Employees' Descriptions of the HR Department within Their Employer Organization ($n = 725$)

Employees' descriptions of their HR department	Frequency (%)
More management-oriented	188 (25.9)
More employee-oriented	154 (21.2)
Neutral	352 (48.5)
Did not know	28 (3.9)
Not applicable	3 (0.4)

Ninety-six percent of the agents in the sample state that their employer organization has a system through which employee grievances can be raised, discussed and solved. Some of these avenues include open-forum meetings, 'open-door' policies, intranet discussion forums, counselling, grievance procedures, skip-level meetings, town halls and suggestion schemes (Budhwar et al., 2009; D'Cruz and Noronha, 2006; Noronha and D'Cruz, 2009a; Poster, 2007; Ramesh, 2004; Thite and Russell, 2009). Yet while respondents can easily turn to their team leaders with their grievances, the extent to which the upper echelons of the organizational hierarchy are available to them is unclear (Table 3.23).

Not surprisingly, then, the response of employees towards the HR department was mixed, with only 21 percent of our respondents stating that HR was employee-oriented (Table 3.24).

3.9   Attrition

Attrition rates in the Indian ITES–BPO sector remain high, testifying to the ineffectiveness of HCM practices. NASSCOM (2006b) data suggest that attrition levels within the industry are between 25 percent to 50 percent, making it an issue that warrants urgent attention.

According to Batt et al. (2005b), job characteristics explain the high attrition rates in subcontracted and offshored call centres as compared to in-house call centres. Subcontracted and offshored call centres are more constrained to follow standardized operating procedures and to enforce them via performance monitoring. Batt et al. (2005b) highlight the contradictory characteristics exhibited by work and employment systems in India. On the one hand, employees have high levels of formal education and receive salaries that are considerably above the national market wage. On the other hand, these same highly qualified individuals receive few or no opportunities to use those skills because the work is designed to limit independent decision-making and innovative problem-solving. Employers are thus paying for skills without making effective use of them.

Quitting becomes the preferred option for call centre employees who are dissatisfied with their jobs and who do not see prospects for better career opportunities with their current employers (Batt et al., 2005b). Besides job design and limited growth and career development opportunities (Budhwar et al., 2009; Noronha and D'Cruz, 2009a; Thite and Russel, 2009), Budhwar et al. (2006) point out that difficulty with customers, inadequate job enrichment, burnout stress syndrome (BOSS), better salary and incentives offered by other companies, employees pursuing higher education, favouritism in appraisals and promotions, a closed management system and health and psychological ailments arising out of night shifts result in employee frustration, and ultimately, resignation.

In our sample, approximately 22 percent of the agents want to move out of the ITES–BPO sector to another industry, while 46 percent want to move to another organization within the ITES–BPO sector. The most important reasons agents cite for wanting to leave their current organization are remuneration (40 percent), poor growth opportunities (27 percent), job demands (23 percent) and work–life balance (17 percent). Similarly, the primary reasons put forward by managers in our study to explain agent attrition from the current organization are poor remuneration (61 percent) and poor opportunities for growth (52 percent) (Table 3.25). These reasons for attrition (i.e., remuneration and opportunities for growth) put forward by both managers and employees contest the discourse of professionalism espoused by ITES–BPO organizations highlighting the presence of rhetoric (see Noronha and D'Cruz, 2009a) which results in a sense of distrust between management and employees (Thite and Russell, 2009).

3.10 Collectivization and Union Formation

Citing the adoption of HCM practices by Indian ITES–BPO organizations, NASSCOM underscores that collectivization and union formation are irrelevant in this sector. On the contrary, it asserts that such endeavours would

Table 3.25 Perspectives of Employees and Managers on Reasons Behind ITES–BPO Employees' Desire to Quit Their Current Employer Organization

Reasons behind ITES–BPO employees' desire to quit	Frequency (%)	
	Employees' views	Managers' views
Job demands (qualitative and quantitative parameters) too stressful	122 (22.6)[a]	29 (15.4)[g]
Poor work–life balance	93 (17.1)[b]	23 (12.0)[g]
Monotony, lack of autonomy and other characteristics of the job	27 (5.0)[c]	12 (6.2)[g]
Poor working conditions and facilities	19 (3.5)[c]	10 (5.1)[g]
Poor growth opportunities	147 (27.1)[d]	101 (51.8)[g]
Negative interpersonal relationship at work	25 (4.6)[c]	11 (5.6)[g]
Unsupportive/indifferent management/superiors	17 (3.1)[a]	3 (1.5)[g]
Poor remuneration	217 (39.9)[b]	119 (61.0)[g]
Lack of recognition and respect	53 (9.8)[c]	17 (8.7)[g]
Health reasons	88 (16.2)[c]	14 (7.2)[g]
Shifts	90 (16.6)[c]	23 (11.8)
Travel	34 (6.3)[a]	11 (5.6)[g]
Constant monitoring and surveillance	28 (5.2)[e]	55 (3.1)[g]
Night work	25 (4.8)[f]	7 (3.6)[g]

[a]$n = 541$; [b]$n = 544$; [c]$n = 542$; [d]$n = 543$; [e]$n = 539$; [f]$n = 525$; [g]$n = 195$

hamper sectoral growth and development, which has achieved significant milestones in the absence of unions (NASSCOM, 2006c).

Notwithstanding NASSCOM's perspective, a substantial number (45 percent) of managers in our study were either neutral (26 percent) or not against (19 percent) the idea of a union being formed in the ITES–BPO sector, underscoring the fact that managers did not form an ideological monolith. For those who were in favour of unions, the most important reason was to save on the high costs of remuneration that ITES–BPO organizations had to bear as compared to the remuneration offered by unionized organizations in the non-ITES–BPO space. The second most important reason was that employees required an independent voice. The mean scores for these two factors were 1.43 and 1.62, respectively, on a scale of 1 indicating to a large extent and 4 indicating not at all. For the other factors, the mean scores pointed in the moderate direction (Table 3.26).

The motivation for employees to favour union formation in the ITES–BPO sector emerges from the constant pressure from clients to reduce operating costs and to increase service levels, which results in a sacrificial HR strategy whereby employees' well-being and job satisfaction are compromised in order to achieve organizational objectives (Wallace, 2009). Not surprisingly,

Table 3.26 Perspectives of Managers on the Desirability of Unions in the Indian ITES–BPO Sector ($n = 37$)

Reasons why unions are desirable	Response of 'to a large extent'	
	Frequency (%)	Mean score
Employer organization has to offer higher salary and benefits	27 (59.5)	1.43
Economic cost of keeping unions out is high	11 (29.7)	1.89
Lack of structure for handling grievances, safety issues and so on	7 (18.9)	2.08
Fear of unionization is a constant worry	6 (16.2)	2.08
Employer organization has to work harder at communication	9 (24.3)	1.86
Management has not been able to reduce attrition	8 (21.6)	1.89
Employees require an independent voice	16 (43.2)	1.62

then, a large group of agents in our sample (43 percent) believe that unions are necessary to protect their interests, especially in matters of salary and physical security, while 26 percent say that there should not be any unions (31 percent did not know how to respond to the question).

Table 3.27 Reasons for ITES–BPO Employees Wanting Unions

Reasons for wanting unions	Response of 'very important'	
	Frequency (%)	Mean score
Duration of workday/shift	153 (48.6)[a]	1.64
Work pressure	138 (43.9)[b]	1.65
Travel time	117 (37.5)[c]	1.91
Health and safety issues	204 (65.2)[d]	1.46
Employees' physical security	209 (66.8)[d]	1.38
Favouritism	69 (22.0)[c]	2.33
Need for employee voice	126 (40.5)[e]	1.77
Difficulties in quitting the job created by employer organizations	137 (44.1)[e]	1.71
Targets	121 (38.7)[d]	1.83
Salary	204 (65.2)[d]	1.38
Bonuses and other benefits	178 (57.0)[c]	1.49
Job insecurity	189 (60.4)[d]	1.49
Demanding superiors	109 (34.8)[e]	1.83
Management reneges on its promises	170 (54.8)[f]	1.52
Abusive customers	66 (33.3)[g]	2.04

[a]$n = 315$; [b]$n = 314$; [c]$n = 312$; [d]$n = 313$; [e]$n = 311$; [f]$n = 310$; [g]$n = 198$.

For those wanting unions, salary and physical security, both of which had mean scores of 1.38 (on a scale of 1 to 4, with 1 being very important and 4 being not important) seemed to be the most important reasons. These were followed by the need for bonuses and other benefits and for job security, which had mean scores of 1.49 each (Table 3.27).

Given that the feeling of wanting to have a union may be very different from the action required on part of employees to actually organize as a collective, it is not surprising that only about 9 percent of employees in our sample knew about the presence of a union in the Indian ITES–BPO sector. This was in spite of several collective bodies such as the Union for ITES Professionals (UNITES Professional), the West Bengal Information Technology Services Association (WBITSA) and the Young Professionals Collective

Table 3.28   Reasons for ITES–BPO Employees Not Joining a Union

Reasons for not joining a union	Response of 'very important'	
	Frequency (%)	Mean score
Employer organizations oppose unions	57 (31.5)[a]	2.17
ITES–BPO employees see themselves as professionals	79 (43.2)[b]	1.76
ITES–BPO employees do not believe in trade unions	77 (42.1)[b]	1.80
Unions in ITES–BPO sector damage sectoral growth	106 (58.2)[c]	1.66
Workforce is young and inexperienced	63 (34.8)[a]	1.92
ITES–BPO employees think that joining a union will affect their careers	63 (34.8)[a]	2.03
ITES–BPO employees fear that employer organizations may terminate their services if they join a union	78 (42.9)[c]	1.96
ITES–BPO employees believe that employer is all they need	72 (39.6)[c]	1.86
ITES–BPO employees believe that any problem they have will be resolved by managers	80 (44.2)[a]	1.80
ITES–BPO employees' 'heart and minds' are with their company	81 (44.5)[c]	1.82
ITES–BPO employees believe that they get a high salary	74 (40.7)[c]	1.77
ITES–BPO employees feel they are better off as compared to their parents	69 (38.3)[d]	2.19
ITES–BPO employees think that they will be promoted	79 (43.6)[a]	1.85
High attrition poses difficulties	57 (31.5)[a]	1.91

[a]$n = 181$; [b]$n = 183$; [c]$n = 182$; [d]$n = 180$.

(YPC) having emerged in India. Moreover, researchers have put forward various reasons why Indian ITES–BPO employees have been reluctant to join unions. These include managerial policies focusing on individualism, travel arrangements peculiar to the Indian context, work systems, the acquired professional identity, fear of employer backlash, avoidance of conflict and attrition (Noronha and D'Cruz, 2006; Ramesh, 2004; Taylor et al., 2008). Among our respondents, the most important reasons for not joining a union (on a scale of 1 to 4, with 1 being very important and 4 being not important) were that unions would hamper the growth of the Indian ITES–BPO industry (mean score of 1.66) and that ITES–BPO employees saw themselves as professionals who did not require unions (mean score of 1.76) (Table 3.28).

3.11 Conclusions

Overall, the findings of our study underscore Indian ITES–BPO employees' dichotomous experiences at work. Positive and negative experiences co-exist, bringing simultaneous well-being and strain. Positive experiences are associated with personal growth, satisfaction and a positive self-concept, resulting in well-being. Negative experiences are associated with distress and dissatisfaction, indicators of strain. Our earlier research on telemarketing agents (Noronha and D'Cruz, 2007b) not only resulted in similar findings, but also demonstrated how respondents tried to work out a balance between positive and negative experiences through various problem-focused and emotion-focused coping strategies so that positive experiences were never overshadowed by negative experiences.

3.12 Recommendations

- Ensuring the effectiveness of HCM practices is an important first step for Indian ITES–BPO organizations. Adopting and implementing developmental and humanistic HR practices, along with due attention to job design elements, would go a long way towards creating and sustaining the organizational image of being a good employer rather than being obsessed with the idea of wanting to keep unions at bay.
- Improved adherence to the existing legal framework in matters pertaining to employee rights and well-being would help Indian ITES–BPO organizations address the issues of attrition and work–life balance, to the advantage of both employers and employees. Under such circumstances, employees benefit in terms of better work systems and work–life balance, while employers benefit from an improved supply of labour resulting from better working conditions.
- The engagement of realistic job previews as a means of styming attrition cannot be overlooked. The current practice of unrealistic job previews, especially with regard to salary and career advancement opportunities

(see Noronha and D'Cruz, 2009a), while enticing young employees with little experience in the short run, only leads to unmet expectations and turnover in the long run.

• The priority for unions in the Indian ITES–BPO sector is to focus on co-ordinating among themselves and intensifying campaigns that highlight their presence. While stepping up awareness and organizing activities, they cannot ignore the professional identity of employees (see Noronha and D'Cruz, 2009b). Indeed, Indian ITES–BPO organizations would do well to keep Penfold's (2008) point in mind. She states that if the Indian ITES–BPO sector is rife with good HR practices, as NASSCOM and employer organizations claim, then trade unions should pose no threat. Rather, trade unions may assist employer organizations to ensure that the work they generate has the broadest possible benefits and that employee rights are properly recognized.

Notes

1. Interview with Ameet Nivsarkar, Vice-President, NASSCOM, on February 26, 2008.
2. Interview with Ameet Nivsarkar, Vice-President, NASSCOM, on February 26, 2008, which indicated that as per rough estimates, 25% of the Indian ITES–BPO employees are located in Bangalore, 16% in Mumbai, 21% in New Delhi and NCR, 10% in Chennai and 7.5% in Hyderabad.
3. NASSCOM is India's National Association of Software and Service Companies, the premier trade body and the chamber of commerce of the IT (information technology) software and services industry in India. As of December 31, 2005, NASSCOM had over 950 members, of which over 150 are global companies from the US (United States), UK (United Kingdom), EU (European Union), Japan and China. NASSCOM's member companies are in the business of software development, software services, software products and ITES–BPO services. A not-for-profit organization, NASSCOM's primary objective is to act as a catalyst for the growth of the software-driven IT industry in India. Other goals include facilitation of trade and business in software and services, encouragement and advancement of research, propagation of education and employment, enabling the growth of the Indian economy and providing compelling business benefits to global economies by global sourcing (NASSCOM, 2006a).
4. That is, one that does not require traditional administrative procedures.
5. The calculation in this section is at the exchange rate of US $1 = Rs 46.
6. 'Creamy Layer' is a common, colloquial term used, in India to imply that a person or group is privileged in some way(s). In terms of caste, it implies the general category.
7. The issue of caste is a sensitive topic and not at the core of this chapter or the book. The reference here is merely used to identify one socio-economic factor in employment and hiring decisions in this industry in India.
8. The master screen of the team leader and other superiors refers to their computer screens which, because of the software employed, enable them to track agents' work in real time. Information about work pace, etc. will appear on the master screen of the team leader indicating work rates, etc.

4
Offshored Work in Philippine BPOs

Maragtas S.V. Amante

4.1 Introduction and Objectives

This chapter offers a glimpse of the highly globalized BPO 'industry': the customer or client is in the US or any other English-speaking country, while the employee sits with a computer in a cubicle in some remote corner of Manila in the Philippines. This study identifies key aspects of the interaction between new technology and people and processes in information technology-enabled services (ITES). This section describes employee characteristics, patterns of work organization, working conditions and employment practices in offshored work in Philippine business process outsourcing (BPO) companies.

The goals of this chapter are to

- describe the business environment behind offshore work in Philippine BPOs;
- examine the links between the Philippine labour market and the increasing demand for employment in offshored work;
- analyse the conditions and terms of employment in offshored work in the Philippines' patterns of work, with a focus on health and safety, pay, employee voice and employment relations;
- provide data for comparative analysis of offshored work, to contribute towards capturing essential global patterns; and
- identify policy gaps in offshored work in the Philippines and offer conclusions useful for deriving recommendations to address labour policy issues in offshored work.

The discussion here provides in-depth analysis and inferences derived from employee characteristics in relation to their working conditions and terms of employment, with significant implications for the nature of work in this industry sector. Conclusions deal with the gaps that need to be filled in order to promote a better working environment, particularly with regard to health and safety, voice and industrial relations.

4.2   Business Environment in the BPO Industry

Virtually unheard of a decade ago, the Philippine BPO industry has grown dramatically in scope and significance. A recent estimate cites US $3.3 billion in revenues from BPOs, which is about 3 percent of the gross domestic product (GDP).[1] This contribution has grown significantly compared to a few years ago, but it still amounts to less than a third of the remittances from overseas Filipino workers (OFW) and seafarers, which was recorded at US $12.7 billion in 2006 and was predicted to reach US $14 billion in 2007.[2] In contrast, income from the BPO sector remains far below the country's top exports, electronics and semiconductors, which totalled $27 billion and $29.5 billion in 2005 and 2006, respectively.[3]

In the view of local managers, BPO firms are companies with clients who 'sliced off' their labour-intensive, noncore activities for relocation to other sites or countries. Offshore business models are often copies of contact centres in the source country, including operation manuals, scripts and procedures. In this sense, the problems of these work processes were also relocated to their new sites, including the Philippines.

Handling customer calls usually takes place in a different time zone from the source country, during the night or the so-called graveyard shift from midnight to early morning, in order to coincide with the daytime hours of overseas customers. Offshore contact centres operate 24 hours a day, 7 days a week (24/7). Work shifts overlap, with shifts consisting of 8–9 hours each. There is a constant change in employee work schedules, with consequences for employees' health, as well as their social and family lives.

Few call centre agents reveal themselves to customers as Filipinos, or that their workplace is located in the Philippines. 'Customers in the US still think that the Philippines and its people live in backward conditions,' said one call/contact centre team leader. Those allowed to admit that they are Filipinos are still required not to reveal their Philippine location, but instead give the main US address of their outsourcing (client) company (Pico, 2006). Many Filipino call centre agents say that they are not used to, and probably could not even understand, racist comments from callers in the US or other western countries. Nonetheless, being the target of insults, complaints and angry calls is still a source of distress.

Philippine BPO agents know that their 'customers' are people based mostly in the US, Canada, Australia, the UK, New Zealand and other English-speaking countries. These customers patronize the products or services of the client and thus must be given special treatment. An HRD manager in a call centre candidly shares his experience:[4]

> One of our CSRs specializes in what we call 'escalation calls from India.' These are calls routed to a Filipino operator, who has an American accent

due to training. He sounded like a real American. The call was routed to satisfy the US customer, who wanted desperately to talk to an American operator. The customer was of course satisfied that his demand was complied with. Little did he know that he was in fact talking to a Filipino operator, well trained in American diction, from a call centre in the Philippines.

4.3   Research Methodology

Research for this study used various sources to generate primary data on the Philippine BPO sector. These sources included several focus group discussions and interviews with employers, as well as an employee questionnaire survey.

4.3.1   Focus Group Discussions and Interviews

The focus group discussions (FGDs) held on November 10 and 17, 2007, dealt mainly with trends in the BPO sector, terms and conditions of employment, compensation and the application of labour laws to the industry. There were seven or eight participants in each FGD, with three managers and three or four customer service representatives and agents. In-depth interviews with five BPO HR managers took place in October and November 2007.

4.3.2   Employee Questionnaire

A questionnaire for BPO employees was designed, pilot-tested, finalized and circulated in September and October of 2007. The questionnaire had items on demographics, education, recruitment, work experience, compensation and benefits, work and life balance, stress, job satisfaction and views about work in the BPO industry. In return for their cooperation, respondents were promised full confidentiality of both their name and company identity. Respondents ($n = 329$) from the sample BPO firms filled out the questionnaires during limited breaks from their work days. When no response was given to certain questions, these nonresponses were excluded from the analysis.

4.3.3   Questionnaire for Employers

An extensive questionnaire for employers gathered information regarding services, the profile of employees, human resource practices, hours of work, recruitment and staffing, operational performance and employment relations. There were 12 employers who responded from the original list of 15 companies; 5 of the responses were incomplete, since these employers cited 'confidentiality' specifically regarding information concerning pay and productivity.

4.3.4   Sampling and Data Limitations

From an existing directory with updated addresses and contact phone numbers, 15 companies were included in the sample, which is 12 percent of the population of 125 BPO firms. Sampling was limited to metropolitan Manila. A sample of five large BPO firms, with multiple sites, and ten small and medium-sized companies were chosen. Due to time and resource constraints, a target of 300 employees was allocated to the sample firms, weighted by the percentage of total employees. Sample firms who refused cooperation or were difficult to follow-up with were replaced by another firm within the list. The final sample consisted of $n = 329$ questionnaires filled in by employees, which is 10 percent more than the target sample. Several questionnaires were not included due to incomplete information.

Follow-up to retrieve questionnaires was done in late October and November 2007. Checking, encoding, rechecking and data analysis followed immediately. Then statistical package for social sciences (SPSS) software was used to code, generate tables and analyse the data. During data analysis, the SPSS statistical software automatically separated questionnaires with no responses or with missing information on the target variable. No response or missing cases were indicated in the statistical tables.

4.4   Overview of the Labour Market[5]

The Philippine population is estimated at 88.5 million in 2007, to grow to 92 million in 2009. The population grows at an average annual rate of 2.0 percent. The Philippine labor force is 36.45 million in April 2008, with an unemployment rate of 8 percent. In April 2009, young workers (aged 15 to 24 years old) comprised one-half (50.6 percent or 1.433 million) of the total unemployed workforce. Youth unemployment rate at 17.4 percent was more than twice the national average. This rate was lower compared with the 18.6 percent recorded in 2008.

The number of unemployed persons in April 2008 was reported to be 2.9 million, placing the unemployment rate at 8 percent. The proportion of males among the unemployed (62.5 percent) was higher than that of females (37.5 percent). Among unemployed persons, those who had attained high school level comprised 45.3 percent, of which 32 percent of the total unemployed were high school graduates. About 40 percent of the total unemployed had reached college level and 14.0 percent had only attained elementary level.

The government documents 1.1 million OFW working for foreign employers. The government also estimates that in 2004 there were 8 million Filipinos working overseas as permanent, temporary or undocumented migrants. These OFW and migrants provide the Philippines with a critical lifeline for balancing the payments deficit, with remittances amounting to US $16.4 billion in 2008 – an increase of 13 percent over the previous year.

Table 4.1   Growth of Philippine BPO Firms (2000–2009)

	Contact centers	All BPO firms	Estimated employees, contact centres	Estimated employees, all BPOs	Employment growth*	Estimated revenues* (US $ millions)	Revenue growth
2000	4		2,400			24	
2001	13		5,600		133%	56	133%
2002	31		12,000		114%	120	114%
2003	60		32,000		167%	320	167%
2004	72		67,000	100,500	109%	1,024	220%
2005	108		112,000	163,250	62%	2,375	61%
2006	114	404	160,000	235,575	44%	3,207	35%
2007	124	531	198,000	298,953	27%	4,816	50%
2008	178	618	227,000	371,965	24%	6,061	26%
2009	191	641	280,000	450,000	21%	7,500	24%

Source: Gigi Virata, Executive Director for Information and Research, Business Processing Association of the Philippines (BPAP), and various news reports. Figures for 2009 are preliminary. Simple rates of growth computed by the researcher.
* Employment and revenue growth from 2000 to 2004 are for contact centers only. From 2005 to 2009, growth is for all BPOs.

In terms of employment, the BPO sector contributed an estimated 450,000 new jobs in the Philippines as of 2007, which is significant with regard to the political goal of creating at least 6–10 million jobs by 2010. With more call centres and BPO firms expected to be established, the government expects that by 2010, more than a million Filipinos could be employed in call centres and other BPO firms. By 2012, the industry forecast is to generate $12 billion in revenues, which will be almost equivalent to the remittances from OFW.

Industry leaders also report that demand in the BPO industry continues to increase. There were 641 BPO firms listed in 2009, compared to 404 firms in 2006 (Table 4.1). There have also been BPO firms that were unable to compete, leading to bankruptcy and job losses, but there is no data available in this regard. There is optimism that the industry might create more than a half-million new jobs even before 2010. The positive outlook for the BPO sector as a source of sustained job creation, however, does not factor in key dimensions of this segment of the labour market. For instance, managers indicate that BPO firms suffer from a relatively high turnover of employees. Some managers state that Philippine BPO firms have 40–50 percent annual attrition of employees. In addition, for every 100 job applicants, only 3–5 are accepted. Most of them are rejected due to a lack of the English communication skills required by call centre jobs.[6]

4.5   The BPO Employers

The data in this section are from interviews and questionnaires returned by managers from a sample of call centres and back-office firms. There were

Table 4.2   Philippine BPO Firms in the Survey Sample

BPO	Years in operation	Main business	No. of Employees	
			2007	2005
AAA	10	IT desk, customer service	80	60
BBB	3	Medical transcription, legal transcription	125	26
CCC	7	Call centre	800	n.d.
DDD	6	Financial customer service	1300	n.d.
EEE	1	Customer service and call centre, IT desk	400	n.d.
FFF	5	Call centre	1200	800
GGG	3	Online English tutorial	32	20
HHH	4	Customer service, inbound healthcare voice applications	1500	500
III	4	Call centre	10,500	2500
JJJ	6	Call centre	15,000	1600
KKK	7	Call centre	8000	7000
LLL	15	Call centre	15,000	n.d.

Note: Several managers returned incomplete questionnaires, citing confidentiality. No data: n.d.

11 managers who returned fully completed questionnaires, and four who returned partially complete ones, citing confidentiality. Indeed, most of the sample firms confirm that employment in this sector significantly increased each year between 2005 and 2007. For instance, one call centre (JJJ) reported they now have 15,000 employees, which is more than a ninefold increase from 1600 seats in 2005.[7] Smaller back-office firms likewise reported significant annual increases in their workforce between 2005 and 2007, such as HHH which reported an increase of 130 percent, and AAA, which reported a 30 percent increase (Table 4.2).

4.6   Employee Characteristics

Philippine BPO employees are young, single, mostly female and college graduates from social sciences, engineering or business courses (see Table 4.3). Males are on average a year older (26 years old) than females (25 years old). They are recruited directly and respond to job advertisements. Good pay is the most common reason why they decide to be BPO employees.

Male respondents plan to work longer in BPO companies compared to females. Respondents expect to continue working in their BPO jobs for an average of an additional 33 months (2.75 years).

Most of the respondents were from call centres (65 percent) and the rest from other BPO firms (35 percent). Many of the firms in the sample have

Table 4.3 Average Age of Employee Respondents (years)

	Mean age	Std. deviation	Minimum	Maximum	N	% of total N
Male	26.15	3.812	20	43	131	41.1
Female	25.41	4.784	19	49	188	58.9
Total	25.72	4.419	19	49	319	100.0

Note: $n = 10$ cases had no response on 'age' and were excluded from the analysis.

both call centre and back-office processing units. There were more female respondents (59.3 percent), compared to males (40.7 percent).

The most common jobs held by females are customer service representatives (CSR), technical support eRepresentatives (TSR or eREP) or client business analysts. On the other hand, many males are technical support engineers (TSE), team leaders (TL) or quality officers. A sample task for TSRs is for the job holder to 'provide quality voice support and respond to clients' issues and queries.'

While most respondents were single, they reported 2.4 dependents, people who depend upon them for financial support. Only 3 percent reported they were 'solo parents.' There were also few cases of 'live-in' or 'separated' respondents, although, due to the sensitive nature of the topic, some underreporting was expected. In separate interviews, BPO company managers said that the number of employees who are solo parents was actually higher than reported, ranging from 15 percent in one top call centre, up to 40 percent in another top back-office firm. The youngest child of BPO employees was 4.5 years old on average.

4.7 Education

The Philippine education system consists of 6 years of compulsory elementary education, 4 years of secondary (high school) education and 4–8 years of college. Most of the young people whose families are well off also have an option to acquire 2 years of pre-elementary schooling (1 year in nursery school, 1 year in kindergarten), if they have the means to finance preschool enrolment. High school graduates have the choice to enter a vocational or technical course, ranging from 1–3 years. College courses usually take 4 years to finish, but some specializations such as engineering require 5–6 years. A law degree requires a college diploma and another 4 years of law education. A medical degree likewise requires 4 years of college and another 4–5 years in medical school, plus an internship. Those individuals who are unable to afford tertiary education join the workforce in agriculture or blue-collar jobs.

Most of the respondents had completed college (80 percent). Many had studied social sciences (27 percent), as well as business and commerce (26 percent). There were also many respondents who had studied engineering and technical courses (27 percent). A significant few had a background in the sciences (5 percent) and the health professions such as nursing (9 percent). BPO firms also attract graduates from other professions, and it is possible that this situation may have contributed to the worsening of the labour market in general, particularly for those who came from engineering or the sciences.

4.8   Work Experience

Respondents were asked whether their job was their first and whether it was their first BPO company. While many of the respondents (39.2 percent) said that their current job was their first work experience, most said (54.7 percent) that their current place of employment was their first BPO company. On the other hand, many employees transfer from one company to another, changing jobs. Those who had worked for two or more BPO firms represented 45.3 percent of the sample. With so many BPO employees changing companies and jobs, the perception may be that they are not loyal. However, the more significant implication is that BPO employees always search for a better workplace, given the availability of alternative positions and the high intensity of stress in these jobs. There is no significant difference between males and females in the frequency of changing companies or jobs.

Males plan to work significantly longer in BPO firms compared to females. While females plan to stay for 27 months more (2.25 years), males said they would continue in their jobs longer, for an additional 40 months (3.3 years). These findings have significant implications for the sustainability of BPO firms in the Philippines and for the design of appropriate programs

Table 4.4   How Long Do You Plan to Continue Work in BPO? (by work shift)

	Mean (months)	Std. deviation	N	% of total N
Regular day shift	37.57	34.823	30	13.3
Evening shift	30.03	36.601	61	27.1
'Graveyard' shift	35.28	39.041	107	47.6
Variation in work hours I choose	30.00	16.541	6	2.7
Variation in work hours company chooses	27.13	21.067	15	6.7
Others	16.83	8.256	6	2.7
Total	32.99	35.912	225	100.0

Note: No response/missing cases are not included in the analysis.

by employers to increase job commitment, given the enormous demand to recruit recent college graduates for offshored positions.

Why would employees choose not to stay long in their BPO jobs? Those who do regular shift work are expected to stay slightly longer (38 months more), compared to those working the regular night ('graveyard') shift, who plan to stay in their BPO jobs for 35 months more (see Table 4.4).

4.9 Recruitment and Training

Many respondents indicated that it is relatively 'easy' or 'very easy' to find jobs in BPO firms (52.7 percent). Most were recruited by applying directly to the BPO firms, which advertised vacancies. The influence of peers (e.g., classmates, friends) was important in their decision to work in a BPO company. Friends (27.7 percent) and relatives (6.8 percent) play an important role as guarantors or 'backers' of BPO candidates. Due to high attrition rates, job advertisements in print, broadcast and web media are almost always dominated by BPO firms. BPO firms spend heavily on advertising and job recruitment postings in both print and electronic media. Major cities, especially in Metro Manila are plastered with huge banners and billboards of call centre companies near major thoroughfares and railway stations, beckoning job applicants. Job-hunting fairs in shopping malls for call centres are a regular event to attract new college graduates to the industry.

After submitting their application, job applicants are told to 'wait for our call,' which will never come to most of them. Call centres require skills not only in English, but also in typing, data coding and written composition. All BPO firms place a premium on English proficiency. Interviews are conducted entirely in English. An HR manager in a call centre says a 7-minute interview is sufficient to determine whether to accept or reject an applicant. Applicants spend more time waiting in line for the interviewer than in the interview itself.

Graduates and even undergraduates who pass the preliminary exams undergo several days of English skills training and product training for 2–3 weeks. The trainee is then put on the floor to attend to mock calls for assessment. Agents are also supposed to be able to type at least 25 words per minute.

4.10 Legal and Regulatory Framework

4.10.1 Industry Legislation

In 1995, the Philippine Congress updated the Omnibus Investment Code to attract foreign investors, including ITES. This updated foreign investment law became the backbone for the development of the country's BPO industry as a preferred area for business, consistent with the open-economy policy, as well as policies on deregulation and trade liberalization.

The critical elements in the updated legal framework are incentives to foreign investors – including financial, infrastructure and support services – with a special purpose of attracting IT service exporters. The government, through the Department of Trade and Industry (DTI), developed programmes to support the Philippine offshore work as a 'sunrise industry.' The goal of the government policy framework was to create more IT-enabled jobs and tap potentials in other business outsourcing sectors.[8] The government also enacted legislation on cybercommerce: the Electronic Commerce Act of 2000.

With the rise of the BPO industry, a key focus of the government's legal framework is to provide support by developing 'ready' locations – special economic zones and IT parks – for foreign investors who are IT service exporters. Through Executive Order 226, as mandated by the investments law, the government specified incentives to ITES and other BPO firms as part of the Investment Priorities Plan.[9] Government provided more incentives for ecozone and IT investors, developers and operators, such as: tax holidays; exemptions from duties on imported capital equipment, spare parts, supplies, raw materials; permanent resident status for foreign investors and their families; employment of foreign nationals in supervisory, technical or advisory posts; and other special support services such as grants for skills training.

The Philippines also passed a law on data protection, based on the European regulatory framework, since data could now flow in and out of the country without restriction. The Electronic Commerce Act of 2000, however, provides civil and criminal penalties for unauthorized access to computer systems and imposes legal obligations of confidentiality on persons who receive electronic data, keys, messages or other information. The Philippines also accepted the Asia-Pacific Cooperation (APEC) Privacy Principles, recognizing the rights of data owners and providing a reasonable forum for achieving redress in security or privacy issues. Most BPOs handle private and sensitive data from financial institutions, customer accounts and monetary transactions. According to the Department of Trade, the Philippines intends to enact privacy and security laws to provide assurance to global clients, to protect business information and trade secrets.

4.10.2   Labour Legislation

The Philippines ratified the fundamental Conventions of the International Labour Organization (ILO) on freedom of association and collective bargaining as early as 1953.[10] These commitments to international norms are reflected in part or in whole through the Philippine Constitution, as well as various labour laws and social legislation enacted through the years. As a commitment to international norms, the Philippine Constitution guarantees the rights of workers:

It shall guarantee the rights of all workers to self-organization, collective bargaining and negotiations, and peaceful concerted activities, including the right to strike in accordance with law. They shall be entitled to security of tenure, humane conditions of work and a living wage. They shall also participate in policy and decision-making processes affecting their rights and benefits as may be provided by law.[11]

Philippine labour laws provide for standards on minimum wages, hours of work, compensation for night work, holiday pay premium, Social Security and health and safety, among other things.[12] Labour law prohibits night work for women, but most call centre employees are women in the 'graveyard shift' from 10:00 pm to 6:00 am, and all centres have been granted exemptions by the Secretary of Labour and Employment.

As understood by most Philippine BPO industry leaders, the term *outsourcing* means the contracting out of jobs by another company or person to do particular functions that are typically not the core competence of the business. The *Philippine Labour Code* regulates the contracting out of jobs, through Article 106 which reads in part:

> ART. 106. *Contractor or subcontractor.* [. . .] In the event that the contractor or subcontractor fails to pay the wages of his employees [. . .] the employer shall be jointly and severally liable with his contractor or subcontractor to such employees to the extent of the work performed under the contract, in the same manner and extent that he is liable to employees directly employed by him. [. . .][13]

How does the legal and regulatory framework measure up to the realities of employment in BPOs? The guarantee of labour protection to women in night work is a good test of the congruence and continuing relevance of such protection. The Philippine Constitution guarantees protection of working women, and[14] the Philippine Labour Code implements this guarantee through a blanket prohibition of night work for women (see Article 130 below).

> ART. 130. *Nightwork prohibition.* No woman, regardless of age, shall be employed or permitted or suffered to work, with or without compensation: (a) In any industrial undertaking or branch thereof between ten o'clock at night and six o'clock in the morning of the following day; [. . .]

Given that the majority of the BPO workforce consists of young females serving customers in different time zones, BPO employers had lobbied to repeal this prohibition of night work. However, there are many industries aside from BPO firms where women would be vulnerable if they were to work at night. A repeal would also violate the Philippines' commitment to

ILO Convention No. 89 (1949).[15] Nonetheless, the law provides for exceptions (Article 131), as determined by the Secretary of Labor, through appropriate regulations. Upon application with the Secretary of Labor, BPO firms almost always have been exempted from this law. Indeed, night work for women in BPO firms is a situation where the 'exception becomes the rule.'

Another test of the vitality of the legal and regulatory frameworks is in the application of the laws that guarantee decent work conditions, including the right to unionize. Philippine BPO firms are not unionized, and many managers say that they prefer a 'no union' environment. This anti-union attitude of management, however, is in direct opposition to the views of almost half of BPO employees.[16] On the other hand, Article 255 of the Philippine Labour Code provides that employees have the right to elect their representatives in labour management committees, enabling employees to participate in policy and other decisions that affect their rights, benefits and welfare, except those rights covered by collective bargaining agreements.

4.11   Working and Employment Conditions

4.11.1   Wages and Benefits

The questionnaire asked respondents to indicate the range of their basic monthly pay. Nonbasic pay (e.g., meal and transport allowances, attendance and performance bonuses, etc.) was a separate question, and respondents chose from relevant items in a checklist. Wage regression analysis uses the human capital model (Becker, 1993), with years of education, months on the job and civil status as variables.

Most BPO employees indicated that their monthly pay is in the range PhP 15,000–20,000 (US $357–476) (Table 4.5).[17] The estimated average basic monthly pay of PhP 16,928 ($402) is 53 percent higher than the prevailing minimum wage paid to Filipinos of the same age employed in other industries. The equivalent minimum wage in Metro Manila is US $262, including pay on rest days and holidays.[18] Before the advent of BPO firms, the most common available jobs for new college graduates were dead-end, fixed 6-month contractual jobs, usually renewed continuously, in sales or warehouses in the shopping malls. Shopping mall employees are paid just

Table 4.5 Average Monthly Pay of BPO Employees

Sex	Mean	US $	Minimum	Maximum	N	Ratio avg/min. wage
Male	18,308	$436	9750	47,500	117	1.7
Female	15,990	$381	9750	37,500	172	1.5
Total	16,928	$403	9750	47,500	289	1.5

Note: Figures in PhP. Missing case/no response not included. US $1 = PhP 42 as of November 30, 2007. Equivalent monthly minimum wage (Manila) = $262 per month. The simple regression result is: Basic pay = 18,307.602–2317.867 (female = 1).

about the minimum wage, and with less take-home pay due to compulsory deductions for social security and health insurance.

4.11.2 Pay Differentials by Gender

There is a significant differential in average wages between men and women, with men having a 13 percent advantage in the BPO firms. Simple regression analysis shows that being male or female explains only 5 percent of this variation in pay. This means that 95 percent of the variations can be accounted for by other factors. In their recruitment policies, many BPO firms specifically say that they are an 'equal opportunities employer' and do not discriminate in pay or employment opportunities. HR managers of BPO firms explain that most males have technical or engineering jobs. These positions are paid higher. Females are mostly sales agents or customer service representatives, who are paid less. This clearly shows that Philippine BPO firms need to seriously examine the congruence of nondiscrimination policy and practice as far as pay is concerned.

Managers from five large BPO firms provided comparable data, which confirm trends in basic pay among employees. On average, a typical BPO employee earns PhP 16,800 basic monthly pay, plus PhP 7625 allowances or a total of PhP 24,425 monthly ($582). On the other hand, managers' pay is 224 percent higher than the pay of typical employees. A typical manager receives on average PhP 39,600 (US $943) in basic monthly pay, plus PhP 15,125 ($363) allowances or PhP 54,725 ($1,303) in average total monthly pay (Table 4.6).

Table 4.6 Typical Monthly Pay of BPO Employees and Managers

Company	Typical employee		Typical manager	
	Basic pay	Allowances	Basic pay	Allowances
TTT	PhP 17,000	10,000	PhP 75,000	PhP 30,000
OOO	16,000	10,000	50,000	15,000
GGG	18,000	2500	22,000	4500
MMM	18,000	8000	21,000	11,000
KKK	15,000	n.d.	30,000	n.d.
Average	PhP 16,800	7625	39,600	15,125
US $1 = PhP 42	US $400	$182	US $943	$363
Total pay = basic + allowance	PhP 24,425		PhP 54,725	
US $1 = PhP 42	US $582		US $1303	

Note: Figures in Philippine pesos (PhP). US $1 = 42 PhP as of November 30, 2007. No data, n.d.
Source: Response by BPO managers to the survey questionnaire.

Some BPO employees are aware of the pay differentials with their foreign counterparts:[19]

> We are paid US $8 per day, while we are told that our American counterparts are paid $8 per hour. Premium [pay] for extra working hours [is] not paid. Commissions are often based on unachievable sales targets. Discrepancies in the pay slip are often not explained.

A productivity incentive scheme based on sales therefore needs to consider the dollar revenues of the BPO company. There are restrictions on access to information and other data on dollar revenues. In this regard, a local HR manager said that he finds it very difficult to design and explain productivity schemes which facilitate the understanding and commitment of the employees. These schemes require transparency and integrity of data sources.

4.11.3 Pay Differentials by Level of Education

A college degree does matter for the pay of BPO employees, but only slightly. The average pay of college graduates in BPO firms is PhP 17,093 (US $407), which is 8 percent higher than employees who did not finish college. Post-graduate education, through masters-level studies, brings in a slight 2 percent advantage in average pay over college graduates (Table 4.7). However, the low coefficient of determination (R-squared) of a simple wage regression where college education is the sole explanation indicates that this variable alone might account for only 1 percent of the differences in pay among BPO employees.[20]

4.11.4 Pay Differentials by Work Experience

Does work experience lead to pay advantages? (See Table 4.8.) The results show that, indeed, work experience does provide a pay advantage over new

Table 4.7 A College Degree Matters for Pay of BPO Employees

Education level	Mean, PhP	Avg US $	Minimum, PhP	Maximum, PhP	N	% of total N
Below college	15,786	376	9,750	22,500	35	12.3
College graduate	17,093	407	9,750	47,500	234	82.4
Post-graduate MS, MA, MBA	17,500	417	9,750	22,500	15	5.3
All	16,953	403	9750	47,500	284	100.0

Table 4.8 Average Pay: Work in BPO Is First Job or Not

	Mean, PhP	US $	Minimum, PhP	Maximum, PhP	N	% of total N
Work in BPO is first job	16,602	395	9750	37,500	118	41.4
Not first job	17,175	409	9750	47,500	167	58.6
All	16,938	403	9750	47,500	285	100.0

Table 4.9 Simple Regression Analysis of BPO Employees' Pay

	Unstandardized coefficients		Standardized coefficients (beta)	t	Sig.
	B	Std. error			
(Constant)	15,655.34	1011.57	—	15.476	.000
Months current job	30.55	7.17	.257	4.264	.000
College = 1	1110.93	888.08	.076	1.251	.212
With job exp = 1	48.03	638.55	.005	.075	.940
Female = 1	−1924.12	612.55	−.188	−3.141	.002
Married = 1	705.24	714.95	.062	.986	.325

Wage function: basic monthly pay $= f$ (months on the job, college $= 1$, with job experience $= 1$, female $= 1$, married $= 1$, otherwise $= 0$). R-squared $= 12.3$, $F = 6.967$ significant (sig.) at alpha $= 0.00$.

job holders, but only slightly – a mere 3 percent differential. The age profile of respondents shows that there is a 3-year difference between new job holders and those with work experience. Wage regression analysis (Table 4.9) confirms that internal work experience within the same BPO company has a significant wage premium. Work experience in other firms is not significant in explaining pay variations. In other words, past work experience brings no wage premium. Therefore, there must be other significant reasons why some BPO employees move from one job to another – such as career advancement or stress – rather than just seeking higher pay in other BPO firms.

4.11.5 Wage Regression Results

Wage regression analysis indicates the variables that are significant in explaining variations in pay. In the survey's sample of respondents, the regression results show that pay variations among BPO employees can best be explained by *months on the job* and by *being male or female*. Staying longer on the BPO job will significantly increase employees' pay. If there is no discrimination in pay among male and female employees, the regression coefficient should be insignificant. The results, however, show that being female is penalized by lower pay, as indicated by a significant negative coefficient.

The following variables are not significant in explaining pay variations: college education, previous work experience and marital status. Altogether, wage regression analysis explains only 12 percent of the variations in pay among BPO employees (see Table 4.9).

Why are BPO jobs so attractive, yet with a high turnover? BPO agents acknowledge that, aside from basic pay, other benefits and perks give an added boost to the positive image of the job. One agent in ICT Philippines said that he enjoyed a monthly PhP 2500 (US $60) food and transportation allowance and a performance appraisal bonus amounting to PhP 4000 (US $95). Employees are also offered nonmonetary incentives such as appliances, cellular phone loads and gift checks in return for higher performance. There are creative schemes to boost the sales-per-hour performance of employees. For example, whoever is the first agent to achieve five sales per hour for the night wins a prize. An agent who hits the target quota sales gets an additional PhP 11,500 commission plus a 30–50 percent night differential. Call centre agents who achieve higher performance levels have a gross monthly income that can be twice the basic pay.

In addition to the benefits mandated by Philippine labour law, the most common incentives indicated by BPO employees are meal (64 percent) and transportation allowances (62 percent). 'Pay for performance incentives'

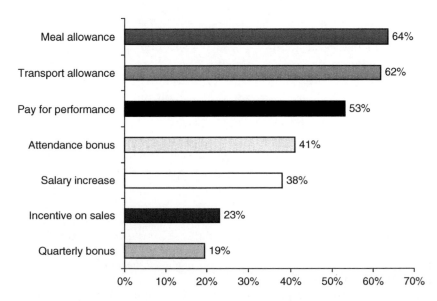

Chart 4.1   Most Common Incentives Given to BPO Employees

are also common (53 percent) (Chart 4.1). A few respondents said that they also receive the following benefits: 'clothing, voice and technical allowances'; 'rice allowances'; 'medical allowances'; 'car loans'; 'language allowances'; 'retention allowances'; 'employee stock options' and 'referral incentives.'

HR managers said that 'it is very difficult to design productivity incentive schemes given restrictions on access to dollar revenues of US or foreign-based BPOs.' In confidence, one BPO manager explained that, given the strategies of transfer pricing within units of the same multinational BPO organization, profit sharing and similar productivity incentive schemes are very difficult to explain to employees.

4.11.6   Working Hours and Shift Work

A key requirement of most BPO jobs in the Philippines is the 'willingness to rotate shifts and work during holidays, including Christmas, New Year's, Lent, weekdays, weekends, evening and morning shifts. To some respondents, it is their impression that during the job interview, recruitment staff only wish to hear them say "Yes, I agree to shift work."' According to one 25-year-old female BPO employee:

> Most call centre agents are women. They leave for work late at night, and they could be vulnerable to attack or harassment. The call centre I work with is far away from public transport. Most call centres have sleeping quarters. There is also a shuttle bus to ferry employees from [the] office to drop-off points in the transport route. Working hours and shift are announced often at the last minute.[21]

The average weekly working hours for BPO employees in the Philippines are 44.7 hours per week. However, average weekly hours for workers on the night ('graveyard') shift are lower, averaging 38 hours per week.

Although the percentage of males working the night shift is greater than females, there is no significant difference in the distribution of males or females by shift type (chi square $= 4.68$, significant at $p = 0.46$). BPO firms operate mostly in the evening and night-time hours, to correspond to day-time hours in the countries where most of their customers are located. While there are some exceptions, variations in work hours are not prevalent. In addition, changes in work schedules are still mainly determined by the company, not by the employee, and thus do not qualify as 'flexitime.'

The work schedule of most BPO employees changes moderately (36.4 percent). However, married employees (27.3 percent) who said their work schedules change frequently are significantly greater in proportion compared to single employees (15 percent) (see Chart 4.2).

A visit to a call centre during the night shift provides an idea of the stress that these employees experience in their jobs. In the company's canteen

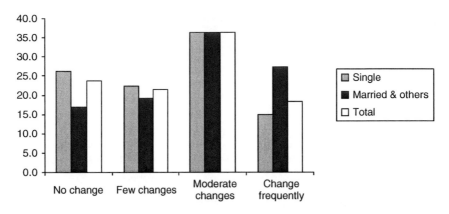

Chart 4.2   How Often Does Your Work Schedule Change? (percentage)

and rest areas, agents have access to a steady supply of coffee and cigarettes. Restaurants, spas, videoke (karaoke with videos) bars, coffee shops, billiard halls and gyms have proliferated, with a booming business in the vicinity of BPO areas, particularly in those 'hubs' where they are concentrated: Makati, Ortigas, Gateway and Libis in Quezon City and near the malls in Pasay City, Manila. Coffee shops and restaurants have specified outdoor smoking sections, where young agents can be seen chain smoking or drinking large mugs of coffee, one after another. Call centre agents say that they need the coffee to stay awake during the 'graveyard' shift and then drink alcohol to drown out the shift's negative events, such as irate calls from customers. Customer service representatives must respond to about 70–80 calls in one shift. They need to be in both a strong mental and emotional state, in order to deal with the potential for curses, insults and rambling, unintelligible conversation from some difficult customers, who may be of diverse ages, races and nationalities.

How do BPO employees deal with work during the 'graveyard' shift, which can begin at 12:00 midnight and continue to 8:00 am? BPO HR managers often tell the night shift employees to 'think it is [a] routine normal day.'[22] A clipping about the night shift is prominently displayed on the bulletin board of one BPO:

How to deal with night shift work? Establish a new pattern for working hours, sleeping hours, and 'everything else' hours. At the end of the night shift, an employee goes home, makes breakfast, and sleeps while everyone else wakes up. For many night agents, it takes time to 'flip' one's internal clock. When they switch back to a 'normal' schedule, their body bioclocks need a few weeks to adjust back to daytime hours.

Another technique for working a late shift is to keep busy, by giving call centre agents extra work or training to fill off-peak hours, when it gets quiet.

4.11.7 Work Intensity, Autonomy and Performance

In call/contact centres, agents are commonly called 'customer care specialists.' On behalf of a client, they receive, forward or refer customer calls or emails on issues ranging from complaints to simple queries; they also promote products or services. The size of a call/contact centre is referred to in terms of 'seats,' instead of 'agents,' since phone operators commonly work in three shifts to adjust to different time zones from which calls originate.

Calls handled by agents are either inbound or outbound. Telemarketing, advisories, sales verification, credit and collection, reaction or reinstatement of accounts, loyalty program benefits, customer services and order entry are covered by outbound calls. On the other hand, inbound calls include inquiries, requests for technical advice or assistance, transcription, complaints, customer service, support, sales, marketing and billing. Agents must know by heart the necessary information, do multiple tasks, make critical decisions, manage data with a minimum of errors and process work quickly while being monitored by their managers.

The most common work activities performed by respondents in this survey are customer service (55 percent) and technical support (29 percent). Inbound sales are handled by only 11 percent of all respondents, and very few employees make outbound sales calls (3 percent) (see Chart 4.3).

There is particularly high pressure for BPO agents engaged in direct sales. They must be 'persuasive and willing to sell,' and must be 'goal oriented.' In addition, they must possess superior listening skills and an ability to deliver information 'at [the] customer's knowledge level in an understandable manner.' For this purpose, the employee must also have basic computer and keyboard skills. 'Excellent communication skills' include a confident and courteous tone of voice and the ability to handle irate customer situations effectively and empathize with the customer.

The most common measures of performance outcomes identified by the respondents are performance appraisals (45.3 percent) and the monitoring of the target times to finish serving the calls of clients or customers (44.7 percent) (see Chart 4.4).

Customer service representatives dealing with inbound business must accommodate an average of 78 calls per day; it is common for an agent to deal with more than 100 calls. It is also common to set a goal to respond to at least 91 percent of these calls within 22 seconds. About 90 percent of these calls are dealt with, but about 6 percent of calls must be abandoned. In addition, employees must deal with work-related emails, by either answering or simply reading them (Table 4.10).

In the case of medical transcription, there should be 100 percent turnaround time (TAT) within 24 hours. There are about 300 files per day that must be processed. A medical transcription call can take from 1 minute to 1 hour.[23]

How do BPO employees perceive the degree of freedom to do their work? Autonomy in doing one's work includes discretion to schedule the tasks

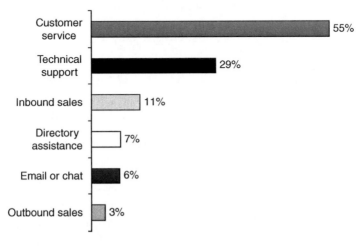

Chart 4.3   Philippine BPO Services

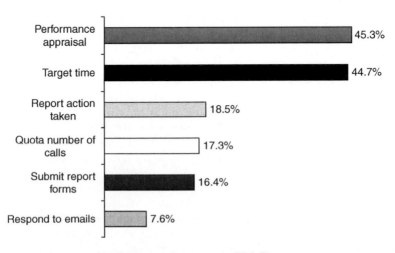

Chart 4.4   Measures of Performance Outcomes in BPO Firms

Table 4.10   Operational Performance in Sample BPO Firms

Company	Percent target calls to answer	Target time to answer (sec)	Percent target calls answered	Average duration of calls (sec)	Average calls per employee per day	Percent calls abandoned	Work-related emails
TTT	90	10	95	285	100	5	0
UUU	85	30	90	120	150	10	50
CCC	100	–	75	–	–	–	50
VVV	80	20	85	300	40	3	5
GGG	100	30	93	540	20	–	–
KKK	–	–	100	100	–	–	–
Average	91	22.5	90	269	78	6	35

needed to produce results and how it is to be done, within a specified time frame. In effective job design, greater autonomy gives employees more responsibility to deliver results, and therefore increases work motivation. Too little or too much autonomy can lead to employee dissatisfaction, and the variations are significant by age. On the one hand, younger BPO employees say that they prefer more direction from their managers. On the other hand, older employees feel that they are often too tightly controlled. Others said that to have more freedom in doing their work, they need more training about how to handle their tasks, learn more about their software and control their equipment.

BPO firms are in the forefront of technical innovation, but they are also under tremendous pressures from global competition. BPO firms in the Philippines tend to be flat organizations, with autonomy at lower levels and with functional work teams. How autonomous are Philippine BPO employees, in having freedom of judgement to decide and act on their tasks? On a scale of least autonomous (1 = not at all) to most autonomous (5 = a great deal), Philippine BPO employees score slightly below moderate, with an average overall score of 2.99 for all the dimensions measured. The level of employee autonomy is relatively high in the following areas: determining one's pace or speed of work, setting daily tasks and dealing with customers. Employee autonomy is least in setting work breaks, changing work methods and the use of new technology.

4.11.8 Stress, Health and Safety

BPO employees are under pressure to meet specific call quotas per day. Customer service associates must meet the average handling time (AHT) per call which is 5–6 minutes. Technical support providers are given 12–15 minutes per call. They cannot say 'no' and 'wait' or 'stop' if they are tired. Stress comes from the pressure from these call quotas, the number of products or services that must be sold and the required time, which is monitored, to process and respond to the calls. Stress also comes from call monitoring. Physical symptoms of stress include: muscular tension, muscle spasms and tics, rapid heart beats, shortness of breath, high blood pressure, cold hands and feet, backaches, headaches, neck ache, stomach problems, indigestion, irritable bowel and ulcers, fatigue, irritability, lack of concentration, insomnia and bulimia and other eating disorders (Occupational Safety and Health Center, 2005).

BPO HR managers admit that 'agents have little discretion over their tasks, which are determined by the company, through managers and team leaders. There are sanctions, including nonrenewal of the employment contract, if there is failure to comply with the standards set by the Quality Assurance and Training Department.'[24]

At the top of the list of health concerns of BPO employees are eye strain (69.6 percent); physical strain in terms of neck, shoulder and back pains (66.6 percent); and voice problems (56.2 percent). Stress is also a major concern (49.2 percent). To help agents cope with stress, HR managers in this survey said that they provide quiet rooms, Internet cafés, cable TV and game rooms. There are rewards and recognition programmes. Agents are rewarded with high-tech gadgets such as computers and iPods, which are raffled off during a meeting, training or game. Promotional giveaways include company jackets, pens and trinkets. In one BPO company, high-performing agents are rewarded with symbolic 'company dollars' which are accumulated and used as a basis for promotion, recognition and other awards. Through a Health and Safety Committee, one HR manager organized basketball teams and tournaments with employees at different sites.

The survey instrument asked BPO employees what specific items caused them stress at the workplace. The top causes of stress for Philippine BPO employees, among items in the work environment, are related to interpersonal relations. The top causes are harassment from angry clients (46.2 percent), lack of recreation facilities (42.6 percent) and lack of bonding (36.5 percent). There are also complaints about poor work stations (33.4 percent) and lack of a health clinic (30.1 percent) (see Chart 4.5).

On the other hand, the top psychosocial symptoms of stress among Philippine BPO employees are insomnia (47.7 percent), overeating or loss of appetite (37.4 percent) and boredom (36.2 percent) (see Chart 4.6).

Philippine BPO employees suffer from the following health problems: headaches (61.7 percent), fatigue (53.8 percent) and eye strain (50.5 percent). There were many who complained of chest and back pain (47.1 percent) and voice problems (33.7 percent). A number of workers also mentioned hearing problems (15.2 percent), ulcers (14.6 percent), hypertension (14 percent) and urinary tract infections (UTI) (10.3 percent) (see Chart 4.7).

Many BPO employees also cited eyesight problems, due to exposure to longer use of visual display units (VDUs). IT service programmers are likely

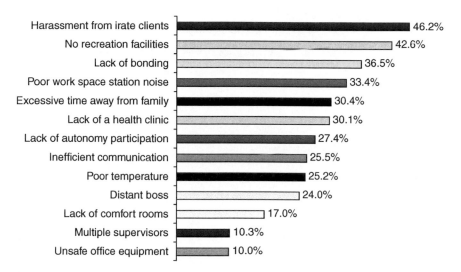

Chart 4.5   Causes of Stress: Working Conditions

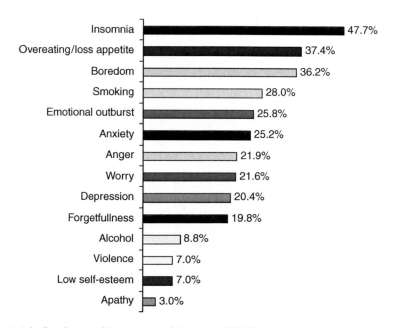

Chart 4.6   Psychosocial Symptoms of Stress in BPO Firms

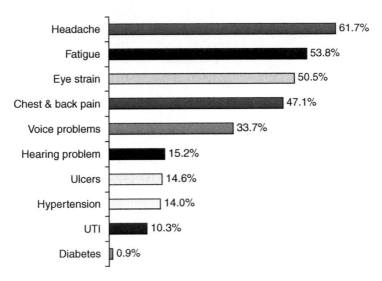

Chart 4.7   Health Problems of BPO Employees

to use VDUs much longer than the others and thus they have higher eyesight risks. However, unlike contact centre employees, IT technical representatives and engineers can take a break at will. Call/contact centre agents don't have much freedom of choice regarding the timing of their breaks. Staring longer at a video or computer monitor tends to drop blink rates and delubricates the eyes, which can cause severe symptoms over a longer period.

Long hours of sitting, with a tendency to slouch in front of computer and video monitors causes backache and muscle and neck problems. There is also a high incidence of digestive disorders, either through overeating or loss of appetite. Many BPO employees said that stress from work is the main reason, although others speculated that this situation may be due to the mass catering of food. Employees troop to company canteens by the hundreds, even thousands. BPO employees also wrote complaints about unsanitary practices by food processing and handling workers, as well as caterers in their canteens and cafeterias. They felt powerless, since the company was unable to act on their feedback – the food caterers were also outsourced contractors, catering to other companies in the same building. Some employees said that as night shift workers, they have specific nutrition and diet requirements.

Finally, as can be seen in Chart 4.7, there is also a high incidence of voice and hearing problems. BPO employees, especially those working in call/contact centres and in medical transcription activities, must wear headsets for a longer period than other employees – 8 hours or more per working day, for 5–6 days a week. The BPO job is half-listening and half-talking. Voice problems arise due to incessant talking and the continuous use of the vocal chords and other face muscles. There is no standard practice or policy on how to maintain the health and vitality of these muscles or the voice. There are no standards on room temperature, the provision of cold or hot water, the use of ice cubes and consumption levels of tea, coffee, soft drinks, other beverages or alcohol. Research on better head and voice sets needs to be accelerated, in order to provide better equipment to protect the voice and the ears of BPO employees.

Box 4.1 Stress, Gender, Disobedience and Punishment

A recent case decided by the Philippine Supreme Court highlights the gaps that need to be addressed in promoting better working conditions and employment relations in offshored work. The dispute concerns the dismissal of a female training manager for telemarketing, as punishment for disobedience to an emailed opinion of a male senior vice-president (SVP). The dispute also highlights ethics in company policies in impersonal cyberspace. The facts cited in the decision – a public document with details such as names, job titles, companies and locations – narrate the stress and pressure from sales quotas put on telemarketing agents. There is also a gender dimension to the dispute, since the subordinate manager is female, while the senior manager is male – a usual pattern in Philippine BPO's organizational structure.

The employee was hired on April 18, 2001, as a senior training manager at a call centre, with a monthly salary of PhP 38,000 (US $905). In March 2002, she was assigned to prepare a new training process for the company's telesales trainees. After review, the company's SVP for business development found that there were no changes that they had discussed earlier, and thus the training was not ready. The vice-president sent instructions through e-mail to postpone the presentation and the implementation of the new training process. The employee emailed back to say that training on the new process would go on as planned, since the module on 'how to get leads both local and abroad' would be covered in the presentation. It would be a 'simple presentation,' she noted, and there was no need to make 'simple things complicated.'

In response, the SVP sent the employee a memo stating that he found her message to be a clear act of insubordination and that he had lost his trust and confidence in her as training manager. He requested an explanation as to why she should not be terminated. Meanwhile, no presentation of the training module was made. The

Box 4.1 (Continued)

company subsequently terminated the employee, without waiting for her explanation. The employee went to the labour court, who declared the employment termination as valid. The case went several layers up, with twists, from the National Labour Relations Commission (NLRC), to the Court of Appeals (CA) and finally to the Philippine Supreme Court. The Supreme Court agreed with the labour arbiter and the NLRC that the employment dismissal was lawful.

The dispute started in 2002 and finally resolved in the highest court in 2007 – after 5 years of litigation. This slow and expensive process, which drains energy and emotion, is enough to discourage any employee from bringing a dispute to court. Toxic gaps between law and practice in cyberspace emerge from the analysis of this case, to promote better working conditions such as the provision for basic grievance procedures in BPOs. Companies whose managers have good training in HR usually have clear company policies on discipline, with a matrix of offences and corresponding graduated penalties. Disobedience as a first offence is usually penalized with suspension, not outright dismissal from employment. This is a significant gap in the decision of the highest court – a possible mistake for future reversal. Employers could ensure better results if they are trained in the tools of decent work, corporate social responsibility and social accountability, in order to prevent workplace disputes such as this case from becoming full-blown, costly court battles.

Source: Condensed from the Philippine Supreme Court decision on *ePacific Global Contact Center* vs. *Maria Lourdes Cabansay*, GR Number 167345, November 23, 2007.
Note: Comments by the researcher.

4.11.9 Attrition and Job Satisfaction

In spite of being well-publicized as a 'sunshine industry,' back-office firms and call/contact centres often encounter issues such as a lack of competent middle and upper management personnel, a low hiring rate due to high standards of communications skills and a high attrition rate of call centre agents.

Among the respondents in this study, first-time BPO job holders are greater in percentage (61 percent) than those with experience in other BPO firms (39 percent). Among those with previous BPO work experience, the top reasons for leaving their previous BPO company are the following: noncompetitive compensation (meaning, low pay) (22.2 percent) lack of professional growth (21.6 percent) and high stress (17 percent). The least cited reasons are extensive monitoring, unpleasant physical working conditions and unpleasant interpersonal relations within the organization (see Chart 4.8).

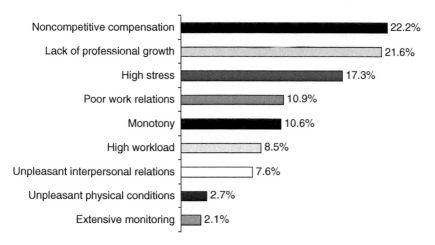

Chart 4.8   Reasons for Leaving Previous BPO

Employee turnover or attrition rates vary. The employee turnover (attrition or separation) rate is the ratio of the number of employees who leave the organization, compared to the number of total employees within the same period. A BPAP survey of 72 employers indicates that turnover appears manageable for most firms. BPAP reported that '30 percent of respondents indicated moderate turnover between 5 percent and 10 percent,' while 'another 46 percent experience turnover between 11 percent and 25 percent.'[25] However, the responses from four BPO managers in the sample BPO firms in this study indicate that the attrition rate in these companies was on the high side, ranging between 20 and 30 percent per year.

Comparing the BPO employee turnover rate to other industry sectors, the average turnover rate for all sectors was 7.8 percent in the second quarter of 2007. High attrition rates were in construction (17.4 percent), trade (14.7 percent) and in education (12.2 percent). Low separation rates of 1.6 percent were reported in large utilities (electricity, gas and water).[26]

BPO industry leaders are confident that the high rate of attrition will taper off, as the BPO labour market takes a foothold in the economy. They believe that when employees start to realize that there is a career in the industry, and also as they gain more work experience, the turnover rate will also somehow reach a plateau. The high turnover rate in the industry leads to an increase in the service fees of sourcing agencies, headhunting firms and recruitment companies. More than simply documenting the rate of attrition, it is important for companies to determine the level of what they would consider to be a healthy rate of turnover. BPO firms should likewise inquire into the reasons why employees leave their companies and identify the existing turnover patterns as a basis for designing effective interventions. To deal with attrition, it was proposed that the BPO industry adopt a Code of Ethics to prevent rampant poaching or a 'war of talents' among companies. Some call/contact centres already have an informal agreement against poaching from one another, which are known as 'noncompete clauses.'[27]

4.11.10   Employee Voice and Industrial Relations

What are the main sources of worry for BPO employees? (See Chart 4.9.) Career worries, through poor chances of promotion (36.5 percent) dominate the list. In addition, BPO employees are worried about working with different people (34.7 percent). Many also feel they do not receive adequate training (24 percent). It should be noted that 'career growth,' which can be provided through training, is a top reason why employees continue working in their current BPO firms. Sources of worry can also be addressed through counselling at the workplace, which provides areas for possible action by managers, in order to respond to these concerns and thus reduce employee turnover.

One important negative finding of the research is that most BPO employees (55.9 percent) did not experience participation or involvement in any committee, forum or venue to express their concerns or problems. This situation is very anomalous: despite their high level of communications technology, most BPO firms are short on the concept of employee involvement. For those companies that do promote employee involvement, the most common avenues are sports (16.7 percent), productivity (13.1 percent) or quality teams (10.9 percent).

The Philippine Constitution and labor laws guarantee the rights of employees to form or join unions and engage in collective bargaining and

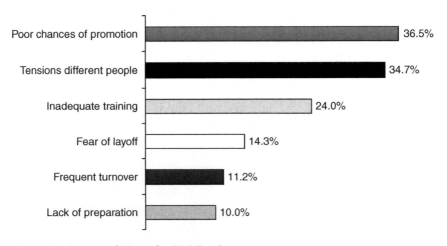

Chart 4.9   Sources of Worry for BPO Employees

negotiations to improve working conditions, working hours and pay and to settle grievances at the workplace. A wide variety of policies, procedures and laws provide for the exercise of these rights, to promote decent work conditions and good industrial relations in BPO firms. Yet, even after 15 years of BPO industry growth, there is still no union and, as a consequence, there is no collective bargaining agreement in call centres and other BPO firms in the Philippines.

A dominant mindset among many HR managers is to adopt a 'proactive attitude.' In response to the question, 'Do you think that the exercise of workers' rights could help increase employee motivation, commitment and productivity in BPO firms and call centres?' one BPO manager said: 'Not necessarily. BPO firms/call centres are very competitive, and most offer very good compensation and benefits. They also provide the best work environment.' A prevailing outlook among BPO managers is to prefer not to have a union in the company:[28]

> The company has already given so much. Having a union would just divide the employee and employers.

Another manager argued:

> If the company follows the 'modern' organization and culture, there is no need for a union. A union in an 'IT' organization does not fit. A 'union' is an antiquated organizational structure for political purpose with a self-serving structure.

Yet, upon being made aware of the country's fundamental framework of industrial relations which guarantees the right to freedom of association and collective bargaining, a manager said that she would welcome a union if 'if there is really a need, and if it will make employees feel that they are well-represented.'

A common attitude among managers is 'to fit labour laws with the realities of the BPO industry.' Indeed, many labour laws were enacted when the BPO sector was not yet prominent. 'Our company policies are often aligned with irrelevant labour laws and policies, but there is no guarantee that there will be discipline, proper work attitudes, and high productivity. Companies need to streamline policies, and provide fair implementation.' A flaw in this argument is clear: the framework of industrial relations should not be bent in favour of just the BPO sector alone. Labour laws can only provide a regulatory framework and not the 'magic formula' for effective HRM to reduce employee turnover or to improve work motivation and employee performance.

BPO employees feel that even if they are part of a team:[29]

...decisions are made in the United States. The local call centre managers are just emissaries to implement the decisions. We feel we don't have a part in making major decisions on pay adjustments, performance appraisal, and performance incentives.

One reason may be a lack of awareness, knowledge of labour laws and leadership skills for union organizers. The courage and commitment to organize a union can only come from being sure of one's bedrock principles, as guaranteed by the fundamental legal framework:

I have not heard of a union being organized among call centres. Management is always anti-union, and discourage the formation of unions. Another factor perhaps is that this type of job is new. There tends to be high turnover of workers, and the lack of long-term career growth. Employees have not thought of organizing unions to protect their rights and improve their working conditions.[30]

Half of the employees in the survey (49.2 percent) agreed, and an additional 4 percent said 'maybe' on the need to have a union. In contrast, only 17 percent of the respondents opposed the idea of a union. A significant number (30 percent), however, has no comment on or response to this question.

Many BPO employees expressed a desire to exercise their rights. A TSE said:

I think it is a good suggestion for employees in BPO firms to form and join labour unions, to voice grievances. The union and the management can [together] create a more productive work environment, [and] motivate employees to do their job better.

4.12   Conclusions

The Philippine BPO industry is relatively young and started only in the 1990s. The growth of the sector is a creation of globalization and new, advanced information and communications technologies (ICTs). On the demand side, there are competitive pressures among BPO source companies in English-speaking countries such as the US, Canada, Australia and the UK. These source companies need to reduce costs, including labour costs. On the supply side, the Philippines has labour and other costs that are much lower than in the source countries, plus a huge educated 'army' of 2.8 million unemployed, 4.1 million 'visibly underemployed,' with new university graduates close to 300,000 every year. The new ICTs link the two sides together.

Call centres currently dominate the BPO industry in the Philippines, with about two-thirds of the total BPO employment in the country. However, other BPO segments, such as back-office work, medical transcription, software development and animation are gaining ground and are predicted to dominate BPO employment by 2010. The BPO's contribution to the Philippine economy increased from an insignificant revenue share in its early years to US $6.1 billion in 2008, which is approximately 2 percent of the Philippine GDP. Employment in the BPO sector has grown significantly, from several hundred employees in the 1990s to an estimated 500,000 employees in 2009. Employment growth, however, peaked in 2003 and the growth rate was slowing until the onset of the global economic crisis, but appears to be increasing once again.

This study highlights the work organization, working conditions and employment practices in Philippine BPOs. BPO employees are 26 years old, on average and predominantly female. The estimated average monthly basic pay of a typical BPO employee is PhP 16,928 ($402), which is 53 percent higher than the prevailing minimum wage paid to young Filipinos of the same age who are employed in other industries. Typical college graduates earn an entry pay about 25–30 percent higher than the minimum wage. Thus, BPOs tend to attract more fresh college graduates as applicants. However, there is a significant differential in basic wages between male and female employees in BPO firms, with men having a 13 percent pay advantage over women.

Working hours in the BPO industry are relatively moderate, with an average of 44.7 hours per week. Yet, over half of all BPO employees work the night shift and have work schedules that change on a moderate or frequent basis. BPO employees also typically have short fixed-term contracts.

Nearly half of Philippine BPO employees suffer from stress. The top causes are harassment from angry clients, lack of recreation facilities and lack of bonding among employees and supervisors. Philippine BPO employees also experience the following health problems: headaches, fatigue, eye strain, neck and back pains and voice problems. Managers confirmed the high rate of employee turnover in BPO firms, at 20–30 percent per year. Most of the reasons for leaving a company cited by employees indicate stress, as well as some concerns about working conditions. Other top reasons for leaving are 'uncompetitive compensation' compared to other BPOs who constantly attract new employees and 'lack of prospects for professional growth' (Chart 4.8).

Most BPO employees did not experience participation or involvement in any committee, forum or venue to express concerns about or problems with their jobs. This situation is anomalous: despite the high level of communications technology in the industry, most BPO firms are short on the concept of employee involvement. Half of all BPO employees also agreed that there is a need to have a union in the industry, and only 17 percent were opposed, although a substantial proportion of employees indicated that they had no opinion on this question. Nonetheless, there are many statements from the research to the effect that the exercise of these rights could improve employee performance, reduce stress, lower attrition and fully harness the capacity of Philippine BPO firms to provide better working conditions and promote decent work.

The question of the deficit in employee voice and representation stands as a crucial issue, given that employees would prefer to have a union. In contrast, the dominant employer attitude is to remain union-free. Managers' lack of knowledge and skills to negotiate workplace disputes fuels BPO employer hostility to labour laws which form the basis of Philippine industrial relations. Some BPO employers said that they need to increase awareness about the fundamental framework of industrial relations and collective bargaining as guaranteed by the Philippine Constitution and labour laws.

Other critical features of the workplace that determine successful performance of employees in Philippine BPOs include proper accessories such as ergonomic chairs, tables, keyboards and VDT screens to ensure the protection and maintenance of workers' health. There is an urgent need to develop expertise on the health and safety of BPO employees, which needs to be integrated into the development of industry practices and regulations and company policies, as well as management systems and procedures.

Notes

1. Press statement by the Office of the President, 'PGMA boosts training of call center agents with allocation of P350 million,' www.gov.ph, November 7, 2007. The World Bank country profile in 2006 indicates that the Philippines had a GDP of US $116.9 billion in that year.
2. Department of Labour and Employment (DOLE) Press Statement, 'Global OFW deployment to reach 1 million, remittances to approach $14b in 2007,' September 12, 2007.
3. *CITEM Newsletter*, 'Boom in wireless communications seen to boost the Philippine electronics industry,' March 2007.
4. Interview with Mr. Wenceslao San Jose, former HRD Manager of Teletech Philippines, October 22, 2007, at the University of the Philippines, School of Labour and Industrial Relations.
5. Statistics in this section are from the following: Philippine Statistics Office, www.census.gov.ph; Bureau of Labour and Employment Statistics, www.bles.dole.gov.ph; and the Philippine Overseas Employment Administration, www.poea.gov.ph. Accessed July 10, 2009.
6. *Philippine Daily Inquirer*, 'Outsource industry seen growing,' February 18, 2006; *Manila Bulletin*, 'Cyber services as key to economic empowerment,' October 15, 2007.' Also *Philippine Daily Inquirer*, 'Call centers dangle paychecks for a skilled few,' September 7, 2007.
7. *Philippine Daily Inquirer*, 'Teletech reaches 15,000 workers, to open two more sites,' December 8, 2007.

8. National Economic Development Authority (NEDA), *Philippine Medium-Term Development Plan 2004 to 2010.*
9. Philippine Economic Zone Authority, 'Incentives to foreign investors,' www.peza.gov.ph. Also see Board of Investments, Department of Trade and Industry, www.dti.gov.ph/contentment/9/60/65/206.jsp). Accessed December 12, 2007.
10. Freedom of Association and Protection of the Right to Organise Convention, 1948 (No. 87); Right to Organise and Collective Bargaining Convention, 1949 (No. 98).
11. Article XIII, Section 3, paragraph 2, 1987 Philippine Constitution.
12. Philippine Labour Code, 1974, as amended.
13. Article 106, on contracting and subcontracting, Philippine Labour Code.
14. Article XIII, Section 4 of the 1987 Philippine Constitution.
15. Night Work (Women) Convention (Revised), 1949 (No. 29). Accessed November 12, 2007. See http://www.ilo.org/ilolex/cgi-lex/convde.pl?C089.
16. Please refer to Section 4.11.10 of this chapter dealing with 'Employee Voice and Industrial Relations,' where it is stated that almost half of BPO employees would prefer unions and to engage in collective bargaining to improve their terms of employment and working conditions.
17. Computed at the foreign exchange rate US $1 = PhP 42 as of November 30, 2007. The average monthly basic pay is computed by using the standard method for grouped data.
18. Effective August 28, 2007, the daily minimum wage in Metro Manila is PhP 362 ($8.62) multiplied by 365 days (including pay on 51 rest days, 11 holidays and 3 special days) and divided by 12 months.
19. Statement by a 26-year-old female BPO agent, during focused group discussion, November 17, 2007, University of the Philippines, School of Labour and Industrial Relations.
20. The simple regression result is basic pay = PhP 15,785.71 + 1331.76 (college graduate = 1); T values: (17.857) (1.410) R-squared = 0.01 F = 1.99.
21. Statement by a 25-year-old female BPO technical service eRepresentative (eREP), in a focused group discussion on November 10, 2007, University of the Philippines, School of Labour and Industrial Relations.
22. Statement by a 28-year-old female night shift manager in one of the biggest call centres, interviewed October 7, 2007.
23. Statement by Mr. Ryan Paguntalan, a medical transcription manager, interview on November 17, 2007, at the University of the Philippines, School of Labour and Industrial Relations.
24. Statement by a male BPO HR manager, November 17, 2007, during a focused group discussion at the University of Philippines, School of Labour and Industrial Relations.
25. Outsource2Philippines (O2P) in cooperation with the Business Processing Association of the Philippines (BPAP), 'Survey shows improved country image, political stability, English proficiency top-of-mind for BPO industry, investors,' press release dated November 13, 2007.
26. Bureau of Labour and Employment Statistics (BLES). 2007. *2nd Quarter Labour Turnover Survey.* Manila: BLES – Department of Labour and Employment.
27. Statement by a female BPO HR manager, in a roundtable discussion on Philippine call centres, organized by the University of the Philippines, School

of Labour and Industrial Relations, June 21, 2006, in Diliman, Quezon City. The summary is reported by Albert F. Haw, Jr., HR Manager, People-Support 'Managing Attrition Rate in the Call Center Industry.' Please see http://www.pmap.org.ph/article/articleview/194. Accessed November 7, 2007.
28. Responses from five managers of BPO firms and call centres in this survey.
29. Statement by a 25-year-old female BPO technical service eRepresentative (eREP), during a focused group discussion on November 10, 2007, at the University of the Philippines, School of Labour and Industrial Relations.
30. Statement by a 33-year-old female BPO team leader, during a focused group discussion on November 10, 2007, at the University of Philippines, School of Labour and Industrial Relations.

5
Remote Work in Brazil

Selma Venco

5.1 Introduction and Objectives

With constant pressure to find new ways to make their organizations more profitable, companies have examined all internal work functions in order to determine which can be carried out more efficiently by other organizations, including firms in other countries. As earlier chapters in this book have already highlighted, developing countries have seen their ability to deliver services in this industry rise at a much faster pace as information and communication technologies (ICTs) within these countries have become less expensive. In this context, Latin America has become a prime destination for organizations sourcing business functions via ICTs, and the result has been the development of a growing BPO industry in countries such as Argentina, Brazil and Chile. Of these countries, Brazil has undoubtedly been at the forefront of BPO expansion.

This chapter considers the development of the BPO industry in Brazil, its current status, and what this means for the Brazilian economy – in particular, its ability to attract so-called remote work. It will also examine the implications this has had for the development of the labour market throughout this industry, and what actions will be needed globally in order for the industry to continue its development. Most importantly, the chapter examines what conditions of employment exist in the Brazilian BPO industry, which is intended to help fill the existing research gap and contribute to policy discussions about how to improve employment conditions in the industry worldwide.

5.2 Research Methodology

This chapter is based on a country study conducted in Brazil for the International Labour Organization (ILO). The study itself was based on a qualitative investigation of the Brazilian BPO industry using semistructured interviews with senior-level managers from these companies, as well as labour union and service sector employer representatives. In addition, a range of secondary data was obtained from the Brazilian federal government. Two professional categories of remote worker have been specifically analysed: teleoperators in call centres serving both the financial services and telecommunications industries, and physicians working in the emerging field of telemedicine. It should be noted that the Brazilian country study was completed in early 2008 and, therefore, the reported findings do not reflect changes that have resulted from the global economic crisis that emerged in the autumn of that year and have continued in many parts of the world through the publication of this book.

Accomplished Interviews (January 2007–March 2008)

Company	Position	Area
A	Director of Operations Planning, Business Workforce and Capacity Management	BPO
B	Senior Account Manager, International Business	Call centre
B	Manager of Human Resources	Call centre
C	COO South America	Software factory
D	Director/CEO	Telemedicine
E	Communications Advisor Medical Manager (Imaging) Director (Diagnostics Centre)	Telemedicine
F	Director of Human Resources	Software factory

Unions	Position	Area
Telemarketing operators (SP)	President	Call centre
Telemarketing operators (SP)	Secretary of Communications	Call centre
Telecommunications workers (SP)	President	Call centre
Telecommunications workers (SP)	Secretary of Health	Call centre
Telecommunications workers (SP)	Secretary of Women's Affairs	Call centre

Organization	Position	Area
Services Federation from the State of São Paulo	President	Service companies
Brazilian Association of Software and Service Export Companies (BRASSCOM)	Executive Director	Software and services companies

Originally the aim of the study was to gather data through a survey of employers and workers in this 'industry' in Brazil. However, due to the fact that the industry is still in its emerging stages (comparatively), the competitive concerns of BPO companies remain considerable. In spite of this, it was determined that there were enough willing participants to employ a case study methodology to gather further information. Individuals, on conditions of anonymity, participated in interviews with the author. This method, in conjunction with the available literature in Portuguese, forms the foundation of this chapter. As literature on working and employment conditions in BPO industries is relatively scarce outside of Brazil, it is hoped that this chapter will help to fill the lacuna in the academic literature and provide a basis for future research.

5.3   The Business Environment for Outsourcing and Offshoring ITES Functions

5.3.1   The Global Environment for Outsourcing and Offshoring of ITES Functions

The concept of globalized companies is not new. As Chesnais (1996) saliently points out, Singer and OTIS could be regarded as examples of globalized companies, and they have been in operation since the nineteenth century. What is new about this form of globalization, according to both Ianni and Chesnais, is that the adaptations to develop the current form of globalization are based on technology, financial institutions that operate on a global scale, internationally divisible work and the use of an 'official' worldwide language (i.e., English) (Ianni, 1995; Chesnais, 1996). Organizations that can operate in this manner are then capable of using flexible geography in order to address their operational functions in a cost-effective manner, which includes relocating organizational functions to countries with the cheapest skilled labour required to handle those functions.

Globalization can help organizations to accelerate their growth around the world, but the reasons they may choose to outsource offshore can vary. According to research by Mouhoud, these reasons may include defensive reasons (i.e., when threatened by competition, organizations send part of their production activities abroad); induced or forced (suppliers follow where producers are located); margin (manufacturers and distributors reduce costs by working from offshore, but reduced production costs do not carry over to consumers); offensive reasons (to strengthen competitive advantage with domestic competitors by offshoring production); and rationalization (separating production and development based on the logic of innovation and learning) (Mouhoud, 2006, p. 24). Thus, organizations can have a number of different rationales to outsource and offshore processes or functions, all of which can result in them having a presence around the world.

With regard to service sector offshoring or outsourcing, traditionally organizations looking to relocate components of their work would look more to local, regional or national service providers to cut costs, but still try to keep functions readily accessible when needed. With rapid infrastructure development and the growth of skilled workforces in developing countries, traditional matrices of decision-making regarding where and how business functions were to be performed have changed. The international division of work through the use of information technology has given a 'new face' to the outsourcing phenomenon. While called different things in different languages (e.g., *offshoring* in English, *délocalisation* in French), the growth of offshore outsourcing of service functions from industrialized countries to developing countries has gathered pace over the last 20 years and looks set to continue in the future. In this context, Brazil has seen a lot of development in recent years as a significant destination for the BPO industry.

5.3.2   The Brazilian Economy and Business Environment

The annual economic growth rate for Brazil during the period 1995–2002 was only about 2.4 percent, but this situation changed in 2003. In the period between 2003 and 2007, the average growth rate rose to 3.8 percent, which represents total economic growth of approximately 60 percent during the period. This was the highest rate of growth since 2004, when the economy grew at a 5.7 percent rate, although this was stimulated by family consumption, which increased to 6.5 percent in 2007, marking the fourth consecutive year of growth (IBGE, 2008).[1]

These results can be viewed as quite positive, as the macroeconomic policies of the Brazilian government at the time were essentially the same as those of its predecessors. The aim of these policies has been to maintain the basic surplus and high interest rates.[2] The main reason successive governments had chosen such policies was based on the fact that until the mid-1990s the Brazilian economy was paralysed by numerous attempts to control inflation that had taken root in the economy during the 1980s. Successive governments sought to correct this problem by indexing the economy, which meant that any change in prices had repercussions on all productive activities. Thus, productive investments fell, but the financial system benefited from the currency being indexed. Inflation, which during its worst periods was over 1000 percent per year in the 1980s, was progressively reduced to much more reasonable levels in the 1990s. The Brazilian Institute of Geography and Statistics (IBGE) determined that the National Consumer Price Index fell from 21.9 percent to 5.2 percent in the period from 1995 to 2007 (IBGE, 2008). In the same period the national price index (INPC) fell from 21.9 percent to 5.2 percent, and the extended national consumer price index (IPCA) fell from 22.4 percent to 4.5 percent (IGBE, 2008).

As this monetary stabilization policy continued throughout the 1990s, it had profound repercussions for companies, institutions and others in the Brazilian economy. This type of economic growth and low inflation has not been seen in the Brazilian economy for a long time. The loosening of the basic interest rate in recent years has resulted in greater confidence in the economy demonstrated by expanded investments and growth in the capacity to supply goods and services. Owing to this, it is perhaps not surprising that the main goal of the government remains price stability. Monetary stabilization led to a noticeable change in Brazil's macroeconomic environment and advanced the process of business reorganization to take advantage of these macroeconomic circumstances (Proni, 2005, p. 98).

While the macroeconomic situation tells part of the recent story of the Brazilian economy, it does not tell it all. Structural, productive and financial variables also need to be considered. Expansion in commerce and foreign direct investment (FDI) is the result of financial and exchange rate liberalization. The influx of FDI to Brazil represents the potential for expansion of productive activities and the creation of new workplaces. For example, according to one of the managers interviewed for this study, Brazil has already reached a high degree of maturity (approximately 10 years of experience) in call and customer service centres and, therefore, is able to sell its services to foreign companies (Senior Account Manager, International Business, Company B, 2007). Brazil remains an important location for customer service centres. Large multinationals tend to concentrate their customer service centres in Brazil in order to secure profits of scale. This remains the case even though the some of the costs may actually be higher in Brazil when compared with some other countries in Latin America, as shown in Table 5.1 below.

Table 5.1 Simulation of Operational Costs per Year (in US $)

	Monterrey, Mexico	Tijuana, Mexico	Campinas, Brazil	San Jose, Costa Rica	City of Panama, Panama	Santiago, Chile
Average salary/hour	3.42	3.59	3.46	3.5	3.62	3.38
Annual payroll	3,255,840	3,417,680	3,293,920	3,446,240	3,332,000	3,217,760
Benefits	1,074,427	1,127,834	2,075,170	1,654,195	1,432,760	965,328
Total of annual work costs	4,330,267	4,545,514	5,369,090	5,100,435	4,764,760	4,183,088
Commercial rent	371,250	405,000	326,250	495,000	267,750	270,000
Equipment	1,320,000	1,320,000	1,320,000	1,320,000	1,320,000	1,320,000
Travel	20,915	21,736	31,056	23,284	24,218	32,933
Total	6,042,032	6,292,250	7,046,396	6,938,719	6,376,728	5,806,021

Source: Boyd Company, 2005.

5.4   The Labour Market in Brazil

The labour market in Brazil has been changing in recent years, owing in part to greater economic stability and changes in the main sources of employment, such as the growing BPO industry. There are several labour market indicators that will be examined in this section, which will help to provide further insights into how the indicated changes have influenced growth in service sector employment.

5.4.1   The Overall Employment Situation

Examining employment by sector in Brazil, the data indicate changes in recent years in a number of factors, including those affecting the information technology-enabled services–business processing outsourcing (ITES–BPO) industry. In the period 1996 to 2006, there was a decrease in agricultural employment from 28.6 percent to 21.7 percent (IBGE, 2008). In the same period, industrial employment was steadily growing from 16.3 percent to 16.5 percent (IBGE, 2008). However, service sector employment during this period grew from 26.9 percent to 31.3 percent (IBGE, 2008). According to Gonçalves, the new demands for productive processes, technological advances and policies created in response to the economic crisis in the 1990s led to the growth in the demand for services in the Brazilian labour market (Gonçalves, 2005, p. 195).

Examining the disaggregated data, there were some notable differences in employment rates for men and women. In the period 1996–2006, women's labour market participation rate grew from 48.1 percent to 52.6 percent (IGBE, 2008). Men's labour market participation rate during the same period declined slightly from 75.3 percent to 72.2 percent (IGBE, 2008). Yet despite this growth in labour market participation by women, the rate of men's participation is still far higher. A number of rationales have been identified that explain these circumstances, but perhaps the most important is the use of traditional gender roles in Brazilian society. Traditionally, men in Brazilian society were primarily viewed as the breadwinners and women as family caregivers. However, this appears to be changing a bit. The data related to the evolution of women's jobs in Brazil suggest that this old breakdown no longer reflects reality as the labour market participation rates of women have increased consistently over the last 30 years (Abramo, 2007).

When examined by sector the working patterns of men and women vary somewhat (see Charts 5.1 and 5.2 below). Men still dominate in the agricultural, industrial, construction and commercial sectors. Women's employment rates in these sectors are either low, or in the case of agriculture (22.4 percent in 1995 to 14.4 percent in 2006) continue to fall. At the same time, the sector where women have been dominant, and continue to dominate, is in the services sector, which in the period from 1995 to 2006 grew from 51.5 percent to 56.3 percent.

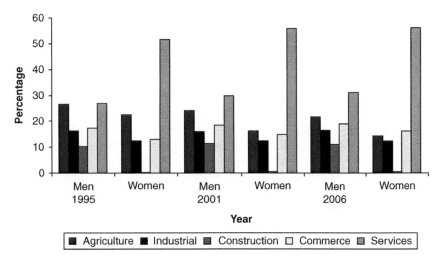

Chart 5.1 Distribution of Occupations by Gender, Segments of Activity or Primary Work (1995–2006)

Source: Ministry of Planning and Budget, Brazilian Institute of Geography and Statistics (IBGE), Department of Research, Coordination of Labour and Income, National Survey by Household Sampling. Years: 1995–2006.

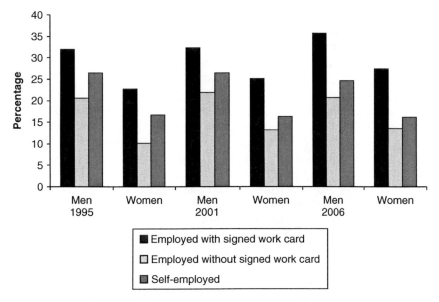

Chart 5.2 Distribution of Employment by Gender and Category of Employment (1995–2006) (percentage)

Source: IBGE, National Survey of Households 1995–2006.

5.4.2 Formal Employment

The Labour Code in Brazil (Consolidao des Leis do Trabalho of 1943 or CLT) stipulates that formal sector workers sign a standard work contract that is ratified by the Brazilian Ministry of Labour. A record of these contracts is then kept by the worker in a 'work card' (*carteira de trabalho*). The law further mandates that all workers have this 'work card' (which is normally in booklet form) in which individual contracts and changes are registered with the employer. Thus, a worker with a work card signed by the employer is considered a formal worker. If a worker works with a work card unsigned by their current employer they are generally considered to be informal (sem carteira assinada). The data gathered by labour and statistical authorities is used to contextualize formal and informal employment in Brazil (as demonstrated below).

The data in Chart 5.2 indicate the degree of formalization among employed workers. When the data are disaggregated by gender, men's employment remains stable, whereas there is a notable growth in women's employment. For men, in the period 1995–2006, there is little variation in formal, and what might be called informal, employment.[3] The data suggest an increase during the same period in the percentage of women in both formal employment (going from 22.7 percent to 27.5 percent) and informal employment (10.1 percent to 13.6 percent). The growth in formal employment may reflect the increase in surveillance by the Ministry of Labour of employers and businesses in an effort to curtail informal employment throughout the Brazilian economy.

5.4.3 Unemployment and the Issue of Informality in Employment

Brazil has historically endured high rates of unemployment. The series of economic crises that began in the 1980s eliminated thousands of workplaces, resulting in greater unemployment. In the 1990s, rather than experiencing job growth, more jobs were eliminated as organizations reorganized. While the job market in the post-1990s improved somewhat, unemployment rates still hover currently around 10 percent, with rates in some Brazilian state capitals, such as Salvador and Recife, reporting rates above 20 percent (IBGE, 2008). When the figures are disaggregated by gender, it is perhaps unsurprising that during the period 1995–2006, women in the Brazilian labour market generally suffered from unemployment more than men (IBGE, 2008).

Yet the figures themselves may actually under-represent the real unemployment situation in Brazil. The methodology used by the IBGE, as with most national statistical services, considers the unemployed to be those looking for but unable to find work. These statistics do not take into account those individuals in the so-called black economy, which is made up of persons who are either unable to find work and are not actively looking, or who are in precarious work arrangements. Informality is a hallmark of the Brazilian labour market and the main alternative for those who cannot find legal work.

5.5   The Labour Law in Brazil

Formal employment in Brazil is governed by the Brazilian Consolidated Labour Law (CLT) (Decree 5452, from May 1, 1943).[4] This legislation is the foundation for all contractual agreements in the workplace. It also addresses Social Security issues relating to work. While the legislation does establish many legal rights and protections, some aspects of working conditions between workers and employers are more open to negotiation. These include certain conditions negotiated within professional category groups, such as minimum wages and some benefits. The legislation also provides the basis for collective bargaining between employers and trade unions.

Although the Brazilian (CLT) is meant to address most employment relationships in the labour market, within the context of this chapter it is important to understand the collective dimension of this legislation. The organization of workers and professionals into trade unions generally takes place on political and institutional levels, while union organization in municipalities takes place on political and geographical levels. A major consequence of this arrangement is that companies takes a more active approach in defining and arranging professional categories and limiting the definition of the trade union to a working region or area in order to derive more benefits for the company. For example, a call centre company might try to get telemarketers to be registered as telephone operators because of that category's lower salary and benefits. The company might also try to find the best form of work regulation to achieve the flexibility it desires.

With regard to severance or termination of an employment contract in union settings, companies and unions must agree. Companies looking to sever or terminate employment contracts must submit those contracts to trade unions to review, but this is only in cases when employees have worked for the company for more than 1 year. If employees have worked for a company for less than 1 year, the company can terminate contracts unilaterally. Under the Brazilian Labour Law, severances, work claims and other issues that relate to employment conditions that cannot be agreed on by all the parties must be submitted for resolution by a specialized judicial body.

Cases that thus need to be decided by the judiciary create a cost that Brazilian companies term the *Custo Brasil* (Costs of Brazil).[5] Companies blame the *Custo Brasil* as one factor that compels them to outsource as many functions as they possibly can. For example, in the banking and financial systems, outsourcing is used in security services, registry of insufficient funds, money transport, insurance and sales, among other things. These banking and financial firms also use temporary agencies to circumvent both the Brazilian Labour Law and Social Security legislation, as workers for these cooperatives are not protected by this legislation.

In addition to cooperatives, there has also been a growing use of 'consultants' in many industries, particularly in the service sector. Consultants have no employment or labour rights, particularly with regard to the customer company, as they are considered to be independent contractors. Consultants have also been increasingly used to replace the disguised self-employed worker. Through this type of subcontract, the hiring company is not legally responsible for a long list of working and employment conditions; for example, Social Security contributions, year-end bonuses (i.e., 13th month salary), employee individual statutory pension accounts (a monthly value which, in the case of unfair dismissal, leads to a fine of 40 percent of the deposited value), an additional one-third salary when an employee goes on vacation, the right to a vacation, disability compensation, a public transportation voucher, a luncheon voucher, the basic food basket, participation in (company) profit schemes and education aid. For women who are consultants, maternity protection can be added to this list of unavailable protections.

As employment relationships in Brazil include all or some variation of these benefits, it is not uncommon for a number of lawsuits to be filed as parties seek to assert their rights. However, administrative follow-up to a court decision may be the greatest challenge for workers who succeed in their case against their employer. Labour Superior Court Minister Ronaldo Loyal Lopes admitted that this was the greatest challenge to the Labour Judiciary in 2003, when he noted:

> The execution of a labour claim in Brazil is a real 'Calvary'[6] for the worker. The claim can be decided fast but, when it comes time for the worker to receive his money, is when 'Calvary' begins: many companies disappear or change partners and, when the citizen looks for his employer, the employer does not exist anymore or is not there anymore.

Another government initiative promoted by the Ministry of Labour focuses on employees in call centres/telemarketing activities. It was discussed and enacted into law after tripartite consultations with employers and workers. The result was Attachment I of NR 17 Standard which stipulates the following:

- 'assures workers, with prior authorization, at least one weekly paid day off and a Sunday of each month given independent of goals, absence and/or productivity';
- '[T]he work organization will need to be arranged so there would be no activities on Sundays and holidays, either total or partial, except for companies previously authorized by the Ministry of Labour, as foreseen in the "caput" of Article 68 of the CLT and the activities foreseen by law' (idem);
- '[T]he working hours can only go beyond the terms of the law in exceptional cases, by *force majeure*, overriding need or to finish services that cannot be postponed or when the not fulfilling service can cause expressed damage, as written in the Article 61 of the CLT, and

communicating the responsible authority, as seen in §1st of the same Article, in the stated period of 10 (ten) days.'

Another portion of Attachment I of NR 17 Standard addresses daily rest and break periods:

- 'The rest and coffee break for call centre/telemarketing activity must be of 20 minutes';
- '[T]he breaks must be granted: (a) out of the workstation; (b) in 2 (two) periods of 10 (ten) continuous minutes; (c) after the first and before the last 60 (sixty) minutes of work in call centre/telemarketing activity';
- '[T]he institution of breaks does not harm the right for rest and feeding breaks foreseen in §1st of Article 71 of the CLT.'

The ability to take regular rest breaks during the course of a workshift has been an important development in these workplaces. In workplaces that abide by this portion of the law, it helps to avoid awkward situations such as a worker needing to formally request a break to use the toilet. The law emphasizes that, 'In order to meet their physiological needs, companies must allow the operators to leave its work place any time during the day, without repercussions on their evaluation and remuneration' (Attachment I of NR 17). This point is especially salient as some organizations have been known to increase pressure on employees to eliminate dead time between tasks, limit down time for workers, overlap tasks to maximize productivity or increase the speed required in executing the work (Durand, 2004, p. 267).

While the above regulation would appear to fully address the fundamental issues of working conditions, particularly working hours and paid days off, the wording of the text leaves a large amount to be interpreted between managers and workers.

5.6 The BPO Industry in Brazil

5.6.1 Background

The BPO industry in Brazil has demonstrated a significant rate of growth in the last 4–5 years. Most of the notable financial corporations in the country are national conglomerates, with banking institutions as their entry point. They have over time expanded their businesses to credit operations, retail financing, leasing of durable goods, credit cards and insurance. The banking system in Brazil is recognized worldwide as one of the most modern, well-structured industries of its kind, and it has been critically important to the country. It was one of the few industries to grow even during the economic crisis in the late 1990s to early 2000s.

There are a number of large companies that offer IT services in Brazil. According to the Ministry of Development, Industry and Foreign Commerce, out of the 15 largest IT companies in Brazil, the top five are American multinationals, but of the remainder six are Brazilian. Moreover, as the Ministry and BRASSCOM (the Brazilian IT industry association) point out, Brazil is a country where foreign organizations concentrate their Latin American operations. Three of the largest IT companies have located operations in Brazil and a number of multinationals have chosen to locate regional offices in the country.

The objective for the creation of the Brazilian Association of Information Technology and Communication Companies (or BRASSCOM) in 2004 was to stimulate and support Brazilian IT and ITES exports. BRASSCOM's strong links to Brazilian federal, state and municipal governments makes it possible to represent the industry when policies are made focusing on service exports. At the same time, it offers qualification programs and similar activities to affiliated professionals.

Companies in the financial services sector such as banks, credit card operators, financing and leasing companies and insurance companies have outsourced customer service functions using call centres, in both a receptive (i.e., taking calls for information) and an active capacity (i.e., seeking new customers). Banks have also made greater use of the Internet for customer services and partnered with credit card companies to solicit new customers by telephone. Retail networks are most active in leasing and financing, though in insurance there is little active prospecting for new customers through call centres.

5.6.2   Brazil: A Major Destination for Business Services

The status of the IT industry in Brazil as a major international destination for exports has only recently been recognized. According to a report by the consultants A.T. Kearney, in the comparatively short period between 2005 and 2007, Brazil went from tenth place to fifth place in the ranks of business attractiveness in this industry (A.T. Kearney, 2007a, p. 9). In 2004, Brazil was listed as the fourth highest destination for outsourcing among industrial organizations (A.T. Kearney, 2004, p. 9).

Another A.T. Kearney study indicates why Latin America was so attractive for offshoring and nearshoring operations by North American and some European companies (A.T. Kearney, 2007a). Among the qualities were: the work force's language skills, in English and Spanish; low costs; cultural affinity; and the wide availability of workers at an active age. In addition to being a desirable destination for these reasons, Brazil (and also Argentina) also benefited from territorial proximity and similar time zones with offshoring countries. Moreover, Brazil has developed a market for services, high standards of service quality, strong technical IT qualifications, as well as strong technical backgrounds in other disciplines that can be outsourced such as engineering, pharmaceutical and financial areas. In part based on these factors, Brazil has become a global centre for IT and shared services for companies such as IBM, HSBC, GM and Nestlé (A.T. Kearney, 2005). From 1999 to 2001, Brazilian software and IT services exports rose from US $60 million to US $120 million. In the 3 subsequent years (2002–2004), they increased 160 percent, to US $314 million.

According to the OECD estimates (based on data from the World Information Technology and Services Alliance, WITSA), Brazilian exports in services grew at 155 percent in the period 2004–2007 (OECD, 2007). A recent article suggested that Brazil is, among emerging economies, a country where large profits from IT services companies are generated (Information Forum, 2007).

5.6.3 Telecommunications in Brazil

Regulation of the telecommunications systems in Brazil has been marked by several pieces of legislation developed and implemented in the 1960s. Law 4117 (from August 27, 1962)[7] established the Brazilian Telecommunications Code, which governs the industry. During the military dictatorship that followed, TELEBRAS was legally created (Law 5972 from July 11, 1972)[8] in order to centralize Executive Control over all communication decisions. More recently, the General Telecommunications Law of 1997 established the right of access to telecommunications for the entire population at 'reasonable prices' (Federal Law No. 9742/97). Technological developments and free competition among companies were meant to help reduce costs, shorten the installation period and help people with lower incomes gain access to telephone services.[9]

In 2007, the federal government of Brazil began auctions of broadband frequencies that ended in the middle of 2008 in order to stimulate third-generation telecommunications. ANATEL, the Brazilian Agency of Telecommunications, divided the country into 11 areas and put up for sale 44 licenses, in order to have four telephone companies per area.[10] Eight companies entered the competition for the licenses: Vivo, TIM, Claro, Oi, Brasil Telecom, Nextel, Telemig Cellular and CTBC. The forecasts estimated that the collection from the federal government with these sales would reach R $6 billion, and that the companies would invest another R $6.5 billion through 2009. Out of this amount R $4 billion would be invested in infrastructure expansion and modernization and R $2.5 billion for the expansion of the service in order to reach 1836 cities that are not assisted by the mobile telephony, benefiting more than 17 million people. At present, 3728 cities are integrated into the existing mobile telephony infrastructure.

5.7 Working and Employment Conditions in the BPO Industry in Brazil

The remainder of this chapter will examine the working and employment conditions in different segments of the BPO industry in Brazil. Customer service centres were established in the 1960s, principally to receive customer complaints. While change was progressive, deep modifications took place in the 1990s as organizations looked to increase productivity and reduce costs through the greater use of technology. This technology used telecommunications combined with computer sciences, and thus allowed the types of work performed by these centres to grow in number and further the ability of work to be done from more distant locations (Venco, 2003, p. 38).

Within the call centres, other technology such as the axial tool helped to organize work by distributing calls to unoccupied operators for longer periods of time, measuring call lengths, producing productivity reports and recording complete calls. As a result of these developments, customer centres turned into multitasking facilities covering communication with customers, measuring customer satisfaction, addressing customer loyalty and soliciting new clients. This 'new economy' allowed organizations to address the 'customer culture' within their firms, while at the same time continuing to look for ways to cut costs through the use of technology or location, or some combination of the two (Caïazzo, 2000).

5.8 The Financial Services Industry in Brazil

The financial services industry is emblematic of the growth in the use of technology and concentration of services in more remote locations. Downsizing in the Brazilian financial system coincides with the growth in the use of customer service centres by banks. Consolidation of work has eliminated a significant portion of jobs in branches, especially back-office functions. Cost reductions in banking services in Brazil are in line with the trend in shifting work away from branches and the cost savings from doing so would be about 50 percent.[11]

It is not therefore a surprise to find that the financial services industry, notably banking services, are the main customers of call centre company services in Brazil (Venco, 2006).[12] The new dimension is the international scope that is now developing in these centres as large foreign banks strive to create customer service centres in Latin America to address customer needs in other parts of the world.

While there is some growth in Brazil in these service centres, there have been limitations to unfettered growth. To begin by looking back, it has been suggested that Brazil has historically been one of the most competitive and organized professional segments in banking (Bicalho, 1978; Segnini, 1988). Even during the economic turmoil of the 1980s and 1990s the banking industry had higher demand for workers – with around one million employees in 1986 – than other parts of the economy (Venco, 2003). However, the concentration of financial institutions such as banks, insurance companies, credit card operators and finance companies, among others, in São Paolo, has meant that worker representatives have played an important role in negotiating collective agreements. This to some extent has limited the creation of customer service centres for offshore support as employers have sought greater working hour flexibility and scheduling, an end to the minimum wage, and substitution of current contracts with ones based on the number of hours worked, which have been opposed by worker representatives.

The financial system is the main customer of the companies that use call centre services in Brazil. Many big foreign banks want to open call centres in Latin America to serve customers from around the world. However, negotiations between unions and entrepreneurs have not always been successful in the installation of call centres for offshore outsourcing, as the owners have demanded greater flexibility in work schedules and the end of a minimum wage.

5.9 The Telecommunications Industry

Oliveira (2004), among others, highlighted that in the telecommunications industry prior to privatization there was strong formal employment. Eighty percent of workers were registered as being formally employed; another 11 percent of workers were public servants, which accounts for approximately 89 percent of workers in telecommunications in regular registered employment. However, in the first year of privatization, downsizing reached about 12 percent of the workforce (Oliveira, 2004, p. 87). Table 5.2 shows the distribution of workers in the telecommunications industry.

Privatization in the telecommunications industry took place during the 'telecoms auction,' and while this benefited the winning companies, it also stimulated the establishment of third-party companies, or customer service centres. These companies and the customer service centres then proceeded to change the terms and conditions of employment for the workforce that before this point had enjoyed some measure of employment security. These changes for workers included diminished employment security, reductions

Table 5.2 Workers in Telecommunications (in thousands)

	2000	2006	3rd Q/2007
Industry	26.7	27.9	28.2
Implementation	46	52.2	50.6
Services	118.2	106.1	107.9
Call Centres Controlled by Telecom Companies	10.5	116	124.5
Total	201.4	303	311.2

Source: Ministry of Labour. Annual Social Information Report (RAIS) up to 2005 and General Report of Employed and Unemployed, 2006.

in wages and a reduced variety of job types as part of the transformation to an outsourcing service (Oliveira, 2004).

There appears to be a great deal of convergence between call centres and the privatized telecommunication services, in that they both appear to be using outsourcing to go beyond simple call services to become much larger service providers. For example, the biggest telephone assistance contractor companies are related to telephone/telecoms companies. Two companies are responsible for more than 15 percent of these contracts in Brazil.

One of the telecom companies noted in 2005 that they had service providers who could speak Spanish, English, French and Japanese (Venco, 2008). According to one employer, this type of multilingual service work is better for the operators, because their earnings are doubled compared with those who can only speak Portuguese (Venco, 2008). Thus, the ability for customer services to be performed in multiple languages is as important as the cost savings for companies in other countries.

5.10   Call Centres and Customer Service Centres in Brazil

5.10.1   Background: The Emergence of Call and Customer Service Centres in Brazil

The growth of call centres has increased greatly over the course of the past decade. Advances in technology and communication systems have allowed companies to innovate in terms of the services they provide, the locations from where their services are provided and in the ways they lower costs.

Call centres, much like other firms that underwent profound reorganization in the 1990s, are now beginning to experience their first changes. Yet the circumstances are somewhat antithetical: companies foresee greater growth and new deals at a time when more mergers are taking place between local–local and local–international firms. This is exemplified by Tivit, a subsidiary of the Votorantim Group, which has in recent years acquired other companies while at the same time discussing organic growth and growing its international presence. According to Pablo Enrique de Oliveira Santos (CEO and Chairman, Board of Directors), '[W]e (the company) will continue to organically grow in a sustainable manner and through selective acquisitions that come to consolidate and to complement our service portfolio.' (Telecomonline, 2007).

Call centres in Brazil are experiencing two distinct forms of change that are taking place at the same time. The experience of workers might best be captured by a worker from another era and workplace in Brazilian history: 'I knew I could complain or quit, because I could just cross the street and I would find another job.'[13] Over the last 7 years call centre service companies have engaged in significant hiring. Considering that this growth is rather new, it is difficult to make predictions regarding what types of jobs will be available in the future.

Despite the fact that mergers in financial services are similar to those in customer service centres, there are plenty of opportunities for development in domestic and foreign markets. On a positive note, it is unlikely that there will be a negative impact on the creation and development of customer call service centres. As noted earlier, most of the negative developments have already taken place in the earlier part of this decade (Venco, 2003, 2006). The growing use of more advanced technological systems, such as electronic menus, also will reduce the need for live intervention by call centre staff members. An example of improved services is that banks in Brazil nowadays are allowed to extend loans up to a certain value to customers without the need for a bank clerk (Venco, 2003).

Changes may be in store, however, for both workers and employers in this industry. An initiative proposed in a document by the Ministry of Labour in Brazil has suggested an incorporation of the 'telemarketing operator' profession in the Brazilian Classification of Professions (CBO). The ministerial action has consequences on a number of levels. It serves as legal instrument of definition for workers and employers and becomes a category for the organization of official statistics in the Annual Social Information Report (RAIS) produced by the Ministry of Labour each year.[14] However, a point of contention is that there is no observed relationship between the number of jobs declared by the associations, unions and companies and the statistics presented thus far. Background data from the Brazilian National Survey by Household Sampling (PNAD) suggest in 2002 there were 132,286 telemarketing operators and in 2004 the number had grown to 215,232.

One chief business officer described variations in call centre services as being done by workers with different roles. These include active workers (i.e., calling out to solicit work), receptive workers (i.e., customer service representatives), bilingual workers (whose specialization is their language skills) and hybrid operation workers (i.e., they do both passive and active work) (Venco, 2006).

The function of telemarketing operators is to establish contact, exclusively by telephone, with users and customers, seeking sales, problem-solving and offering technical support, real-time research or registration. To perform this work they must always follow 'guides or scripts that are planned and controlled to catch, retain or to recover customers' (CBO, 2000). In order to perform these functions the operators must have at least a high school education and basic courses of professional qualification of up to 200 lesson-hours.[15] Physiologically, the basic requirement for the work is good speech and hearing (Venco, 2006). According to this CBO, personality traits that are important are the ability to work under pressure, to be patient, to manage conflicts between the customer and company and to work as part of a team in the workplace (Venco, 2006).

5.10.2   Composition of the Call Centre Workforce

The composition of customer service operators varies between centres, notably those that focus on the Brazilian market and those that address international markets. Those working in centres with a national focus tend be 18–25 years old, with 45 percent of them in their first job (Oliveira et al., 2005). Most who are working in international facing customer service centres have international experience, good command of Portuguese, but may have been underemployed when working abroad and have returned to Brazil. As a manager in this industry has pointed out:

> They are young, but not as young as the average staff (member) working in call centres. We are talking about 22–23 year olds [...] who have come back to Brazil and are trying to get in the market. Even though they have lived abroad and mastered the language, they may not have finished university yet [...] and have difficulty (working in another language) [...] this happens for a majority who come to work here claiming to speak English. As for Spanish, most in City W have parents (who speak the language), whereas here and in City Y they tend to be people who study abroad. (Senior Account Manager, International Business, Company B, October 15, 2007)

The gender distribution of the workforce in the national operations is predominantly female (76.2 percent) according to Oliveira and in the outsourcing service companies the percentage is 80 percent (Venco, 2006; Oliveira et al., 2005). These companies hire women who place value on qualities they expect women to have, including: understanding social order, patience, ability to listen and courtesy when interacting with customers (Venco, 2003, 2006). The reason women are treated this way is because, it is argued, men in Brazil are not conditioned to handle a Taylorist organized service workplace (Hirota, 2002; Kergoat, 2001). Another important consideration is that by reducing the status of work to tacit attributes of gender, the work performed can be reduced in value.

Yet when it comes to customer service centres that have international operations, the evidence suggests that staffs are 60 percent male (Venco, 2006). The reason for this may be because the work is considered more important or influential and is also better compensated, even if the differential is not terribly great. For example, compensation for a telemarketing operator in São Paolo is R $558.62, while bilingual operators earn R $800.00, and trilingual operators earn R $1,000.00.

5.10.3   Working Conditions in Brazilian Call and Customer Service Centres

Interviews conducted for a recent study with workers in a customer service centre in a rural area in the state of São Paolo offer some insights into the scheduling of working hours and how the regulations can be circumvented (Venco, 2007). The customer service centre fixes the work schedule in shifts grouped by period. The first shift goes from 7:30 to 14:00 and the second shift from 14:00 to 20:30. Supervisors are often known to 'invite' the first shift to return to work from 18:00 to 22:00, when call demands go up. As the law (CLT) allows only two extra hours per day, the payment of these hours is made in instalments to circumvent the law and prevent labour litigation. This would appear to be a continuation of the behaviour observed when the same firm was studied in 2006:

> Operators with higher seniority who worked the established six hours and fifteen minutes in the morning shift (which ends at 15:00) were invited to come back at 18:00 and remain until 21:00 (when there was better chance for sales) occupying the rookie PA. The rookie PAs were monitored by the more experienced operator listening to calls, which the company considered its training method for new employees. What is significant is that the company had no sales commission policy, offering only the possibility of job promotion. (Venco, 2006, p. 162)

Studies of call centres have also uncovered persistent concerns in the workplace, notably regarding management's ability to monitor the workforce. In an effort to increase productivity and efficiency, managers have implemented policies and technology to monitor individual workers on a continuous basis. Research by Venco (2006) and Marinho-Silva (2004) have highlighted that many customer service centres have computerized systems to control call flows and average service time; other devices appear on operator work screens if they exceed the call time determined by management to be sufficient. One notable technological system indicates the number of calls waiting to be answered by the customer service operator on their computer screen as well as simultaneously on the floor manager's screen, which can increase the tension to speed up service (Venco, 2003). In a similar vein, another study has highlighted the use of a colour coding system on customer service monitors, which is meant to make the time pressure on operators explicit (Silva, 2004).[16]

Concerns arising from this research within the industry subsequently led to changes in legislation covering call centres. The legislation now requires that monitoring of calls to speed up workers can only be done with the operator's knowledge and further prevents use of mechanisms monitoring production, such as messages in video monitors; light, colour-coded, or sound signs; or indications of time. If they exist, they can only be used at the worker's discretion (Attachment I of NR 17).

Rest days have also been a point of contention in customer service centres. The use of a day off is normally a legal right, not one acquired as a reward. Yet, due to the fact that Saturday is a normal work day in customer service centres, workers (especially young ones) viewed this day off concession as a reward given for good returns during the week. The customer service companies 'traded' on worker aspirations by requiring higher goals to be met during the week in exchange for two consecutive days off during the weekend (i.e., Saturday and Sunday). However, research indicated that because the decision by management in some firms did not come until Friday, workers who were eligible would not be able to make plans for the day off when they were awarded. As a customer service operator summed up:

> What a customer service operator wants the most is to have Saturday off. They (managers) say: If you sell this many cards, you have Saturday off, but when 9:00 PM on Friday arrives and it is time to leave, they (managers) decide you will not get the day off. I mean, you make plans... And this happens a lot during the holidays... they (managers) say that, if you beat the target, you will have a day off just before the holiday and at the last minute (change their mind). (Telemarketing operator, Company Y, interview 2004)

These so-called motivational strategies appear to be widely used in customer service centres, though they are technically illegal under the law.

Another 'motivational strategy' used by management in customer service centres is a system called 'happy days.' On so-called happy days managers choose a theme and expect all call centre operators to work wearing costumes. In the words of a recently hired operator:

> It is very nice, because it is very relaxing. One day chosen was panama 'happy day' (operators all wore panamas at the workplace during that shift). Imagine, I call your house and I am wearing my panamas [...] it is a bit of fun. Another day my supervisor dressed as a witch [...] (because) it's Carnival, everybody gets in the mood...we get down! [...] And it works, because it is the day that we sell more! There are days when people are more excited, we really sell. When we want to sell, we rock!' (Telemarketing operator, Company Z, interview June 6, 2005)

Among those with more seniority, the 'happy day' set-up made some employees feel ridiculous. They felt that only those who did not feel embarrassed and chose to should participate. However, for those who did not participate, their nonparticipation meant that they lost points in their evaluation because they did not demonstrate appropriate team spirit (Venco, 2006).

These types of 'motivational' strategies often contain hidden systems to change the production requirements of the workforce. In describing one such strategy used in Brazilian industry, Hirata noted that companies developed 'production Olympics.' Conducted in two stages, the first is set up to change the productivity parameters defining the best times. The next stage is meant to exceed the first stage. According to Hirata, the result of these games as tools subliminally compelled workers to produce more than what was required (Hirata, 2002, p. 36).

Worker concerns regarding the use of these managerial tactics to stimulate over-production compelled changes in the law. The law from the Ministry of Labour recommends (Attachment I of NR 17):

4.11. It is forbidden the use of methods that cause work pressure, moral harassment, fear or constraint, such as:

- Stimulus to competition among workers or work groups/teams;
- To demand that the workers use in a permanent or temporary fashion, accessories, costumes and clothes with promotion or advertisement objective;
- To publicly display the operators' performance evaluations.

Moreover, there are other mitigating factors that can make working in customer service centres less than ideal. Intense pressure from management to speed up service, mistreatment by customers, exposure to embarrassing situations and repetitive and highly standardized work are some of the concerns operators in these centres give for leaving the work. From an occupational point of view, operators in this industry have limited possibilities for promotion. This may provide context to the findings by Oliveira, which indicate that in Brazilian customer service centres 13.4 percent of the workers resigned, 15.7 percent were fired and little less than 5 percent were promoted (Oliveira et al., 2005). One company in this study indicated that their turnover was 80 percent per year (Venco, 2006).

In spite of these expressed concerns, there is still a labour market for this industry in Brazil. The reason is that although some companies do not offer the best working conditions, working in companies in this industry offers a chance for formal employment, signified in Brazil by having an employer signed card. As labour markets in Brazil have a high degree of informality, this is not an insignificant consideration, particularly for those who are beginning their careers, such as educated young men and women. As one company manager in this study noted:

Although call centre is the first job for young people in city X, it is the first entrance (to the labour market). Why do we say this? Because today company B employs around 1 percent of the population and if you talk about PEA [economically active population], among those with legal and registered work, we are talking about almost 10 percent of the population. Then, it is the city's (W) best entrance into formal work. And here in city W you see that people already worked at other call centres. But perhaps they don't have the same patience to wait for a promotion, so they go jumping from call centre to call centre and when they have the chance to use some skills, some different ability (like a second language or computer knowledge) or such. They remain a little more time in the company if they don't continue jumping from job to job and won't stay in the company longer. Here in city W the number of people who remain in the job is very low. (Senior Account Manager, International Business, Company B, interview October 15, 2007)

5.10.4   The Brazilian Paradox in Call and Customer Service Centres

In addition to this, there is a paradox that operates in the call and customer service centre industry in Brazil: While the market is large and growing, very little of it is targeted beyond the domestic market in Brazil itself. According to a manager of a call centre company interviewed for this study and an examination of their organizational information, six in ten of their employees are working in telecommunications, but only 1 percent of them work in customer service in other countries (Senior Account Manager, International Business, Company B, 2007). One manager noted the striking contrast between this industry in Brazil and India:

Today in Brazil around 65 percent of what is outsourced in call centres is between the financial industry and telecom companies, half and half. These are the great outsourcers. [...] In this context Brazil is the third largest call centre country in the world. The first one is the U.S.A., the second is England, and then comes Brazil. Brazil (industry) is bigger than India, but in Brazil less than 1 percent is offshore and in India 70 percent is offshore. If American or English companies stop outsourcing call centre (functions) to India, then this industry (in India) ends, but not in Brazil. (Senior Account Manager, International Business, Company B, interview October 15, 2007)

5.10.5   Telemedicine: An Emerging Field for Remote Work

Telemedicine is not often considered as a form of service sector outsourcing or offshoring. Yet this line of work has been established in different parts of the world, including Brazil, and may be an area of future growth. As countries look to reduce health care costs, the use of such mechanisms may become more common and may further compel changes in traditional professional and doctor–patient relationships. In this study, two laboratories in Brazil were identified as offering different services for the US and Portugal. Pathology examinations starting in the US were sent to one lab in Brazil (via the internet), and radiology materials were sent from Portugal to another lab in Brazil.

Telemedicine is not a new concept, but one that has moved forward with developments in technology (Royal College of Pathologists, 2005). Telemedicine allows those making medical decisions to be in a different location than the patients being examined. Advances in computer graphic design in the 1980s allowed for better image diagnoses, thus leading to the possibility of a new model of analysis. Changes in technology from analogue to digital further enhanced the possibility of remote diagnosis much easier. In addition to images that can be transferred, improvements in technology have also led to the ability to engage in different forms of robotic medicine, such as surgical procedures or observation of surgical techniques.

However, the most commonly used form of telemedicine is *telepathology*, in which medical images are transferred to other locations outside of the surgical room for analysis, which can be in the same hospital or to another hospital in another country. Such innovations have often been used in remote areas where medical professionals are scarce, such as in Scandinavia where some of this technology was pioneered.

Unlike other forms of service sector provision described in this chapter, the development of telemedicine was not initially guided by a desire for cost reductions, but to expand knowledge of medical techniques to remote locations. As time has passed, health providers have begun to use the Internet as a vehicle to treat patients. The model used is called 'health risk control,' which aims to reduce costs (particularly for chronic users) by reducing interpersonal contact and replacing it with the management of health indicators transmitted through the Internet.

The ability to provide and obstacles impeding offshore health operations vary according to the employer's service country. For example, through interviews, it was learned that Portugal would allow flexible outsourcing of some medical services to other countries. In one case, a European company visited sites of Company E in Brazil to examine the stability, tradition and technology used by the Brazilian firm, and concluded that it could expand the use of image-related medicine such as ultrasound. However, another company located in the US must operate within strict limitations defined by law, though there is some variation by specialty. For the contact companies in both the US and Brazil, interaction is strictly monitored and takes place where the responsible doctor for the diagnosis in Brazil has attended a 3-year specialization course in the state of the employing company (Medical Manager, Company E, 2008).

These legal links can slow the advance of offshore diagnostic service operations, but it is important that health standards be observed. Brazilian services tend to look for professionals with the background required in the country they will be dealing with from offshore. Because the work these professionals do is obviously quite specific and the countries they provide advice to have requirements, the service firm is not limited by geography in identifying professionals who can perform the tasks because the high profits can cover the costs.

Curiously, in spite of the high qualifications necessary to perform such work, linguistic barriers can still be a concern. For health services that are done in Portuguese, hiring a Brazilian company makes sense. Language is exceptionally important in diagnostic services, as one mistake can lead to an inaccurate diagnosis or treatment that can pose injury risks for a patient. A Portuguese clinic that had tried to outsource its radiology function to India found that language was too much of a barrier to overcome and instead looked to find such services in a Portuguese-speaking country (Director of Diagnostics Centre, Company E, 2008). At the same time, the Brazilian health service group with which the contract was made believes the Portugal contract has opened up their ability to expand services to other European countries provided from Brazil.

It is difficult to measure the degree of cost reduction that takes place by internationally outsourcing certain health care functions (Medical Director, Company E, 2008). The reason suggested for this is that private network services in Brazil receives a fixed and pre-established amount set by the national price table (in Portugal) for examining the information. Automation of the reporting may also help to increase productivity in this segment (Medical Director, Company E, 2008). Among those interviewed in Brazil, the offshoring of medical services to Brazil drops the costs in Europe seven to ten times lower than if they were done in the European country (Director Diagnostics Centre, Company E, 2008; Medical Manager, Company E, 2008; Director Company D, 2008).

This form of offshore outsourcing, although growing and important, is without doubt very different from other forms mentioned in this book. It requires very high qualifications, but its growth will depend on the ability to interpret the images sent between service purchaser and service provider. One factor that is expected to play a large role in systematizing this segment of the industry will be improvements in technology to enhance images that can be relayed between parties (Director Diagnostics Centre, Company E, 2008; Medical Manager, Company E, 2008; Director Company D, 2008).

An unintended consequence of the remote provision of health care services is that it may actually influence some hierarchical dimensions of medical decision-making. Some medical services that are vital but tend in practice to be invisible to patients, such as radiology and pathology, are the ones most likely to be offshored and outsourced. It is also notable that there is a gender dimension to this situation as women, at least in Brazil, are more likely to be radiologists or pathologists (Venco, 2008).

Finally, and not to be diminished, telemedicine touches on a subject that does not directly affect other dimensions of offshoring or outsourcing so profoundly, namely ethics. Shifting certain medical functions offshore (or outsourcing them) may appear to make a certain financial sense overall, but it is of questionable justification in countries where there are sufficient medical professionals available to perform the specialized task. Working relationships that take place in the physical workplace may not be replicable with offshore (or outsourced) medical staffs, which in this case could compromise patient care. Moreover, a patient's right to privacy may be compromised if they are not only unsure of who is providing the medical advice but have no way to ensure that the medical advice is being transmitted and examined privately. These are ethical concerns that may pose greater challenges to increased demands and may have consequences for this line of offshore or outsourced service provision.

5.11 Conclusions

It is clear that in Brazil the development of the BPO industry has proceeded at a steady pace. In particular, companies are giving greater consideration to nearshoring. According to one of the businesspeople interviewed, such modality tends to replace the current offshore model, since the activities developed in the information technology area need more and more interactivity. In this sense, countries such as India and China would reduce their participation in this market segment, and Brazil would tend to broaden its activities due to its time zone geographical position, in addition to being identified as culturally closer to Europe and the US. Furthermore, political stability, the distance from terrorist conflicts and similar dangers, and the absence of catastrophic natural phenomena that could endanger sensitive equipment, are extremely valued.

Although Brazil does not have amongst its main languages the ones required for the kinds of work demanded by the international division of labour, firms often favour Brazil due to the large number of qualified workers available with acquired skills in other languages, due to formal education and resulting from European immigration patterns in the twentieth century. The growth rates of Brazilian exports of software and IT services reinforce its desirability, with projected growth rates of 11 percent over the period from 2008–2011. The total value of spending on IT products and services could pass $30 billion in 2011 (M2 Presswire, 2009).

The creation and development of call and customer service centres in Brazil is based on decisions made to open certain sectors of the economy, namely financial services and telecommunications as highlighted in this chapter. As a result the teleservice sector (ITES–BPO) sector has grown without interruption since the beginning of 2000. While the current financial and economic crisis may have some impact, the early indications are that there is much space for growth and expansion of this industry in Brazil. There may still be resistance to offshoring of operations by organizations that have yet to do so, but as the market in Brazil continues to develop this may change organizations' decisions in the future. However, the call and customer service segment in Brazil exists in an environment of ongoing contradictions: a domestic industry strengthened by experience, yet challenged by mergers and buyouts from abroad; a sector that is based on deregulation yet still is discovering how to address labour issues and union disputes through existing and evolving law.

Telemedicine, in turn, has distinguished itself as a new element in the service exportation scenario. Recognized as a high-skill activity, telemedicine is based on new technologies that make it feasible to develop offshore operations. It is implied here that this segment of the industry will experience more growth as a whole because there is already an established a patient–professional relationship.

In summary, the BPO industry in Brazil is generally seen as a provider of good-quality, formal employment. However, the wages and working conditions appear to depend greatly on whether the particular remote work positions are primarily serving the domestic market or international markets; the pay and conditions tend to be better in the latter than in the former. In the context of this industry, less-than-optimal working conditions can be found, including antisocial work schedules, insufficient breaks and stress due to high workloads and intensive electronic monitoring.

Brazilian policymakers have tried to address these circumstances through legislation, and only time will tell the extent of their impact on the working conditions found in the industry. Ironically, the other factor that may improve working conditions may take place as the BPO service centres address more international clients, because conditions in these workplaces would appear to be better than in others that only address the Brazilian market. Finally, because of the costs, location and capacity of this industry in Brazil, coupled with the need for international organizations to cut costs, it seems unlikely that the financial crisis of 2008 will have a profound negative impact on the overall development of this industry in Brazil.

Notes

1. Brazilian Institute of Geography and Statistics (IBGE) Department is responsible for national statistics. The department is linked to the Brazilian Ministry of Planning and Budget.
2. This is the use of rigorous economic policy to control expenditures by means of elevated primary surplus and monetary policy, which keeps the basic interest rates of the economy high in order to hold down inflation.
3. Formal employment is employment in which the employer signs the work card of an employee, and informal employment in this context is being employed without having the work card signed by the employer.
4. Published in the Official Federal Government Gazette on August 9, 1943. Available at: http://www.trt02.gov.br/geral/tribunal2/legis/CLT/INDICE.html. Last review on March 11, 2008. Accessed on March 20, 2008.

5. According to Otaviano Canuto, the term 'Custo Brasil' has been used across the board to refer to all factors that are problems for competitiveness between areas and companies within the Brazilian economy. Labour is one factor, but others will be identified in the next section.

6. 'Calvary' is a Christian reference relating to the suffering in the final hours before the death of Christ. In this context, it is meant to signify an intense amount of effort, sacrifice and suffering that may or may not have a desired or successful conclusion.

7. This law is available at http://www.planalto.gov.br/ccivil/LEIS/L4117.htm. Accessed on March 10, 2008.

8. This law is available at http://www.planalto.gov.br/CCIVIL_03/Decreto-Lei/1965-1988/Del2134.htm. Accessed on March 10, 2008.

9. While growth did take place, it did not translate into lower costs for people.

10. Available at www.agenciabrasil.gov.br/noticias/2007/12/20/materia.2007-12-20.5696758798/views. Accessed on March 10, 2008.

11. These percentage increases significantly when compared respectively to automatic teller machines, or ATMs (75 percent), home banking (80 percent), or to Internet banking (90 percent) (Venco, 2003).

12. According to a research conducted by Brazilian Association for Corporate and Customer Relations (ABRAREC) and the company E-consulting, financial and telecommunication services were responsible for 56 percent of the call centre demand in 2006; according to the president of one of the largest companies in the sector (Atento) the banking area showed the highest growth in the demand for collecting and financial services. Available at www.abrarec.com.br. Accessed on March 18, 2008. Moreover, according to a research by Oliveira, Jr., et al. (2005, p. 13), banks are the second biggest client of support centres. It is implied here that the discrepancies among the sources relate to sampling, because of the diversity of companies used in the study. The Brazilian Association of Teleservices website also shows that banks are the main call centre client. Available at: http://www.abt.org.br/pesquisa.html. Accessed on March 22, 2008.

13. A steelworker in the 1980s (Venco, 1991).

14. This includes official statistics about work and unemployment for this type of work.

15. It is unclear whether this company provides this training or not.

16. One location used the following system: blue for less than 20 seconds; yellow for 20–25 seconds and red for 25 seconds or more (Silva, 2004, p. 25).

6
Remote Work and Global Sourcing in Argentina

Andrés López, Daniela Ramos and Iván Torre

In recent years new export opportunities have appeared for developing countries mainly due to the development of information and communication technologies (ICTs), which allow long-distance provision of a larger number of services (accountancy, finance, logistics, computer and information services, etc.) – the so-called information technology-enabled services (ITES).

For developing countries, service exports not only generate currency income, but also generate a number of employment opportunities (with often low investment requirements) and human capital improvements. Moreover, though perhaps different from what happens in some developed countries, the emergence of these new work modalities may provide employment and training opportunities for people in low and medium-low social and income classes. These factors help to explain why many countries are openly and aggressively competing to attract investments in these areas.

Labour costs are usually a key determinant when it comes to deciding on locations for new investments in ITES-related activities.[1] This is especially the case in developing countries. In fact, for a developing country to engage in global service value chains, the costs must be such that they allow the country to be considered an attractive location by multinational corporations (MNCs). However, investments associated with services exports are usually 'footloose.'[2] Hence, when integration in global service value chains rests only upon low labour costs, competitiveness in the end depends on the fact that the wages of the respective countries do not rise compared to other possible locations (López et al., 2008). It is thus pragmatic for countries to offer local environments where investors can find valuable assets (e.g., specific human resources skills, technological capabilities, etc.) and maintain stability in their investments.

Argentina has been rapidly gaining attractiveness as a supplier of ITES. This trend began relatively recently and in fact is mainly related to the mega-devaluation of the Argentine peso that took place in early 2002, which in turn translated into a dramatic decline in local costs. Due to the heavy recession that the country faced during 2001, unemployment surged to 21.5

percent, a fact that blocked any possible large increases in wage levels owing to changes in the exchange rate and the inflation shock that followed. Nominal wages grew only 5 percent between December 2001 and December 2002 (INDEC, 2004). To understand the extent of the fall of local wages, a look at the dollar exchange rate reveals that one US dollar rose from ARS 1 to ARS 3.50 in the same period. Local inflation was 40 percent between December 2001 and December 2002, so real wage levels had sharply reduced. Other costs such as rents and electricity also fell considerably in dollars. Construction and real estate activity collapsed, and with the rest of the country in a deep crisis, prices dipped to an almost 20-year low (Cetrángolo et al., 2008). Utilities tariffs were frozen by the government at their 2001 level, making Argentina one of the Latin American countries with some of the cheapest energy prices in the region.

The currency devaluation combined with the deep recession in the domestic market was a stimulus for a number of domestic and foreign firms of the software and information services (SIS) sector to begin to explore the possibility of exporting services, due to the significant capabilities that had been accumulated over previous decades. Soon after Argentina's economy entered into rapid economic growth in 2003, the country received growing attention as an attractive location for providing not only SIS, but also for other services, by installing call and contact centres (CCCs) and SSCs as well as service provision in other areas such as business processes, health, engineering, finance and so on. A large part of the expansion of ITES activities was due to the growing investments of a number of large MNCs looking for new locations where skilled and relatively low-cost human resources were available and also where different services could be supplied efficiently.

Owing to these circumstances the national government, as well as many provincial and city governments in the country, have begun to try fostering investments in ITES activities through a number of fiscal incentives and through direct subsidies and provision of infrastructure development. The existence of attractive business opportunities in the ITES area has in turn generated often fierce competition for human resources among other areas. This had led to rapid growth in wages rates and to an increase in labour turnover, both of which have impacted mainly domestic firms.

The main objective of this chapter is to analyse the dynamics of employment and human capital in the emerging services export activities in Argentina. The aim is to develop a better understanding of the employment and working conditions prevailing in firms exporting ITES; to learn about the differences in employment and working conditions among firms according to their size, ownership, business segments and market orientation (i.e., exports vs. local market); and to analyse to what extent working and employment conditions, including aspects related to labour legislation and staff turnover, are currently damaging or fostering Argentina's competitiveness in the ITES sector. The chapter will concentrate on the cases of business and computer services. The first group comprises the provision of business process outsourcing (BPO) services, as well as SSCs and CCCs. The second group comprises the provision of SIS.

The chapter is organized as follows: Section I explains the methodology used in the discussion. Section II analyses services in Argentina, focusing on the export of business services and SIS. The section concludes with a description of the public policies in force that impact on these sectors. Section III examines employment and working condition in ITES. The discussion begins with an investigation of the overall situation and the recent evolution of the labour market and employment conditions in Argentina. The section also outlines the main features of the country's labour legislation. The analysis then turns to labour issues in the BPO and SIS sectors, examining wages, labour relationships, working conditions and unionization, among other things in these sectors. Section IV provides some concluding observations.

6.1   Methodology Used for This Study

The methodology used in our work was that of a case study. We took into account several factors. First, the nature of the topic we addressed – namely, the dynamics of labour and human resources in the services exports sector – is still relatively unknown and, thus, any kind of quantitative analysis is wrong-headed since the variables and mechanisms that may play a role in this context are not certain. A case study approach allows us to explore the different aspects of the dynamics involved and contributes to give a more precise image of the phenomenon we want to analyse. A quantitative study may, thus, follow this case study approach, but not precede it. Another reason to conduct a case study approach was the lack of quantitative data at the firm level. We nevertheless were kindly provided some of this information by the Ministry of Labour and Employment, although on a limited scale.

We conducted interviews with human resources managers and department heads in our fieldwork. We selected the most important companies in the sector based on information provided by sector analysts and business chambers. Not all the companies accepted an interview; however, we estimated that we covered at least the most important companies in the call centre business and the business outsourcing sector. The software sector is made up of several small and medium-sized companies, which would have been impossible to cover in our fieldwork. Nevertheless, Andrés López and Daniela Ramos, part of our team, improved knowledge of the sector by conducting several interviews with software companies and were able to provide extra information towards our work.

The interviews conducted were based on a questionnaire but allowed for the inclusion of information, views and opinions not covered in it. A list of the interviews that were conducted during the fieldwork is presented at the end of this chapter (see section 6.5). Due to a confidentiality agreement we signed with the interviewees, we can disclose neither their names nor the companies for which they work.

6.2 Recent Trends in Trade in Services in Argentina

6.2.1 Trade in Services in Argentina: An Overview

There are no precise figures regarding world trade in services, due to a number of factors that prevent accurate measurement and are essentially related to the fact that services are intangible. The same difficulties apply to Argentina. In light of this, and aiming to improve the available data, the International Accounts National Direction, which is in charge of compiling balance of payments statistics, enlarged the sample of firms it used to quantify trade in services in 2002. Although this clearly ameliorated the representativeness of the trade figures, it has also made the comparison of the information before and after that year infeasible.

Bearing this in mind, the available statistics can now be analysed. A first look at the data shows a great growth of services exports between 2000 and 2007 (Table 6.1), which allowed the country to narrow the enormous deficit it showed in 2000 (US $4 billion) down to US $500 million in 2007. A large part of this growth was due to the impressive performance of 'other business services.' whose share in services exports passed from 6.6 percent in 2000 to 28.8 percent in 2007. While this increase may be to some extent the result of the abovementioned improvement in the compilation of statistics, it is clear that business services exports have increased strongly. Also notable is the growth of exports of computer and information services, which amounted to slightly less than US $500 million in 2007, a figure that is more than triple the level in the year 2000.

There are different factors behind the growth in the export of these activities. As we already mentioned, the high real exchange rate regime established from 2002 onward has significantly contributed to positioning the country as a low-cost provider of services. This competitive advantage was an important driver both for the arrival of many export-oriented service MNCs to the country (or the expansion of those already established) and for many local companies to start export activities. Policies for the promotion of services exports were only adopted later on.

The cost-based competitive advantage has been gradually eroded by a rapid growth in wages in recent years, but so far this has not been a setback for services exports. Sector experts repeatedly underline the highly skilled human resources available in the country as a key asset driving services exports. Argentina would appear to be another example of a country where MNCs 'went for cost, stayed for quality' (Dossani and Kenney, 2003). However, cost increases are a source of concern for firms exporting ITES and may become a problem in the future.

Table 6.1 Argentina Services Exports (2000–2007)

Type of service	2000		2007		Total growth rate (%)	Cumulative average annual rate (%)
	Million dollars	Share (%)	Million dollars	Share (%)		
Transport	1145.2	23.2	1666.8	16.2	45.5	5.5
Travel	2903.7	58.8	4313.6	42.0	48.6	5.8
Communication	174.5	3.5	312.8	3.0	79.3	8.7
Construction	7	0.1	38.4	0.4	448.6	27.5
Insurance	12.4	0.3	0	0.0	—	—
Financial	6.2	0.1	9	0.1	45.2	5.5
Computer and information	147.1	3.0	491.3	4.8	234.0	18.8
Royalties and licenses fees	36.8	0.7	79.5	0.8	116.0	11.6
Other business services	324.4	6.6	2959.5	28.8	812.3	37.1
Personal and cultural Recreational	18.1	0.4	281.3	2.7	1454.1	48.0
Government	160.2	3.2	130.3	1.3	-18.7	-2.9
Total	4935.5	100.0	10282.5	100.0	108.3	11.1

Source: International Accounts National Direction, Ministry of Economy.

Table 6.2 Other Business Services Exports by Destination (2000–2007)

2000		2007	
Country of destination	Share (%)	Country of destination	Share (%)
US	56.5	US	49.8
Brazil	10.5	Chile	8.1
Spain	6.2	Spain	7.8
France	5.0	Brazil	5.0
Chile	3.4	Belgium	4.9
Paraguay	2.5	UK	3.9
Peru	2.4	Mexico	2.2
Germany	2.2	Uruguay	2.2
UK	1.9	Switzerland	2.2
Uruguay	1.6	Germany	2.0
Percentage of exports reporting information	82.8	Percentage of exports reporting information	51.6

Source: International Accounts National Direction, Ministry of Economy.

The available information also permits a partial examination of the destination of service exports.[3] The US is the main destination for exports of computer and business services (Tables 6.2 and 6.3). However, its relative importance has diminished in recent years, particularly in the case of computer services exports (from 70 percent in 2000 to 54 percent in 2007). In the case of destinations for business services, Chile has moved into second

Table 6.3 Computer and Information Services Exports by Destination (2000–2007)

2000		2007	
Country of destination	Share (%)	Country of destination	Share (%)
US	70.0	US	53.9
Mexico	7.5	Spain	10.5
Chile	4.3	Mexico	9.4
Brazil	3.0	Chile	5.2
Venezuela	2.9	Netherlands	4.0
Netherlands	2.6	Uruguay	3.7
Uruguay	2.5	Venezuela	2.3
Canada	2.3	Brazil	2.0
Spain	1.6	UK	1.6
Bolivia	0.9	Ecuador	1.3
Percentage of exports reporting information	71.3	Percentage of exports reporting information	74.6

Source: International Accounts National Direction, Ministry of Economy.

place after being in the fifth place in 2000 (although its 8.1 percent share is far behind the almost 50 percent corresponding to the US). Spain also raised its share as a destination of business services exports from 6.2 percent in 2000 to 7.8 percent in 2007, but its growth was more impressive in the case of computer services exports (from 1.6 percent to 10.5 percent in the same period). Mexico came in third place as destination of these exports in 2007, after gaining a 2 percent share during the same period. These data are noteworthy in that the trends in both sectors reveal a growing presence of Spanish-speaking countries as export destinations.

6.2.2   Business Services Offshoring

Different locations have emerged as primary destinations for service offshoring. India is the most important, but China, Russia and other nations in Asia, as well as in Eastern and Central Europe are gaining relevance. Although Latin America is also becoming a relatively important player in this field, the region as a whole lags behind in the competition for attracting investments in these activities. A study covering only US companies showed that the region's share in offshoring destinations was 13 percent (Mexico representing 4 percent), a figure higher than that of Eastern Europe (7 percent), but well behind India (43 percent) and China and the Philippines combined (20 percent) (Lewin et al., 2005). Perhaps a more worrying fact is that, according to a survey done to more than 500 European and US firms, Latin America is mainly chosen as a destination for offshoring simple functions based on lower costs and not as a region where activities requiring higher skills can be carried out (Couto et al., 2006). This is probably the result of the relatively recent entrance of the region into the service offshoring business and the weaknesses in the availability of human resources with expertise in those functions that are technologically more complex.

Some specific information about Argentina's situation can be found in A.T. Kearney's *Global Service Location Index 2007*, which consists of a ranking that positions each country according to its attractiveness for offshoring. Argentina's position was 23rd over the 50 locations ranked (Table 6.4). The country is not very well positioned in the Latin American context: in fact, Brazil was in 5th position, Chile in 7th position, Mexico in 10th position and Uruguay in 22nd position, just ahead of Argentina. Argentina ranks better in human resources (due to its availability of skilled people) and financial attractiveness (because of low costs measured in US dollars).

Comparison of this ranking with the one published in 2004 (which covered only 25 locations) is interesting: Brazil and Chile rose two positions each. Mexico also rose from the 14th position to the 10th position. Argentina, on the contrary, fell from 15th position to 23rd position. This fall reflects the deterioration of the index of 'financial attractiveness' in light of the rising wages as labour demand (together with inflation) grew considerably during the last few years. In spite of this, the country has improved

Table 6.4 Global Service Location Index (2007)[4] (in index numbers)

Country	Human resources	Business environment	Financial attractiveness	Global index	Position in world ranking
India	2.34 (2)	1.44 (19)	3.22 (5)	7.00	1
China	2.25 (3)	1.38 (20)	2.93 (10)	6.56	2
Malaysia	1.26 (9)	2.02 (5)	2.84 (13)	6.12	3
Thailand	1.21 (11)	1.62 (12)	3.19 (6)	6.02	4
Brazil	1.78 (4)	1.47 (18)	2.64 (17)	5.89	5
Indonesia	1.47 (7)	1.06 (25)	3.29 (2)	5.82	6
Chile	1.18 (12)	1.93 (8)	2.65 (16)	5.76	7
Philippines	1.23 (10)	1.26 (21)	3.26 (3)	5.75	8
Bulgaria	1.04 (18)	1.56 (15)	3.16 (7)	5.75	9
Mexico	1.49 (6)	1.61 (13)	2.63 (19)	5.73	10
Singapore	1.51 (5)	2.53 (1)	1.65 (24)	5.69	11
Slovakia	1.04 (17)	1.79 (10)	2.79 (14)	5.62	12
Egypt	1.14 (14)	1.25 (23)	3.22 (4)	5.61	13
Jordan	1.78 (4)	1.47 (18)	2.64 (17)	5.61	14
Estonia	0.98 (21)	1.54 (17)	3.09 (8)	5.60	15
Czech Rep.	0.96 (22)	2.2 (3)	2.44 (22)	5.58	16
Latvia	1.1 (15)	2.05 (4)	2.43 (23)	5.55	17
Poland	0.91 (24)	2 (6)	2.64 (18)	5.55	18
Vietnam	0.99 (19)	1.22 (24)	3.33 (1)	5.54	19
Unit. Arab Emir.	1.17 (13)	1.79 (11)	2.59 (20)	5.51	20
US	0.86 (25)	1.92 (9)	2.73 (15)	5.51	21
Uruguay	2.74 (1)	2.29 (2)	0.48 (25)	5.47	22
Argentina	**1.3 (8)**	**1.26 (22)**	**2.91 (11)**	**5.47**	**23**
Hungary	0.95 (23)	1.98 (7)	2.54 (21)	5.47	24

Source: A.T. Kearney, 2007b.

its position in the index of 'human resources,' now in 8th position after being in 19th position in 2004. The index in which Argentina is worst positioned is in 'business environment,' where it is well behind most other Latin American countries, probably because of doubts regarding the soundness of the institutional architecture and the protection of property rights.

Lewin et al. (2005) examined other determinants for the selection of offshoring destinations: co-localization (with other activities), language and expertise. Latin America's main advantage is language (many experts state that for tasks requiring contact with foreign customers, the region's English accent is better accepted than the ones found in Asian countries). The main perceived weakness is the lack of technical expertise. Beyond the above-mentioned factors, a general advantage for most Latin American countries is that the region's time zone is relatively aligned with those of the US and is not far behind those of Western Europe, allowing firms from developed countries to have real-time control of their providers' operations, instead of locations such as India where provider and customer operate from different time zones (A.T. Kearney, 2007a).

Although no hard data exist on investments in Argentina in this sector, we know that several companies are now exporting business services. The main companies providing BPO services are IBM, Deloitte, Accenture and Cubecorp, among others. Concerning CCCs export activities, the main companies are local affiliates of the French firm Teleperformance, US firms Teletech and Apex Sykes, the German firm Arvato and local companies such as Actionline and Audiotel, among others. Regarding SSCs, the following companies have set up at least one of them in Argentina: ExxonMobil, Chevron, InBev, McDonald's, Cargill, IBM, Google and SAP.

6.2.3   Software and Information Services

Although the SIS sector is concentrated in developed countries, some developing countries have gained significant shares in international markets, India being the most noteworthy case. Other successful 'late' entrants to the sector include Ireland and Israel. Latin America is far from exhibiting the export figures of those countries. Nevertheless, there are substantial differences within the region. For example, in Brazil the industry is large but very inward-oriented (similar to Mexico, the region's second producer). On the other hand, Costa Rica and Uruguay have smaller yet more open sectors. Argentina lies between these cases, since its local market is not as large as those of Brazil and Mexico, but it does offer attractive opportunities for SIS firms. Hence, the export propensity of the SIS industry in Argentina ranges between both groups (Table 6.5).

The competitive advantages of Argentina in this sector are not very different from those in the export of business services, mainly because the location determinants are basically the same in both cases. These advantages include: (i) the high real exchange rate which has lowered local costs, including labour costs; (ii) the dynamism that the local SIS industry has shown in recent years; (iii) the existence of a stock of relevantly skilled human resources; (iv) the cultural affinity with most of the Western world; (v) the time zone, particularly if the activities involve real-time operations with customers in developed countries; (vi) the availability of a very good communication infrastructure, mainly an inheritance of investments made in the 1990s; and (vii) the existence of an internationally harmonized legislation on data protection (López and Ramos, 2008). Moreover, according to information from the Software Engineering Institute, there has been a growing trend in the number of CMM or CMMI[5] certifications obtained by firms located in Argentina (in 2005 there were only 12 certifications, while in 2007 that figure had gone up to 47).

Table 6.5   SIS Sector Statistics in 'Late'-Entry Countries (2006) (or last available year)

	Sales (1) US $ million	Exports (2) US $ million	(2/1) %	Employment
Ireland	30,000	28,500	95	24,000
India	30,000	22,900	76	1,300,000
Israel	4100	3000	73	15,000
Costa Rica	173	80	46	4800
Uruguay	265	104	38	4900
Argentina	1870	400	21	45,700
China	13,300	700	5	190,000
Brazil	9900	308	3	200,000
Mexico	2870	125	4	48,000
Colombia	340	10	3	32,000
Ecuador	90	11	12	4500
Chile	1385	69	5	25,000

Source: López and Ramos (2008), Bastos Tigre and Marques (2007), NASSCOM, Enterprise Ireland's National Informatics Directory, Israel Association of Software Houses, Caprosoft and China Software Industry Association.

There are a number of potential challenges the industry in Argentina faces, including: (i) loss of investments to other economies with higher costs, such as Chile, because of macroeconomic and institutional instability in Argentina; (ii) the labour market is showing supply restrictions, resulting in large wages increases that push up overall costs, which are separate from limited growth in the sector due to a lack of skilled professionals; (iii) the energy shortages and the lack of adequate maintenance of the communication infrastructure are starting to worry many investors; and (iv) negative perceptions of people interviewed for this and other studies regarding Argentine workers, suggesting that while their technical qualities are not in question, they appear to be unable to work in groups and follow organizational norms (López and Ramos, 2007).

The Argentine SIS industry – following a path of inward-oriented development (the result of a growing domestic market in the 1990s combined with an overvalued exchange rate and the absence of government policies aimed at fostering services exports) – started to export more actively at the beginning of the present decade, which was initially propelled by the recession in the local market and helped by the devaluation of the peso. This was also stimulated by the existence of qualified human resources and the experience gained by many companies in the local market as providers of privatized utilities and the banking sector. A group of local companies was thus able to very rapidly refocus its business strategy to foreign markets (López and Ramos, 2008).

Nowadays, according to CESSI (the Software and Information Services Chamber), the Argentine SIS industry comprises around 1000 firms, to which a presumably large but unknown number of one-person and informal firms must be added. Between 2003 and 2005 the rate of creation of new firms in the SIS industry was 11 percent, which is the second highest rate among all the sectors in the economy and double the average rate for the country (Castillo et al., 2007).

In recent years, MNCs (some of which were already well established in the country and others which are more recent arrivals) have gained weight in SIS exports. These companies have located in Argentina driven mainly by the depreciation of the real exchange rate and the existence of skilled human resources. Secondary factors include the cultural affinity of the country with the Western world and the existence of a good ICT infrastructure. Based on information from interviews carried out for this chapter and from previous research (López and Ramos, 2007, 2008) considerations about local legislation (either tax- or labour-related) were not relevant at the time of deciding to locate in the country, although they could have played a role in determining the specific location within the country (more on this below).

A number of MNCs have been established in Argentina for some time now. The most notable is IBM, which now employs more than 7000 people and actively exports SIS and BPO services through three global delivery centres, having attained the CMMI 5 and the level 4 eSourcing Capability Model for Services Provider (eSCM-SP)[6] certifications. Other MNCs exporting SIS from Argentina include recent arrivals such as EDS, Tata Consultancy Services (TCS), Google, Motorola and Intel. Of this group, Motorola and Intel are also noteworthy. Both firms have recently established affiliates in Argentina in order to develop software related to their hardware production (which is not produced in Argentina). In 2001, Motorola established a software development centre for cell phones in the province of Cordoba, and in the following year it began to export. Nowadays the local affiliate has attained a CMM 5 certification. Intel set up a software development centre in Córdoba in 2005. The Intel centre is important because it aims to provide a very high level of technological services in Argentina as it develops the whole life cycle of a project, from inception to the final production stage.

Among the successful cases of local companies that export services we find the ASSA group, which has about 1000 employees, has offices in Brazil and Mexico, and specializes in consulting and maintenance of software produced by global firms such as SAP and Oracle. It also performs similar functions for Globant, a provider of IT outsourcing established in 2003, which has offices in Boston, Silicon Valley, London and Mexico employing more than 1000 employees worldwide.

6.2.4   Public Policies for Services Exports

In recent years, there has been a growing interest from the national level down to provincial states to promote the SIS sector. The policies carried out cover diverse type of instruments, some of them oriented towards the promotion of the industry's development, others towards the improvement of the provision of critical inputs (e.g., human resources) and others aimed at fostering local demand. The first two groups of policies are of special concern in this chapter (policies related to fostering the supply of human resources will be analysed in section 6.3).

In 2003, the Ministry of Economy created the SIS Competitiveness Forum, aimed at opening a debate on the policies needed to improve competitiveness. The Forum was made up officials from federal, provincial and municipal governments, as well as representatives from the private and academic sectors. The result of this Forum was the *Strategic Plan for Software and Information Services 2004–2014*, which identified problematic issues and opportunities for the industry as well as defining concrete actions to be carried out.

Subsequently, in 2004, two laws promoting the SIS sector were authorized. Law No. 25.856 establishes that software production is to be considered an industrial activity with regard to tax exemptions, credit benefits and other type of provisions. This law exempts the sector from paying the provincial sales tax. Law No. 25.922 provides fiscal benefits to SIS companies and creates a Software Industry Promotion Fund (FONSOFT) aimed at financing R&D expenditures in SMEs, universities and research centres. The benefits of this legislation apply to those firms that prove expenditures in R&D, quality certifications and software exports. These benefits include: (1) the establishment of a fiscal stability regime for 10 years; (2) the exemption of 60 percent of the taxable benefits used to the determine the income tax payments; (3) the possibility of using an amount equivalent to 70 percent of the paid Social Security taxes to offset other tax burdens (including the value added tax) and (4) the elimination of foreign currency transfer restrictions for the import of hardware and other components needed for software production. By February 2008, 213 firms had benefited from the application of law No. 25.922 according to official information.

Regarding provincial SIS promotion policies, many Argentine provinces are offering extra benefits (apart from those extended by the two national pieces of legislation previously mentioned) to those companies that invest in their territories. The most active districts in this context are the province of Córdoba and the city of Rosario, in Santa Fe province. In both cases the activities that fall under the promotional policies include those related to business services exports.

For instance, Motorola decided to invest in Córdoba in 2000 after the provincial government offered to pay for the construction of the buildings and provided a subsidy for each job created. Other MNCs such as Intel and EDS also received attractive subsidy packages. The incentives granted to these corporations raised some criticism in the local communities as these public policies appeared to favour large *foreign*, as opposed to domestic, companies (López and Ramos, 2008). On the other hand, the province of Córdoba currently provides tax exemptions (mainly on sales tax) to all SIS firms.

In the case of Rosario, the government did not provide any tax exemption or subsidy to stimulate the establishment of companies. Their strategy instead is to generate a favourable environment for the development of the industry's business activity. The rationale behind this policy is to promote investments that will generate local spillovers and not become a platform for service exports that are driven only by the existence of low costs (López and Ramos, 2008). In spite of this, the three MNCs established in Rosario would appear to fit more into the kind of investment projects the city government would apparently want to avoid. Ironically, the MNCs that could create a potential spillover for the local industry (e.g., Intel and Motorola) have decided not to invest in Rosario but in Córdoba, where tax exemptions and subsidies are given by the provincial government.

6.3   Working Conditions and Employment in Light of the New Trends in Services Exports in Argentina

6.3.1   An Overview of Argentina's Labour Market

The origins of the recent evolution in Argentina's labour market can be traced back to the beginning of the Import Substitution Industrialization (ISI) stage. The large expansion of the manufacturing industry between 1930 and 1945 gave a huge boost to trade union activity. During the same period, the government expanded its weight in the economy, empowering unions by providing long-term employment relationships (Galiani and Gerchunoff, 2003). The pro-labour measures taken by Juan Peron as a member of the military government from 1943 to 1946 and then as president from 1946 to 1955 also favoured the development of unions and established a legal system of collective and individual labour legislation.

The State's intervention in the labour market was one of the most salient characteristics of all the ISI stages (until 1976). The main factor was the State granting the trade unions the legal capacity to engage in collective bargaining (called *personería gremial* in Spanish). Hence, the State decides which trade union can engage in collective bargaining and which cannot. Since in each industry only one trade union can be the signatory of collective bargaining, the State in essence decides which union will be entitled to have monopoly rights over the bargaining process.

Argentina's inward-looking development strategy gradually became unsustainable as the result of a periodic balance of payments crisis which finally resulted in recessionary periods, large devaluations of the domestic currency and the growth of inflation rates that reached more than 200 percent annually in 1975. The bargaining structure was not helpful in this context, as it was extremely inflationary itself, as trade unions engaged in competitive behaviour between themselves as a result of the lack of bargaining coordination (Galiani and Gerchunoff, 2003).

The socioeconomic crisis the country faced during the mid-1970s ended tragically with a coup d'état in March 1976. The period starting in 1976 can be characterized as one in which official policies have sought to make the labour market more flexible, which was only achieved in the 1990s due to the increase in product market competition brought about by trade liberalization (Galiani and Gerchunoff, 2003). This policy, in addition to a massive programme of privatization, has been particularly helpful in reducing wage pressures and creating union discipline since the 1990s.

There were no great changes in the institutional setting of the labour market during this period, except for the creation of unemployment insurance and the extension of trial periods in employment contracts. Some reforms introduced in those years (e.g., the introduction of a variety of fixed-term contracts in 1991 and the decentralization of bargaining in 2000) were quickly reversed, probably because of disappointing results (Galiani and Gerchunoff, 2003).[7]

The main characteristic of the last stage (from the 1990s to early 2000s) was a huge rise in unemployment. In 1994, for the first time since the 1930s, the unemployment rate exceeded 10 percent, and in 1995 it reached a historic peak of 18.4 percent. There was a short-lived decline that reduced the rate to 13 percent in late 1998, but in 2002, in the midst of the country's worst economic crisis since 1890, unemployment reached 21.5 percent. The economic recovery that followed brought a huge fall in unemployment. The most recent information on unemployment indicates that in the third quarter of 2008 the unemployment rate stood at 7.8 percent, which though relatively high may actually understate the problem as it does not include those in the Program for Unemployed Male and Female Heads of Households (Plan Jefes y Jefas de Hogar Desocupados), which was implemented after the 2001 crisis.[8] This is based on the premise that in the second quarter of 2008, if the people in this Heads of Household programme were counted, it would have added 0.4 points to the unemployment rate.

Throughout the years of high unemployment (1995–2003) there were repeated attempts to make the labour regime more flexible but, as noted previously, they were quickly reversed or had no significant effect. In fact, the large fall in unemployment that followed the economy's recovery from 2003 and after happened within the context of pro-labour policies (such as the automatic doubling of severance pay because of an 'economic emergency' in the country). All in all, the labour legislation now in force is roughly similar to the one inherited from the previous period, although the degrees of protection for registered workers may be lower.

Another phenomenon that is particularly characteristic of the present stage in the labour market's historical evolution is the high level of informality. In this context informality refers to the high level of unregistered workers who enjoy no labour rights and benefits because their employment relationship is informal, with no signed employment contract. According to INDEC's last available information (4th quarter of 2006) the rate of informality was of 42.9 percent, computed as a percentage over the total number of wage earners. In Greater Buenos Aires, where one-third of the country's population is concentrated, the rate was 43.7 percent in the same quarter, while in 1991 it was 31.1 percent (FCS-UBA, 1999).

Both Beccaria (2008) and Galiani and Gerchunoff (2003) point out that one of the most relevant features of the Argentine labour market in the 1990s and even today is 'job insecurity': the extent to which the informal employment relationship has become common in the labour market has led to greater job instability. Galiani and Gerchunoff (2003) note that between 1986 and 1998 the 1-year retention rate in the first year of tenure for all jobs decreased 12 percentage points in Argentina.

Curiously, though changes in labour legislation have not been significant, working conditions have continued to worsen in recent years as informal work and associated 'job insecurity' gained greater relevance. This might suggest that existing labour legislation is diminishing in importance with regard to providing a stable and formal job for Argentine workers, although it has not apparently been an obstacle for job creation since unemployment has both risen and fallen during the actual regime. In this sense, the flexibility that policymakers were looking for during the 1990s would appear to not have come through changes in labour legislation itself, but by a progressive *de facto* deterioration in contractual status and, in turn, general working conditions for Argentine workers.

All of this happened in circumstances characterized by a notable retreat in trade union power (albeit transitory, since it is not the case currently), which was not a result of an institutional change but mostly based on a defensive attitude implemented in the face of trade liberalization during the 1990s (Cruces and Gasparini, 2008). Etchemendy and Collier (2007) nevertheless suggest that in recent years there has been a rise of what they call 'segmented neocorporatism' – that is, trade unions have regained power, but in a context of a dismal segmentation of the labour market between formal and informal workers. There have been enormous wage gains by the 'insiders' (formal workers), enlarging the gap with the 'outsiders' (informal workers).

Table 6.6 shows the composition of employment in Argentina for the last available period (2nd quarter of 2006). At least 53 percent of the people employed are in rather 'insecure' and informal jobs (this figure includes the percentage of unregistered wage earners and nonprofessional self-employed persons in addition to owners of firms that employ fewer than 6 people).

Unemployment, informality and job insecurity affect particularly young people and those with limited education. More than 85 percent of those with no high school degree 18–25 years of age are either unemployed or

Table 6.6 Employment Structure in Argentina (2nd Quarter 2006)

Type of employment	Percentage of total employment (%)
Registered wage earners	44
Owners of firms that employ more than 6 people	1
Self-employed professionals	2
'Secure' and formal employment	47
Unregistered wage earners	31
Rest of self-employed and owners	22
'Insecure' and informal employment	53

Source: Beccaria (2008), based on EPH, INDEC.

had an informal job in the 2nd quarter of 2006, and almost 75 percent of that age group, independent of their education status, were also part of that group (Beccaria, 2008). This fact is especially important because, as seen below, a large part of the workers in services exports come from that age group. Moreover, almost 40 percent of the people with a college degree are either unemployed or in 'insecure' working conditions (the percentage is 67.2 percent for those with at least high school degree but no college degree).

The growth in employment has been accompanied by an increase in real wages. On the eve of the 2001–2002 crisis, the average real wage was about the same level it had been in October 1991. The sharp rise in inflation (40 percent annually in 2002) after devaluation of the peso made real wages fall almost 30 percent by October 2002, as the nominal wages were stable in the same period. Immediately after the economy began its recovery, in late 2002, employment and real wages started to grow: by the end of 2006, real wages were less than 5 percent below their precrisis level. There is no credible information for the evolution of real wages after that date since official inflation figures have been contested. The recovery of real wages has been weaker among registered wage earners, who in 2006 were still 11 percent below the October 2001 level – partly due to the lag in wage increases in the public sector. In fact, the nominal wages paid in the private sector to registered workers were, by far, those who had the most strong increase vis-á-vis the late 2001 levels – in fact, they report a 125 percent growth in the period (INDEC, 2006). Because inflation was 90 percent between December 2001 and December 2006, actual real wages for private sector registered wage earners should have risen 18 percent. In contrast, the salaries of public sector workers grew only 45 percent in that same time period, which implies almost a 24 percent fall in their real wages.

The recent situation in the Argentine labour market can be summed up by the following features: (i) a low unemployment rate with respect to the last decade, but roughly around (or slightly above) the historical average; (ii) widespread informality and 'job insecurity' that affects 61 percent of those active in the labour market, especially young people and/or those without secondary education; (iii) rising real wages, particularly among registered wage earners in the private sector; (iv) a trade unions system still strong due to the administration of the workers' health insurance system; and (v) despite the reforms attempted in the 1990s, a limited flexibility labour regime, inherited mostly from what had been created in the 1940s–1950s.

6.3.2   Labour Legislation in Argentina

Argentine labour legislation is organized around several laws that address different aspects of labour relations. On one side, covering what is called the individual labour law, there is the Contract of Employment Law No. 20.744. On the other side, covering what is called the collective labour law, there are Law No. 23.555 for professional associations and Laws Nos. 23.545 and 23.456 for collective bargaining. There are other laws that cover both categories, such as Law Nos. 24.013, 25.013, 25.877 and also 24.557 for working accidents.

The main law in the context of this chapter is the Contract of Employment Law No. 20.744. This law (which unified previously existing and diverse legislation) was passed in 1974, though the actual text dates from 1976 when the military government limited some rights granted in the original text. The law has suffered subsequently from several changes in the ensuing years. As pointed out by Levaggi (2006), one crucial aspect of this law stipulates that the employment relationship between employee and employer begins when the former actually joins the firm and not when the contract is signed. The sole act of providing any kind of labour services to a firm supposes the existence of a contract, unless proven otherwise.

The main type of contract promoted by the law is the permanent employment contract (literally 'indefinite time' contract) (García, 2005), but other types of contracts exist: fixed-term, seasonal and work-team employment contracts. Law No. 24.013, passed in 1991, created other types of employment contracts (e.g., employment contracts for young people or for the promotion of a specific activity), which were eliminated in 1998 by Law No. 25.013. Law No. 24.465 enacted in 1995 included part-time contracts, which are actually a form of permanent contract defined as an employee working less than two-thirds of the full-time working hours in the activity.

Of notable interest in the context of this work are fixed-term and seasonal contracts. As García (2005) points out, these types of contracts are not actually emphatically promoted by the law, which, as previously noted, states that all employment contracts are permanent unless otherwise stated. The law establishes the same legal framework for both types of contracts. In each case, when the term (which can be no longer than 5 years) expires, a new contract should be signed as there is no automatic renewal of the old employment contract. Even if the date of expiry is known in advance, the employer should give notice to the employee at least a month in advance. If no notice is given in the time frame, the contract is automatically converted to a permanent one. The severance pay for fixed-term contracts includes not only the pay corresponding to a permanent contract (a month of salary for each year worked, or a fraction of 3 months) but also payments based on the general severing of the contract. This is based on the loss of future earnings, which can be calculated as the salaries to be paid until the actual expiry of the contract (García, 2005).

One subject addressed by proposed reforms to the labour law over the last two decades is the trial, or probationary, period for employees. The termination of the employment relationship after that period does not require the payment of severance. Different changes in the legislation in the 1990s had allowed the probationary period to extend up to 6 months, but Law No. 25.877, which was passed in 2004, limited this period to up to 3 months.

The Contract of Employment Law also addresses certain aspects of the working day. The law provides that the actual duration of the working day will be decided by each 'professional statute' (i.e., specific legislation for each professional activity), but establishes an implicit limit of 12 daily hours by stipulating at least 12 hours of difference between each working day. Regarding work hours at night, this law establishes that work between 9 pm and 6 am should not exceed 7 hours a day. If an activity is classified as unhealthy, the maximum duration of the working day is 6 daily hours or 36 weekly hours. Work is forbidden between 1 pm on Saturday and 12 am on Monday, though if an employee is requested to work during this period, the law requires double-time payment for each hour worked.

With regard to collective labour legislation, several laws exist. As a brief overview, the 'historical model' of Argentine collective labour relationships consisted of a great deal of State intervention (the state having the authority to both decide which trade union is able to engage in collective bargaining and to terminate strikes and labour conflicts), vast authoring over almost every aspect of the employment relationship and a trade union model based on the existence of a single union for each industrial sector (Goldin, 2001). Although this last point is not explicit in the legislation, Law No. 23.555 indicates that the sector's trade union with the status of *personería gremial* (the legal capacity to represent the sector's workers and to engage in collective bargaining) has exclusive control over almost all possible functions that correspond to a trade union (Goldin, 2001). In particular, trade unions with *personería gremial* are the exclusive representatives of the workers inside the firms, including those workers not affiliated to the trade union.[9]

Among the firms in the BPO, CCC and SIS industries, it is noteworthy that most of those interviewed for this study considered labour legislation as neither a factor favouring exports or investments, nor an obstacle to improving competitiveness (interviews, López and Ramos, 2008).

6.3.3   Employment in the Business Services Export Sector

Information about employment in the business services export sector[10] in Argentina is very limited. Although growing, business services exports are still small in comparison to inward-oriented activities. In this sense, the available statistics of employment in business services are not representative for the purposes of this study. The lack of information is particularly severe in the case of BPO services and SSC, and no studies have been yet conducted about employment in these activities. By contrast, figures about employment in CCCs are available thanks to the existence of a chamber that groups the main companies in the sector.

Based on the available qualitative research conducted for this study, the overall impression of the evolution of employment in BPO services and SSC in Argentina is that of high growth in the recent years, particularly in early 2002 after the devaluation of the Argentine peso. However, employment growth was not immediate: though some companies started as early as 2004, most companies interviewed for this study set up their BPO exports or their SSC from 2005 onward. This almost 2-year gap suggests that the decision to set up the business export activities involved in BPO and SSC (not those related to CCC, as will be seen below) was taken only after the exchange rate advantage gained in 2002 was perceived as having stabilized. This is reflected in the different rate of employment growth in both sectors during recent years: while export-oriented CCC companies employed 42 percent more people in 2007 than in 2005, BPO and SSC companies employed 72 percent more people in the same period (Table 6.7; see also Table 6.8 where it can be seen that BPO/SSC companies are those with the greatest increases in the average workforce).

Offshore BPO providers in Argentina are generally large foreign-owned companies, and their numbers are small, suggesting a great deal of concentration in this market. These companies each employ 4000–7000 people, and the share of exports in their total sales exceeds 50 percent. The growth rate of employment in these companies has been enormous: IBM, for instance, employed 3400 people in March 2005, while in October 2008 it employed around 7200. Another company interviewed for this study employed around 2500 people in 2005 and 4200 in 2008 (interviews, López and Ramos, 2008).

The major growth in employment in this sector was also possible due to the availability of a great number of professionals with skills suited for these activities. The qualifications and skills required for the export of BPO services, it should be noted, are very high compared to those required in offshore CCCs. Offshore BPO providers and the SSC industry look for graduates (or advanced undergraduates as it can take around 5 years for a university education in Argentina) mainly in accountancy, economics and business management. These disciplines are the most popular among Argentine students and according to information provided by the Ministry of Education

Table 6.7 Salaries and Employment in the Services Export Sector (sample of representative large firms)

Group	Number of firms in the sample	Year 2005		Year 2007		Change, 2005 to 2007	
		Average monthly salary (ARS)	Employment	Average monthly salary (ARS)	Employment		
BPO and SSC*	11	4939	3698	4473*	6371	-9%*	72%
SIS	18	2852	4234	4379	6966	54%	65%
Export-oriented CCCs	10	975	13,324	1280	18,974	31%	42%
Local market-oriented CCCs	13	858	3886	1141	4711	33%	21%

*This group is growing and many firms included in the 2007 sample were not present in 2005. We have not been provided wage figures for a comparable group of firms in both years, so the reported decline in average wages may be a statistical artefact derived from the sample enlargement. Changes in the skills profile of the labour force employed in this sector might also be behind the decline in average wages.
Source: Ministry of Labour and Employment, OEDE, based on SIJyP (Integrated System of Pensions).

Table 6.8   Average Workforce in the Services Export Sector (2005 and 2007) (sample of representative large firms)

Group	Average workforce		Change (%)
	2005	2007	
BPO and SSC	740	1187	60
SIS	282	457	62
Export-oriented CCCs	1332	1897	42
Local market-oriented CCCs	389	469	21

Source: Ministry of Labour and Employment, OEDE, based on SIJyP (Integrated System of Pensions).

almost 19,000 students graduated with qualifications in these disciplines in 2005, or almost 22 percent of the 87,000 students that graduated in the same year (SPU, 2006). Other disciplines such as law or medicine rank behind this group.

In spite of this, it is knowledge of the English language that constrains the availability of qualified professionals in this industry. According to experts, the number of English speakers in Argentina is relatively high compared to other countries in the region, but it still fails to be adequate in terms of quality (interviews, López and Ramos, 2008). There is no standard measurement of English proficiency in Argentina so this information is quite anecdotal, yet all those interviewed agreed with this assessment (interviews, López and Ramos, 2008). This deficiency becomes more serious as the level of English required in BPO exports is very high.

The job market for BPO and SSC has thus begun to show some signs of stress as labour supply has become scarcer. The wages in these sectors are clearly higher than the national average: in 2007, the average monthly salary in large firms of the SSC sector was about ARS 4400 (or US $1375) and ARS 4500 (or US $1405) in the BPO sector (Table 6.7); these figures should be compared with an average salary for 2007 in the private sector of ARS 2434 (or US $760). This difference may hence reflect not only the high qualifications needed in these sectors but also the growing difficulties in finding personnel in the face of the rapid expansion in this industry.

According to information obtained during our interviews, the typical profile of people employed by offshore BPO providers and SSCs appears to be the following: young (22–35 years old); men and women (men:women ratio around 1:1); a recent graduate in accountancy, economics or business management; a good knowledge of English; and middle-class social background (interviews, López and Ramos, 2008). Working in services export activities does not appear to particularly improve their social status since most of these employees already come from families that are not near being impoverished.

Working conditions in offshore BPO providers and SSC do not differ very much from the average conditions in any office-based work. The working shifts generally last 9 hours (which includes an hour for lunch) and people work 5 days a week, with weekends free. Because the main export market (the US) shares roughly the same time zone, the times of work correspond roughly to those of Argentina – that is, from 9 am to 6 pm. There are, of course, some exceptions: firms with customers on the west coast of the US may start working later, around 11 am, while those with customers in Europe may begin work earlier, around 4 am. In these special cases, some companies hire private transport to pick up their employees at their homes. The job contracts are of unlimited duration according to the general labour legislation.

One fact that concerns firms in this industry is the high turnover rate, with 20–30 percent of employees leaving their company each year. According to the employees interviewed, this may be attributed to two main factors: first, the pressures in the labour market (with wages rising steeply to about 15 percent per annum in the firms interviewed for this project,[11] although this is behind the real inflation rates) which leads to strong competition for relatively scarce human resources, and second, the nonconformism of the so-called Y generation, which includes those younger than about 27 years old (interviews, López and Ramos, 2008). Apparently, many young people are reluctant to establish long-term employment relationships with any company and aspire to be self-employed. Stress or 'burnout' from work does not appear to be a particular determinant of the high turnover rates observed in these types of firms (interviews, López and Ramos, 2008).

In face of this high turnover problem, companies carry out diverse strategies to retain their employees. Most such strategies aim to improve employee welfare. Some companies set up relaxation rooms, yoga classes, internal soccer tournaments and days free for birthdays, for instance (interviews, López and Ramos, 2008). Strategies concerning monetary bonuses are less extensive since they are generally awarded based on employee hierarchy.

The situation of employment in CCCs is very different to the one depicted in the previous discussion. The number of employees in this sector is between 45,000 and 50,000 (CICOMRA, 2007; Del Bono, 2008), although there are no precise figures about the number actually working in export activities. What is known is that around 30 percent of the sector's sales correspond to exports (Del Bono, 2008). This percentage may well represent the upper limit for a possible estimation of the share of employees in the sector working in export activities.

The recent evolution of employment in this sector shows a strong positive trend beginning in 2002, when only 6000 persons were employed. In the 2 years following the devaluation of the peso in 2002, the number of employees tripled, reaching 20,000 in 2004. Between then and 2007, that figure more than doubled again, reaching a total of 45,000 employees (Del Bono, 2008).

There are a large number of companies operating in the sector, but those that export services are in general large, foreign-owned firms – namely Teleperformance (France), Teletech (US), Atento (Spain), Apex Sykes (US) and Arvato (Germany). All these companies employ from 600 to 2500 people. Local large companies, some of which employ up to 3000 people, also have export activities, but the share of sales to foreign customers over total sales is notoriously lower than in the case of foreign-owned companies for which exports represent the main source of income. Regardless, export-oriented CCCs are, on average, the largest firms among the different types of companies in this study (and their average workforce is four times higher than that of the domestic market-oriented CCCs, followed by those dedicated to BPO and SSC (Table 6.8).

A crucial point to consider when examining wages is that the wages paid in export activities differ fundamentally according to the language in which the work is carried out, which may actually matter more than the job tasks. Wages paid for jobs in foreign languages (mainly English, but also Italian, German and Portuguese) are higher (about double) than those for jobs in Spanish (e.g., CCCs that export their services to Spain) (interviews, López and Ramos, 2008). Wages in export activities oriented to Spanish-speaking markets are roughly the same as those paid to people working for the local market. In this sense, the difference in wages arises not from the export nature of the job but from the qualifications needed to do that job, namely the knowledge of foreign languages.

The overall level of wages is lower than the one observed in BPO activities: the average monthly wage paid in CCCs oriented to the local market (a proxy for the wage of those exporting services in Spanish) was about ARS 1141 (US $356) in 2007, while the monthly wage paid to those working in export-oriented companies (mixing those working in foreign languages and those working in Spanish) was about ARS 1280 (US $400) (Table 6.7). To correctly identify the wage premium paid to foreign-language speakers, HR managers were asked about it: those interviewed estimated that the monthly wage paid for an English speaker was around 2000 ARS (US $614) for the same shift of a Spanish speaker (interviews, López and Ramos, 2008). Job contracts are in general of unlimited duration, but in some cases seasonal spikes in work require workers on fixed-term contracts.

The profile of employees in the CCC sector shows some differences depending on the language in which the activity is performed. The proportion of men to women is roughly the same and the average age is around 25–26 years old. In Spanish-speaking jobs, the employees come from a comparatively lower-class background than those of foreign-language-speaking jobs. Some employees seek their job as a means of improving their social status, while others see the job as a way of acquiring financial independence from the family while pursuing a university degree (Del Bono, 2008). The employees' educational status is, in fact, different across these two subsectors: in Spanish-speaking jobs most of the employees have attained a high school degree and nothing more, while in foreign-language-speaking jobs the prevailing status is that of undergraduate university students.

Many CCCs operate 7 days a week, 24 hours each day. The working shifts are on average 6 hours long, but there is a great deal of flexibility if the employee requests it. It is not unusual for some employees, mainly university students, to have shorter shifts of about 4 hours, while others may request longer shifts, ranging from 7 to 8 hours. In the case of foreign-language-speaking jobs, the flexibility may be even greater than in Spanish-speaking jobs, where the labour supply is obviously larger.

The percentage of employees working during the night depends on the time zone to which the service is exported. As the main destinations of exports are either the US (where different time zones are, at maximum, 4 hours behind the Argentine time zone) or Europe (5 hours ahead during the austral winter and 4 during the austral summer), the hourly distribution of employees on average does not differ from the Argentine working times.

The most important problem currently facing the sector, according to persons interviewed for this study, are high turnover rates (interviews, López and Ramos, 2008). The figures are remarkable: one interviewed call centre reported an annual rotation rate of 150 percent for its English-speaking jobs, while another call centre, specialized in providing service in Spanish for Spain, computed 100 leaves and 100 entries per month over a total of approximately 400 employees (interviews, López and Ramos, 2008).

Views vary as to the reasons behind these high rotation rates. Most of the firms interviewed for this study discarded the widespread opinion of 'burnout' syndrome as the main driver of leaving a call centre job, relying instead on motives such as the existence of good job opportunities outside the sector and, as in the case of BPO services, the nonconformism of the so-called 'Y generation' (interviews, López and Ramos, 2008). It should also be noted that working in a call centre is often seen as a first step in the industry labour market, which may be useful for later employment consideration in BPO or SIS activities. However, it could be argued that this view of the phenomenon may be biased as available literature, based on employee interviews, shows that stress and fatigue are identified as the main reason behind the high rotation rates (Del Bono and Bulloni, 2008).

Among the service activities being considered, it is only in the CCC sector where employees are evaluated online, in order to control their performance. In the other sectors, evaluations are performed mostly to make decisions regarding promotions and/or annual bonuses (as well as for learning about possible ways to improve efficiency), and they are basically an *ex post* evaluation of work.

Finally, concerning the status of unionization, there is a difference between the BPO sector and the CCCs sector. In the BPO sector, unionization is practically nonexistent, and employees lie outside of any kind of bargaining agreement (firm-based employee organizations are also nonexistent). The situation in CCCs is different: although human resources managers said that most of the employees were not affiliated with any trade union, the sector is included in the collective bargaining agreement of the Commerce trade union. The managers said that the activity was nevertheless limited, mainly due to the high turnover rates observed in the sector which undermine any possibility of gaining beyond a certain measure of support among workers.[12]

6.3.4   Employment in the SIS Sector

As in the case of business services, human capital also plays a key role in SIS exports.[13] For example, a study conducted by CICOMRA (2007) for the ICT sector in Argentina estimates that in 2006 the average ratio of total wages to sales was 55 percent. Hence, employment-related variables are crucial in determining the sector's competitiveness.

According to a study conducted by CICOMRA (2007), the total employment in the SIS sector in Argentina in 2008 was estimated to be around 55,800 jobs. This figure has been steadily rising over recent years: according to the same study, the sector employed about 37,500 people in 2006 and 46,100 in 2007, a growth of about 20 percent per annum. Tables 6.7 and 6.8 also demonstrate that employment in a representative sample of large SIS firms grew more than 60 percent both in absolute as well as in average terms between 2005 and 2008. This very rapid growth, which is similar to what happened in the business services sector, is also having a collateral consequence: increased competition for increasingly scarce resources in the labour market.

This labour shortage in the services sector in Argentina is based on a steady supply in the face of booming demand. This situation is not exclusive to Argentina, but it is based on demand from western countries. According to sector experts, the current shortage of qualified personnel would appear to challenge further growth of Argentina's SIS sector (interviews, López and Ramos, 2008).

A report prepared by the Ministry of Science, Technology and Innovation offers a good depiction of the characteristics of the labour demand in the SIS sector. First, SIS labour demand competes with two other groups of employers, private users (firms whose principal activity is not SIS-related) and state agencies (which actually pose no threat[14]). In turn, the SIS labour demand is itself divided into different groups: (i) SIS MNCs, a small group of large firms, the main activity of which is the sale of foreign software and the provision of computer and consultancy services; (ii) globalized software development companies, either local or foreign-owned; and (iii) local and regional IT companies. The firms of group (i) and group (ii) employ people with very high qualifications and often 'poach' skilled labour from group (iii), which is unable to afford the high wages offered by the other two groups. Companies in groups (i) and (ii) tend to be parts of larger global corporations that are capable of offering higher wages as their point of reference due to the fact that these costs reflect headquarters or other similar centre costs rather than the local or international labour market costs (MINCYT, 2008).

In turn, as previously noted, as the whole SIS sector faces the competition for private users it appears to be a 'relaxed territory' for IT human resources, since jobs are mainly filled and very well paid (MINCYT, 2008). Nevertheless, professional development possibilities inside these companies are limited as their main business is outside the ICT area.

The growth of IT labour demand between 2007 and 2008 is estimated by CICOMRA to be around 26,000 jobs, of which 19,300 are considered to be 'critical' or, in other words, essential for the productive process (CICOMRA, 2007). The SIS sector, as expected, appears to be particularly dependent on 'critical' IT jobs that compose the bulk of the sector's employment. The supply of IT labour, comprised of graduates from university and tertiary institutes as well as undergraduates and self-schooled people with adequate knowledge,[15] has been estimated to have grown by 12,500 people (CICOMRA, 2007). A gap of around 6800 IT staff arises from the difference between the 'critical' demand and the supply for the year 2008. According to the same study, in the period between 2007 and 2009 this accumulated gap amounted to 21,300 (CICOMRA, 2007).

Another aspect of this problem is the fact that SMEs in this sector are unable to employ people with the educational degrees they would prefer due to competition for human resources from large companies. For instance, a survey conducted by Observatorio Pyme-OPSSI revealed that SMEs would prefer that 58 percent of their employees hold a university degree or higher, while in reality 45 percent of their employees do so (Observatorio Pyme-OPSSI, 2008). On the other hand, they would prefer that 25 percent of their employees have an incomplete university or tertiary degree, while the percentage of employees that do so is around 34 percent (Observatorio Pyme-OPSSI, 2008).

The lagging supply of IT labour is due mostly to the lack of interest young people have in the IT field. López and Ramos point that this may partly be the result of flaws in secondary education, such as poor performance in mathematics in Argentine schools according to the PISA assessments (López and Ramos, 2008). According to these authors, another factor behind this situation may be the existence of imperfect information about the market labour conditions, thus failing to reflect the growing demand for IT professionals. In this sense, as seen below, sector business associations such as CESSI have been carrying out public campaigns among young people to try and change the misperceptions about the sector.

The government has been taking action to promote IT degrees to loosen this bottleneck. The main programmes aim not only to raise the number of university graduates (mainly via scholarships), but also at expanding tertiary and technical secondary education. Among the first group of initiatives, at the end of 2005 the CESSI and the Ministry of Education, Science and Technology launched the 'Invest in Yourself' ('InverTI en vos') programme, aimed at promoting new work and education possibilities in technological degrees in Argentina among high school students, relying mostly on a scholarships programme.

These scholarships include a programme (Becas Bicentenario) that would give up to 30,000 scholarships for students in the following fields: natural, agricultural and applied sciences as well as engineering and 'hard' disciplines (such as physics, mathematics and chemistry). Investment in the programme is expected to be about ARS 1.5 billion (US $470 million) during the next 5 years. Another programme in the same direction is the PNBTIC (Programa Nacional de Becas para Carreras de Grado en Área TICS), which gives scholarships to students in ICT-related degrees.

In May 2005, the Ministries of Labour and Employment, Economy and Education signed a National Training Agreement for the SIS sector. This agreement paved the way for the start of the first stage of the Professional Education National Plan for SIS Workers, including the creation of the public–private Fund for the Improvement of Computer Teaching (FOMENI). This fund aims to provide resources and evaluate and control the education programmes proposed by the diverse business and educational organizations.

Policy initiatives concerning the promotion of technical education have also been established through legislation. The programme of improvement in technical education was created following the enactment in 2005 of Law No. 26.058, and according to the latest information available from the institution in charge (INET, the National Institute of Technological Education), the investment in 2007 was ARS 270 million (US $84 million).

A public–private campaign called 'IT Generation' ('Generación TI') was recently launched, aimed at encouraging young people to pursue IT-related degrees. This campaign aims to raise awareness of the need for more professionals in the SIS sector. The campaign involves advertisements, presentations in schools and talks with professionals in order to transmit the idea that studying 'hard sciences,' engineering and applied mathematics is less difficult than what most people think. This campaign is very new, and hence its results are still not known.

The strategy being carried out by the government and some private companies to address the IT labour supply has encountered some difficulties. Some of the sector's experts point out that many IT graduates have a very good grasp of the specialization they have studied but seriously lack non-technological capabilities (e.g., management, marketing, project management). An IBM executive publicly explained to government officials in October 2008 that the sector demands increasingly 'T-shaped' human resources (i.e., people who have deep technical knowledge but also a broad view of the business). Some interviewees in this study mentioned that they found substantial differences in these kinds of capabilities depending on the educational institution from which the person graduated (interviews, López and Ramos, 2008).

Furthermore, it should be noted that some persons quoted in the study carried out by MINCYT (2008) highlighted that another problem with human resources in Argentina was 'not their deficit but their use.' This statement may have more merit than has been previously acknowledged. A study conducted by Borello et al. (2006) indicated that around 22.5 percent of the IT employees in Argentina perform tasks for which they are overqualified, while 15.4 percent perform tasks for which they are underqualified. The first group generally is comprised of self-schooled workers, while the second group consists mainly of managers over 40 years old who have obsolete technological knowledge, but nonetheless possess valuable managerial capabilities.

Working conditions do not differ according to the market orientation of the activity (i.e., exports vs. local market). Shifts generally last 8 hours, with an additional hour for lunch. The working time depends, as in the other cases, on the type of activity being performed (whether it involves real-time operations or not) and the time zone of the country of destination. Firms specialized in IT consultancy or in customized software development usually work during the standard Argentine working day (that is, from 9 am to 6 pm). Companies that provide support and maintenance services for foreign customers either operate 24 hours a day during the weekdays (sometimes the whole week) or 8 hours shifted to fit the time zone of the destination country. Job contracts are usually of unlimited duration. In this regard, some people agree with the view that Law No. 25.922, by giving SIS firms the option of using part of the labour taxes paid to reduce VAT and other national tax payments, favoured the 'formalization' of labour relationships in this sector.

The profile of the people employed in exporting firms is that most are young men around 27 years old with a recent university or tertiary degree in computer engineering, systems engineering, systems analysis and related domains. Women only represent about 24 percent of the total employment in the software sector (Castillo et al, 2007). However, it is not uncommon for many young people to abandon their university studies because they are seduced by the high wages paid in this sector, preferring instead to work full-time. This fact is a cause of concern insofar as it lowers the advanced skill levels available in the country's labour market in the long term (i.e., it is a solution for the shortage of human resources in the short run, but it could be a problem in the long run since these people do not complete their advanced-level education).

Very few of the people employed in this sector have a post-graduate degree (this is also a cause of concern as it prevents investments aimed at developing activities with a high degree of technological complexity in Argentina). Knowledge of English in this sector is usually suboptimal, which according to sector experts is a critical barrier for those involved in activities that require direct interaction with foreign customers.

As a result of high qualifications requirements and a shortage of professionals, wages in the sector are high. The constant rise in wages, above the inflation rate at least until 2007, has managers concerned about the sector's competitiveness in international markets. Undergraduates in trainee regimes are paid monthly around ARS 1500 (US $461) for a 6-hour shift, while those in a regular work may be paid up to ARS 2500 (US $769) for an 8-hour shift. This wage level was already higher than the average salary in the Argentine private sector for 2007, which paid ARS 2434 (US $760). Recent graduates have a base salary of between ARS 3000 (US $923) and ARS 3500 (US $1076). These salaries correspond to software analysts and developers. Software architects are paid from ARS 4000 (US $1230) to ARS 5000 (US $1538). In turn, the average salary paid in a sample of representative large companies of the sector was ARS 4379 (US $1368) (Table 6.7). This pattern holds true in the sector SMEs, where the average wage is about 1.7 times the average wage of industrial SMEs (Observatorio Pyme-OPSSI, 2008).

Another consequence of tension in the labour market is worker turnover. According to information obtained during our interviews, turnover rates are considerably lower than those observed, for instance, in the CCC sector, but are still high in absolute terms – around 20 percent of the employees leave their companies each year (interviews, López and Ramos, 2008). It must be noted that in this sector it is common for many employees to quit their jobs and create their own firms, so the turnover rates observed may also reflect this. However, it is probably the case that the bulk of the observed turnover is due to people leaving their jobs because they are offered higher wages.

Competition for scarce human resources is made more difficult for local SMEs, because they cannot offer the same wage levels, image or reputation that MNCs operating in the same market can provide. According to the information provided by the Ministry of Labour and Employment for a representative group of large SIS firms in Argentina, wages paid by MNCs were on average 37 percent higher than those paid by local firms (though this might be explained to some extent by a different profile of skills that are required in both types of firms).

It should also be noted that on average MNCs are much bigger than large domestic SIS firms in terms of their workforce (for the same abovementioned group of representative SIS firms, it is estimated that foreign firms employ four times more personnel than large local firms). This may help to explain why local firms are concerned about the presence of MNCs, insofar as these firms have a high demand for labour.

MNCs are sometimes blamed for adopting 'predatory' recruiting practices (e.g., offering money to employees they hire if they convince former colleagues to leave their jobs). As MNCs often attract the best employees in the first place, this practice can further limit the competitive strength of local firms. However, workers who leave do not always come up 'smelling of roses.' According to a number of local firms interviewed for this study, many employees who quit working for domestic firms in order to go work for an MNC affiliate or subsidiary, end up performing work tasks that are less technologically complex than the jobs they left (interviews, López and Ramos, 2008).

Nevertheless, all companies are concerned about high turnover and are pursuing many welfare and professional development programmes to retain their employees. Some of these organizations suggest that these programmes have been successful, reducing the turnover rates to below 10 percent (interviews, López and Ramos, 2008).

On the issue of trade union activity, the situation in the SIS sector is pretty much similar to the BPO sector. Unionization is nonexistent and there are no collective bargaining agreements because there is no trade union for the sector (firm-based employee organizations do not exist either).

6.4 Conclusions

Services exports have boomed in Argentina in recent years. This boom has been strongly associated with the offshoring of business processes, as well as with the provision of information services and software products. The rapid increase in these exports has resulted in many new jobs and has led to significant wage increases in a context of demand growing at a faster pace than the supply of qualified labour (this was especially the case for jobs directly related to ICT skills as well as for those requiring decent English or other foreign languages skills).

Although relatively low labour costs measured in US dollars was a key factor in attracting investments aimed at exporting services from Argentina, it would seem that these investments have not led towards a deterioration of employment conditions in these sectors. Of course, this does not mean that these conditions are the same as those in developed countries, but firms exporting services appear to comply with the local labour legislation (which is more aligned with the European rather than with the US labour standards) and pay higher wages than the economy's average (the exception being the CCC industry). Moreover, during interviews with HR managers of firms exporting services from Argentina, none had complaints about the local labour legislation in the country (interviews, López and Ramos, 2008). In any case, Argentine labour legislation *per se* has not appeared to be a factor limiting investments and exports from Argentina (in other words, there would appear to be no 'race to the bottom' in terms of labour standards in these sectors in recent years).

In fact, at least within the companies interviewed for this project, it can be said that employment conditions are better than Argentina's average. This is particularly the case with the increased rate of formalized labour contracts on offer in this sector, especially to young people who are often the segment of the labour market most affected by unemployment and labour market informality.

Among the sectors analysed in this study, the situation of CCCs must clearly be distinguished from that of BPO and SIS activities. Wages in the first group are notably lower than in the other two industries. Workers are seldom interested in developing a professional career in a CCC, and demanding working conditions can lead to stress or fatigue. Hence, it comes as no surprise to find that turnover rates in the CCC sector are resoundingly high.

Another difference between both groups of sectors is that trade unions have a role in CCCs (though no specific organization exists for the sector, the employees working in CCCs belong to the Commerce trade union), while unionization is almost nonexistent in BPO and SIS. A notable factor explaining this situation might be that in Argentina workers with a university degree are rarely unionized (except for special cases such as physicians working for the public sector). Trade union activity in CCCs is seemingly weak and unionization has not apparently led to better working conditions than in nonunionized activities.

Beyond the above-mentioned differences, it is worth noting that the profile of people employed in activities in this sector is clearly heterogeneous. Most people employed in the CCC sector have at most a high school degree or are university students. As stated before, it is rarely the case that these people aim to develop a professional career in the sector. In spite of this, firms do not appear to be overly concerned by the high turnover rates since the skills they need are relatively easy to find in the market (an exception to this rule are people with foreign language skills, who are offered higher wages for this skill set).

The situation is very different in the BPO and the SIS sectors. In this case, almost all employees have studied or are studying for university or tertiary degrees, and many of them have developed skills that are often scarce or specific for the firms in which they work. Hence, firms in these industries are more uneasy about turnover (especially domestic SMEs, which find it harder to retain their best workers). They compete not only through salaries and wages, but also through welfare and professional development programmes (this is specially the case for ICT professionals) as selecting and training a new employee is often costly. In turn, the situation for workers in the SIS sector also differs as they face not only the possibility of changing employment due to a better compensation offers, but are also capable of opening their own firms (spin-offs) which is not realistically feasible in the BPO and CCC sectors.

Wage increases have in any case gradually eroded a key competitive advantage for these sectors. Although the skills of Argentine workers are usually praised (and interviews made for this project were not the exception to this rule), it is rather clear that the country only began to be considered as an attractive location for exporting services after the 2001 devaluation, which strongly lowered domestic costs (not only labour ones) measured in US dollars.

In addition to the effects of the current international crisis on services exports from Argentina (firms in these sectors are worried, and perceive a deceleration of foreign demand), the rise in local costs (due to the peso appreciation in recent years combined with the aforementioned strong wage increases in the BPO and SIS industries) will make it increasingly difficult for the country to compete for investments and exports unless other competitive advantages (i.e., greater availability of specific skills and knowledge sets) are built and developed.

Hence, Argentina first needs to encourage more people to engage in careers related to these sectors (especially ICT) and dramatically improve the proficiency levels in foreign languages (particularly English). This would help to slow worker turnover and could pave the way for new investments in Argentina to take advantage of the export opportunities available compared with the international market.

In the long run, Argentina cannot rely solely on relatively low labour costs to compete in these sectors. The need to build distinctive competitive advantages remains. Beyond the need to improve on areas in which Argentina is not very well-positioned in the international offshoring rankings (e.g., business environment), it will continue to be important to provide continuity in service export activities performed in Argentina in order to carry on developing the trust of foreign investors and customers in the quality of Argentine services. Such activities have generated specific knowledge and skill sets, and further efforts along these lines can continue to reinforce this positive process, though this is not meant as an end in itself. Argentina also needs to move up the value chain in the BPO and SIS sectors, not only to consolidate its attractiveness as a location apt to provide services exports, but also to increase the level of value added of those exports. In this way, these industries will not only help to create employment for young educated people, but will also generate more spillovers in terms of human capital development and accumulation of technological knowledge within the country.

Annex: Interviews Conducted for This Chapter

- Human Resources Manager, SSC, Buenos Aires, August 19, 2008.
- Head of Human Resources Department, Software and Computer Services Company, Buenos Aires, August 29, 2008.

- Human Resources Manager, Call Center Company, Buenos Aires, September 15, 2008.
- Human Resources Manager, Software and Business Outsourcing Company, Buenos Aires, September 22, 2008.
- Human Resources Manager, Call Center Company Buenos Aires, September 22, 2008.
- Human Resources Manager, Call Center Company Buenos Aires, September 29, 2008.
- Head of Human Resources Department, Software and Computer Services Company, Buenos Aires, October 6, 2008.
- Human Resources Manager, Call Center Company Buenos Aires, October 6, 2008.
- Human Resources Manager, Business Outsourcing Company, Buenos Aires, October 10, 2008.
- Human Resources Manager, Call Center Company Buenos Aires, October 23, 2008.
- Head of Human Resources Department, Software and Computer Services Company, Buenos Aires, November 10, 2008.

Notes

1. In the call centre sector, for instance, labour costs may represent up to 75 percent of total costs (Hansen, 2007).
2. 'Companies running SSCs should regularly re-evaluate their location decisions. Therefore, it appears likely that preferred off-shoring locations will change if relative cost advantages of existing off-shore locations diminish and companies can achieve additional cost reductions by moving their SSCs to new, even cheaper locations' (KPMG, 2007, p. 4).
3. We say 'partly' because not all the transactions report the country of destination or origin For instance, according to information provided by the International Accounts National Direction of the Argentine Ministry of Economy, in 2000, 82 percent of business services exports and 71 percent of computer and information services exports reported that information, while in 2007 the figures were 51 percent and 74 percent, respectively. The fall may be a side effect of the expansion of the sample used for compiling trade statistics, although this is only a hypothesis.
4. The first component, 'financial attractiveness,' considers variables such as labour costs, taxes, regulations and so on. The second component, 'human resources,' includes work experience, qualifications and educational degrees. The third component, 'business environment,' comprises the political and economic environment, the protection of property rights and the cultural adaptation and infrastructure indicators.
5. The so-called capability maturity model (CMM), developed by the Software Engineering Institute, describes the basic practices associated with the development of trustable and reusable software that can be created according to the time and budget constraints originally established. The CMM establishes five 'maturity' (or excellence) levels for software production. In 2002, the SEI developed a new

model, called capability maturity model integration (CMMI). CMM and CMMI certifications are key credentials to compete at a global level in the SIS sector.

6. This certification is used in the BPO sector.
7. For instance, Cruces et al. (2008) report that the drastic reduction in the payroll tax from 27.5 percent in 1994 to 15 percent in 2000 had no effect on local employment creation.
8. INDEC was intervened by government officials in January 2007. According to the press and former workers of the institute that were fired after the intervention the figures of inflation, unemployment and economic growth are being forged; a judicial process is being carried out so as to clear any doubts. In the case of unemployment, after the first quarter of 2007 the basic information that allows calculating unemployment rates has not been made available publicly, hence doubts regarding the official figures have emerged. The last incontestable official information for unemployment is that of the 4th quarter of 2006, when the corresponding rate reached 8.7 percent.
9. This limited framework of trade union freedom has been repeatedly criticized by the International Labour Organization (ILO) and has recently been challenged by the Argentine Supreme Court's decision to declare unconstitutional one of the articles of Law No. 23.555, namely that only the trade union with *personería gremial* can have worker representatives in the firms. It must be noted that this is the first time in modern Argentine history that the labour relationship system has been challenged by the judicial system in such a direct way.
10. Unless other source is explicitly quoted, this section is based on primary information gathered during interviews to human resources managers of firms in this sector.
11. Since the nominal exchange rate was almost fixed during these years, this increase was practically the same in magnitude both in pesos as well as in dollars.
12. Unionization in CCCs has been a recent issue in the public agenda since there was in 2005 a great dispute between the Telephone Workers' Union and the Commerce Trade Union that triggered some strikes in Telefonica's Call Center affiliate Atento (see *La Nación*, December 4, 2005, http://www.lanacion.com.ar/nota.asp?nota_id=761928)
13. Idem footnote 10.
14. According to MINCYT (2008), state agencies are unable to compete at the wage level with other users, and its provision of human resources comes, in general, from agreements with public universities. State agencies appear to be a relatively relaxed place to work while completing undergraduate studies.
15. Many people employed in the SIS sector hold no university or tertiary degree, but have the same skills and qualifications as people who do have them. This is the result of widespread on-work training and self-schooling.

7

A Comparative Analysis of the Business Environment, Job Quality and Work Organization in Offshored Business Services

Jon C. Messenger and Naj Ghosheh

7.1 Introduction

Earlier chapters in this book described how developments in information technology-enabled services (ITES) provided by business process outsourcing (BPO) companies have played out in different countries. First, we discussed the major 'source' countries for BPO – including the US, the UK and Canada. We then examined developments in several of the most important 'destination' countries for global sourcing of ITES, or, as it is more commonly known, 'offshoring' – India, the Philippines, Brazil and Argentina (in chapter order). These four chapters identified the most important trends in ITES–BPO in each country, including the size, scope and features of those companies using remote work enabled by ICTs; the size and characteristics of the BPO 'industry' and the workforce engaged in remote work arrangements (RWAs); the organization of work and the working and employment conditions in these companies; and a few important indicators of firm performance – especially the key issue of staff turnover.

In this chapter, we attempt to synthesize the material from the various studies of individual countries and integrate it with the (limited) existing literature on the labour market and working conditions in the BPO industry. The aim will be to identify some common patterns and important differences among those developing countries with substantial BPO 'industries' – with a particular emphasis on the four BPO destination countries that are the main focus of this volume.

Following this brief introduction, the first major part of this chapter will examine a number of macro-level environmental factors that have influenced business decisions regarding the outsourcing and offshoring of business functions in ITES, and by extension, the working and employment conditions that exist in the BPO industry in destination countries. The first section of this first part will set the stage by briefly profiling the global BPO industry, considering both its industrial composition and the characteristics of the BPO workforce. Following this industry profile, the next section will analyse the labour law provisions regarding working and employment conditions that are applicable to the BPO industry in different countries, and explain why these laws have not been viewed as a barrier to industry growth. The workplace environment in the BPO industry and its implications for working and employment conditions in BPO destination countries are treated in the following section. Finally, the last section of this part will attempt to make sense of this diversity by developing a categorization of the most important types of RWAs that exist in the global BPO industry.

Moving from the macro environment down to the micro level, the second part of this chapter will examine the quality of jobs in the BPO industry. BPO jobs providing ITES are often considered to be prized jobs in many countries, although this view has been challenged in some places. This section will therefore provide a brief overview of the concept of job quality and identify the specific dimensions that will be used for an analysis of job quality in the BPO industry. The analysis will then examine the quality of the jobs in this industry in terms of the employment conditions and work organization that exist in a number of major BPO destination countries. This job quality analysis will also consider how the working and employment conditions vary by different categories of RWAs, such as call centres versus back-office work, to the extent permitted by the available data.

Following the job quality analysis, the chapter will conclude with a summary of our main findings regarding job quality in RWAs. This will set the stage for the concluding chapter, which will offer some suggestions for government policies and company practices that hold the potential to both improve job quality in RWAs and enhance the performance of BPO companies as well.

7.2 Global, National and Organizational Environments of BPO Companies

7.2.1 The Global BPO Industry: Its Industrial Composition and Workforce Characteristics

Our analysis begins by briefly profiling the industrial composition and workforce characteristics of the global BPO industry. In most countries, the BPO industry is not considered to be an industrial grouping in its own right, but rather is made up of specific segments within a number of other major industries – particularly financial services (including insurance) and telecommunications. For example, according to the Sutherland Global Survey on BPO (2007), the specific sectors that have the largest representation within the cross-cutting BPO industry are, in order of importance: insurance (43 percent), banking (28 percent), telecommunications (16 percent) and retailing (13 percent) (Sutherland, 2007, p. 7).

Although the specific proportions vary by country, this basic industrial composition is confirmed by the country studies conducted for the International Labour Organization's (ILO's) Remote Work and Global Sourcing Project. For example, Taylor (Chapter 2 in this volume) citing data from Contact Babel (2006), reports that in the US – the largest source country for BPO – four industries are the most important: finance (including insurance), retail/distribution, telecoms and outsourcing[1] account for 55 percent of all employment in the BPO industry. For the UK – the second largest source country for BPO – Taylor (Chapter 2 in this volume) reports a similar industrial breakdown for the BPO industry, albeit in a slightly different order: financial services is the largest industry (in terms of total employees), followed by telecoms, retail/distribution, utilities and transportation/travel. And in Spain, perhaps the most important non-English-speaking source country for BPO, a report by Datamonitor (2004) listed the following industries (in order) as being the most important for BPO activities: the outsourcing sector, financial services and telecommunications.

From the perspective of major destination countries for the global sourcing of business services, not surprisingly, the country studies commissioned by the ILO in developing countries reveal a very similar industrial/sectoral breakdown within their BPO 'industries.' In India, the largest destination country for BPO globally, the most important service categories include: finance and accounting, customer interaction (i.e., telecommunications) and human resource administration (D'Cruz and Noronha, Chapter 3 in this volume). In the Philippines, the second largest BPO destination country globally, the telecommunications industry is dominant with most BPO services focused on call and contact centres, although other parts of the Philippine BPO industry (e.g., accounting and medical and legal transcription services) have been growing more rapidly than call/contact centres in recent years (Amante, Chapter 4 in this volume). In Brazil, the financial services and telecommunications industries predominate, although they are largely (as noted above) serving the internal Brazilian market (Venco, Chapter 5 in this volume).[2] Argentina, although with a much smaller BPO industry, exhibits similar characteristics (López et al., Chapter 6 in this volume).

Turning now to the characteristics of those workers employed in the BPO industry, we likewise find a remarkably similar profile of the BPO workforce in very different countries. Table 7.1 provides information on the characteristics of the BPO workforce in a range of countries from different regions of the world. As can be seen from this table, perhaps the most prominent feature of the global BPO workforce is that it is extremely young: the majority of this workforce is between 20 and 30 years old. It is also predominantly female: with a few notable exceptions, such as Mexico, where the BPO work-force is mostly male, and especially India, where the BPO workforce is split between men and women (with the best available estimates suggesting a 60/40 male/female ratio), women constitute the vast majority of all workers in the BPO industry in nearly all of the countries in the table.

The other defining characteristic of the global BPO workforce is that workers in this industry also have a relatively high level of education – particularly by the standards of a developing country. Despite the nega-tive picture painted by some observers (e.g., the use of the derogatory term 'cybercoolies' to describe call centre workers in India), in all of the countries shown in Table 7.1 the typical BPO employee has at least completed a sec-ondary school education and often has some college (university) education as well. Interestingly, in the two countries with the largest BPO industries – India and the Philippines – the majority of all BPO employees are actu-ally college graduates, and typical BPO employees are college graduates in Argentina, Costa Rica, Canada and Spain as well.

Finally, in terms of languages spoken, we can see from the table that in the vast majority of countries, BPO employees use English as their primary language for work purposes. Spanish is also an important language for BPO employees in a number of countries. Moreover, the BPO workforce in those countries in Latin America serving the US market, such as Argentina, Costa Rica, Guatemala and Mexico, is bilingual in Spanish and English.

7.2.2 National Labour Laws and Their Implications for BPO Labour Markets

The growth of the BPO industry in developing countries has not taken place in a vacuum. Labour legislation and the labour market in this industry are related, as in any other sector of the economy. It is important to begin by separating out the different, but important, dimensions of labour law. One important area of labour law as it relates to the BPO industry is the employment relationship (or employment contracts) that are common in the industry. The other important dimension is the labour laws regulating the conditions of employment, such as wages, working hours, and so on, and their application in these industries. These two different dimensions of labour law can have a profound influence on the labour market, and specifically on working and employment conditions.

7.2.3 Labour Laws Governing Employment Relationships

With regard to labour laws governing employment relationships, there are different varieties that exist in different countries and that have been applied in different ways in the BPO industry, as compared to other industries. For example, the law governing employment relationships in Argentina is the Contract of Employment Law (No. 20.744), which provides that the employ-ment relationship between an employer and an employee begins when the

Table 7.1 Characteristics of the Global BPO Workforce (by country)

Country	Age Mean (Stand.Dev.)	Gender (%, male/female)	Education level (%) [Secondary /under-graduate/graduate]	Education level (modal value)	Languages
India[a]	24.5	60/40	2.7/3.2/94.6	College graduate	English
Philippines[b]	25.7	40.7/59.3	0.6/11.7/87.6	College graduate	English
Brazil[c]	18–25	23.8/76.2	N/A	High school graduate	Portuguese (with some English and Spanish)
Argentina[d]	22–35	50/50 (est.)	N/A	College graduate	English/Spanish
Chile[e]	25	25/75	N/A	—	Spanish
Costa Rica[f]	—	—	51/46/N/A	College graduate	English/Spanish
Guatemala[g]	20–25	50/50	N/A	Some college	English/Spanish
Mexico[h]	18–30	66/34	N/A	Some college	English/Spanish
Poland[i]	No data	41.6/59.4	64.5/43.4/31.6	High school graduate	German/Polish
Ghana[j]	No data	30/70	N/A	—	English/French
Australia[k]	23[l]	32.0/68.0	51.0/20.4/6.1	High school graduate	English
USA[m]	27	34/66	N/A	High school graduate	English
UK[n]	31.8	31/69	76(+3)/21/0	High school graduate	English
Netherlands***[o]	<25****	39/61	76/24/0	High school graduate	Dutch/English

Canada[p]	—	30.9/69.1	45.9/54.1/0	College graduate	English
Spain[q]	18–35**	24/76	10.2/54.6/35.2	College graduate	Spanish
Malaysia[r]	—	45/55	N/A	—	Malay/English
South Africa[s]	N/A	43/57	84(+3)/13/0	High school graduate	English

** 74.5 percent of sample.

*** Numbers reflect the data in the subcontractors category.

***** 39 percent of sample.

[a] D'Cruz, P., and Noronha, E. (2008a). *ILO Country Studies: India*.

[b] Amante, M.S.V. (2008). *ILO Country Studies: The Philippines*.

[c] Venco, S., Moriyama, J.K., and Teixeira, M.O. (2008). *ILO Country Studies: Brazil*.

[d] López, A., Ramos, D., and Torre, I. (2008). *ILO Country Studies: Argentina*.

[e] DiMartino, V. (2004). *Teleworking Start-up: Telework in Latin America and the Carribbean*. Geneva, September 2004. International Development Research Centre, Ottawa, Canada. Project #102374, 45 pp.

[f] Ernst, C., and Sanchez-Ancochea, D. (2008). *Offshoring and Employment in the Developing World: The Case of Costa Rica*. Geneva: ILO.

[g] Cuevas, M., and Bolaños, L. (2007). *Oportunidades y riesgos en la liberalización del comercio de servicios: El caso de Guatemala*. Centro de Investigaciones Económicas Nacionales (CIEN) and International Centre for Trade and Sustainable Development.

[h] Rocha Lawton, N. (2005). Traditional union organizing methods confront young workers reality: a case-study of a Mexican call-centre workforce. 23rd Annual Labour Process Conference.

[i] Piskurek, E., and Shire, K. (2005). *Callcenter in Polen*. Institut für Soziologie, Universität Duisberg-Essen, Duisberg, Germany.

[j] Ampah, M. (2008). *Providing business opportunities for women in the ITES and BPO industry: The case of eGhana*. World Bank.

[k] Australian Graduate School of Management. (2005). *The Australian Call Centre Industry: Work Practices, Human Resource Management, and Institutional Pressures*.

[l] ACTU. (2002). *On the Line: The Future of Australia's Call Centre Industry*.

[m] Batt, R., Doellgast, V., and Kwon, H. (2005a). The US call centre industry 2004: National benchmarking report, CAHRS Working Paper #05-06. Cornell University, School of Industrial and Labor Relations, Center for Advance Human Resource Studies (CAHRS), Cornell, NY, USA.

[n] Holman, D. (2002). Employee well-being in call centres. *Human Resource Management Journal*, 12, 35-50.

[o] De Grip, A., Sieben, I., and Van Jaarsveld, D. (2005). *Employment and industrial relations in the Dutch call centre sector*. Maastricht: ROA.

[p] Canadian call centre report

[q] Spanish benchmarking report

[r] Ng, C., and Mitter, S. (2005). Valuing women's voices: Call centre workers in Malaysia and India. *Gender Technology and Development*, 9, 209–33.

[s] Benner, C, Lewis, C. and Omar, R. (2007). *The South African Call Centre Industry: A Study of Strategy, Human Resource Practices and Performance*. Sociology of Work Unit, University of the Witwatersrand, Johannesburg, South Africa.

former actually joins the firm and not when the contract is signed (López et al., 2008). Thus, the provision of services to a firm by an individual assumes the existence of an employment contract, unless proven otherwise.

Argentine labour law tends to promote permanent employment contracts, but the law also addresses other employment relationships including fixed-term, seasonal and work team contracts (López et al., 2008). Nonetheless, even these latter contract types in Argentina may be more secure than similar contracts of employment found in the labour law of other countries. One example is that contracts for part-time workers, which are governed by Law No. 24.465, are actually permanent contracts in which the employee works less than two-thirds of the normal hours of a full-time work contract (López et al., 2008). With regard to these contracts, the law further provides that when the term, which cannot last for more than 5 years, expires, a new contract must be signed. Contract renewal is not automatic, but if the employer does not give 1 month's notice that the employment contract is about to expire, then the contract automatically becomes permanent. If the permanent contract is severed, then the severance pay is not only for the corresponding contract (1 month for every year worked), but there are also additional payments associated with breaking the contract and the loss of future earnings until the end of the contract (López et al., 2008).

The law covering formal employment in Brazil is codified in the Brazilian Labour Code, CLT (Decree, 5452 of August 9, 1943), which addresses employment relationships and working conditions legislation that also apply to the BPO industry. However, the situation with regard to employment relationships and the labour law in Brazil is a bit different from the one in Argentina. Due to the requirements of the Brazilian Labour Law, especially as regards the severance of employment contracts and the costs involved in terms of severance pay, companies in the BPO industry appear to have tried a number of different means to circumvent the application of the labour law and its associated costs.[3] For example, telemarketing agents in Brazilian call centres are frequently registered as telephone operators due to lower salary and benefit costs, which presumably are also less in cases of severance (Venco, 2008).

The 'coop' system in Brazil, which resembles the function performed by employment agencies in other countries, provides another approach to attempt to get around the labour law, as workers in coops are not covered by the Brazilian Labour Law (Venco, 2008). Another tactic is to hire workers in this industry through 'consultancy' firms. These 'consultancies' hire workers whom they refer to as 'consultants,' who are then assigned to a company that does ITES work (Venco, 2008). Much like employment agencies, the consultancy firm is responsible for ensuring the legal rights of, and financial obligations to, these workers, rather than the company to which they are assigned. However, if affected workers seek to address their labour rights through the consultancy, they may begin an arduous process that has been called 'Calvary,' in which the consultancy companies disappear or change partners to avoid making payments to the workers (Venco, 2008, p. 41).

As opposed to the circumstances in Brazil, there does appear to be a different perception of the labour law as it applies to the employment relationship in India. Technically, ITES–BPO employees in India are engaged on an ongoing employment contract of unlimited duration (Pengold, 2008, p. 583). However, while the Indian national government believes that the Industrial Disputes Act (IDA) of 1947, which defines 'workers' and provides them with stronger employment protection, is applicable to workers in the BPO industry, there is a different interpretation at state level. A number of state governments in India have instead used the Shops and Establishment Acts to regulate the employment conditions in this industry, which offer workers less protection than the IDA of 1947 (Noronha and D'Cruz, 2008a). The disagreement on the applicable labour legislation hinges on whether these employees fall into the category of 'workman' or can be classified differently. This has in all likelihood created some inconsistencies among different Indian states in terms of what protections are available to BPO employees, depending upon the employment relationship. In this uncertain legal situation, employers may have actually created some their own solution, since most contracts in the Indian ITES–BPO industry now include terms addressing termination and providing advance notice of 2–4 weeks; however, these contracts can also be terminated if a project ends (Pengold, 2008). Employees have a right to appeal against dismissal without reasonable cause and they may be entitled to either reinstatement or compensation, although it is left up to the employer to decide which sanction they choose to take (Pengold, 2008).

One of the main complexities in the applicability of labour law in the BPO industry in the Philippines is that both most of its BPO employers and nearly all of their customers reside outside of the country (Amante, 2008). Perhaps owing to this situation, the legislation applicable to employment relationships in the Philippine BPO industry is located in provisions of the Philippine Labour Code that address contracting and subcontracting. Article 106 of the Philippine Labour Code governs the contracting out of jobs, stipulating that ' "labour-only" contracting is where a person supplying workers to an employer does not have a substantial investment in capital or tools [...], and the workers recruited and placed by such a person are performing activities which are directly related to the principal business of such employer ([the] worker is considered an agent of [the] employer and [is] to be treated the same way as if the worker was directly employed).' This means that Philippine labour law will be applicable in BPO firms in which the work is performed by Filipino workers in the Philippines, even if the work is for a firm located overseas. This is not necessarily a variation on the employment relationships found in the labour law of the other countries noted previously, but it does clarify the employment relationship and the responsibilities of workers and employers in a type of relationship that can be unclear if it is not specifically addressed.

7.2.4   Labour Laws Regulating Working and Employment Conditions

With regard to labour laws regulating working and employment conditions, most of the same pieces of legislation are applicable to employment conditions in the BPO industry, just as they would be to workers in the rest of the economy.[4] Thus, the Argentine Contract of Employment Law, the Brazilian Consolidated Labor Law and the Philippine Labor Code all address the conditions of employment, as well as the employment relationships noted above. There are a few unique aspects in the cases of Brazil and India. In Brazil, the Brazilian Consolidated Labor Law addresses general employment conditions in the country. In addition, however, there is a Special Brazilian Regulation for Call Centres (NR 17 Standard), which was developed and implemented specifically to address working conditions (e.g., work days, rest breaks harassment) in call centres.

In the case of India, the Shops and Commercial Establishments Act is the applicable legal instrument regarding the working conditions in the BPO industry. What is unusual about India is that while the national Shops and Commercial Establishment Act has provisions addressing working conditions, most notably on working time (e.g. regulations restricting night work), exemptions have been given at state level so that companies can run around the clock (Noronha and D'Cruz, 2008a). Some states in India have further adopted a self-certification system, which means that an employer provides a written statement certifying that no employee will be deprived of the benefits extended under various labour laws, mainly in the context of compensation (Noronha and D'Cruz, 2008a) Once these 'self-certificates' are furnished to the authorities by employers, then the authorities stop routine inspections of BPO firms, although the authorities can return for an inspection if they receive complaints or it is believed that management is deviating from the applicable labour laws.

Overall, one important point to make regarding the implications of labour law for the labour market in the BPO industry is that its impact to date has been far more limited than one would normally expect. This is not to suggest that there are not violations of different dimensions of labour legislation in this industry in the respective countries. With regard to employment conditions legislation, for example, violations of working time laws have in fact taken place in this industry in a number of countries, such as exceeding daily limits on working hours in Brazil (Venco, 2008).

Yet, in spite of the existence of some violations, there is not much evidence to demonstrate that workers are pursuing their rights through legal channels. This is not necessarily because they are unable to do so, but often due rather to the scarcity of the skills required by the BPO industry and the resulting fluidity in the industry labour market in these countries. Whether in Argentina,

Brazil, India, the Philippines or other developing countries, there are short-ages of available workers with the desired skill sets for ITES work, such as being multilingual or possessing certain technical skills (e.g., accounting, engineering, computer programming, etc.). The skills required to perform ITES work require a higher degree of education and/or training than is the case in many other industries in developing countries, and linguistic and technical capabilities are essential for such work. These skill shortages have permitted workers in the BPO industry to exercise some choice as to the companies where they work. As Kuruvilla saliently points out, the issue of skills shortages is not a new one, but has happened when a new industry develops in a place that has little or no previous experience with it, such as the early development of the Japanese silk industry, the US auto industry and the period when areas in Asia such as the Republic of Korea and Taiwan (China) moved up the value chain in manufacturing (Kuruvilla, 2008). As the BPO industry matures in these countries, it will likely mean improved workforce skills, but also the need for better protection from labour laws as the supply of skilled workers increases, skill shortages decrease, and the labour market tightens.[5]

A final important factor in how the BPO labour market functions in these destination countries can to some extent be explained by the nature of the business functions that companies perform and for whom. The work done in the BPO industries in Argentina, India and the Philippines is, for the most part, performed for markets outside of these countries. There is some ITES work that is performed for domestic firms within these countries, especially in India, but for the most part the work is done for clients or organizations in industrialized countries. This common characteristic is reinforced by the paradox of Brazil: the Brazilian BPO industry, while large in size, has devel-oped mainly to serve the internal domestic market in this vast country. There has been some limited ITES work in Brazil performed for overseas clients, and where such work has taken place, it has been mainly in high-end BPO work such as telemedicine, which is one type of KPO (Venco, 2008). Nonetheless, the Brazilian BPO industry has a primarily domestic focus, and due to this orientation, the skills required are not always as high as in the other coun-tries studied in this volume. Therefore, while the Brazilian BPO industry can employ more workers, they do not typically have to be as highly skilled: the average BPO employee in Brazil has a secondary school education and speaks only Portuguese. This situation has important implications for employment conditions, as we will see later.

7.2.5 The Workplace Environment in the BPO Industry and Some Implications for Working and Employment Conditions

The workplace environment in the BPO industry can vary substantially depending on the activities and tasks being performed and to some extent on management issues (as was extensively discussed earlier in this volume). Nonetheless, call and contact centres form an important segment of the

BPO industry, and as such they provide an illustrative example of the pressures faced by some of the workers in this industry, as well as a point of comparison with workers in other segments of the industry.

The nature of the work in call centres is highly repetitive. The pace of work can vary, but is usually very demanding. This pace can be made worse in third-party offshore providers in which a vendor agreement or contract is in place requiring a fixed or a target number of calls to be made within a given period. One notable study has indicated that the average target call time in call centres globally is 3 minutes and 10 seconds (Holman et al., 2007, p. 10). To achieve such tight goals, call centre managers typically engage in intensive monitoring of the workforce, usually involving electronic monitoring systems designed to control the quality of the calls, as well as checking on compliance with established scripts and procedures. Such intensive monitoring can raise the stress levels of workers, as evidenced in research conducted in Indian call centres, which indicated that workers felt pressure based on the number of calls that they made, meeting their performance targets, the lack of turnaround time between calls and the obligation to deal with difficult individuals on the phone (Noronha and D'Cruz, 2008a, p. 69).

In sharp contrast, BPO employees working in back-office positions are not generally subject to such stringent controls. In Argentina, for example, for those BPO employees who do *not* work in call centres, 'evaluations are performed mostly to decide about promotions and/or annual bonuses [...] and then they are basically ex-post' (López et al., 2008, p. 55). Thus, we have two different types of remote work arrangements with two very different sets of working conditions – call centre functions and back-office work – with very different implications for employee stress, a subject to which we will return later in the chapter.

Managers in call centres may also tightly regulate rest breaks, lunch breaks and even toilet breaks in order to ensure sufficient coverage of the phones (Kuruvilla, 2008; Noronha and D'Cruz, 2008a; Amante, 2008). Recent research in both Brazil and India indicates that coffee/tea breaks in call centres were 15 minutes each, while lunch and dinner breaks were 30 minutes each; the timing and the duration of these breaks were strictly enforced (Venco, 2008, p. 63; Noronha and D'Cruz, 2008a, p. 7). In addition, the work of call centres in India and the Philippines is normally performed for customers in North American or European markets – which requires extensive night work as well (Noronha and D'Cruz, 2008a; Amante, 2008).

Once again, the conditions of BPO workers in back-office positions appear to be very different from those of call centre employees: none of the ILO country studies suggests that back-office workers are subject to the tight controls on rest, meal and toilet breaks seen in call centres, although their overall workloads may be just as heavy. Nonetheless, this is an important difference: relatively heavy workloads can be manageable if employees possess a sufficient level of job discretion (Karasek, 1979). In addition, given the nature of most back-office activities – which do not require 'real-time' interaction with customers – night work is generally unnecessary for those workers performing back-office work, which is also a very important difference compared with call centre work.

In addition to the stresses resulting from the use of demanding performance targets and electronic monitoring – which will be analysed in the next part of this chapter – there are two additional stressors that are common to call centre work, but which are not often considered in-depth. The first stressor appears to be specific to call centres that are serving English-speaking countries, and it concerns changing workers' accents on the phone. Because customers communicating with call centres are not accustomed to foreign accents, call centre agents are often required to change their accents to match more widely acknowledged accents in English-speaking countries (i.e., typically either American or British accents). One recent study in India noted that 58 percent of responding call centre workers underwent voice and accent training (Noronha and D'Cruz, 2008a, p. 50). Philippine call centres also go to great lengths to try and convince customers that they are not 'foreign,' often using their client's North American address if they are asked for information about their location (Amante, 2008). Maintaining these accents can be an additional source of strain for call centre agents, who must differentiate between their work accent and their home accent. It is not unheard of for this to result in forms of psychological problems (e.g. identity crisis) for workers who must constantly adjust the way they speak depending on the environment they are in.

The second additional stressor in call centre work is emotional stress. This form of stress results from performing 'emotional labour,' which can be defined as 'the effort, planning and control needed to express organizationally desired emotions during interpersonal transactions' (Morris and Feldman, 1996, p. 98). In other words, workers in call centres are expected, as part of their jobs, to demonstrate pleasant emotions at all times when engaging with customers on the other end of the phone. As indicated above, the pace of call centre work can be daunting, and under these circumstances, the requirement to constantly maintain a positive persona can be a heavy strain on workers during the course of a working day. This strain is made worse if they have to endure hostile remarks or insults from difficult customers, as has been noted by call centre agents in the ILO study for the Philippines (Amante, 2008).

While these working conditions would be challenging in the best of circumstances, they take on a new dimension when the managers or owners of the outsourced offshore call centres engage in poor or even abusive management. Poor management practices compound the stressful nature of the work and can create an unpleasant climate in the workplace and among the workforce – a phenomenon referred to by some as 'lousy boss syndrome' (Kuruvilla, 2008, p. 56). In badly managed workplaces, possibly because the owner or manager has over-promised regarding deliverables and cannot achieve the required results, workers may be required to work overtime unnecessarily, or they may not get their rest breaks in a systematic fashion. In more extreme cases, managers may even make promises that they have no intention of keeping. For example, the ILO study for Brazil highlighted instances in which call centre managers promised that if a certain level of work was achieved then the workers would get a 2-day weekend (which is a right rather than a reward according to Brazilian law); then systematically, on the day before the final day of the work week, the workers would be told that they had not reached the required performance level, and thus would not get the promised extra day off (Venco, 2008). Abusive management practices such as the one illustrated here tend to undermine morale in the short term, and may also increase the possibility of workers leaving the company, as well as undermining the quality of service that workers provide to customers.

One of the interesting paradoxes regarding the BPO industry is that, of all the skill sets required by the industry, the one that is the least talked about, but perhaps is of the greatest importance, is managerial skills. In all the developing countries highlighted in this volume, one of the most critical skill shortages in the BPO industry is for trained, experienced managers who are nationals of their respective countries. Because most managers come from companies based in industrialized countries, and the skill sets sought by companies in developing countries have been mainly linguistic or technical (as discussed earlier), there has been a critical shortage of 'home-grown' managers in destination countries. This problem is compounded by the fact that the BPO industry is so youth-oriented (as was seen in Table 7.1) and also that there is such high turnover among workers (especially in call centres); therefore, there is relatively little time to train workers to become effective supervisors (Kuruvilla and Ranganathan, 2008). The problem has best been summed up as 'trying to create 10-year-old Scotch in 2 years' (Kuruvilla and Ranganathan, 2008, p. 56).

7.2.6   Categorization of RWAs in the BPO Industry

The final section of this first part of the chapter attempts to identify the different categories of RWAs that exist within the BPO industry, which may, in turn, potentially influence the quality of the jobs in each category.

The most fundamental distinction among different categories of RWAs is between call/contact centre arrangements and IT-enabled back-office services. The former type of arrangement focuses primarily on voice-based ITES, such as inbound customer service, outbound sales and technical support, while the latter category includes a variety of nonvoice ITES, ranging from basic data entry/processing (e.g., credit card processing, payroll) to professional business services (e.g., accounting, human resources, etc.). It is quite likely that there are also important job quality distinctions within these two broad categories of RWAs, such as between technical call centre positions and other types of call centre positions, typically handling either inbound calls, outbound calls or both. The limited evidence available suggests that technical call centre jobs are typically of higher quality, particularly in terms of factors such as task complexity, variety and job discretion/autonomy (see, e.g., D'Cruz and Noronha, 2007). The back-office service RWA category is even broader, and although focused mainly on business process services (BPS), this category also includes knowledge process outsourcing (KPO), which provides services requiring domain-specific knowledge, such as R&D and market analysis.

Another important distinction among RWAs is that between ITES that are provided by offshore subsidiaries, commonly known as 'captive' units, and those delivered by third-party offshore providers. As discussed earlier in this chapter the former category consists of RWAs in MNCs in destination countries. In fact, this type of RWA, although considered part of the BPO industry, is not actually outsourced at all. On the other hand, third-party service providers (i.e., subcontractors) are companies specialized in delivering BPS; other firms outsource their business processes to these companies, which typically provide a wide range of such services to many different companies.

The final major distinction among RWAs that will be explored in the remainder of this chapter is the one between international-facing outsourcing of BPS and domestic-focused outsourcing. In this case, the main difference is simply whether or not the particular company or subunit is providing ITES primarily to customers in other countries or to customers in the same country.

We now turn to the issue job quality in RWAs, and the specific factors that will be examined in order to make a determination regarding the quality of these positions.

7.3 An Analysis of Job Quality in RWAs

In the previous part of this chapter, we reviewed and analysed the national and organizational business environments affecting the BPO industry, considering the profile of the industry across countries; the national legal frameworks applicable to this industry; and also the environment in the BPO workplace and its implications for working and employment conditions. Finally, we developed a basic categorization of the major types of RWAs that currently exist in BPO companies.

In this part, we will narrow our focus to concentrate on the quality of jobs in BPO companies, and to the extent possible given data limitations, within each RWA category identified in the previous section. The aim of this analysis will be to assemble the available evidence, in order to answer two main questions:

1. To what extent can remote work positions in general be considered to be 'good' jobs or 'bad' jobs?
2. How does the quality of BPO jobs vary by category of RWA?

7.3.1   Job Quality: A Summary of Key Literature and Its Application to RWAs in the BPO Industry

We begin our analysis of job quality in RWAs by first briefly reviewing some of the key pieces of literature regarding job quality. As the job quality literature is vast, we will concentrate primarily on those studies that are quite recent and/or have proven to be particularly influential, as well as the handful of existing studies (most of them quite recent) that have attempted to apply the concept of job quality to examine positions in the BPO industry.

At its core, job quality is a concept that refers to the extent to which the characteristics of a particular job are considered to be positive or negative from one perspective or another. Having said that, it is immediately obvious that this concept raises serious questions regarding both: (1) what job characteristics should be considered in evaluating job quality, and (2) for any given characteristic, what specific factors should be considered in order to make a determination as to whether a particular job is 'good' or 'poor' on that dimension. In general, job quality can be viewed from either a subjective perspective based entirely on the views of the employee (e.g., job satisfaction), or alternatively, from a more objective perspective, which is the more common approach and focuses on a given set of criteria for evaluating job quality.

The specific criteria that are used to evaluate job quality vary widely across individual research studies, and indeed the question regarding how to define a good job or a bad job remains unresolved, since the concept is highly dependent on the point of view from which the analysis is done. For instance, a job may be considered a good job in a particular country or labour market, but at the same time it may be classified as a bad job if it is compared with jobs in other countries or other labour markets. Certainly, the wages of BPO industry employees in India would be considered poor by the standards of developed countries, but yet (as we will see), they are actually quite high by Indian standards. Also, the quality of the same type of job (e.g., call centre operator) can be very different even in the same country, since the specific circumstances in the workplace may vary widely across employers. Moreover, the specific set of criteria used to evaluate job quality are the key determinants of what the quality results will be, and which criteria are used in any given study of job quality appears to depend largely on which social science discipline is conducting the study. The following quote succinctly captures this reality:

> Social scientists approach the study of job quality in different ways. Economists tend to focus on aspects of economic compensation such as wages or fringe benefits. [...] Sociologists generally study occupational prestige within a system of social stratification as well as the degree of autonomy and control that workers have over their jobs. Psychologists more often emphasize the noneconomic aspects of work [...] and assess the variety of psychological sources of job satisfaction. Each of these perspectives is useful but only partially so: understanding job quality requires a multidimensional approach that takes into account economic as well as noneconomic sources of variation in the goodness of jobs; these components of job quality all constitute significant foci for research. (Kalleberg and Viasey, 2005, p. 432)

Our review of the job quality literature would lead to the same conclusions.[6]

One important exception to this rule is the recent work by Francis Green (2006) on job quality in developed economies. Although Green is an economist, in that volume he takes a much more multidisciplinary approach to job quality, examining a range of different dimensions, including wages, skills, job discretion, job security, workload/work intensification and worker well-being. Along similar lines, a recent article critiquing the EU job quality indicators, the so-called Laeken indicators (Davoine et al., 2008), also calls for a multidisciplinary approach, and recommends a set of indicators focused on four main aspects of job quality: socioeconomic security, including decent wages; skills and training; working conditions; and the ability to combine work and family life, including the promotion of gender equality.

Despite the vastness of the job quality literature in general, studies focusing on job quality in the BPO industry are actually quite rare, and the few existing studies focus on call centres. The first of these studies, *The Global Call Centre Report*, considered job quality as one small component of a large-scale, comprehensive study focused on management strategies and human resource practices in call centres (Holman et al., 2007). The job quality component of that study defined job quality rather narrowly as follows: 'a high-quality job will combine high job discretion with low performance monitoring' (Holman et al., 2007, p. x). Based on this definition, the report found that around one-third of all the call centres studied had either high to very high quality jobs (32 percent) or low to very low quality jobs (38 percent). Nonetheless, overall about two-thirds of call centre agents worked in low to very low quality jobs, mainly because lower quality jobs were in the larger call centres (ibid.).

Another significant study on job quality in the BPO industry was recently undertaken in Australia. An article by these Australian researchers (Hannif

Table 7.2   Job Quality Elements for the Call Centre Context

Job Functions	Work organization	Workplace relationships/ initiatives	Protective mechanisms
Aspects of the job Identification with work	Income Work hours Work–life balance Employment status	Relationships with co-workers Managerial style and strategies Training and development opportunities	Occupational safety and health Unionization

Source: Hannif et al., 2008, Table 1, p. 277.

et al., 2008) outlines their planned research program to evaluate job quality based on company case studies in two call centres in that country. The authors' approach for assessing job quality is based on a range of job characteristics, which identify the primary elements of job quality, as outlined in Table 7.2 below.

Finally, Valvderde et al. (2007) suggest a classification of those factors that should be considered in defining job quality – essentially another job characteristics approach, only with a somewhat different set of characteristics. Valverde et al. then select a subset of five of these factors – the characteristics of the contract (the percentage of temporary employees who become full-time, permanent employees, and the percentage of employees with a permanent contract versus those with a temporary contract); job stability or security (the length of tenure of agents with a company, and the number of employees with more than 5 years of tenure with a company); access to training and career development opportunities; and gross annual salary plus benefits – and convert these factors into an index. Their results indicate that the majority of Spanish call centres are at the lower-to-middle levels of job quality on the scale established by the index. (For a complete list of the job quality factors in this classification, see Valverde et al., 2007, Table 1, p. 149.)

Based on the data and materials available for our analysis, we have decided to use a variant of these job quality frameworks for our analysis of job quality in RWAs in the BPO industry. Thus, the job quality indicators to be examined in this section will include a mix of 'hard' (objective) and 'soft' (subjective, self-reported) measures, but focus mainly on working and employment conditions, occupational safety and health and work organization and control – the latter being key issues in the BPO industry. The resulting measures are as follows:

- average wages and employee nonwage benefits;
- hours of work, work schedules and work–life balance;
- job stability, that is the length of time that employees have been in their current jobs, and job security, in terms of the characteristics of the employment contract, specifically whether it is time-limited or indefinite in length;
- various aspects of the physical working environment and workers' health and safety concerns; and
- work organization, workload and job discretion – in particular, the use of electronic monitoring and performance targets for work control, and the effects of these aspects on (self-reported) employee stress.

Throughout the analysis, any significant gender differences will be identified and (to the extent that adequate data is available) analysed, in order to determine the reasons for these differences and their potential effects on both female and male employees.

7.3.2   What Is the Quality of the RWAs in the BPO industry?

This subsection of the chapter presents an analysis of the job quality indicators identified above for RWAs in the BPO industry, mainly emphasizing those destination countries presented in the previous chapters of this volume. In addition, to the extent permitted by the available data, including from employee surveys, this analysis will also consider these same job quality indicators for the different major categories of RWAs identified in Section 2.5, which are as follows: (1) back-office business service RWAs versus positions in call/contact centres; (2) RWAs in 'captive' units of MNCs (subsidiaries) in destination countries versus those RWAs with third-party offshore providers and (3) RWA positions in international-facing outsourcing versus those RWAs in outsourcing focused on domestic markets.

7.3.3   How Much Does the Job Pay? Wages, Salaries and Employee Benefits

From the perspective of workers, it seems fairly obvious to state that their wages, salaries and nonwage benefits are fundamental conditions that help determine the quality of their jobs. For example, a substantial majority of respondents from the BPO employee surveys conducted in both India (63.6 percent) and the Philippines (62.0 percent) reported that workers' primary reason for joining their current company was a financial one (D'Cruz and Noronha, Chapter 3 in this volume; Amante, Chapter 4 in this volume).

From the perspective of workers in most BPO destination countries, the vast majority of ITES positions offer wages that are quite high by local standards. NeoIT (2006) analysed the level of salaries for 20 key destinations for the IT offshoring (ITO) industry,[7] and for both voice-based and nonvoice-based BPO. The results of NeoIT's analysis are presented in Table 7.3, which

Table 7.3 Comparison of Average Annual Wages per Agent Among BPO and ITO Destinations (US $) (2005)

Country	ITO	BPO
Brazil	15,935	13,163
Canada	43,841	34,462
China	10,095	7634
Costa Rica	21,083	17,420
Czech Republic	22,500	17,438
Hungary	25,174	21,553
India	9896	7779
Ireland	57,072	43,732
Malaysia	21,823	16,935
Mexico	22,484	17,899
Philippines	12,522	9844
Poland	29,393	24,874
Romania	15,743	12,691
Russia	21,018	16,313
Singapore	41,512	34,295
Slovakia	17,395	13,481
South Africa	36,696	29,588
Thailand	11,340	8806
Vietnam	6131	5188

Source: neoIT, 2006.

shows wide variations in wages in the BPO and ITO industries across 20 destination countries, demonstrating the substantial potential cost savings that can be achieved via offshoring; for example, the table shows that average wages for a BPO agent in India are less than one-quarter of those for an agent in Canada. Nonetheless, it is also obvious that the wage levels in these industries are relatively high by the standards of most developing countries, where it is well-known that a large proportion of the population earns under $2 a day.

The wages of BPO employees, in general, appear to be higher than the average wages in developing countries, but to confirm this situation it is necessary to compare the average salaries of BPO employees with the average salaries of all workers in the same countries. The Philippines provides an illustrative example: the average monthly salary (base pay) of a typical BPO employee in that country was only US $413 per month in 2007 (based on data from the Philippine country study), but that was 53 percent higher than the prevailing wage paid to Filipinos of the same age employed in other industries (Amante, Chapter 4 in this volume; see also Table 7.5 later in this section). Likewise, even though the average monthly salaries in the Indian BPO industry are quite low by global standards (an average of

US $346 per month in 2007, based on data from the India country study) – especially given the high level of qualifications of the Indian BPO workforce – they are nearly twice as high as the average monthly wages in other sectors in the country, which are only US $184 (ILO Wage Database, 2008). Indian BPO employee wages are also several multiples of the typical Indian State-mandated minimum wages (D'Cruz and Noronha, Chapter 3 in this volume).

The same pattern of higher-than-average wages found in India and the Philippines also holds for Argentina as well. In the Argentine BPO industry, back-office employees earn about ARS 4400–4500 (US $1374–1405) per month and call centre employees earn around ARS 1280 (US $400) per month on average, although English-speaking call centre reps earn substantially more, approximately ARS 2000 (US $614) (López et al., 2008). All of these wage figures (even for call centres) are more than the average wage in Argentina, which was US $368 in the same year (ILO Wage Database, 2008).

The exception to this general pattern in our destination countries is Brazil. While no data are available on average monthly wages for the BPO industry as a whole, a study of call centres in Brazil (De Miranda Oliveira Júnior et al., 2005, p. 8) noted that the average wages for employees in call centre RWAs in Brazil were US $4513 per year or US $376 per month – which was actually *lower* than the average monthly wage of US $450 for all workers in the country in the same year (ILO Wage Database, 2008). While the reason for this apparent anomaly is uncertain, the most likely explanation is the 'Brazilian paradox' described earlier in this chapter: the fact that, with a few notable exceptions (e.g., telemedicine), the Brazilian BPO industry serves a predominantly domestic market, and thus the skill requirements are generally less than for those workers serving international markets (Venco, Chapter 5 in this volume).

Moreover, even in Brazil, those BPO workers serving international markets earn higher salaries. For example, in São Paulo – a major hub of the Brazilian BPO industry – the average monthly salary of a telemarketing operator who is bilingual or trilingual is much higher (800 and 1000 Brazilian Reals, or approximately US $450 and US $562, respectively) than the average salary of an operator who speaks only Portuguese (which was only 559 Brazilian Reals, or about US $314)(Venco, 2008, p. 71). Thus, the BPO wage situation in Brazil suggests that one important job quality factor – wages – is likely to be higher in RWAs serving international markets, such as most BPO positions in Argentina, India and the Philippines, than in RWAs serving domestic markets, such as most of the BPO positions in Brazil.

Within the BPO industry, the wages in different types of remote work positions vary according to the skills required to perform the job and also according to the complexity of the functions performed by the worker. For example, the wages of BPO employees appear to vary by the type of remote

Table 7.4   Comparison of Annual Wages Among BPO and ITO Destination Countries, Selected Positions (2007)

Country	Average wages (US $)	Call centre representative compensation (US $ thousands)	IT advanced programmer compensation (US $ thousands)	F&A agent compensation (US $ thousands)
Chile	6552	11–13	25–27	12–17
Colombia	6408	8–10	18–20	8–12
Argentina	5268	8–10	16–19	7.5–10
Panama	5217	6.5–8.5	19–21	7.5–11
Uruguay	5137	8–10	15–18	8–11
Brazil	5028	7.5–10	25–27	10–14
Mexico	3936	10–12	25–27	11–14
Costa Rica	3864	8–10	19–21	8–12
India	2220	3.5–5	7–11.5	6–10
Philippines	1752	4–6	8–13	9–12

Source: A.T. Kearney, 2007b.

work arrangement, and a recent industry report by A.T. Kearney (2007) sheds some light on wage differences among different types of RWAs. Based on this report, Table 7.4 above provides comparative information on the average annual wages in BPO and ITO destination countries for three types of positions: call centre representative, IT advanced programmer and finance and acquisitions (F&A) agent – the latter is a fairly typical back-office position. Not surprisingly, the IT programmers received the highest annual salaries among the three groups, but it is interesting to observe that the wages of the F&A agents – that is, the group of back-office employees shown in this table – are also somewhat higher than those of the call centre reps in nearly all of the destination countries shown in this table.

An analysis of the studies commissioned for the ILO's Remote Work and Global Sourcing Project, particularly the employee surveys conducted in India and the Philippines, was conducted to determine if a similar pattern could be found.[8] In both India and the Philippines, there was no statistically significant difference in the base salaries of back-office and call centre employees, as shown in Table 7.5 below. However, in Argentina, back-office employees earn salaries three times higher than those of call centre agents, approximately ARS 4400 to ARS 4500 (US $1374 to US $1405) compared with an average of around ARS 1280 (US $400) for call centre employees (López et al., 2008).

Turning now to employee benefits, the results indicate that back-office RWAs in India are of higher quality than call centre RWAs, in that the former positions provide more extensive employee benefits. Specifically, as shown in Table 7.6 below, significantly higher proportions of back-office RWAs offer

Table 7.5 Average Salaries in the BPO Industry by Country and RWA (2007)[a]

	India			The Philippines		
	All BPO	Back office	Call centre	All BPO	Back office	Call centre
Total	346.05	343.26	350.56	413.22	418.51	390.37
Male	349.37	350.68	348.52	440.50*	438.40	440.82*
Female	339.54	354.37	331.74	393.06	373.42	398.76

* Significant at level $p < 0.01$.
[a] Data in US dollars, exchange rate as of December 31, 2007 (www.exchangerate.com).

Table 7.6 Employee Benefits in the BPO Industry by Country and RWA (2007) (percent of employees receiving benefits)

	India[a]			The Philippines[b]		
	All BPO	Back office	Call centre	Overall	Back office	Call centre
Benefits	99.2	100.0	98.7	96.7	95.3	97.0
Attendance bonus	—	—	—	41	37.5	41.9
Education subsidies	44.7	50.2	41.3	—	—	—
Incentive on sales	—	—	—	23.1	6.3**	27.2
Retirement benefits	51.2	59.5*	46.1	61.7	—	—
Meal allowance	77.9	87.6**	71.9	65.3	71.9	61.5
Medical allowance	73.6	77.1	71.4	—	—	—
Performance incentives	81.6	81.8	81.5	53.2	23.4**	60.4
Quarterly bonus	—	—	—	19.5	1.6**	23.8
Referral bonus	49.5	48.0	50.4	—	—	—
Regular salary increments	90.2	95.3**	87.1	38.0	34.4	38.9
Transport allowance	77.9	81.1	75.9	61.7	65.6	60.8

* Differences are significant using chi-square analysis at $p = 0.05$.
** Differences are significant using chi-square analysis at $p = 0.01$.
[a] Data from the India country report.
[b] Data from the Philippines country report.

regular salary increments, educational benefits and meal allowances than call centres. In contrast, in the Philippines there are only small, insignificant differences between back-office RWAs and call centre RWAs for most types of employee benefits, with the exception of performance-based incentives such as quarterly bonuses, which call centre employees in that country were *significantly more likely* to receive than those in back offices. This is a difficult phenomenon to explain – although one possible explanation is that, faced with high levels of staff turnover and so-called poaching by other firms, call centre employers may believe that providing regular bonuses are a necessary (if not sufficient) condition for minimizing staff turnover, given that (as noted earlier) the number one reason for joining a BPO company is a financial one.

Regarding other key differences in wages and employee benefits by RWA category, we found that, as anticipated, both wages and employee benefits were typically higher for 'captive' units (subsidiaries) than for third-party offshore providers, and also for international-facing RWAs compared to those RWAs focused on the domestic market. For example, for BPO employees surveyed in India, the reported salaries were substantially higher for employees working in in-house/'captive' RWAs than in third-party providers (US $399 vs. US $356), and the difference was even greater (US $375 vs. US $263) for employees in international-facing RWAs compared with domestic-focused ones. BPO employees in 'captive' RWAs earned more than those employees working for third-party providers in Brazil and South Africa as well (De Miranda Oliveira Júnior et al., 2005; Benner et al., 2007). These findings are also in line with findings from the *Global Call Centre Report,* which indicated that, on average, wages for in-house call centres were 18 percent higher than those for third-party (subcontractor) providers (Holman et al., 2007, p. viii). Regarding employee benefits, workers in in-house RWAs in India were more likely to receive education subsidies, meal allowances and regular salary increments than those working for third-party providers. Likewise, according to employee survey data from India, employees in international-facing Indian RWAs were significantly more likely to receive these same benefits than those workers in RWAs serving the domestic market; workers in international-facing RWAs were also more likely to receive retirement benefits as well.

Finally, from a gender perspective, we find a few important differences between women and men in wage and employee benefit outcomes in the countries studied. Beginning with India, we see no significant differences in that country between the salaries earned by women and men in the BPO industry. By contrast, in the Philippines, men in the BPO industry earn significantly more than women – 13 percent more – and '[b]eing female in the Philippine BPO industry means a lower wage profile, with a significantly negative coefficient, all other factors being equal' (Amante, Chapter 4 in this volume). Interestingly, however, despite (or perhaps because of?) the lower overall salaries, women workers in the Philippines are actually *significantly more likely* than men to receive regular salary increases.

7.3.4   When Do You Work? Hours of Work, Work Schedules and Work–Life Balance

Beyond wages, other employment conditions also impact job quality. Working time – that is, both the total *number of hours of work* required for the position and the *work schedules*, that is the *timing* of when those hours are required to be worked – also have profound implications for the quality of work in a specific job. In particular, it is well established that regular long hours of work have negative effects on workers' health, workplace safety and work–life balance. Many studies suggest that these negative effects begin to manifest themselves when regular working hours exceed 50 hours per week (see Note 9 and also Spurgeon (2003) for a summary of the literature).[9] It should also be noted that other studies indicate the negative impact of excessively long hours on employees' work–life balance as well:

> [T]he greatest effect of long working hours is on work–life balance: three times as many workers working long hours compared to other workers feel that their working hours do not fit in with their social and family commitments. (European Foundation for the Improvement of Living and Working Conditions, 2007, p. 9)

Moreover, the work schedule, or the timing of the work, can also have important effects: in particular, night work is well known to have potentially serious effects on workers' health (e.g., breast cancer in women) and workplace safety (depending critically upon the individual's ability to adapt to the disruption in normal circadian rhythms caused by night work), while irregular and unpredictable work schedules can result in greater interference between work and family life (see, e.g., Spurgeon 2003; Fagan, 2004).

Turning now to the actual situation regarding working time in the BPO industry, we can see that the hours of work in BPO positions appear to be quite moderate by developing country standards – where regular hours of work in excess of 50 per week are commonplace (see Lee, McCann and Messenger, 2007). Average weekly hours in RWAs in those countries that are the main focus of this volume are typically 40–50 hours per week. As can be seen from Table 7.7 below, Indian BPO positions, for example, average 46.5 hours (although working hours are slightly higher for call centre employees) and average weekly hours of BPO employees are 44.7 in the Philippines. Average weekly hours are slightly lower among BPO employees than the average for all workers in India and slightly higher for BPO employees than for all workers in the Philippines, but these differences are not statistically significant.[10] It should also be noted that there are no significant differences

Table 7.7   Weekly Hours in the BPO Industry by Gender and Type of RWA (2007)

	India[a]				The Philippines[b]			
	Work hours[c]	Mean	Back-office	Call centre	Work hours[d]	Mean	Back-office	Call centre
Total	47.2	46.49	45.64**	47.02	41.7	44.70	43.55	44.98
Men	47.1	46.64	45.75**	47.22	41.4	44.70	43.77	44.86
Women	46.9	46.03	45.22	46.45	42.1	44.67	43.30	45.07

** Significant at level $p < 0.01$.
[a] Data from ILO country study
[b] Data from ILO country study
[c] Data from Labour-related establishment survey in Laborsta, data only reflect hours in manufacturing in 2005
[d] Data from The Labour Force Survey in Laborsta; data reflect average hours of work in 2007.

in hours of work by gender that emerge from the employee surveys in these two countries.

In other destination countries, back-office employees in Argentina work 9 hours per day (including an hour for lunch, which is not typically counted as working time) and 5 days per week, with 2 days of rest on the weekends (López et al., 2007). Call centre workers in Argentina actually have more variable shifts than those in back-office RWAs, but – despite the fact that the call/contact centres themselves generally have 24/7 operations – average shifts are only about 6 hours per worker, and 'there is a great deal of flexibility at the employee's request. For example, it is not unusual for some people, mainly university students, to have shorter shifts (e.g., 4 hours) while other ask for longer ones – perhaps 7 or 8 hours' (López et al., 2007, p. 54). In Brazil, a maximum shift of 6 hours for teleoperators (excluding meal breaks), with 1 paid weekly rest day, is required by law; these shorter-than-normal work shifts are designed to help workers recuperate from the stressful nature of call centre work (Venco et al., 2008).[11]

In terms of weekly overtime hours, based on data from the country studies, overtime work in these positions also appears to be quite modest as well: it amounts to only approximately 1 hour per week (e.g., 0.97 of 1 hour per employee in India; 1.12 hours per employee in the Philippines). And the typical remote worker in the BPO industry enjoys between 1 and 2 rest days per week: an average of 1.75 rest days in India; 1.45 rest days in the Philippines; 2 full rest days in Argentina; but only 1 weekly rest day in Brazil. These figures would suggest that BPO employees in these destination countries are not typically being subjected to the excessively long weekly hours of work that are common in many industries in developing countries, such as hotels and restaurants, and the textile and garment industries (Lee, McCann and Messenger, 2007).

Table 7.8 Work Schedules in the BPO Industry by Gender and Type of RWA (2007) (in percentages)

	India			The Philippines		
	Overall BPO	Back-office	Call centre	Overall BPO	Back-office	Call centre
Day shift	25.7	27.2	24.7	14.0	43.5**	11.0
Evening shift	33.9	36.4	32.3	29.2	17.4**	37.3
Night shift	40.3	36.4	43.0	42.6	39.1**	51.7
	Overall	Male	Female	Overall	Male	Female
Day shift	25.7	25.7	25.6	14.0	14.5	17.1
Evening shift	33.9	32.5	38.7	29.2	30.8	36.6
Night shift	40.3	41.8	35.7	42.6	54.7	46.3

** Significant at level $p = 0.01$.

With regard to work schedules, however, the job quality situation in the BPO industry appears to be somewhat less favourable. As can be seen from Table 7.8, night work is relatively common in the BPO industry – affecting between one-third and one-half of all employees in both India and the Philippines. Night work disproportionately affects employees in call centre RWAs – reaching 51.7 percent of these workers in the Philippines. Although men are more likely than women to work night shifts, these differences are not statistically significant. As explained above, such common and frequent use of night work is likely to lead to employee health concerns, such as sleeping disorders or insomnia – which, in fact, affect nearly half of all BPO employees in the Philippines, particularly those working in call centres (as will be discussed later in the subsection on occupational safety and health), as well as potential safety hazards associated with increased fatigue levels. In sharp contrast, night work is not a significant concern in the BPO industry in either Argentina or Brazil because both of these countries have time zones that are much more similar to those of their customers in North America and Europe than is the case in India and the Philippines. Also, in the case of Brazil, the industry is in fact serving a largely domestic market sharing similar time zones.

In addition, irregular work schedules are quite common in BPO jobs: more than half of all BPO employees surveyed in both India (59.6 percent) and the Philippines (54.5 percent) reported that their work schedules change on either a 'moderate' or a 'frequent' basis, as shown in Table 7.9 below. As can also be seen from the table, irregular work schedules are significantly more common in call centres than in back-office work. Such frequently changing schedules at short notice are disruptive to all workers, but especially (as noted above) they can exacerbate interference between paid work and family life, as well as compounding job-related stress. Irregular work schedules

Table 7.9   Irregular Work Schedules in the BPO Industry by Type of RWA (2007) (in percentages)

	India			The Philippines		
	Overall	Back-office	Call centre	Overall	Back-office	Call centre
No change	39.0	50.7*	31.7	23.5	48.4*	17.6
Few changes	1.4	0.7	1.8	21.4	11.3*	23.8
Moderate changes	43.2	38.2*	46.3	36.2	16.1*	41.8
Frequent changes	16.4	10.3*	20.2	18.3	24.2*	16.9

* Significant at level $p < .001$.

are thus likely to be particularly problematic for those workers with family responsibilities, and given the existing domestic division of labour in nearly all countries, this disproportionately means women. Therefore, it appears that work–life balance problems are more likely to affect women than men in the BPO industry.

7.3.5   How Secure Is the Job? Job Stability and the Employment Relationship

One of the most enduring popular perceptions of the BPO workforce, particularly in call centres, is that it is highly unstable, and thus typical BPO employees have very short job tenure. And unlike many popular perceptions, the available data appear to confirm that the reality in the industry is actually quite similar to these perceptions. For instance, the *Global Call Centre Report* found that for those call centre employees studied, about one-third had less than 1 year of job tenure with their current employer (Holman et al., 2007, p. ix); from almost any perspective, this is quite a high proportion of employees with very short job tenure. Data from the country studies conducted for this report show a similar pattern: tenure with the current employer averaged only 15.8 months for BPO employees in India and 17.0 months in the Philippines (D'Cruz and Noronha, Chapter 3 in this volume; Amante, Chapter 4 in this volume); average tenure in Brazil was somewhat higher at 2.4 years; however, nearly 44 percent of BPO employees in that country had less than 1 year of tenure with their current employer (De Miranda Oliveira Júnior et al., 2005, p. 8). In India, workers in back-office RWAs have significantly longer job tenure than workers in call centre RWAs, although it is still quite short (17.0 months vs. 15.1 months), while there is no difference in tenure between these two groups in Brazil or the Philippines.

Extremely short job tenure with a specific company provides an indication that the positions in that company may be unstable, and hence that workers may lack security. The fact that project-based work – in which employment contracts are typically for the duration of a specific project – is common in call centres could be one factor affecting employees' job tenure. Nevertheless, at least two of the countries studied in this volume, Argentina and India, in accordance with applicable labour laws, offer virtually all BPO employees contracts of unlimited duration (D'Cruz and Noronha, Chapter 3 in this volume; López et al., 2008). Moreover, even where temporary workers are widely used – such as in Brazil – only 26 percent of the call centres studied use temporary workers (De Miranda Oliveira Júnior et al., 2005, p. 6).

Staff turnover in the BPO industry is endemic. One study in India reported that the average turnover rate in the BPO industry there was 50–60 percent annually (Kuruvilla, 2008, p. 51). A similar study in the Philippines found a 20–30 percent turnover rate in the BPO industry in that country (Amante, 2008, p. 64). Staff turnover rates in the call centre industry are comparatively high in all of these destination countries, with the Argentine country study reporting an annual turnover rate of 100 percent or more for some call centres in that country (Lopéz et al., 2008, p. 55).

While high staff turnover rates are common in the BPO industry in nearly all countries, especially in call centres, the factors that drive this instability appear to be quite varied. For example, age might be a factor that helps to explain the extremely short job tenure of BPO employees: BPO employees in Argentina, Brazil, India, the Philippines and other developing countries with important BPO 'industries' are typically between 20 and 35 years old (see Table 7.1 earlier in the chapter), and younger workers generally have weaker labour force attachment than prime-age and older workers. In addition, younger workers are often more willing to change jobs, in order to obtain higher salaries and/or secure a promotion.

Nonetheless, despite the youth factor, there are reasons to believe that there are also other important factors at work in the relatively low levels of job stability among BPO employees. The reasons for this high turnover are remarkably similar across the BPO industry, regardless of the country. For instance, in Argentina, many BPO workers initially seek job experience and then later seek higher compensation with another company (Lopéz et al., 2008). Poor career growth opportunities, noncompetitive compensation and high job pressures (e.g., customer demands and mistreatment by customers) were all cited as reasons for the high employee turnover rates in the BPO industry, and particularly call centres, in Brazil, India and the Philippines (Venco, 2008; Noronha and D'Cruz, 2008a; Amante, 2008).

Given the relatively high (by local standards) levels of remuneration in BPO jobs, it is difficult to imagine that wages are really the main issue here, although high demand for skilled, experienced workers by BPO employers, combined with employee concerns about lack of professional growth, may encourage those who are already in the industry to continuously seek better positions (Amante, Chapter 4 in this volume). Along these lines, Noronha and D'Cruz (2007b; see also Chapter 3 in this volume) postulate that the fact that remuneration and growth opportunities are, simultaneously, the main reasons for joining and also for leaving BPO firms, suggests that agents are 'reconciling dichotomous demands' because the positive aspects of ITES–BPO jobs in India, such as pay and employee benefits, are indeed quite attractive, but the negative aspects, such as job demands and stress, are also quite substantial. Under these circumstances, the fact that employees' ability to advance their careers, at least within the same company, is far more limited than their aspirations, may result in frustration, and ultimately, cause them to seek better opportunities elsewhere.

Thus, in this case, the limited evidence available suggests that the relatively low levels of job stability in remote work positions are not necessarily indicative of poor job quality; they may instead be due to a mix of both positive and negative factors, including health concerns (which will be discussed in the next subsection), in an overall context of tight BPO labour markets that have enabled workers to move between jobs with relative ease. Nonetheless, it should be noted that such workforce instability also results in higher costs for companies, particularly for recruiting and training new employees.

7.3.6 What Are the Conditions in the Workplace? The Physical Working Environment and Occupational Safety and Health

No review of job quality issues can be considered complete without at least some discussion of occupational safety and health (OSH) issues. The literature regarding the effects of working conditions on OSH in the BPO industry is rather limited, and nearly all of the extant literature is focused on call centres. What literature exists, however, points to several potentially important OSH issues in call centres – with stress being the most widely observed problem (see, e.g., Hannif and Lamm (2005) for a summary of the existing OSH literature related to call centres).

However, the extent to which these problems manifest themselves in a particular call centre appears to depend on a variety of firm-specific factors. Also, on a broader level, there is a question as to whether many of those OSH issues that exist for call centres are as significant in back-office operations; for example, there is no inherent reason to believe that employees in back-office RWAs should suffer from voice problems – which are an obvious OSH risk for workers in call centres. In this section, we will briefly review some important aspects of OSH in the BPO industry that are related to the physical working environment, while in the next section we will focus on psychological aspects of OSH in BPO firms – especially stress, which appears to be closely linked with the organization of work in these companies.

The main source of data on the physical aspects of OSH in the BPO industry is focused on call centres, particularly those in developed countries such as Australia and the UK. The existing literature (e.g., Hannif and Lamm, 2005; Charhotel et al., 2008; UCROT, 2000) suggests that the following types of worker health issues are prominent in call centres: visual fatigue and eye strain from spending long hours looking at video display monitors (VDMs); musculoskeletal complaints, such as back, shoulder and neck problems from sitting upright in the same position; vocal and auditory fatigue (e.g., voice problems) from alternately speaking and listening non-stop throughout the workday; repetitive strain injuries such as those from extensive keyboarding (e.g., carpal tunnel syndrome); sleep-related disorders stemming from regular night shift work serving customers in remote time zones and psychological stress (which, as noted above, will be discussed in the next section).

The broad pattern that we see in the limited data on self-reported OSH problems from the country studies is quite similar to what one would expect from the OSH literature on call centres. For example, in India, data from the country study indicates that the top health-related problems reported by BPO employees are physical strain, such as back, shoulder and neck problems (55.4 percent); sleep and related problems (33.5 percent); eye strain (22.1 percent); and voice problems (15.9 percent). In the Philippines, headaches and fatigue topped the list of BPO employees' health concerns (61 and 54 percent, respectively), followed closely by eye strain (50.5 percent); sleeping disorders or insomnia (47.7 percent); physical strain, such as neck, shoulder, chest and back pains (47.1 percent); and voice problems (33.7 percent). Along similar lines, in South Africa, interviews with Cosatu's Naledi Research Institute raised concerns that the BPO industry – although not affected by many classic OSH concerns – possesses a different set of health risks than in traditional industries such as mining (Patel and Dziruni, 2009). For example, long periods on the phone performing emotional labour can be 'mentally exhausting' – even more so if accent changes are required – and many hours spent on the phone can lead to or exacerbate back and neck problems, and may also contribute to obesity and related concerns.

In addition, the data from the ILO country case studies suggest that certain OSH issues are more likely to affect employees in call centre RWAs than those in back-office RWAs. Specifically, based on the results of the country studies commissioned for this volume, call centre workers in both India and the Philippines are significantly more likely than back-office employees to experience voice problems and sleep-related problems – the latter most likely linked with the much higher proportion of call centre employees who work night shifts (D'Cruz and Noronha, 2008a; Amante, 2008). Interestingly, eye strain is a problem that is more likely to affect back-office employees than those in call centres (although this relationship is only significant in India), which makes sense when one considers that back-office workers (e.g., accountants) in the BPO industry are typically reviewing and processing large numbers of documents.

7.3.7   How Much Pressure Is There? Work Organization, Workload and Job Discretion: The Use of Performance Targets and Electronic Monitoring, and Their Effects on Stress

The organization of work within each BPO company is another key element that affects the quality of remote work jobs. Much has been written about the application of the Taylorized, so-called mass production model of work organization to call centres (e.g., Taylor and Bain, 1999) and, more recently, of its application in Indian call centres (e.g., D'Cruz and Noronha, 2008a, D'Cruz and Noronha, Chapter 3 in this volume). The following description in the ILO country report for India (D'Cruz and Noronha, 2008a, p. 58) provides an excellent description of this view:

> Thus, barring agents working in technical call centres and higher-end back offices, the majority of respondents in our sample worked in contexts that resembled [the] mass service/engineering model [...] that emphasize[s] factory-like division of labour [...] with jobs being characterized as dead-end, with low complexity, low control, repetition and routineness. [...]

As noted in the above quotation, Indian call centres may well constitute an extreme example of this type of 'mass service/engineering model' – with certain important exceptions, such as technical call centres, which by their nature (as discussed earlier), possess high task complexity and high levels of job discretion (see D'Cruz and Noronha, 2007). However, that does not necessarily mean that this type of work organization model is dominant in call centres in all countries, much less the entire BPO industry. For example, the *Global Call Centre Report* has documented substantial differences in work organization practices in call centres for a number of countries (Holman et al., 2007).[12] To suggest that a Taylor-type 'mass production model' is the dominant form of work organization everywhere in the BPO industry, or even just in call centres, strains credulity. Nonetheless, as we shall see, this model does appear to be relatively widespread – particularly in call centre RWAs.

In the context of the BPO industry, there appear to be two key factors that affect employees' workload (i.e., their job demands) and employees' discretion in responding efficiently and effectively to those job demands (i.e., their job control). These factors are, respectively: (1) *the type and level of performance targets* that employees are required to meet and (2) *the forms and frequency of electronic monitoring* that are used by specific BPO companies. Performance targets have been widely used in call centres in developed countries such as the UK, and some influential authors, particularly Taylor and Bain (see Taylor and Bain, 1999, Bain et al., 2002), have argued that the use of performance targets in call centres to measure not only the *quantity of calls* in a given period of time, but also the *quality of employee–customer interactions* during those calls, represents 'new developments in the Taylorization of white-collar work' (Taylor and Bain, 1999, p. 115).

Not surprisingly, performance targets are also widely used in the BPO industry in all of the countries studied in this volume – especially, although certainly not exclusively, in call centre companies. For example, call centre employees in the Philippines are required to meet specified call quotas each working day, including an average handling time (AHT) per call of 5–6 minutes for customer service agents and 12–15 minutes for technical support staff (Amante, Chapter 4 in this volume). Average service time per call is also widely used as a performance target in call centres in Brazil, and in that country it has been reinforced by a colour-coding system that monitors the length of calls in real time, with the colour on the employee's video monitor changing from blue to yellow to red as the length of the call increases (Venco, 2008; Venco, Chapter 5 in this volume). And although managers in Argentina interviewed for the ILO study in that country explicitly rejected 'burnout' as an explanation for the very high turnover rates in Argentine call centres – as high as 150 percent per year in one company – Argentine studies related to this issue clearly suggest 'that stress and fatigue may be an important reason behind the high attrition rates' (Del Bono and Bulloni, 2008, as cited in López et al., 2008, p. 55).

While the extensive use of performance targets can intensify job demands, the use of electronic monitoring can substantially reduce an employee's discretion in responding efficiently and effectively to those demands – that is, it can reduce their job discretion or control. Electronic monitoring comes in two general forms: performance monitoring and behaviour monitoring (Couvert et al., 2005). Performance monitoring typically focuses on task-specific measures (e.g., number of calls taken or number of claims handled per unit of time); it can also include listening in on telephone conversations in order to determine the extent to which work procedures are being followed. Work behaviour monitoring, on the other hand, takes the form of electronic surveillance or 'eavesdropping' (e.g., unobtrusively listening in on phone conversations), and typically focuses on workers' personal behaviours in the workplace (e.g., web sites visited, number and duration of toilet breaks) – which, in turn, generates concerns about privacy (Couvert et al., 2005).

The end result of these extensive forms of monitoring and control mechanisms should logically be relatively low levels of employee job discretion. Not surprisingly, when questions about job discretion (as measured on a five-point Likert scale) were asked to BPO employees in India and the Philippines, their responses indicated mid-to-low levels of job discretion (with average scores of around 3.0 or below) on most work-related activities. As can be seen

Table 7.10   Job Discretion (5-point Likert Scale: 1 = not at all, 5 = a great deal) (Mean scores for BPO employees surveyed)

	India (N = 710)	The Philippines (N = 298)
Setting daily work tasks	2.61	3.15
Pace or speed of work	3.36	3.28
Setting breaks	2.60	2.60
Revising work methods	3.15	2.65
Handling additional requests	2.34	3.05
Settling customer complaints	2.43	3.10
Plan the work	2.89	—
Set work targets	2.63	—
Work overtime when wanted	1.93	—
Design and use of technology	—	2.87
Tools, methods and procedures to use	—	3.02

in Table 7.10, these include employees' discretion over daily work tasks, setting work targets, the pace or speed of work, break times and various other work-related activities.

The main point to emphasize here is that the BPO industry is characterized by the use of advanced technologies that permit sophisticated electronic tracking and monitoring of all stages of work activities, which, in turn, can be used to tightly control work processes and thus workers. This seems to be particularly true for call centres: for example, the Argentine country study emphasizes that among all the BPO and ITO activities that they examined in the study, 'it is only in the CCC [call centre] sector where employees are evaluated online, in order to control their performance. In the other [BPO] sectors the evaluations are […] basically ex-post' (López et al., 2008). Computer-generated data provide real-time information on agent performance (and strong motivation to respond to waiting calls), including statistics on work availability, (i.e., time logged into the system), numbers of calls taken, average length per call and total call handling time (Russell, 2002). According to Russell:

[T]he same suite of technology then is not only an information tool that is used by CSRs [customer service representatives] in responding to incoming queries, but also a source of information about agent work effort and a manufactured database that can be 'mined' by CSRs as part of their work routine. In theory at least, this technology could deliver a winning 'trifecta' for employers, a tool that provides real-time information for CSRs, on CSRs, and on consumers. (p. 38)

In addition to this quantitative electronic monitoring, qualitative electronic monitoring of BPO employees' performance is also common in voice services. Such qualitative monitoring may assume two forms. The first is side-by-side monitoring, a situation in which a supervisor 'double-jacks' with a worker and provides feedback on the calls being handled by the employee. Alternatively, remote or silent monitoring can be used. In this case, the agent may be unaware that his/her call is being listened to. Again, calls are evaluated against the desired characteristics, and feedback is provided to the worker. In the case of some call centres in Australia, for example, the work tasks monitored and displayed include a variety of factors such as the length of the phone call, the time period between calls, the degree of politeness towards customers, the content of calls, agents' adherence to scripts, adherence to established procedures and various types of customer satisfaction measures (Van Den Broek, 2002).

While performance targets and electronic monitoring can provide certain advantages for employers, they also raise serious concerns about employees' overall workload and their pace of work (work intensity). These two factors, taken together, can create constant time pressure on employees – in effect, *continuous deadlines* – which has important implications for employee stress. These implications are neatly captured in the following quotation: '[D]emanding performance standards paired with electronic performance monitoring is a recipe for stress' (Couvert et al., 2005, p. 310). This type of 'high-strain work organization,' characterized by both high job demands and low job discretion or control (European Foundation for the Improvement of Living and Working Conditions, 2007), appears to be quite common in call centres across a wide range of different countries. For example, all of the country studies summarized in this volume, including the multicountry synthesis (Taylor, Chapter 2 in this volume) analysing key developed economies that are major sources of BPO work (which covers the US, the UK, Canada and Spain), describe forms of work organization featuring a high level of job demands and relatively low levels of job discretion or control.

Along similar lines, the *Global Call Centre Report* found that two-thirds of all call centre employees worked in jobs that combined low job discretion with high levels of performance monitoring (Holman et al., 2007, p. x). This is a key issue because this 'high-strain work organization,' with its high job demands but low job discretion/control, can be expected to produce relatively high levels of job-related stress, as was first suggested by Karasek (1979).

Nonetheless, to our knowledge no study to date has attempted to look beyond call centres to see if workers in other types of BPO companies or functions – specifically, back-office operations or the emerging KPO activities – were subject to similar forms of work organization as those that appear to be widespread in call centres. However, it appears that BPO employees in back-office RWAs, and particularly those involved in KPO activities, are far more likely to work in more traditional office work environments and to be managed using less intensive methods (see, e.g., López et al., 2008). Such environments may vary substantially in the amount of job discretion accorded to individual employees; nonetheless, when one considers the typical kinds of work activities that back-office employees are performing (e.g., accounting, HR functions, etc.), it seems likely that, while these employees may have high job demands, they would be much less likely to be subjected to the kind of continuous, and often invasive, monitoring techniques typically used with call centre employees.[13]

Grounded in this perspective, two of the ILO country studies – those in the two largest BPO destinations, India and the Philippines – gathered data from BPO employees in both call centre and back-office RWAs regarding their perceptions of stress stemming from different sources. The potential sources of stress included a number of specific factors related to: interpersonal relations, specific working conditions, the organizational environment and changes (or potential changes) in the workplace. The potential stress factors that BPO employees were asked to consider and the proportions of employees reporting that they are affected by these factors are shown in Tables 7.11–7.14 below.

Although far from definitive, the results presented in these tables provide a general indication of which stress factors are the most widespread among BPO employees in India and the Philippines, and whether these factors affect call centre employees, back-office employees or both. Perhaps most importantly, they provide a basic framework for future research on the critical issue of stress in the BPO industry. Given these limitations, the results indicate that interpersonal factors, such as harassment from irate clients, distant

Table 7.11   Stress from Interpersonal Relations (percentage of employees affected)

	India ($N = 687$)			The Philippines ($N = 329$)		
	Overall	Back office	Call centre	Overall	Back office	Call centre
Harassment from irate clients	36.7	11.3**	50.2	45.6	34.4*	48.3
Distant, uncommunicative supervisor	34.2	20.9**	42.4	23.7	20.3	24.5
Excessive time away from family	29.8	23.7**	33.5	30.1	15.6*	33.6

*Significant at level $p = 0.05$.
** Significant at level $p = 0.01$.

Table 7.12 Stress from Specific Working Conditions (percentage of employees affected)

	India ($N = 722$)			The Philippines ($N = 329$)		
	Overall	Back office	Call centre	Overall	Back office	Call centre
Excessive and tedious workload	—	—	—	41.0	50	38.9
Monotony and meaningless tasks	23.8	12.0*	31.1	33.7	31.3	34.3
Regular night work	26.6	16.9*	34.2	33.4	28.1	34.7
Constant changes in work schedule	—	—	—	25.2	32.8	23.4
Infrequent or lack of discretion over breaks	21.6	7.2*	30.6	19.5	6.3*	22.6
Performance demands	50.3	37.5*	58.2	37.4	32.8	38.5

* Significant at level $p = 0.01$.

Table 7.13 Stress from the Organizational Environment (percentage of employees affected)

	India ($N = 724$)			The Philippines ($N = 329$)		
	Overall	Back office	Call centre	Overall	Back office	Call centre
Lack of autonomy	17.5	13.4*	20.1	27.1	32.8	25.7
Voiceless and inefficient communication	—	—	—	25.2	25	25.3
Multiple supervisors	—	—	—	10	7.8	10.6
Lack of bonding activities	—	—	—	36.2	31.3	37.4

* Significant at level $p = .05$.

and uncommunicative supervisors and excessive time away from family, are all important reported causes of stress among BPO employees.

Likewise, certain working conditions are also widely reported by BPO employees as factors that cause them stress. The conditions most often cited as stress-inducing include: excessive and tedious workload, monotony, regular night work and performance demands. Other factors that were frequently reported by BPO employees as causes of stress include: poor

Table 7.14   Stress from Workplace Changes (percentage of employees affected)

	India (N = 721)			The Philippines ($N = 329$)		
	Overall	Back office	Call centre	Overall	Back office	Call centre
Fear of layoff	—	—	—	14.3	12.5	14.7
Frequent personnel turnover	—	—	—	10.9	7.8	11.7
Lack of preparation for technological changes	7.9	6.2	8.9	9.7	9.4	9.8
Inadequate training	19.8	6.2**	28.1	23.7	25	23.4
Poor growth opportunities	—	—	—	36.2	40.6	35.1
Tensions brought about by colleagues	19.1	10.2**	24.6	34.3	35.9	34

** Significant at level $p = 0.01$.

growth opportunities, tensions with colleagues, inadequate training, lack of autonomy and a lack of activities to promote 'bonding' with other employees.

Interestingly, however, back-office employees appear to be less subject to stress from most of the sources identified in Tables 7.11–7.14, both in India and the Philippines. For example, workers in back-office RWAs are less likely to experience stress from interpersonal relations than workers in call centres. Back-office employees are also significantly less likely to report stress from specific working conditions, including monotony, regular night work and performance demands in India, and significantly less likely to feel stressed by infrequent breaks or lack of discretion over breaks in both India and the Philippines. Finally, although this applies only to India, employees in back-office RWAs are significantly less likely to experience stress from a lack of autonomy, inadequate training or tensions brought about by colleagues.

In terms of gender, there were actually very few stress factors in either India or the Philippines about which significant differences were observed between men and women. This may well be due, at least in part, to the low sample sizes of the employee surveys, particularly in the Philippines. Nonetheless, as shown in Table 7.15 below, the only factors that showed significant differences by gender in the proportions of workers affected were those regarding stress from the following working conditions: regular night work, infrequent breaks or lack of discretion over breaks and performance demands. A significantly larger percentage of female employees than male employees reported experiencing stress from those three factors, but only in India.

Table 7.15 Stress from Specific Working Conditions and Gender (percentage of employees)

	India (N = 722)			The Philippines (N = 329)		
	Overall	Male	Female	Overall	Male	Female
Excessive and tedious workload	—	—	—	41.0	40.6	41.2
Monotony and meaningless tasks	23.8	24.0	23.3	33.7	38.3	30.9
Regular night work	26.6	16.9**	34.2	33.4	32.3	34.5
Constant changes in work schedule	—	—	—	25.2	28.6	22.7
Infrequent or lack of discretion over breaks	21.6	19.6*	28.0	19.5	21.8	18.0
Performance demands	50.3	47.9*	57.7	37.4	32.8	38.5

* Significant at level $p = 0.05$.
** Significant at level $p = .01$.

7.4 Conclusion: Summary of Job Quality in the BPO Industry

Based on the analysis presented in this chapter, we find that, overall, the quality of the jobs in the BPO industry in developing countries and in particular the working and employment conditions that exist in remote work positions in the destination countries examined in this volume are generally better than the quality and conditions of typical jobs in the same countries. In other words, in the developing country context, remote work positions are 'good jobs' overall – in stark contrast to similar jobs in many developed countries – albeit with some potentially negative aspects, such as high levels of stress, in particular for certain types of RWAs such as those in call centres. This is perhaps not so surprising when one considers how the governments in various developing countries have worked to attract the sourcing of ITES functions, particularly from multinational corporations based in the major source countries.

Within the BPO industry, as expected, we find a few important distinctions in job quality between different types of RWAs. First, we find that back-office RWAs are typically of higher quality – that is, they have better wages and working conditions – than call centre RWAs. This important difference in the quality of jobs between the two major categories of RWAs in the BPO industry appears to be due both to the generally higher skills and qualifications required for many back-office positions, as well as to the extensive use of performance targets and intensive electronic monitoring in call centre functions – which, in turn, is reported as higher employee stress levels on a number of factors.

Second, we find that job quality in terms of wages and working conditions in 'captive' unit (in-house) RWAs are typically superior to similar positions with third-party service providers – a conclusion that has already received considerable empirical support for call centre RWAs (see e.g. Holman et al., 2007). This situation is likely due, at least in part, to the contractual agreements between companies sourcing ITES functions and third-party offshore providers, and the myriad management issues (which were discussed in the Introduction to this volume) that are likely to arise in such contracts – exacerbated by the critical shortage of experienced managers in the BPO industry in many developing countries.

Finally, we also observe that those RWA positions 'facing' international markets, such as the US, UK and Spain, appear to have better quality jobs, including substantially higher wages and better working conditions, compared with those RWAs focused on domestic markets. This is likely to be the result of the higher level of skills (e.g., languages) required in international-facing positions. Perhaps the most striking example of this situation is the 'Brazilian paradox': unlike other BPO destination countries studied, the Brazilian BPO industry is mainly focused on the domestic market, and therefore, its skill requirements are lower and its job quality (e.g., wages) is below average overall, particularly for domestic call centre positions.

Thus, we conclude that remote work positions in the global BPO industry are, for the most part, 'good jobs.' Nonetheless, many of these positions do have certain negative aspects that need to be addressed. In the final chapter, we will consider what government policies and company practices can help to address these concerns, as well as their broader implications for improving job quality in developing countries.

Notes

1. In the US, Spain and some other countries, outsourcing is now considered to be a separate industry in its own right.
2. It should be noted that ITO service providers in Brazil (e.g., software firms) are more likely to be serving customers in other countries than BPO service providers in that country. However, as noted earlier, the focus of this volume is on the business process services provided by the BPO industry, not IT services.
3. The cost of labour litigation is called the 'Custo Brasil' by employers, which refers to the cost of litigating labour disputes with workers in the courts. Disputes can include those over wages, working hours and other conditions, as well as severance payments.
4. It should be noted that some sectors and industries, such as agriculture, may have their own specific legislation governing working and employment conditions in the sector/industry.
5. Economic downturns, such as the current global economic crisis, can be expected to have a similar effect on the BPO labour market from the demand side.

6. An initial draft of this literature review was prepared by Austin Akers in December 2008.
7. The IT Outsourcing (ITO) 'industry' is not a primary focus of this volume.
8. Descriptions of the methodology used for the manager and employee surveys conducted in India and the Philippines are presented in the chapters summarizing these two country studies.
9. Multiple studies regarding health agree that the negative impacts of regular long hours include both short-term and long-term effects (NIOSH, 2004). Acute reactions involve physiological responses such as increased levels of stress, fatigue and sleeping disorders as well as unhealthy behavioural responses such as smoking, alcohol abuse, irregular diet and lack of exercise. Long-term effects include an increased incidence of cardiovascular disease, gastrointestinal and reproductive disorders, musculoskeletal disorders (MSDs), chronic infections and mental illnesses (Caruso et al., 2004, 2006). In addition to these health implications, it is clear that work schedules that regularly involve extended hours decrease workplace safety, as the risk of occupational accidents and injuries rises with increasing length of the work schedule – which obviously is also costly to enterprises (Dembe et al., 2005; Johnson and Lipscomb, 2006).
10. Data on average work hours in India from the Indian Labour-related establishment survey in Laborsta; data only reflect average work hours in manufacturing in 2005 (the closest year for which data were available). Data on average hours in the Philippines from the Philippine Labour Force Survey in Laborsta; data reflect average hours in 2007.
11. However, this report also notes that operators who work in the morning shift are frequently 'invited' to work extra hours in the evening shift, which is busier, but that this overtime work often exceeds the legally mandated limit of 2 hours of overtime per working day (Venco et al., 2008).
12. Not surprisingly, call centre employees in Continental European countries tend to report higher levels of employee job discretion than those in either liberal market economies (e.g., the UK, the US) or in developing counties. Surprisingly, however, liberal market economies actually fare *worse* than developing ones in terms of reported levels of job discretion.
13. As discussed earlier, employees in technical call centres constitute an important exception.

8
Conclusion

Implications for Government Policies and Company Practices

Jon C. Messenger and Naj Ghosheh

8.1 Introduction

Throughout this volume, we have seen that remote work in information technology-enabled services (ITES) has been growing rapidly along with the global business process outsourcing (BPO) industry. Obviously, as noted in the Introduction, the global economic crisis that swept over the world beginning in the autumn of 2008 has profoundly impacted economies and employment in nearly all countries around the world. Nonetheless, the underlying fundamentals that have driven the growth of the global BPO industry – the business imperative to continuously reduce costs; the availability of skilled workers in developing countries at much lower salaries and the desire for access to emerging markets – seem unlikely to change in the near-term, and will most likely accelerate when the global economy recovers.

Moreover, service sector work is undoubtedly the wave of the future in most developing countries. One of the most dramatic changes in the structure of the world's economy over the last 30 years has been the profound 'tertiarization' in the nature of economic activity – that is, the substantial increase in the size of the service sector, particularly in terms of employment.

It is well-known that the sectoral composition of employment in developed countries has shown a strong and continuing secular increase in the service sector's share of total employment. What is less well understood, however, is that this broad historical trend towards an increasing share of employment in services also applies in a wide array of developing countries as well. In fact, a wide range of countries from all over the world witnessed an increase in the size of their service sectors between 1980 and 2000.[1] As is shown in Table 8.1, this includes countries as diverse as Brazil, Egypt, Hungary, Malaysia, Mexico, Namibia and the Philippines. While not all countries have followed this trend, it is clear nonetheless that the

Table 8.1 Share of Total Employment in the Service Sector in Selected Countries (in percentages) (1980, 1990 and 2000)

	1980	1990	2000
Industrialized Countries			
Canada	66.1	71.3	74.1
France	55.4	67.6	73.9
Japan	54	58.2	63.1
Switzerland	55	63.6	69.1
United States	65.9	70.9	74.5
Transition Countries			
Bulgaria	32.9	37.3	45.5
Czech Republic	39.1	42.2	54.8
Hungary	N/A	53.65[a]	58.7
Romania	26.3	27.4	31
Asia			
China	11.7	9.5	12.9
Malaysia	38.7	46.5	49.5
Pakistan	26.8	28.9	33.5
Philippines	32.8	39.7	46.5
Africa			
Egypt	35.7	40.1	49.1
Kenya	55.4	60.5	61.9[b]
Namibia	37.2	29	56
Americas			
Brazil	46.1[c]	54.5	59.2[c]
Chile	65.4[d]	55.5	62.2
Colombia	64.6	67.7	73.3
Ecuador	62[e]	66.3	67.6
Jamaica	N/A	54[f]	60[f]
Mexico	24.1	39.6	55.2

Source: Lee, McCann and Messenger, 2007, Table 5.1, p. 88. Data presented in this table were originally drawn from ILO, *Key Indicators of the Labour Market*, Third Edition, Geneva, Switzerland 2003.
[a] For Hungary, the 1990 figure in fact corresponds to 1992.
[b] For Kenya, the 2000 figure in fact corresponds to 1999.
[c] For Brazil, the 1980 and 2001 figures correspond to 1981 and 2001, respectively.
[d] For Chile, the 1980 figure in fact corresponds to 1982.
[e] For Ecuador, the 1980 figure in fact corresponds to 1988.
[f] For Jamaica, the 1990 and 2000 figures correspond to 1991 and 1998, respectively.

service sector represented nearly half of total employment in many developing countries back in 2000, and it is likely to constitute an even greater proportion of total employment today. Moreover, many of the services industries are also major sources of female employment (e.g., education, health services, retail trade, hotels and restaurants) – and, as we saw in Chapter 7, the global BPO industry is an important and growing source of employment for women as well.

The growing share of service sector employment in developing countries, combined with the importance of services employment for women workers, makes developments in the BPO industry a potential forerunner of future developments in service sector employment in these countries. Moreover, as we saw in Chapter 7, remote work positions in the global BPO industry are, by and large, relatively 'good jobs' in the developing country context. Indeed, there are some positive practices in this industry that merit replication – such as wage levels that are typically far above the minimum wage and reasonable weekly hours. Nonetheless, many remote work positions also do possess certain aspects that have negative implications for working and employment conditions. Government policies and company practices designed to address these factors hold the potential not only to improve working and employment conditions in the BPO industry, but also to serve as models of good practice for the service sector in developing countries.

8.2   Key Factors Affecting Employment Conditions and Possible Responses

8.2.1   Business Strategy Issues

The first set of key factors affecting working and employment conditions in the BPO industry are related to the business strategies of BPO companies. In particular, the relationship, including communications, with the offshore 'captive' unit (subsidiary) or third-party offshore provider, and also the provisions of the vendor agreements or contracts used with third-party providers, are all factors likely to affect working and employment conditions, and hence the quality of BPO jobs.

For example, a detailed contract may establish specific guidelines and rules, including specific deliverables – which may even include specific performance targets. While clear guidelines and deliverables are essential for a successful contractual relationship, if these are unrealistic or too prescriptive, they create enormous pressures on downstream managers to deliver on these targets, regardless of circumstances. On the other hand, if loose or task-based contracts are used, problems may occur if there is any misunderstanding regarding the requirements of the contract between the parties; if this is the case, expectations for delivery will be in a constant state of flux. This latter situation can also complicate the delivery of the ITES function and create substantial pressures on managers to resolve the resulting problems. And, as noted earlier, in either circumstance the so-called rule of organizational gravity applies: Whatever problems affect managers will soon become issues for workers as well.

As was discussed in Chapter 7, offshoring business functions requires managers from both the sourcing organization upstream and the downstream subsidiary or third-party offshore provider to communicate regularly regarding the work performed, how it is delivered, and also to sort out any problems that are encountered. It is essential that these relationships be managed positively and with constant and effective communication. Managers in the sourcing organization need to bear in mind that managers downstream play a key role, not only in the delivery of the service function, but also in managing the workforce to deliver upstream. Clarity of communication, sufficient technical expertise, and being realistic in terms of deliverables, time frames and any specific performance targets can bring benefits for all the parties involved – including better working and employment conditions for workers in offshore operations.

8.2.2 Management Practices

Closely related to business strategy issues are the management practices in the BPO industry and their effects on working and employment conditions. As discussed in Chapter 7, the problems that arise during the ongoing relationship between a company and its offshore subsidiary or third-party provider can have significant consequences for the working and employment conditions in the downstream organizations. For example, if offshore managers (whether in a 'captive' unit or a third-party offshore provider) either have to satisfy unrealistic deliverables and/or performance targets or do not have a clear understanding of what ITES business functions are to be delivered and how they are to be delivered, they may be inclined to ask for greater efforts from the workforce to compensate. Under these circumstances, managers might also increase workloads or increase the monitoring of workers in an attempt to achieve these unrealistic or fluctuating targets, which can in turn raise the stress levels of the workforce; this situation is made even worse if the targets are not adequately explained to workers. This problem and some possible solutions will be further discussed in the section on work organization issues later in this chapter.

Another problem that can arise from this situation is that it can create role ambiguity – unclear or conflicting roles and/or responsibilities for workers in BPO organizations. Role ambiguity for workers occurs when they struggle to provide effective responses to unpredictable circumstances or lack certainty regarding the consequences of the performance of their work tasks (Pearce, 1981). While a range of possible solutions to this problem exist, perhaps the most basic one is to ensure, first, that all employees are provided with information regarding the company's structure, purpose and practices, and, second, that all employees have clear, detailed job descriptions (Leka et al., 2004) that are free of any gender-related or other structural biases.

Of course, the fundamental underlying problem here, particularly in third-party offshore providers, is the lack of experienced, 'home-grown' managers.

There is a pressing need – not only in the BPO industry, but also in most industries in the developing world – to develop managers, including team leaders and other first-line supervisors, and provide them with management training to impart the skills required for effective management. This management skills training should include the following subjects: contracts management; human resource management and team building; labour law, industrial relations and collective bargaining; systems development; health and safety issues; and change management (for some useful suggestions, see Paul and Huws, 2002).

Obviously, management practices are also closely linked to other key factors affecting working and employment conditions in BPO companies. These other key factors, which will be discussed below, include the following: pay and career development issues working time and work–life balance issues and work organization issues.

8.2.3   Pay and Career Development Issues

As we saw in Chapter 7, a substantial majority of respondents from the BPO employee surveys conducted in both India and the Philippines reported that their primary reason for joining their current company was compensation. With the notable exception of Brazil, wages and other compensation in the BPO industry exceed the average wages in the BPO destination countries studied: they are far above minimum wage levels and appear sufficient to ensure that BPO employees can live a comfortable, middle-class lifestyle.

Nonetheless, career development has been a major concern for the BPO industry. For example, in the Philippines, the main reasons that BPO employees voluntarily left their jobs were noncompetitive compensation, lack of professional growth and high stress. And in India, the top reasons that employees left their previous BPO jobs were quite similar: remuneration, poor growth opportunities, high job demands and concerns about work–life balance. Given the relatively high (by local standards) levels of remuneration in BPO positions, compensation *per se* seems unlikely to be the key factor; rather, as was discussed in Chapter 7, the combination of employees' concerns about the lack of professional growth opportunities, the relative youth of the workforce and the high demand for skilled, experienced workers, may encourage those workers already in the industry to continuously seek better positions.

The offer of competitive wages, along with the implementation of human resources practices for the recruitment and selection of BPO employees, commissions and other kinds of benefits, such as contributions towards a pension fund and health coverage, has an immediate impact on the attraction and retention of highly qualified workers (Castilla, 2005). This is particularly the case in the BPO industry, given that compensation is the No. 1 reason for joining a BPO company. The next step is to move beyond pay and other forms of compensation to create career ladders that enable

BPO employees to have opportunities to advance into higher-level positions in BPO companies, as well as offering ongoing training and development courses that enable employees to enhance their existing skills and develop new ones as well. Given the high levels of employee turnover and employers' concerns about losing experienced workers, some type of a shared, industry-wide training facility would appear to make a great deal of sense in the BPO context.

8.2.4   Working Time and Work–Life Balance Issues

As discussed in Chapter 7, weekly hours of work in the BPO industry tend to be quite reasonable in the context of the developing world. Rather, it is various problems with work schedules that are the key working time factors affecting job quality in BPO firms.

The most significant work scheduling issues in the BPO industry fall into three categories: night work, infrequent or irregular rest breaks and irregular work schedules. Night work, as discussed in Chapter 7, is associated with serious effects on workers' health, including sleep-related disorders stemming from regular night shift work serving customers in remote time zones. Night work is well-known to have potentially serious effects on workers' health (e.g., breast cancer in women) and workplace safety (see e.g., Spurgeon, 2003). As will be recalled from Chapter 7, night work is a much more important concern in call centre remote work arrangements (RWAs) than in back-office positions. It is also a much more widely used in countries serving customers in more distant time zones, such as India and the Philippines. In these cases, the ideal solution – avoiding night work altogether – may simply not be feasible for voice services provided from such remote locations, since these services must be provided to customers in 'real time.' Nonetheless, there are a wide range of measures that can be implemented to help protect the health and safety of night workers, such as regular health checkups, many of which are specified in the ILO Night Work Convention, 1990 (No. 171), and accompanying Recommendation. Strong protections for night workers should be a cornerstone of government policies (including appropriate regulations) and company practices in the BPO industry.

The second work scheduling issue concerns infrequent or irregular rest breaks. Once again, this is a factor that mainly seems to affect call centre employees, rather than those in back-office work. In such cases, automated call distribution systems in BPO companies need to be designed to ensure that workers can have 'reasonable flexibility' in the timing and frequency of their breaks (see, e.g., Paul and Huws, 2004). There is also a need for government policies (including appropriate regulations) to ensure that all BPO employees receive at least certain minimum rest periods both during the working day and between shifts – a practice common in national labour laws. By contrast, as was discussed in Chapter 7, weekly rest periods in the BPO industry in the destination countries studied nearly always meet, and often exceed, the 24-consecutive-hour standard of the ILO Weekly Rest (Commerce and Offices) Convention, 1957 (No. 106).

The final work scheduling issue identified by the comparative analysis is irregular and unpredictable work schedules. As discussed in Chapter 7, substantial portions of BPO employees report moderate or frequent changes in their work schedules, and (as noted earlier) such irregular schedules can result in greater interference between work and family life, and thus create substantial challenges for work – family reconciliation (see, e.g., Fagan, 2004). In this case, suggested good practices include a range of flexible working time arrangements that provide workers with a degree of choice, or at least, influence, regarding their work schedules; this may include, for instance, assigning shift schedules based upon workers' working time preferences, in order to allow them to better accommodate their personal needs (Boulin et al., 2006). It is also crucial to provide workers with as much advance notice of their shift schedules as possible, in order to allow them to have sufficient time to plan for how they will handle their family and other personal responsibilities.

8.2.5   Work Organization Issues, Including Ergonomics

As we saw in Chapter 7, work organization issues lie at the very core of job quality in the BPO industry. Generally high and variable workloads underpinned by performance targets, relatively low levels of job discretion (particularly in call centres) with tight rules and procedures enforced via electronic monitoring and often monotonous and unpleasant work tasks (e.g., dealing with difficult customers over the phone), together constitute a tailor-made recipe for stress-related hazards.

On this score, however, it is important to emphasize one of the major conclusions of Chapter 7 – that back-office RWAs are typically of higher quality; that is, they have better wages and working conditions than call centre RWAs. This important difference in the quality of jobs between the two major categories of RWAs in the BPO industry appears to be due both to the generally higher skills and qualifications required for many back-office positions, as well as the much more extensive use of performance targets and intensive electronic monitoring in call centre functions – which, in turn, is reported as higher employee stress levels on a number of factors.

Given this important caveat, the most obvious set of potential solutions to these issues revolves around a redesign of work processes – especially in call centre RWAs – in order to allow BPO employees more discretion to make effective use of their considerable qualifications. A study prepared by the Institute of Work, Health & Organisations (Leka et al., 2004) for the World Health Organization (WHO) recommends a four-pronged approach to work redesign. These four components are as follows: (i) changing job demands, either by changing the work process or sharing the workload differently; (ii) ensuring that employees have the job-specific knowledge and skills for the tasks that they are performing; (iii) expanding employees' control over their work, such as consulting workers regarding the development and operation of performance management and monitoring systems and (iv) increasing the support provided to employees (both in quantity and quality), such as by providing training for managers in 'people management' and encouraging teamwork (Leka et al., 2004, p. 18). These actions to redesign work processes can be usefully complemented by stress management training and related measures.

In some cases, there are also significant ergonomic issues that are related to physical health problems, such as those reported in Chapter 7: visual fatigue and eye strain from spending long hours looking at video display monitors (VDMs); musculoskeletal complaints (e.g., back, shoulder and neck problems) from sitting upright in the same position; vocal and auditory fatigue (e.g., voice problems) from alternately speaking and listening non-stop throughout the workday; and repetitive strain injuries, such as those from extensive keyboarding (e.g., carpal tunnel syndrome). Addressing these ergonomic issues may require changing the layout of work stations or adapting existing ones to minimize or eliminate the underlying factors affecting workers' health. Proper accessories such as ergonomic chairs, tables, keyboards and VDT screens are essential to ensure the protection of workers' health.

8.2.6 Skill Requirements and Shortages, Job Stability and Staff Turnover

Last, but certainly not least, there is the issue of the high rates of staff turnover in the BPO industry. Such high levels of attrition represent a real problem for BPO firms, even though the turnover rate is generally less than in developed countries such as the US, where the attrition rate in call/contact centres is between 25 percent and 45 percent, and in some cases might be close to 100 percent annually (Castilla, 2005). As we saw in Chapter 7, this situation is related to the shortages of skilled workers in the BPO industry in many developing countries, and it has been further exacerbated by the phenomenon of industry clustering – that is, the existence of a few major BPO 'hubs' in each destination country. The costs of such high levels of employee turnover to employers can be very high, particularly in terms of increased recruitment and training costs. On the other side of the coin, job instability can also be a concern for employees as well – particularly if it is driven by the desire to escape poor working conditions, as may well be the case in many call centres (see the discussion of work organization in the preceding section).

A range of potential solutions to the staff turnover issue in the BPO industry have been proposed. For example, call centre training is mostly seen as a complement to previous skills, and consequently, both BPO firms and employees could benefit from training investments because they could help satisfy workers' career development needs and also reduce turnover rates (Sieben et al., 2006; Amante, Chapter 4 in this volume). Another approach, which was proposed by Castilla (2005), is to use a social referral network to help reduce the high rates of staff turnover in call centres. Under this type of scheme, workers are paid to recommend other individuals that they know for a specific position. With such personal referrals, potential workers have a more realistic idea about the positions for which they are applying, and they may also enjoy the job more if they could work with a friend in the same company. Finally, as noted earlier, competitive wages can help to decrease staff turnover rates and can even contribute towards raising worker productivity.

Finally, and most importantly, in the context of high staff turnover in the BPO industry, it is notable that there is a nearly complete absence of any form of worker organization or social dialogue of any kind in the BPO destination countries studied in this volume.[2] The BPO country studies reveal what appears to be a generally negative attitude towards unions among BPO employers and managers in all the destination countries studied in this volume. There is a certain irony in this view given that research in Brazil (De Miranda Oliviera Júnior et al., 2005) and South Africa (Benner, et al., 2007) has suggested that greater levels of unionisation may actually be associated with lower levels of turnover, which is one of the most significant staffing problems for these companies. The chapters on both India and the Philippines (Noronha and D'Cruz, Chapter 3 in this volume; Amante, Chapter 4 in this volume) also document the lack of company mechanisms that facilitate employee participation in firm decisions, such as problem-solving groups, emphasizing that such mechanisms can improve employee morale and performance and reduce staff turnover. Thus, there is a clear need for policies and practices in the BPO industry aimed at improving the workers' collective voice and promoting social dialogue in the industry, which ultimately would benefit both workers and employers alike.

8.3 Concluding Remarks

At various times the global BPO industry has been heralded as the wave of future knowledge work in a service and information economy, and alternatively, demonized as a 'brave new world' of electronic sweatshops and 'cybercoolies.' The reality, as one might imagine, is far more complex. Following this wide-ranging analysis of the global BPO industry, we can conclude that this industry has been generating jobs that are of reasonably 'good' quality by local standards in terms of their working and employment conditions – and which governments in many developing countries have actively sought to promote – but which nonetheless have certain negative characteristics. Therefore, in this chapter, we have also offered some suggestions for government policies and company practices that can make these jobs even better, while also helping to reduce staff turnover. The BPO 'industry' could then offer a model for a future of good quality service sector jobs and high-performing companies in the global economy.

Notes

1. It should be noted that this increase in the size of services as a share of total GDP is, in part, a statistical phenomenon arising due to outsourcing. This situation occurs because, if a particular service is provided within a manufacturing company, it is counted as manufacturing value-added in national GDP, but when it is outsourced, the very same service is then counted as services value-added in GDP.
2. The trade union UNITES in India is a notable exception: it has reached collective agreements with six BPO companies in that country (Penfold, 2008).

Bibliography

Abramo, L. 2007. *A Inserção da Mulher No Mercado de Trabalho: Uma Força de Trabalho Secundária?* Doctoral Thesis, University of São Paulo.

AEECCC (Associación Española de Expertos en Centro de Contacto con Clientes). 2007. *Primer Estudio de Offshore Latinoamérica.* Available at http://www.mundocontact.com/boletines/estudio_offshore_izo_2005.pdf.

Alonzo, P. 1998. Les rapports au travail et à l'emploi des caissières de la grande distribution. Des petites stratégies pour une grande vertu ['The work relationships of checkout operators: minor strategies for a major virtue']. In: *Travail et Emploi,* Vol. 76, pp. 37–51.

—— 2000. *Femmes et Salariat: l'inégalité dans l'indifférence.* Paris: L'Harmattan.

Alves, G. 2002. Trabalho e sindicalismo no Brasil: um balanço critico da 'década neoliberal' (1990–2000). In: *Revista Sociologia e Politica.* Curitiba, Brazil, pp. 71–4.

Amante, M. 2008. *Outsourced Work in Philippine BPOs.* ILO Conditions of Work and Employment Programme, unpublished report.

Anton, J. 1999. *Call Centre Performance Benchmarking Report.* West Fayetteville, IN: Purdue University.

Antunes, R. 1999. *Os Sentidos do Trabalho.* São Paulo: Boitempo.

—— 2006. *Riqueza e Miséria do Trabalho No Brasil.* São Paulo: Boitempo.

Aron, R., and Singh, J.V. 2005. Getting offshoring right, *Harvard Business Review,* December 2005, pp. 135–43.

Arora, A., and Athreye, S. 2002. The software industry and India's economic development, in *Information Economics and Policy,* Vol. 14, No. 2, pp. 253–73.

Australian Graduate School of Management (AGSM). 2005. *The Australian Call Centre Industry: Work Practices, Human Resource Management, and Institutional Pressures. National Benchmarking Report, 2005.* Sydney: AGSM and Hallis, Pty Ltd.

Azucena, Cesario A. 2006. *The Labor Code with Comments & Cases.* Manila: Rex Book Store.

Bain, P., and Taylor, P. 2002. Ringing the changes? Union recognition and organisation in call centres in the UK finance sector, *Industrial Relations Journal,* Vol. 33, No. 2, pp. 246–61.

Bain, P., and Taylor, P. 2008. No passage to India? Initial responses of UK trade unions to callcentre offshoring, *Industrial Relations Journal,* Vol. 39, No. 1, pp. 5–23.

Bain, P., Watson, A., Mulvey, G., Taylor, P., and Gall, G. 2002. Taylorism, targets, and the pursuit of quantity and quality by call centre management, *New Technology, Work, and Employment,* Vol. 17, No. 3, pp. 170–85.

Baldry, C., Bain, P., Taylor, P., Hyman, J., Scholaros, D., Marks, A., Watson, A. Gilbert, K., Gall, G., and Bunzell, D. 2007. *The Meaning of Work in the New Economy,* Basingstoke: Palgrave.

Banco Mundial. 2004. *Fazendo Com Que a Justiça Conte.* Relatório No. 32789-BR.

Banerjee, D. 2006. Information technology, productivity growth, and reduced leisure: revisiting the end of history, *Working USA: The Journal of Labour and Society,* Vol. 9, No. 2, pp. 199–213.

Bardhan, A., and Kroll, C.A. 2003. The new wave of outsourcing, *Fisher Center for Real Estate & Urban Economics Research*, Report Series No. 1103, University of California-Berkeley, Fisher Center for Real Estate and Urban Economics, October 2003.

Barnes, A. 2007. The construction of control: the physical environment and the development of resistance and accommodation within call centres, *New Technology, Work, and Employment*, Vol. 22, No. 3, pp. 246–59.

Bastos Tigre, P., and Marques, F. 2007a. Aspectos económicos del software e implicancias para Latinoamérica, in: P. Bastos Tigre (ed.), *Oportunidades y Desafíos para la Industria del Software en América Latina*, Comisión Económica para América Latina (CEPAL), Oficina de Buenos Aires, Argentina.

Batt, R., Doellgast, V., and Kwon, H. 2005a. *The US Call Centre Industry 2004: National Benchmarking Report*, Ithaca, NY: Cornell University.

—— 2005b. *Service Management and Employment Systems in US and Indian Call Centers*. Ithaca, NY: Cornell University.

Batt, R., Doellgast, V., Kwon, H., Nopany, M., Nopany, P., and Da Costa, A. 2005c. *The Indian Call Centre Industry: National Benchmarking Report*. Ithaca, NY: Cornell University.

Batt, R., and Monihan, L. 2002. The viability of alternative call centre production models, *Human Resource Management Journal*, Vol. 12, No. 4, pp. 14–34.

Beccaria, L. 2008. El mercado de trabajo luego de la crisis. avances y desafios. In: Kosacoff, B. (ed.): *Crisis, Recuperación y Nuevos Dilemas: La Economía Argentina, 2002–2007*, CEPAL Oficina de Buenos Aires, Argentina.

Becker, G.S. 1993. *Human Capital: A Theoretical and Empirical Analysis with Special Reference to Education (3rd edition)*. Chicago: University of Chicago Press.

Belt, V. 2002. Women and social skill and interactive service work in telephone call centres, *New Technology, Work, and Employment*, Vol. 17, No. 1, pp. 20–34.

Benner, C., Lewis, C., and Omar, R. 2007. *The South African Call Centre Industry: A Study of Strategy, Human Resource Practices, and Performance*. Johannesburg, South Africa: The Link Centre and the Sociology of Work Unit, University of the Witwatersrand.

Beshouri, C., Farrell, D., and Umezawa, F. 2005. Attracting more offshoring to the Philippines. *The McKinsey Quarterly*, October 24, 2005.

Bicalho, L. 1978. *O Sindicalismo Bancario em São Paulo*. São Paulo: Simbolo.

Blinder, A.S. 2006. Offshoring: the next Industrial Revolution? *Foreign Affairs*, Vol. 85, No. 2, pp. 113–28.

Boltanski, L., and Chiapello, E. 1999. *Le nouvel esprit du capitalisme*. Paris: Gallimard.

Boulin, J.Y., Lallement, M., Messenger, J., and Michon, F. (eds.). 2006. *Decent Working Time: New Trends, New Issues*. Geneva, ILO.

BPAP. 2009. *What Next? The Philippine IT–BPO Industry*. Manila: Business Process Association Philippines.

Bristow, G., Munday, M., and Griapos, P. 2000. Call centre growth and location; corporate strategy and the spatial division of labour, *Environment and Planning A*, Vol. 32, No. 3, pp. 519–38.

Buchanan, R., and Koch-Schulte, S. 2000. *Gender on the Line: Technology, Restructuring and the Reorganisation of Work in the Call Centre Industry*, Ottawa, ON: Status of Women Canada.

Budhwar, P., Varma, A., Singh, V., Dhar, R. 2006. HRM systems of Indian call centres: an exploratory study, *International Journal of Human Resource Management*, Vol. 17, No. 5, pp. 881–97.

—— 2009. Work processes and emerging problems in Indian call centres. In: Thite, M., and Russell, B. (eds.), *The Next Available Operator: Managing Human Resources in the Indian Business Process Outsourcing Industry* (pp. 59–82). New Delhi: Sage.

Caïazzo, B. 2000. *Les centres d'appels: les nouveaux outils de la relation client*. Paris: DUNOD.

Carroll, W., and Wagar, T. 2009. Strategic human resources management in outsourced call centres in India and Canada. In: Thite, M., and Russell, B. (eds.), *The Next Available Operator: Managing Human Resources in the Indian Business Process Outsourcing Industry*. New Delhi: Sage, pp. 279–305.

Cassen, B. (ed.). 2007. Les dossiers de la mondialisation. *Le Monde diplomatique*, Vol. 91, Janvier–Février.

Castilla, E. 2005. Social networks and employee performance in a call center, in *American Journal of Sociology*, Vol. 110, No. 5, pp. 1243–83.

Castillo, J.J. 2007. *El Trabajo Fluido En La Sociedad De La Informacion: Organizacion Y Division Del Trabajo En Las Fabricas De Software*. Buenos Aires: Miño y Davila.

Castillo, V., Novick, M., Rojo, S., and Tumini, L. 2007. Gestión productiva y diferenciales en la inserción laboral de varones y mujeres: estudio de cuatro ramas de actividad. In: Novick, M., Rojo, S., and Castillo, V. (eds.). *El Trabajo Femenino en la Post-Convertibilidad: Argentina 2003–2007*, Comisión Económica para América Latina (CEPAL), Oficina de Buenos Aires, Argentina.

CCC. 2007. *Contact Centres in Canada: The Implications of Current Trends in Human Resources*, Ottawa, ON: Contact Centre Canada.

Centre for Spatial Economics. 2004. *Customer Contact Centres in Canada: An Employment Profile*, Milton ON: The Centre for Spatial Economics.

Cetrángolo, O., Heymann, D., and Ramos, A. 2008. Macroeconomía en recuperación: la Argentina post-crisis. In: Bernardo Kosacoff (ed.), *Crisis, Recuperación y Nuevos Dilemas: La Economía Argentina, 2002–2007*, CEPAL Oficina de Buenos Aires, Argentina.

Chandrasekhar, C.P., and Ghosh, J. 2007. Recent employment trends in India and China: an unfortunate convergence? *The Indian Journal of Labour Economics*, Vol. 50, No. 3, pp. 383–406.

Charbotel, B., Croidieu, S., Vohito, M., Guerin, A.-C., Renaud, L., Jaussaud, J., Bourboul, C., Imbard, I., Ardiet, D. and Bergeret, A. 2008. Working conditions in call-centres, the impact on employee health: a transversal study. Part II. In: *International Archives of Occupational and Environmental Health*, DOI 10.1007/s00420-008-0351-z.

Chesnais, F. 1996. *A Mundialização do Capital*. São Paulo: Xamã.

Chesnais, F., Duménil, G., Lévy, D., and Wallerstein, I. 2003. *Uma Nova Fase do Capitalismo?* São Paulo: Xamã.

CICOMRA. 2007. *Situación y Perspectivas del Capital Humano TICC En Argentina.*, CICOMRA: Buenos Aires.

Clark, E.E. 2007. Characteristics of work organization in UK and Philippine call centres, *Team Performance Management*, Vol. 13, No. 7–9, pp. 227–43.

Coase, R.H. 1937. The nature of the firm. *Economica*, NS, Vol. 4, No. 4, pp. 386–405.

Cohen, L., and El-Sawad, A. 2007. Accounting for 'us' and 'them': Indian and UK customer service workers' reflections on offshoring, *Economic and Political Weekly*, Vol. 42, No. 21, pp. 1951–57.

Contact Babel. 2006. *North American Contact Centres in 2006: The State of the Industry*, Contact Babel: Sedgefield, UK.

Contact Centre Canada. 2005. *Canadian Contact Centre Survey*, Ottawa.

Couto, V., Mani, M., Lewin, A., and Peters, C. 2006. *The Globalization of White-Collar Work: The Facts and Fallout of Next-Generation Offshoring*, Chapel Hill, NC: Duke University's Fuqua School of Business and Booz Allen Hamilton.

Couvert, M.D., Thompson L.F., and Craiger, J.P. 2005. Technology. In: Barling, J., Kelloway, E.K., and Frone, M.R. (eds.), *Handbook of Work Stress*. Thousand Oaks, CA: Sage.

Cowie, C. 2007. The accents of outsourcing: the meanings of neutral in the Indian call centre industry, *World Englishes*, Vol. 26, No. 3, pp. 316–30.

Cruces, G., and Gasparini, L. 2008. *A Distribution in Motion: The Case of Argentina*, CEDLAS Working Paper No. 78, La Plata, Argentina: UNLP.

Communications Workers of America (CWA). 2004. *The Hollowing Out of America: A Labor Perspective on Outsourcing and Offshoring*, CWA: Washington, DC.

—— 2005a. *Outsourcing and CWA: A Discussion*, Washington, DC.

—— 2005b. *Keeping Customer Service Work*, Washington, DC.

—— 2007. *Telecom News*, Washington, Vol. 67, No. 4 (October–November).

D'Cruz, P., and Noronha, E. 2006. Being professional: organizational control in Indian call centres, *Social Science and Computer Review*, Vol. 24, No. 3, pp. 342–61.

—— 2007. Technical call centres: beyond 'electronic sweatshops' and 'Assembly lines in the head, *Global Business Review*, Vol. 8, No. 1, pp. 53–67.

—— 2008. *Remote Work and Global Sourcing of Information Technology–enabled Services, Country Studies, India Final Report*. ILO Conditions of Work and Employment Programme, unpublished report.

—— 2008. Doing emotional labour: the experiences of Indian call centre agents, *Global Business Review*, Vol. 9, No. 1, pp. 131–47.

Datamonitor. 1999. *Opportunities in US and Canadian Call Centre Markets: The Definitive Vertical Analysis*, New York.

—— 2004. *Call Centres in Spain: Industry Profile*, New York.

—— 2006a. *Emerging Contact Centre Markets: Market Databook*, New York.

—— 2006b. *Contact Centres in Canada: Generating Growth in Contact Centre Markets*, New York.

Davoine, L., Erhel, C., and Guergoat-Lariviere, M. 2008. Monitoring quality in work: European Employment Strategy indicators and beyond, *International Labour Review*, Vol. 147, No. 2–3, pp. 163–98.

De Miranda Oliveira Júnior, M. Hoyos Guevara, A. J. de, Nelmi Trevisan, L., Nogueira, A. J. F., Giao, P. R., Fatima Silva, M. de, Melo, P. L. R. 2005. *Brazilian Call Centre Industry Report 2005* (The Global Call Centre Industry Project). São Paulo: Pontifícia Universidade Católica de São Paulo.

Deery, S., and Kinnie, N. 2004. *Call Centres and Human Resource Management*. Basingstoke: Palgrave.

Del Bono, A. 2008. Producción de servicios orientados hacia la exportación: empleos y trabajos del siglo XXI: los *call centers offshore* en Argentina, *Nova Tesis–ARTRA de Derecho Laboral y Relaciones del Trabajoso*. No. 7 (May–June).

Del Bono, A., and Bulloni, M.N. 2008. Experiencias laborales juveniles: los agentes telefónicos de call centers offshore en Argentina, *Trabajo y Sociedad*, Vol. 9, No. 10, pp. 1–21, Santiago del Estero, Argentina.

Delberghe, M. 2004. Les centres d'appels sont à leur tour tentés par la délocalisation, *Le Monde*, Paris, February 28, 2004.

Di Ruzza, R. 2003. La prescription du travail dans les centres d'appels téléphonique, *Revue de l'IRES* (Institut de Recherches Economiques et Sociales), Paris, Vol. 43, pp. 121–147.

Dicken, P. 2007. *Global Shift (5th edition)*, London: Sage.

Dossani, R., and Kenney, M. 2003. *Went for Cost, Stayed for Quality? Moving the Back-Office to India*. Asia-Pacific Research Center, Stanford University, at http://iis-db.stanford.edu/pubs/20337/dossani_kenney_09_2003.pdf.

—— 2007. The next wave of globalisation: relocating service provision to India, *World Development*, Vol. 35, No. 5, pp. 772–91.

DTI. 2004a. *The Globalisation of Business: Making Globalisation a Force for Good*, London.

—— 2004b. *The UK Contact Centre Industry: A Study*, London.

Durand, J.-P. 2004. *La chaîne invisible: travailler aujourd'hui: flux tendu et servitude volontaire*. Paris: Seuil.

Eisenberger, R. Huntingdon, R., Huntingdon, S., and Sowa, D. 1986. Perceived organizational support, *Journal of Applied Psychology*, Vol. 71, No. 3, pp. 500–07.

El Mouhoub Mouhoud. 2006. *Mondialisation et délocalisation des entreprises*. Paris: La Découverte.

Engman, M. 2007. *Expanding International Supply Chains: The Role of Emerging Economies in Providing IT and Business Process Services: Case Studies of China, the Czech Republic, India, and the Philippines*, OECD Trade Policy Working Paper No. 52, Paris: OECD.

Espinosa, J.A. Cummings, J. N., Wilson, J. M., and Pearce, B. M. 2003. Team boundary issues across multiple global firms, *Journal of Management Systems*, Vol 19, No. 4 (Spring), pp. 157–90.

Etchemendy, S., and Collier, R. 2007, Down but not out: union resurgence and segmented neocorporatism in Argentina: 2003–2007, *Politics & Society*, Vol. 35, No. 3, pp. 363–401.

European Foundation for the Improvement of Living and Working Conditions. 2007. Work organisation (Chapter 6). In: *Fourth European Working Conditions Survey 2005*. (Luxembourg: Office for Official Publications of the European Communities.

Fagan, C. 2004. Gender and working time in industrialized countries. In: Messenger, J.C. (ed.), *Working Time and Workers' Preferences in Industrialized Countries: Finding the Balance*, London: Routledge.

Falquet, J., Hirat, H., and Lautier, B. 2006. Travail et mondialisation: confrontations nord/sud, *Cahiers du Genre*. Paris: L'Harmattan.

FCS-UBA. 1999. El trabajo asalariado: precariedad laboral y desocupación en el Gran Buenos Aires, School of Social Sciences, Universidad de Buenos Aires, Argentina, available at http://lavboratorio.fsoc.uba.ar/textos/1_1.htm.

Filgueiras, L. 2006. O neoliberalismo no Brasil: estrutura, dinâmica e ajuste do modelo econômico. In: Basualdo, E.M., and Arceo, E. (eds.), *Neoliberalismo y Sectores Dominantes: Tendencias Globales y Experiencias Nacionales*, Buenos Aires: CLACSO, Consejo Latinoamericano de Ciencias Sociales.

Fleischer, S.R. 2002. *Passando a América a Limpo o Trabalho de Housecleaners Brasileiras em Boston, Massachussets*, São Paulo: Annablume.

Fransman, M. 2002. *Telecoms in the Internet Age*, Oxford: Oxford University Press.

Friedman, T. 2005. *The World Is Flat*, London: Allen Lane.

FSA. 2005. *Offshore Operations: Industry Feedback*, London: Financial Service Authority.

Galiani, S., and Gerchunoff, P. 2003. The labor market. In: della Paolera, G., and Taylor, A.M. (eds.), *A New Economic History of Argentina*, New York: Cambridge University Press.

García, H.O. 2005. *Autonomía Individual y Estabilidad del Contrato de Trabajo a Plazo Fijo*, Buenos Aires: CTA, Documento de Doctrina Jurídica.

Gardels, N. 2006. Globalização produz países ricos com pessoas pobres. Interview with Joseph Stiglitz. *Global Economic Viewpoint, O Estado de São Paulo*, September 27, 2006.

Gereffi, G. 2006. *The New Offshoring of Jobs and Global Development*, Geneva: ILO (International Institute for Labour Studies).

Goldin, A. 2001. *Continuidad y Cambio en el Sistema Argentino de Relaciones Laborales*, Administration Department Working Paper No. 20, Victoria, Argentina: Universidad de San Andrés.

Goodman, B., and Steadman, R. 2002. Services: business demand rivals consumer demand in driving jobs growth, *Monthly Labor Review*, Vol. 125, No. 4, pp. 3–16.

Green, F. 2006. *Demanding Work: The Paradox of Job Quality in the Affluent Economy*, Princeton, NJ: Princeton University Press.

Hall, P.A., and Soskice, D. (eds.). 2001. *Varieties of Capitalism: The Institutional Foundations of Comparative Advantage*, Oxford: Oxford University Press.

Hammer, M., and Champy, J. 1993. *Re-engineering the Corporation: A Manifesto for Business Revolution*, New York: HarperCollins.

Hannif, Z., and Lamm, F. 2005. *Occupation Health and Safety in the New Zealand Call Centre Industry*, Employment Studies Centre Working Paper No. 2005/8.

Hannif, Z., Burgess, J., and Connell, J. 2008. Call centres and the quality of work life: towards a research agenda, *Journal of Industrial Relations*, Vol. 50, No. 2, pp. 271–84.

Hansen, A. 2007. *Call Centres: Exportación de Servicios*, AmCham – La Cámara de Comercio de los EE.UU. en la República Argentina.

Harvey, D. 1989. *The Condition of Postmodernity*, Oxford: Blackwell.

—— 2001. *A Produção Capitalista do Espaço*. São Paulo: Annablume.

—— 2005. *A Short History of Neo-Liberalism*, Oxford: Oxford University Press.

Henley, J. 2006. Outsourcing the provision of software and IT-enabled services to India: emerging strategies, *International Studies of Management and Organization*, Vol. 36, No. 4, pp. 111–31.

Hirata, H., and Doare, H. 1998. Les paradoxes de la mondialisation. *Cahiers du GedisstNo. 21*, Paris:. L'Harmattan

—— 2002. *Nova Divisão Sexual do Trabalho? Um Olhar Voltado para a Empresa e a Sociedade*, São Paulo: Boitempo.

Holman, D.J. 2003. Call centres. In: Holman, D.J., Wall, T.W., Glegg, C.W., Sparrow, P. and Howard, A. (eds.), *The New Workplace: A Guide to the Human Impact of Modern Working Practices*. Chichester: John Wiley.

Holman, D., Batt, R., and Holtgrewe, U. 2007. *The Global Call Centre Report: International Perspectives on Management and Employment*. Sheffield: Global Call Centre Research Network.

Holman, D., and Wood, S. 2002. *Human Resource Management in Call Centres*, Sheffield: Institute of Work Psychology, University of Sheffield.

HRDC. 2002. *The Canadian Customer Contact Centre Landscape: An Industry in Transition*, Ottawa: Human Resource Development Canada.

Hutchinson, S., Purcell, J., and Kinnie, N. (2000). Evolving high commitment management: the experience of the RAC call centre, *Human Resource Management*, Vol. 10, No. 1, pp. 63–78.

Huws, U. (ed.). 2003. *When Work Takes Flight: Research Results from the EMERGENCE Project*, Brighton: Institute for Employment Studies.

Huws, U. 2003. *The Making of a Cybertariat: Virtual Work in a Real World*. New York: Monthly Review Press e Reino Unido: The Merlin Press.

Huws, U., and Flecker, J. (eds.). 2004. *Asian Emergence: The World's Back-Office?* IES Report No. 409, Brighton: Institute for Employment Studies.

Ianni, O. 1995. A dialética da globalização. In: *Teorias da Globalização*. São Paulo: Civilização Brasileira, pp. 135–62.

IDS. 1997–2005. *Pay and Conditions in Call Centres*, London: Incomes Data Services.

IFAES–AEECCE. 2005. *I Estudio Sobre Call Centers en España*, Madrid: International Faculty for Excutives y la Associación Española de Expertos en Centro de Contacto.

INDEC. 2004. Informe de variación salarial, June.

—— 2006. Informe de variación salarial, December.

Insigna, R.C., and Werle, M.J. 2000. Linking outsourcing to business strategy, *Academy of Management Review*, Vol. 14, No. 4, pp. 58–70.

International Labour Organization (ILO). 2008. *The Global Wage Report 2008/09. Minimum Wages and Collective Bargaining. Towards Policy Coherence*, Geneva: ILO.

Josselin, M.-L. 2004. Dakar se cache au bout du fil du télémarketing. Paris. *Libération*. June 9, 2004.

Kaka, N.F., Kekre, S.S., and Sarangan, S. 2006. Benchmarking India's business process outsourcers, *McKinsey on IT*, Summer.

Kalleberg, A., and Viasey, S. 2005. Pathways to a good job: perceived job quality among machinists in North America, *British Journal of Industrial Relations*, Vol. 43, pp. 431–54.

Kannan, K.P., and Papola, T.S. 2007. Workers in the informal sector: initiatives by India's National Commission for Enterprises in the Unorganized Sector (NCEUS), *International Labour Review*, Vol. 146, No. 3–4, pp. 321–29.

Karasek, J.A. 1979. Job demands, job decision latitude, and mental strain: implications for job redesign, *Administrative Science Quarterly*, Vol. 24, pp. 285–308.

Kearney, A.T. 2004. *Six-Industry Survey*. Chicago: A.T. Kearney.

—— 2007a. *Offshoring for Long-Term Advantage: The 2007 A.T. Kearney Global Services Location Index*. Chicago: A.T. Kearney.

—— 2007b. *Destination Latin America: A Near-Shore Alternative*. Chicago: A.T. Kearney. Available at http://www.atkearney.com/index.php.

Kergoat, D. 2001. Le rapport social de sexe: de la reproduction des rapports sociaux à leur subversion, *Actuel Marx*, Paris Vol. 30, Presses Universitaires de France (PUF).

Kinnie, N., Hutchinson, S., and Purcell, J. 2000. Fun and surveillance: the paradox of high commitment management in call centres, *International Journal of Human Resource Management*, Vol. 11, No. 5, pp. 967–85.

Knights, D., and McCabe, D. 1998. What happens when the phone goes wild?: Staff, stress and spaces for escape in a BPR telephone banking work regime, *Journal of Management Studies*, Vol. 35, No. 2, pp. 63–94.

KPMG. 2007. Managing Performance through Shared Service Centers, white paper, KPMG Switzerland.

Krein, J.D. 2007. *As Tendências Recentes nas Relações de Emprego no Brasil: 1990–2005*. Doctoral thesis, UNICAMP–Instituto de Economia.

Krein, J.D., and Gonçalves, J.R. 2005. Mudanças tecnológicas e seus impactos nas relações de trabalho e no sindicalismo do setor terciário, *O trabalho no Setor Terciário. Emprego e Desenvolvimento Tecnológico*. São Paulo: Campinas, CESIT.

Krein, J.D., and Teixeira, M. 2001. A materialização da flexibilização: as experiências de CCPS, *Cadernos de Debate & Reflexão*, No. 12, Campinas.

Kroll, C. 2005. *State and Metropolitan Area Impacts of the Offshore Outsourcing of Business Services and IT*, University of California, Fisher Center Working Paper No. 293.

Kurvilla, S., and Ranganathan, A. 2008. Economic development strategies and macro- and micro-level human resource policies: the case of outsourcing in India, *Industrial and Labor Relations Review*, Vol. 62, No. 1, pp. 39–72.

Lavinas, L. 2000. *Evolução do Desemprego Feminino nas Areas Metropolitanas*. Texto para Discussão No. 756, Rio de Janeiro: IPEA.

Lee, S., McCann, D., and Messenger, J. 2007. *Working Time Around the World: Trends in Working Hours, Laws and Policies in a Global Comparative Perspective*, Geneva and London: ILO and Routledge.

Leka, S., Griffiths, A. and Cox, T. 2004. Institute of Work, Health & Organisations. *Work Organization and Stress*. Geneva: World Health Organization.

Leone, E.T., and Baltar, P. 2005. Disparidades nos rendimentos do trabalho de homens e mulheres nas metrópoles brasileira. In: *O trabalho no Setor Terciário. Emprego e Desenvolvimento Tecnológico*. São Paulo, Campinas, CESIT.

Levaggi, A. 2006. Historia del derecho Argentino del trabajo, 1800–2000, *Iushistoria*, No. 3, Universidad del Salvador, Buenos Aires, Argentina.

Levina, N., and Vaast, E. 2008. Innovating or doing as told? Status differences and overlapping boundaries in offshore collaboration,' *MIS Quarterly*, Vol. 32, No. 2, pp. 307–32.

Lewin, A.Y., and Furlong, S. (2005). 2nd Bi-annual Offshore Survey Results, Duke University CIBER/Archstone Consulting.

López, A. and Ramos, D. 2007. Oportunidades y Desafíos para la Industria del Software en Argentina, en Paulo Bastos Tigre (ed.), *Oportunidades Y Desafíos Para La Industria Del Software En América Latina*, Comisión Económica para América Latina (CEPAL), Oficina de Buenos Aires, Argentina.

—— 2008. *La Industria de Software y Servicios Informáticos Argentina: Tendencias, Factores de Competitividad y Clusters*, preliminary study prepared for the Project 'Desafíos y Oportunidades de la Industria de Software en Brasil y Argentina,' PEC B-107 FLACSO-IDRC.

López, A., Ramos, D. and Torre, I. 2008. *Remote Work and Global Sourcing in Argentina. Final Report*. ILO Conditions of Work and Employment Programme, unpublished report, Geneva.

—— 2009. Las exportaciones de servicios. ¿Puede América Latina insertarse en las cadenas de valor?, CEPAL Oficina de Buenos Aires, Series Especiales.

M2 Presswire. 2009. *Brazil Information Technology Report Q1 2009* (www.companiesandmarkets.com), Coventry, April 2009 (found on Proquest database December 2009).

Magitbay-Ramos, N., Estrada, G. and Felipe, J. 2008. An input-output analysis of the Philippine BPO industry, *Asian-Pacific Economic Literature*, Vol. 22, No. 1, pp. 41–56.

—— 2007. *An Analysis of the Philippine Business Process Outsourcing Industry*. ADB ERD Working Paper No. 93, Manila: Asian Development Bank.

Mahesh, V.S., and Kasturi, A. 2006. Improving call centre agent performance: a UK–India study based on the agents' point of view, *International Journal of Service Industry Management*, Vol. 17, No. 2, pp. 136–157.

Mais, L. 2006. Brasileiros roubam vagas de norte-americanos, diz sindicato em anúncio, *Folha de São Paulo*, Vol. 26, No. 9.

Malhotra, N., Budhwar, P., and Prowse, P. 2007. Linking rewards to commitment: an empirical investigation of four UK call centres, *International Journal of Human Resource Management*, Vol. 18, No. 12, pp. 2095–2127.

Manitoba Customer Contact Association. 2007. *Industry Profile 2007*, Winnipeg.

Manning, S., Massini, S. and Lewin, A.Y. 2008. A dynamic perspective on next generation offshoring: the global sourcing of science and engineering talent, *Academy of Management Perspectives*, Vol. 22, No. 3, pp. 35–54.

Marinho-Silva, A. 2000. *A Norma Regulamentadora 17: texto normativo integral comentado*, Belo Horizonte (mimeo).

——— 2003. A regulamentação das condições de trabalho no setor de teleatendimento no Brasil: necessidades e desafios. In: SALIM, Celso Amorim et al. (orgs.), *Saúde e Segurança no Trabalho, Novos Olhares e Saberes*. Belo Horizonte, Brazil: SEGRAC.

——— 2004. *A Regulamentação das Condições de Trabalho No Setor de Teleatendimento No Brasil: Necessidades e Desafios*. Dissertação mestrado, Programa de Pós-graduação em Saúde Pública, Faculdade de Medicina, Universidade Federal de Minas Gerais.

McMillin, D. 2006. Outsourcing identities: call centres and cultural transformation in India, *Economic and Political Weekly*, Vol. 41, No. 3, pp. 235–41.

Mehta, A., Armenakis, A., Mehta, N., and Irani, F. 2006. Challenges and opportunities of business process outsourcing in India, *Journal of Labor Research*, Vol. 27, No. 3, pp. 324–38.

Mercer. 2006. *Contact Centres in Canada: The Competitive Landscape for Pay*, Mercer/ Contact Centre Canada.

MINCYT. 2008. *Libro Blanco de la Perspectiva TIC: Proyecto 2020*, Buenos Aires, Argentina.

Minevich, M., and Richter, F.-J. 2005. *Global Outsourcing Report 2005*. New York and Geneva: Going Global Ventures, Inc., and HORASIS.

Miozzo, M., and Soete, L. 2001. Internationalization of services: a technological perspective, *Technological Forecasting and Social Change*, Vol. 47, No. 2, pp. 159–85.

Mirchandani, K. 2003. Gender eclipsed? Work relations in transnational call centers. Paper presented at the *Administrative Sciences Association of Canada 2003 Conference*, Halifax, Nova Scotia.

——— 2004. Practices of global capital: gaps, cracks and ironies in transnational call centres in India, *Global Networks*, Vol. 4, No. 4, pp. 355–73.

Mitter, S., Fernandez, G., and Varghese, S. 2004. On the threshold of informalization: women call centers in India. In: Carr, M. (ed.), *Chains of Fortune: Linking Women Producers and Workers with Global Markets*, London: Commonwealth Secretariat, pp. 165–83.

Morris, J.A., and Feldman, D.C. 1996. The dimensions, antecedents, and consequences of emotional labour, *Academy of Management Review*, Vol. 21, No. 4, pp. 986–1010.

NASSCOM. 2002. *The IT Industry in India: Strategic Review 2002*, New Delhi.

——— 2003. *Strategic Review 2003*, New Delhi.

——— 2005. *Strategic Review 2005*, New Delhi.

——— 2006a. *Strategic Review 2006*, New Delhi.

——— 2006b. NASSCOM asks ITES players to take steps to curb attrition. Accessed 1 March 2010. http://www.nasscom.in/Nasscom/templates/NormalPage.aspx?id=829

——— 2006c. Tech titans tip on farmland debate: NASSCOM wants stake for sons of soil. Accessed 1 March 2010. http://www.nasscom.in/Nasscom/templates/NormalPage. aspx?id=50648

——— 2007a. *India ITES-BPO Strategy Summit 2007: Background and Reference Source*, New Delhi.

——— 2007b. *Strategic Review 2007*, New Delhi.

——— 2008. *BPO Strategy Summit 2008, Conference Guide, Reference Resource Articles*, New Delhi.

——— 2009. *Strategic Review: The IT Industry in India*, New Delhi.

NASSCOM-McKinsey. 2002. *Nasscom-McKinsey Report 2002: Vision for the Indian IT Services and IT-Enabled Services Industry*, New Delhi: NASSCOM-McKinsey.

—— 2005. *Nasscom-McKinsey Report 2005: Extending India's Leadership of the Global IT and BPO Industries*, New Delhi: NASSCOM-McKinsey.

National Commission for Enterprises in the Unorganised Sector (NCEUS). 2007. Report on 'Condition of work and promotion of livelihood in the unorganized sector,' Government of India, New Delhi.

neoIT. 2006. *Offshore Insights: Market Report Series*. Vol. 4, No. 4, June. http://costkiller.net/tribune/Tribu-PDF/OIv4i04_0506 ITO_and_BPO_Salary_Report_2006.pdf

Ng, C., and Mitter, S. 2005. Valuing women's voices: call center workers in Malaysia and India, *Gender, Technology, and Development*, Vol. 9, No. 2, pp. 209–33. New Delhi: Sage.

Noronha, E. 1996. Liberalization and industrial relations, *Economic and Political Weekly*, Vol. 31, No. 8, pp. L14–L21.

Noronha, E., and D'Cruz, P. 2006. Organizing call centre agents: emerging issues, *Economic and Political Weekly*, Vol. 41, No. 21, pp. 2115–21.

—— 2007a. Seeking the future: after-hours telecommuters in India's medical transcription industry, *Labour and Management in Development Journal*, Vol. 8, pp. 14–27.

—— 2007b. Reconciling dichotomous demands: telemarketing agents in Bangalore and Mumbai, India, *The Qualitative Report*, Vol. 12, No. 2, pp. 255–80.

—— 2008. The dynamics of teleworking: case studies of women medical transcriptionists from Bangalore, India. *Gender, Technology and Development*, Vol. 12, No. 2, pp. 157–83.

—— 2009a. *Employee identity in Indian call centres: the notion of professionalism*, New Delhi: Sage/Response.

—— 2009b. Engaging the professional: organising call centre agents in India, *Industrial Relations Journal*, Vol. 40, No. 3, pp. 215–34.

Observatorio Pyme, OPSSI. 2008. Situación y perspectiva de las PyME del sector del software y servicios informaticos en la Argentina: una mirada a la demanda de TI's en el sector PyME Industrial, June 2008, Buenos Aires, Argentina.

Occupational Safety & Health Center (OSHC), Philippine Department of Labor & Employment. 2005. *Case Study on the Health, Safety and Working Conditions in a Contact Center*. Unpublished paper, Quezon City: Occupational Safety & Health Center.

Ofreneo, R.E., Ng, C., and Marisigan-Pasumbal, L. 2007. Voice for voice workers: addressing the IR concerns in the call center/BPO Industry of Asia, *The Indian Journal of Industrial Relations*, Vol. 42, No. 4 (April), pp. 534–57.

Ohmae, K. 1990. *The Borderless World: Power and Strategy in the Interlinked Economy*, New York: Free University.

Oliveira, J. R. et al. 2005. *The Global Call Centre Industry Project. Relatório Brasil*. Pontifícia Universidade Católica de São Paulo.

Oliveira, S.M. 2004. *Reestruturação das telecomunicações no Brasil: uma (re) visão das estratégias de gestão da produção e das relações de trabalho na cadeia produtiva (estudo de caso da telefonia fixa em São Paulo, 1990–2003)*. São Paulo, 376 f. Doctoral thesis, Faculdade de Filosofia, Letras e Ciências Humanas, Universidade de São Paulo.

ONS, 2005. *Labour Market Trends*, Vol. 113, No. 9. London: Office for National Statistics.

Organisation for Economic Cooperation and Development (OECD). 2007. *Offshoring and Employment: Trends and Impacts*, Paris: OECD.

Pal, M. and Buzzanell, P. 2008. The Indian call center experience a case study in changing discourses of identity, identification, and career in a global context, *Journal of Business Communication*, Vol. 45, No. 1, pp. 31–60.

Patel, A., Khalil-Hassen, E., and Dziruni, M. 2009. *Remote Work and ITES Global Sourcing: Country Study for South Africa*. Revised Draft Report. ILO Conditions of Work and Employment Programme, unpublished report.

Patel, R. 2006. Working the Night Shift: Gender and the Global Economy. *ACME: An International E-Journal for Critical Geographies*, Vol. 5, No. 1, pp. 9–27.

Paul, J., and Huws, U. 2002. *How Can We Help? Good Practice in Call Centre Employment*. Brussels: European Trade Union Confederation.

Pearce, J. 1981. Bringing Some Clarity to Role Ambiguity Research, *Academy of Management Review*, Vol. 6, No. 4, pp. 665–74.

Penfold, D. 2008. Off-shoring and decent work: worlds apart? *International Journal of Comparative Labour Law and Industrial Relations*, Vol. 24, No. 4, pp. 573–94.

Penrose, E. 1959. *The Theory of the Growth of the Firm*, Chichester: John Wiley.

Pezé, M. Le geste de travail, entre usure et sublimation. In: *Revue Française de Psychosomatique*. Paris, No. 24; PUF, 2003.

Pico, Ermelo. 2006. Employment in the Philippine Contact Center and Business Process Outsourcing Industry: Issues & Concerns. *Philippine Journal of Labor & Industrial Relations*, Vol. 26, Nos. 1 and 2, pp. 123–42.

Pochmann, M. 2001. *Economia Global e a Nova Divisão Internacional do Trabalho*. Available at http://decon.edu.uy/network/panama/POCHMANN.PDF. Accessed August 27, 2009.

Pochmann, M. 2004. Juventude em busca de novos caminhos no Brasil. In: Novaes, R., and Vannuchi, P. (eds.), *Juventude e Sociedade: Trabalho, Educação, Cultura e Participação*. São Paulo: Editora Fundação Perseu Abramo.

Poster, W. 2007. Who's on the line? Indian call centre agents pose as Americans for US outsourced firms, *Industrial Relations*, Vol. 46, No. 2, pp. 271–304.

Prahalad, C.K., and Hamel, G. 1990. The core competence of the corporation, *Harvard Business Review*, May–June, pp. 79–91.

Proni, M.W. 2005. A modernização econômica do setor terciário no Brasil. In: *O trabalho no Setor Terciário: Emprego e Desenvolvimento Tecnológico*. São Paulo, Campinas, CESIT.

Ramesh, B. 2004. Cybercoolies in BPOs, *Economic and Political Weekly*, Vol. 35, No. 9, pp. 492–97.

Rashbass, J., and Furness, P. 2005. *Telepathology: Guidance from the Royal College of Pathologists*. Available at http://www.rcpath.org/resources/pdf/G026-Telepathology-May05.pdf. Acessed on January 11, 2007.

Rea, A., and Tripier, M. 2003. *Sociologie de l'immigration*. Paris: La Découverte.

Reis, R.R., and Sales, T. (eds.). 1999. *Cenas do Brasil migrante*. São Paulo: Boitempo.

Richardson, R., and Marshall, J.N. 1996. The growth of telephone call centres in peripheral areas of Britain: evidence from Tyne and Wear. *AREA*, Vol. 28, No. 3, pp. 308–17.

Ritter, J. and Anker, R. 2002. 'Good jobs, bad jobs: workers' evaluations in five countries', in *International Labour Review*, Vol. 141, No. 4, pp. 331–58.

Robinson, G., and Morley, C. 2006. Call centre management: responsibilities and performance, *International Journal of Service Industry Management*, Vol. 17, No. 3, pp. 284–300.

Russell, B. 2002. Making, re-making, managing and controlling customer service agents: Brownfield and Greenfield call centre sites, *Research and Practice in Human Resource Management*, Vol. 10, No. 1, pp. 35–52.

Russell, B., and Thite, M. 2009. Managing work and employment in Australian and Indian call centres. In: Thite, M., and Russell, B. (eds.), *The Next Available Operator*:

Managing Human Resources in the Indian Business Process Outsourcing Industry, New Delhi: Sage, pp. 253–78.

Sako, M. 2006. Outsourcing and offshoring: implications for productivity of business services, *Oxford Review of Economic Policy*, Vol. 22, No. 4, pp. 499–512.

San Jose, W. 2006. *Achieving Sustainability of the Philippine BPO Industry through Decent Work and Sound Industrial Relations*. Unpublished paper. Quezon City: University of Philippines School of Labor and Industrial Relations.

Schalk, R., and van Rijckevorsel, A. 2007. Factors influencing absenteeism and intention to leave in a call centre, *New Technology, Work, and Employment*, Vol. 22, No. 3, pp. 260–74.

Schultz, C.W. 2007. To offshore or not to offshore: which nations will win a disproportionate share of the economic value generated from the globalization of white-collar jobs, *Houston Journal of International Law*, Vol. 29, No. 1, pp. 231–70.

Segnini, L.R.P. 1988. *A liturgia do poder: trabalho e disciplina*. São Paulo: Educ-editora da Pontifícia Universidade Católica de São Paulo.

Sennet, R. 2006. *A Cultura do Novo Capitalismo*. São Paulo: Record.

Shankardass, A. 2007. *Latin America: The Next India?* Sitel White Paper, available at http://www.sitel.com/sitel/download/Latin_America_The_Next_India_2008-04-03.pdf.

Sieben, I. 2006. *Training, Technology, and Human Resource Management in Call Centers*. Maastrict, the Netherlands: Research Centre for Education and the Labour Market (ROA), Maastricht University.

Singh, P., and Pandey, A. 2005. Women in call centres, *Economic and Political Weekly*, Vol. 12 (February), pp. 684–88.

Skarlicki, D, van Jaarsveld, D., and Walker, D. 2007. *Getting Even for Customer Unfairness: The Moderating Role of Moral Identity in the Relationship Between Customer Interactional Justice and Employee Retaliation*, paper presented to the Society for Industrial and Organizational Psychology Annual Meeting, New York.

Souza Santos, B. 1995. *A Construção Multicultural da Igualdade e da Diferença*. Palestra proferida no VII Congresso Brasileiro de Sociologia, realizado no Instituto de Filosofia e Ciências Sociais da Universidade Federal do Rio de Janeiro, de 4 a 6 de setembro de 1995. (mimeo)

SPU – Secretaria de Políticas Universitarias. 2006. *Anuario 2006*, Buenos Aires: Ministerio de Educación.

Sutherland Global Services. 2007. *Business Process Outsourcing: The Year Ahead: A Perspective on Evolving Worldwide Requirements*. Rochester, NY: Sutherland Global Services.

Talahite, F. 1998. L'emploi des femmes au Maghreb, *Cahiers du Gedisst*, Paris, Vol. 21, pp. 35–59.

Tate, W.L., and van der Walk, W. 2008. Managing performance of outsourced contact centers, *Journal of Purchasing and Supply Management*, Vol. 4, pp. 160–69.

Taylor, P. 2007. *Multilingual Contact Centres: A Global Overview*, Presentation to NASSCOM ITES–BPO Strategy Summit, Bangalore, August 7, 2007.

Taylor, P., and Anderson, P. 2008. *Contact Centres in Scotland: The 2008 Audit*, Glasgow: Scottish Development International.

Taylor, P., and Bain, P. 1997. *Call Centres in Scotland: A Report for Scottish Enterprise*, Glasgow: Scottish Enterprise.

—— 1999. 'An assembly line in the head': work and employee relations in the call centre, *Industrial Relations Journal*, Vol. 30, No. 2, pp. 101–17.

—— 2003. *Call Centres in Scotland and Outsourced Competition from India*, Scotecon: University of Stirling.

—— 2005. India calling to the faraway towns, *Work, Employment, and Society*, Vol. 19, No. 2, pp. 261–82.

—— 2006. *An Investigation into the Offshoring of Financial Services Business Processes from Scotland to India*, Glasgow: University of Strathclyde.

—— 2008. United by a common language? Trade union responses in the UK and India to call centre offshoring, *Antipode*, Vol. 40, No. 1, pp. 131–54.

Taylor, P., D'Cruz, P., Noronha, E., and Scholarios, D. 2009. Indian call centres and business process outsourcing: a study in union formation, *New Technology, Work, and Employment*, Vol. 24, No. 1, pp. 19–42.

Taylor, P., Mulvey, G., Hyman, G., and Bain, P. 2002. Work organization, control, and the experience of work in call centers, *Work, Employment and Society*, Vol. 16 (March), No. 1, pp. 133–50.

—— 2003. 'A unique working environment': health, sickness, and absence management in UK call centres, *Work, Employment, and Society*, Vol. 17, No. 3, pp. 435–58.

—— 2005. 'Striving under chaos': the effects of market turbulence and organizational flux on call centre work. In: Stewart, P. (ed.), *Trade Union Renewal and the Future of Work*, Basingstoke: Palgrave, pp. 20–40.

Taylor, P., Noronha, E., D'Cruz, P., and Scholarios, D. 2008. Employee voice and collective formation in the Indian ITES–BPO industry, *Economic and Political Weekly*, Vol. 43, No. 22, pp. 37–46.

—— 2009. Union formation in Indian call centres. In: Thite, M., and Russell, B. (eds.), *The Next Available Operator: Managing Human Resources in the Indian Business Process Outsourcing Industry*, New Delhi: Sage, pp. 145–81.

Taylor, P., Scholarios, D., Noronha, E., and D'Cruz, P. 2007. *Employee voice and collective formation in the Indian ITES-BPO industry*. Bangalore: UNITES.

Thite, M., and Russell, B. 2009. Human resources management in Indian call centres/business process outsourcing. In: Thite, M., and Russell, B. (eds.), *The Next Available Operator: Managing Human Resources in the Indian Business Process Outsourcing Industry*, New Delhi: Sage, pp. 33–58.

Todd, P.A., Eveline, J., Still, L.V., and Skene, J 2003. Management responses to unions in Australian call centres: exclude, tolerate, or embrace? *Australian Bulletin of Labour*, Vol. 29, No. 2, pp. 162–76.

UNCTAD. 2004. The shift towards services, *World Investment Report 2004*, Geneva and New York: United Nations Conference on Trade and Development.

UNCTAD. 2009. *Information and the Economy Report 2009: Trends and Outlook in Turbulent Times*. UNCTAD/IER/2009, Geneva and New York: United Nations Conference on Trade and Development.

Union Research Centre for Organisation and Technology (URCOT). 2000. *Call Centres: What Kind of Future Workplaces?* RMIT School of Social Sciences & Planning, Victorian Trades Hall Council, Melbourne, Australia.

USGAO. 2004. *International Trade: Current Government Data Provide Limited Insight Into Offshoring of Services*, Report No. GAO-04-932, Washington, DC: US Government Accountability Office.

USGAO. 2005. *Offshoring of Services: an Overview of the Issues*, Report No. GAO-06-5, Washington, DC: US Government Accountability Office.

Valverde, M., Ryan, G., and Gorjup, M.T. 2007. An examination of the quality of jobs in the call centre industry, *International Advanced Economic Research*, Vol. 13, pp. 146–56.

Van Den Broek, D. 2002. Surveillance, privacy, and work intensification within call centres. In: *WorkSite: Issues in Workplace Relations*, Sydney: University of Sydney.

—— 2004. 'We have the values': customers, control, and corporate ideology in call centre operations, *New Technology, Work, and Employment*, Vol. 19, No. 1, pp. 2–12.

van Jaarsveld, D., Frost, A.C., and Walker, D. 2007. *The Canadian Contact Centre Industry: Strategy, Work Organisation, and HRM*, Vancouver, B.C., Canada: The Global Call Centre Industry Project.

Venco, S. 1991. Pesquisa desenvolvida para o sindicato dos metalurgicos de são bernardo do campo e diadema. *O Metalurgico Hoje* (mimeo).

—— 2003. *Telemarketing Nos Bancos: O Emprego Que Desemprega.* Campinas: Edunicamp.

—— 2006. *Tempos Moderníssimos Nas Engrenagens do Telemarketing.* Doctoral Thesis presented to the Department of Applied Social Sciences, UNICAMP.

—— 2007. O consumidor nas teias do telemarketing. In: Dowbor, Antas, L., Jr., and Mendes, R. (eds.), *Desafios do Consumo*, São Paulo: Vozes (no prelo).

Venco, S., Kratz Moriyana, J., and Teixeira, M. 2008. *Remote Work and Global Sourcing Countries: Brazil.* ILO Conditions of Work and Employment Programme, unpublished report.

Vilela, L.V., and Assunção, A.Á. 2004. Os mecanismos de controle da atividade no setor de teleatendimento e as queixas de cansaço e esgotamento dos trabalhadores, *Saúde Pública*, July–August., pp. 25–31.

Vivek, S.D., Richey, Jr., R.G., and Dalela, V. 2009. A longitudinal examination of partnership governance in offshoring: a moving target, *Journal of World Business*, Vol. 44, pp. 15–30.

Wallace, C. 2009. An overview of the Indian contact centre industry. In: Thite, M., and Russell, B. (eds.), *The Next Available Operator: Managing Human Resources in the Indian Business Process Outsourcing Industry.* New Delhi: Sage, pp. 13–32.

Wegge, J., Van Dick, R.; Fisher, G.K.; Wecking, C.; and Moltzen, K. 2006. Work motivation, organisational identification, and well-being in call centre work, *Work & Stress: A Journal of Work, Health and Organisations*, Vol. 20, No. 1, pp. 60–83.

Weinkopf, C. 2002. Call centre work: specific characteristics and the challenges of work organization, *Transfer*, Vol. 3, pp. 456–66.

Willcocks, L.P., and Lacity, M.C. 2006. *Global Sourcing of Business and IT Services.* Basingstoke: Palgrave Macmillan.

Williamson, O.E. 1975. *Markets and Hierarchies: Analysis and Antitrust Implications.* New York: Macmillan Free Press.

Index

Abramo, L., 140
Accenture, 19–21, 27, 33, 36, 38–9, 57, 170
AHT, *see* average handling time per call (AHT)
AICTE, *see* All India Council for Technical Education (AICTE)
All India Council for Technical Education (AICTE), 68
Amante, M., 12–14, 101–32, 198, 203, 206–7, 214, 223–4, 225, 227, 244
ANATEL, the Brazilian Agency of Telecommunications, 147
Anderson, P., 44
annual wages among BPO and ITO destination countries, comparison of, 214–15
Anton, J., 32
APEC, *see* Asia-Pacific Cooperation (APEC)
Apex Sykes, 170, 184
Argentina
  employment, *see* working and employment conditions, Argentina
  labour market, 174–9, *see also* working and employment conditions, Argentina; labour market, Argentina
  legislation: Contract of Employment Law, 199, 202, *see also* labour legislation, Argentina
  mega-devaluation of Argentine peso, 162, 180
  methodology used for study, 164–5; case study approach, 164; interviews with HR managers/department heads, 164
  salaries and employment in services export sector, 181
  trade in services, *see* trade in services, recent trends in Argentina

trade union, 143, 174, 176, 186, 191; activity, software and information services sector, 191; collective bargaining, 179; segmented neocorporatism, 176
wages, employment in SIS sector: high wages, 190
working conditions, *see also* working and employment conditions, Argentina; business services export sector, 182–3; and employment, 174–91; software and information services sector, 189
Argentine peso, mega-devaluation, 162, 180
Aron, R., 4, 6–7
Arora, A., 12
Arvato, 170, 184
Asia-Pacific Cooperation (APEC), 110
ASSA group, 172
  see also Argentina
Atento, 184
Athreye, S., 12
attrition, 31, 35–6, 40, 43, 45, 62, 69, 72, 82, 99, 105, 109, 227, 243
  career development opportunities, 95
  employee dilemmas in Indian ITES-BPO sector, 94–6
  job characteristics/dissatisfaction, 95
  perspectives of employees/managers on reasons, 96
  Philippines, 126–8; attrition, reasons for, 126; BPO, reasons for leaving previous, 127; Code of Ethics to prevent poaching, 128
  profiling Indian ITES-BPO workforce, 72
  recommendations, 99
  United Kingdom, 45
  United States, 35–6
  see also individual countries

automated call distribution systems, 10, 241

average handling time (AHT) per call, 121, 227

Aviva, 45, 46

back-office
  agent, 71, 91
  and call centre, comparison, 91;
    evaluations, 206; intensive
    monitoring, 206; night work, 207;
    rest breaks, 206
  employees, 61, 72, 78, 82, 216–17,
    220, 225, 229–30
  operations/processes/services, 24, 27,
    32, 45, 51, 60, 63, 107, 208–9,
    224, 229
  organizations, 62
  rationalization, 42
  relocation of, 26
  remote work arrangements (RWAs),
    218, 220, 225–6, 229–30,
    234
  work/activities/functions, 17, 24,
    33, 37, 46, 48, 50, 58, 62, 66,
    131, 148, 197, 206–7, 222, 241
Bain, P., 10, 12, 18, 24, 26, 37, 42, 44,
  46–8, 50, 61–2, 65–70, 82–3,
  226–7
Baldry, C., 44–5
Banerjee, D., 69
banking system in Brazil, 145
Barclays, 43, 45
Bardhan, A., 60–1
bargaining agreement, 112, 129, 186,
  191
Bastos Tigre, P., 171
Batt, R., 9–10, 32, 34–6, 40, 61, 67, 73,
  76, 78, 82–3, 95
Beccaria, L., 176–7
Becker, G.S., 112
Belt, V., 44
Benner, C., 218, 244
Bicalho, L., 148
'black economy', 142
  see also labour market, Brazil
Blinder, A.S., 28
BOSS, *see* burnout stress syndrome
  (BOSS)
Boulin, J.Y., 242

BPO companies, comparative analysis,
  197–209
  categorization of RWAs, 208–9
  global BPO industry, 197–9, *see also*
    global BPO industry, comparative
    analysis; 'cybercoolies', 199;
    industries, finance/retail/
    distribution/telecoms/outsourcing,
    198; perspectives of major
    destination countries, 198;
    workers/workforce, characteristics,
    198–9
  labour laws, *see also* labour laws,
    comparative analysis;
    employment relationships,
    199–204; regulating working and
    employment conditions, 204–5
  national labour laws, implications,
    199
  workplace environment, 205–8, *see
    also* workplace environment in
    BPO industry
  see also individual countries
BPO industry in Brazil, 145–7
  background, 145–6
  BRASSCOM, objective of, 146
  companies in financial services, 146
  IT as major destination for business
    services, 146–7; growth in
    Brazilian exports, 147; reason for,
    146–7
  telecommunications, 147; ANATEL
    (Brazilian Agency of
    Telecommunications), 147;
    General Telecommunications Law
    of 1997, 147; Law 4117, Brazilian
    Telecommunications Code, 147;
    TELEBRAS, 147
  see also Brazil
BRASSCOM, *see* Brazilian Association of
  Information Technology and
  Communication Companies
  (BRASSCOM)
Brazilian Association of Information
  Technology and Communication
  Companies (BRASSCOM), 136,
  146
Brazilian Institute of Geography and
  Statistics (IBGE), 138, 140–2
Brazilian Labour Code, CLT, 202

Brazil
  business environment for outsourcing
    and offshoring ITES functions,
    137–9
  call centres/customer service centres,
    150–9, *see also* call centres
  financial services industry in Brazil,
    148–9; economic turmoil of the
    1980s and 1990s, 148
  financial system, 148
  'health risk control', 157
  hours of work: call centres and
    customer service centres, 152–6;
    working and employment
    conditions, 147–8
  labour laws, 143–5; Attachment I of
    NR 17 Standard, 144–5; Brazilian
    Consolidated Labour Law (CLT),
    143; Brazilian Labour Code, CLT,
    202; 'Calvary', 203; 'coop' system
    in Brazil, 202; *Custo Brasil* (Costs
    of Brazil), 143; employment
    contract/relationships, 143–4;
    hiring workers through
    'consultancy' firms, 202–3;
    subcontract, 144
  labour market, 140–2, *see also* labour
    market, Brazil
  legislation, Brazilian Labour Code,
    CLT, 202; 'Calvary', 203; 'coop'
    system in Brazil, 202; hiring
    workers through 'consultancy'
    firms, 202; Law 4117, Brazilian
    Telecommunications Code, 147;
    Special Brazilian Regulation for
    Call Centres (NR 17 Standard),
    204
  remote work in, 145–7
  research methodology, 135–7;
    accomplished interviews, 136;
    professional categories of remote
    worker, 136
  salary, *see* Brazil
  telecommunications industry,
    149–50; convergence between call
    centres and privatized
    telecommunication services, 150;
    'telecoms auction', 149; workers
    in, 149

trade union, labour law in: collective
    bargaining between employers
    and trade unions, 143
  wages, *see* labour market, Brazil
  working and employment conditions,
    147–8; axial tool, 148; 'new econ-
    omy' and 'customer culture', 148
Bristow, G., 43
Budhwar, P., 61, 73, 75, 78, 83, 86, 92,
    94–5
Building Society Act (1986), UK, 42
Bulloni, M.N., 185, 227
burnout stress syndrome (BOSS), 95,
    183, 185, 227
business process services (BPS), 2–3,
    209
Buzzanell, P., 61

Caïazzo, B., 148
call and contact centres (CCCs), 163–4,
    192, 198, 205
call centres, 9–10
  back-office and: evaluations, 206;
    intensive monitoring, 206; night
    work, 207; rest breaks, 206
  and customer service centres in Brazil,
    150–9, *see also* Brazil; Brazilian
    paradox in, 156; composition of
    call centre workforce, 152;
    emergence of, 150–1;
    telemedicine, 156–9; working
    conditions, 152–6
  dichotomization in, 47
  The Global Call Centre Report, 211, 218,
    229
  location, 10
  mass production call centre, 42
  nearshoring, 10
  and privatized telecommunication
    services, 150
  prominent health issues in, 224–5
  qualified labour, 10
  Special Brazilian Regulation for Call
    Centres (NR 17 Standard), 204
  studies on, 211–12
  survey in Indian cities for employee
    dilemmas, 61–2
  telephone operator call centres,
    9–10
  UK's 'call centre capital', 43

unionized call centres in Canada, 56
Union Network International's Call
  Centre Charter, 30
CallTech, 39
'Calvary', 144, 203
Canada
  Canadian contact centre agent
    positions/agent numbers, 52
  Contact Centre Canada, 53
  dimensions to location/
    relocation, 51
  employment profile, 52
  employment relations, 56; 'low-value
    interactions', 56; pay levels in
    outsourced operations, 56;
    unionized call centres, 56
  location by province/region, 52–3
  national health care system, 54
  nearshoring, 54–5; cost savings, 54;
    proximity to/shared time zones
    with, 54
  offshoring: CEP, 55; customer service
    roles by telecoms companies, 55;
    Dialogue Management
    Group, 55
  salary, pay levels in outsourced
    operations, 56
  sectoral breakdown, 53
  trade union, 56
'captive' unit, 6–9, 79, 209, 213, 218,
  234, 238–9
  see also global captive companies
carpal tunnel syndrome, 225,
  243
Carroll, W., 92
Castilla, E., 240, 243–4
Castillo, J.J., 172, 189
Castillo, V., 172, 189
CCCs, *see* call and contact centres
  (CCCs)
CEP, *see* Communications, Energy and
  Paperworkers' Union (CEP)
CESSI, *see* Software and Information
  Services Chamber (CESSI)
Cetrángolo, O., 163
Champy, J., 26
Chesnais, F., 137
CICOMRA, 183, 186–7
CMM 5 certification, *see* Argentina
Coase, R.H., 4

codifiable processes, 6
Cohen, L., 61
collective bargaining, 40, 48–50, 110–12,
  128–9, 132, 143, 174, 178–9, 186,
  191, 240
collective labour law, 178
  see also Argentina
Collier, R., 176
colour coding system on customer
  service monitors, 153, 227
Communications, Energy and Paper
  workers' Union (CEP), 55
Communications Workers of America
  (CWA), 40
'concession bargaining', 29
'consultancy' firms, hiring workers
  through, 202–3
Contact Babel, 33, 34, 35, 52, 53, 55,
  198
Contact Centre Association, 43
Contract Labour (Regulation and
  Abolition) Act (1970), 69
Contract of Employment
  Law, Argentina, 178–9, 199, 202,
  204
contractual issues/relationships, 7, 26,
  112, 143, 176, 234, 238
Conventions, ILO *see* ILO Conventions
Convergys, 19, 36, 38, 39, 54,
  55
'coop' system in Brazil, 202
cost savings/cuttings, 3–4, 10, 11, 33, 36,
  42, 46, 49, 51, 54, 58, 63, 65, 69,
  148, 150, 214
Couto, V., 168
Couvert, M.D., 227–9
Cowie, C., 61
Cox, T., 253
Cruces, G., 176
CSR, *see* customer service representatives
  (CSR)
Cubecorp, 170
culture, national/organizational/
  operational, 8
customer service representatives (CSR),
  107
customer care specialists, 119
customer service centres/call centres in
  Brazil, 150–9
  Brazilian paradox in, 156

customer service centres/call centres in Brazil – *continued*
composition of call centre workforce, 152
emergence of, 150–1
telemedicine, 156–9; better image diagnoses, 157; degree of cost reduction, 158; 'health risk control', 157; telepathology, 157
working conditions, 152–6
see also Brazil
CWA, *see* Communications Workers of America (CWA)
'cybercoolies', 83, 199, 244

Daksh, 20
Dauer, J.L., 38
Davoine, L., 211
D'Cruz, P., 14, 60–100, 198, 203–4, 206–7, 209, 213, 215, 223–4, 226, 244
decision making, 4, 7, 11–12, 95, 111, 138, 158
matrix of, 7
Deery, S., 49
Del Bono, A., 183–5, 227
Dell, 36, 38, 39, 43, 55, 65
Deloitte, 170
De Miranda Oliveira Júnior, M., 215, 218, 223, 244
Department of Trade and Industry (DTI), 29, 110
Dialogue Management Group, 55
dichotomization in call centres, 47
Dicken, P., 19, 30
distance-shrinking technologies, 25, 34, 42
Doellgast, V., 201
domestic tariff area (DTA), 64
'do more, with less', 3
Dossani, R., 10–12, 26–7, 33, 37, 60, 165
DTA, *see* domestic tariff area (DTA)
DTI, *see* Department of Trade and Industry (DTI)
Durand, J.-P., 145
dynamics, economic/geographical/locational, 25–6
distance-shrinking technologies, 25
Dziruni, M., 225

economic boom (1990s), 33, 36
economic crisis, global, 3, 131, 136, 140, 145, 159, 175
economic recession/dot.com crash, 32
EDS, 20, 33, 38, 172, 173
education
acceptance of English as medium of, 61
AICTE, 68
Argentina: FOMENI, 188; INET, the National Institute of Technological Education, 188; 'Invest in Yourself' programme, Argentina, 188; Professional Education National Plan for SIS Workers, 188
education aid, Brazil, 144
highest education levels in in-house centres, 54
IT, 64
lowest education levels in outbound centres, 54
profiling Indian ITES-BPO workforce, 73–4; education level of ITES–BPO employees and their parents, 73
system, Philippines, 107–8; pay differentials by level of education, Philippine BPOs, 114–15
UK demographic profile of BPO workforce: educational levels of workers, similarities with US, 45
EHTP schemes, *see* electronic hardware technology park (EHTP) schemes
Electronic Commerce Act of 2000, 110
electronic hardware technology park (EHTP) schemes, 64
electronic monitoring, 160, 206–7, 213, 226–9, 233–4, 242
El-Sawad, A., 61
EMEA, *see* Europe, the Middle East and Africa (EMEA)
emergence of ITES–BPO in developing countries, 12–14
Brazilian BPO industry, 13
development in Latin America, 13
emergence of Spain, 13
government influences on BPO, 13–14
historical development in India/Philippines, 12–13

night work and negative
implications, 12
time zone issue, 12
'emotional labour', 207
employee benefits in BPO Industry by
country and RWA, 217
Employees State Insurance Act (1948), 69
employees' workload, factors affecting,
226
'end-to-end customer support', 21
Engman, M., 13
EOU, *see* export-oriented units (EOU)
Equal Remuneration Act (1976), 69
'escalation calls from India', 102
eSCM-SP, *see* level 4 eSourcing Capability
Model for Services Provider
(eSCM-SP)
Espinosa, J.A., 8
Etchemendy, S., 176
EU Data Protection Act, 28
Europe, the Middle East and Africa
(EMEA), 20
Evalueserve
in China, 21
in India, 27
export-oriented units (EOU), 64
extra work or training to fill off-peak
hours, 84, 114, 119

Fagan, C., 219, 242
Fair Debt Collections Act, 38
Feldman, D.C., 207
FGDs, *see* Focus Group Discussions
(FGDs)
Financial Services Act (1986), UK, 42
FirstSource, 21, 65
Flecker, J., 18
'flexitime', 117
Focus Group Discussions (FGDs), 103
FOMENI, *see* Fund for the Improvement
of Computer Teaching (FOMENI)
FONSOFT, *see* Software Industry
Promotion Fund (FONSOFT)
Fransman, M., 27
Friedman, T., 19
Fund for the Improvement of Computer
Teaching (FOMENI), 188

Galiani, S., 174–6
García, H.O., 178–9

Gasparini, L., 176
GATS, *see* General Agreement of Trade in
Services (GATS)
General Agreement of Trade in Services
(GATS), 28
General Telecommunications Law of
1997 (Brazil), 14, 147
Genpact, 21, 38
Gerchunoff, P., 174–6
Gereffi, G., 9
GFAs, *see* global framework agreements
(GFAs)
global BPO industry, comparative
analysis, 197–9
'cybercoolies', 199
industries, finance/retail/distribution/
telecoms/outsourcing, 198
perspectives of major destination
countries, 198
Sutherland Global Survey on BPO
(2007), 197
workforce, characteristics of (by
country), 200–1
workforce/workers, characteristics,
198–9
see also job quality in RWAs
The Global Call Centre Industry Project, 35
The Global Call Centre Report, 211, 218,
229
global captive companies, 20–1
HSBC, 20–1
global framework agreements (GFAs), 30
'globalization' White Paper, 28
global service delivery, 18–19
accessing deeper skills at 'higher-end'
business, 19
'hyperglobalists', 19
leveraging low costs at 'low-end'
business, 19
multilocational, multisite strategies, 18
scale and volume, 18
transformational offshoring, 18
Global Service Location Index 2007
(Kearney), 168
Global Services Index, 22
global services network (GSN), 20
global sourcing, unevenness of, 22–3
diverse locations, attractiveness of, 22
India/Philippines/South Africa, 22
Goldin, A., 179

Gonçalves, J.R., 140
Goodman, B., 33
government influences on BPO, 13–14
  deregulation, 13–14
  'industrial seeds', 14
  industry concentration, 14
government policies and company
    practices, implications for
  factors affecting employment
      conditions/responses, 238–9;
      business strategy issues, 238–9;
      management practices, 239–40;
      pay and career development
      issues, 240–1; skill requirements
      and shortages, job stability and
      staff turnover, 243–4; working
      time and work–life balance issues,
      241–2; work organization issues,
      including ergonomics, 242–3;
      ergonomic issues that are related
      health problems, 243
  female employment, major sources of,
      237
  share of total employment in service
      sector in selected countries, 237
Gramm–Leach–Billey Act, 38
'graveyard shift', 102, 109, 111, 117–18
Green, F., 211
Greenock operation (IBM), 24
grievance redressal
  basic grievance procedures,
      Philippines, 126
  India, 93–4

Hall, P.A., 29, 57
Hamel, G., 4
Hammer, M., 26
Hannif, Z., 212, 225
Hansen, A., 194
'happy days', 154
  see also Brazil
Harvey, D., 19, 27
HCL, 21
HCM, *see* High-commitment
    management (HCM)
HCM practices, 91, 94, 95, 99
Heads of Household programme, 175
  see also working and employment
      conditions, Argentina
health

'health risk control', Brazil, 157
HIPAA, 29, 38
Institute of Work, Health &
    Organisations, 242
issues in call centres, 224–5
management of indicators transmitted
    through Internet, 157
National health care system,
    Canada, 54
OSH, 224–6
problems, Indian ITES-BPO, 90
'risk control', 157
  see also stress; *individual countries*
Health Insurance Portability and
    Accountability Act (HIPAA), 29, 38
'health risk control', 157
Henley, J., 60
Hero-ITES, 21
Hewitt Associates, 19–20
Hewlett-Packard, 36, 65
High-commitment management (HCM),
    91, 94, 95, 99
HIPAA, *see* Health Insurance Portability
    and Accountability Act (HIPAA)
Hirata, H., 155
Holman, D., 7, 45, 57, 201, 206, 211,
    218, 222, 226, 229, 234
Holman, D.J., 82
'home-grown' managers, 208, 239
Hong Kong and Shanghai Bank (HSBC),
    20, 21, 26, 45, 48, 65, 147
hours of work
  Argentina, working conditions, *see also*
      working and employment
      conditions, Argentina; business
      services export sector, 182–3; and
      employment, 174–191; software
      and information services sector,
      189
  BPO companies, comparative analysis:
      labour laws, working and
      employment conditions, 204–5
  Brazil, working conditions: call centres
      and customer service centres,
      152–6; working and employment
      conditions, 147–8
  extra work or training to fill off-peak
      hours, 84, 114, 119

India: extended work hours, 82; odd
working hours, 89; satisfaction
with working conditions, 93
irregular work schedules, by type of
RWA, 222
labour laws, comparative analysis:
working and employment
conditions, 204–5
night work, 220
Philippine BPOs, *see also* Philippines;
change, work schedule, 118; night
shifts, 118–19; 'flexitime', 117;
working and employment
conditions, 112–30; working
hours and shift work, 117–19
stress, comparative analysis: from
interpersonal relations/specific
working conditions, 231; from
specific working conditions and
gender, 233
weekly hours, by gender/type of RWA,
220
working time and work–life balance
issues, 241–2
work schedules, by gender/type of
RWA, 221
see also impacts of
offshoring/outsourcing on
working and employment
conditions
human resources (HR)
administration, 66, 198
India, practices in, 92–5; avenues for
grievance redressal, 93;
employees' descriptions of HR
department, 94; facilities, 92;
HCM practices, 91; intranet
discussion forums, 94; 'open door'
policies, 94; satisfaction with
working conditions, 93; well
organized buildings, 92
management/managers, 109, 113–14,
117–18, 122, 129, 184, 191, 240;
'proactive attitude' of, 129
performance: appraisal, 84, 116, 119,
130; targets/monitoring, 226–7
practices, 91–5, 99–100, 103, 211
strategy, 96
see also recruitment, training
Hutchinson, S., 92

Huws, U., 18, 29, 51, 240–1
'hyperglobalists', 19

Ianni, O., 137
IBM Global Services, 19, 20, 21, 27, 33,
36, 38, 39, 57, 147, 170, 172, 180,
188
ICTs, *see* information and
communications technologies (ICTs)
IDS, *see* Incomes Data Services (IDS)
ILO, *see* International Labour
Organization (ILO)
ILO Conventions: on freedom of
association and collective
bargaining, 110; Night Work
Convention, 1990 (No. 171), 112,
241; Remote Work and Global
Sourcing Project, 198, 216; Weekly
Rest (Commerce and Offices)
Convention, 1957 (No. 106), 242
impacts of offshoring/outsourcing on
working and employment
conditions
boundaries, social and
organizational, 8
good working relationship, 8
manager's task, 8
problems during ongoing relationship,
9; role ambiguity for workers, 9
problems, source of, 9
regular communication, 8
'rule of organizational gravity', 9
Incomes Data Services (IDS), 42, 44,
45, 50
India
attrition, *see* attrition
employee dilemmas, *see* working and
employment conditions, India
'end-to-end customer support', 21
grievance redressal: avenues for, 93
hours of work: extended work hours,
82; odd working hours, 89;
satisfaction with working
conditions, 93
human resources practices, 92–5,
see also human resources (HR)
labour market, 67–70, *see also*
labour market, India;
benchmarking service, NASSCOM,
69–70; Contract Labour

India – *continued*
(Regulation and Abolition) Act
(1970), 69; discussions with
labour commissioners, 69;
Employees State Insurance Act
(1948), 69; employment levels, 67;
Equal Remuneration Act (1976),
69; Industrial Disputes Act (1947),
69, 203; labour cost, 69–70;
labour-related advantages, 68–9;
Maternity Benefit Act (1961), 69;
Minimum Wages Act (1948), 69;
MoU with UGC and AICTE, 68;
NAC, NASSCOM, 68; Payment of
Gratuity Act (1972), 69; Payment
of Wages Act (1936), 69; Shops
and Commercial Establishments
Act, 69; 'trainable' into
'employable' workforce, 68;
Workmen's Compensation Act
(1923), 69
legislation, *see also* labour market,
India; contracts, 203;
self-certification system, 204;
Shops and Establishment Acts,
203
problems, ITES-BPO, 90
recruitment, 76–80, *see also* working
and employment conditions,
India
regulations, *see also* labour market,
India,; Contract Labour
(Regulation and Abolition) Act
(1970), 69
reverse shoring, 21
safety, 93, 97; satisfaction of
employees with aspects of
working life, 74; stop-gap
arrangement, 75
salary: competitive compensation
packages, 75; deductions on
disciplinary mechanism, 86, 87,
88; increments on
performance-based data, 86;
monthly salary of employees,
74–5; overtime rates paid to
employees, 81; Payment of
Gratuity Act (1972), 69
seamless service, 21

sectoral overview, 63–7; advantages,
63; constraints imposed by
country's infrastructure, 65;
export revenues, 63; globalization,
63; relaxation of policies, inbound
and outbound investments, 64;
role of Indian government in
growth and development, 64;
'third-party MNCs', 65
trade union, 62, 68; reasons for not
joining union, 98
union formation, 95–9, *see also* union
formation, India
wages: Minimum Wages Act (1948), 69;
Payment of Wages Act (1936), 69
work-life balance, *see* work-life
balance, India
work systems, 80–90
indicators
BPO business, 15
firm performance, 196
job quality, 16, 211, 213
labour market, 140
Laeken, 211
management of health indicators
transmitted through Internet, 157
individual labour law, 178
see also Argentina
Industrial Disputes Act (IDA) of 1947,
India, 203
'industrial seeds', 14
see also government influences on BPO
INET, the National Institute of
Technological Education, 188
information and communications
technologies (ICTs), 2, 3, 10, 15, 25,
27, 42, 60, 83, 130, 135, 196
in-house offshoring, 7
Insigna, R.C., 3–4
Institute of Work, Health &
Organisations, 242
International Labour Organization (ILO),
110, 112, 135, 198, 205–8, 215–16,
226–7, 230, 241, 242
'Invest in Yourself' programme, 188
irregular work schedules in BPO industry
by type of RWA, 221, 241
'IT Generation' (public-private
campaign), 188
see also Argentina

job discretion, 206–7, 209, 211, 213, 226–33, 242
  comparative analysis, 228
job quality in RWAs, 209–33
  classification of factors for, 212
  in developed economies (Green, Francis), 210–11
  elements for call centre context, 212
  indicators, 213
  job stability and employment relationship: 'reconciling dichotomous demands', 224; short job tenure, 222–3; staff turnover, 223
  Laeken indicators, 211
  literature and its application, 210–11
  measures for issues in BPO, 212–13
  physical working environment and OSH, 224; health issues in call centres, 224–5
  studies on call centres, 211–12
  wages/salaries/employee benefits, comparison, 213; annual wages among BPO/ITO destination countries, 216; annual wages per agent, BPO/ITO destinations, 214; average salaries by country, 217; differences between women and men, 218–19; employee benefits by country and RWA, 217; employee benefits, higher for 'captive' units, 218; exception in Brazil, 215; higher-than-average wages, 215–16; ILO's Remote Work and Global Sourcing Project, 216
  work, hours/schedules and work-life balance: irregular work schedules, by type of RWA, 221; night work, 219; weekly hours, by gender/type of RWA, 219; work schedules, by gender/type of RWA, 221
  work organization, workload and job discretion: electronic monitoring, quantitative/qualitative, 229; factors affecting employees' workload, 226–7; job discretion, 227; 'mass production model', 226–7; performance targets/monitoring, 226–7; stress from interpersonal relations/specific working conditions, 231; stress from organizational environment/workplace changes, 232; stress from specific working conditions and gender, 232; stress, sources of, 230
job stability/security
  comparative analysis: 'reconciling dichotomous demands', 224; short job tenure, 223; staff turnover, 223
  and employment relationship, 222–4
  skill requirements and shortages and staff turnover, 243–4

Kalleberg, A., 211
Karasek, J.A., 206, 229
Kasturi, A., 61
Kearney, A.T., 1, 3, 11, 19, 22, 70, 146–7, 168–70, 216
Kenney, M., 10–12, 26, 33, 37, 60, 165
Kergoat, D., 152
Kinnie, N., 49, 92
Knights, D., 82
knowledge process outsourcing (KPO), 5, 27, 37, 66, 67, 205, 209, 229
KPO, *see* knowledge process outsourcing (KPO)
Kroll, C.A., 41, 60–1
Kwon, H., 201

labour laws, comparative analysis
  Argentina: Contract of Employment Law, 199, 202
  Brazil: Brazilian Labour Code, CLT, 202; 'Calvary', 203; 'coop' system in Brazil, 202; hiring workers through 'consultancy' firms, 202–3
  characteristics of global BPO workforce (by country), 200–1
  'concession bargaining', 29
  GFAs, 30
  global low-cost competition, 29
  governing employment relationships, 199–204

labour laws, comparative
  analysis – *continued*
  India: contracts, 203; IDA of 1947,
    203; self-certification system, 204;
    Shops and Establishment Acts,
    203
  Philippine Labour Code, 203–4
  Shops and Commercial Establishments
    Act, India, 204
  shortages of workers with desired skill
    sets, 205
  Special Brazilian Regulation for Call
    Centres (NR 17 Standard), 204
  Union Network International's Call
    Centre Charter, 30
  working and employment conditions,
    204–5
  work performed for outside markets,
    205
labour legislation, Argentina
  for collective bargaining, 178
  collective labour law, 178
  Contract of Employment Law,
    'professional statute', 178–9
  fixed-term, seasonal and work-team
    employment contracts, 178
  individual labour law, 178
  for working accidents, 178
  see also labour market, Argentina
labour market, Argentina
  characteristics of 1990s to early 2000s,
    175
  collective bargaining, 174
  employment structure, 177
  Heads of Household programme, 175
  informality, 175–6
  inward-looking development strategy,
    174
  job insecurity, 176
  Program for Unemployed Male and
    Female Heads of Households, 175
  pro-labour policies, 175
  'segmented neocorporatism', 176
  socio-economic crisis, mid-1970s, 175
  State's intervention, 174
  see also labour legislation, Argentina
labour market, Brazil
  formal employment, 142; informal
    employment, 142; work card
    method, 142

overall employment situation, 140–1;
    differences in employment rates
    for men and women, 140;
    distribution of occupations/
    employment by gender, 141
  unemployment and issue of
    informality in employment, 142;
    'black economy', 142; Brazilian
    government statistical agency,
    IBGE, 142
  see also Brazil
labour market, India
  benchmarking service, NASSCOM,
    69–70
  Contract Labour (Regulation and
    Abolition) Act (1970), 69
  discussions with labour
    commissioners, 69
  Employees State Insurance Act
    (1948), 69
  employment levels, 67
  Equal Remuneration Act (1976), 69
  Industrial Disputes Act (1947), 69,
    203
  labour cost, 69–70
  labour-related advantages, assessment,
    68–9
  Maternity Benefit Act (1961), 69
  Minimum Wages Act (1948), 69
  MoU with UGC and AICTE, 68
  NAC, 68, 76
  Payment of Gratuity Act (1972), 69
  Payment of Wages Act (1936), 69
  Shops and Commercial Establishments
    Act, 69, 204
  'trainable' into 'employable'
    workforce, 68
  Workmen's Compensation Act
    (1923), 69
labour market, Philippines, 104–5, 108,
    127, *see also* Philippines
  Philippine Labour Code, 203
Lacity, M.C., 5–7
Laeken indicators, 211
Lamm, F., 225
Law 4117, Brazilian Telecommunications
    Code, 147
Lee, S., 219–20, 237
legal and regulatory framework,
    Philippine BPOs, 109–12

industry legislation, 109–10; APEC Privacy Principles, 110; Electronic Commerce Act of 2000, 110; Executive Order 226, 110; incentives to foreign investors, 110; Investment Priorities Plan, 110; law on data protection, 110; Omnibus Investment Code, 109
labour legislation, 110–12; anti-union attitude of management, 112; ILO Conventions on freedom of association and collective bargaining, 110; Philippine Labour Code, 111; prohibition of night work for women, 111
see also Philippines
Legislation
aimed at preventing offshoring, 38
Argentina, *see also* working and employment conditions, /Argentina; Contract of Employment Law, 199, 202; labour legislation/market, 174–9
Brazil: Brazilian Labour Code, CLT, 202; 'Calvary', 203; 'coop' system in Brazil, 202; hiring workers through 'consultancy' firms, 202–3; Law 4117, Brazilian Telecommunications Code, 147; Special Brazilian Regulation for Call Centres (NR 17 Standard), 204
India, *see also* labour market, India; Contract Labour (Regulation and Abolition) Act (1970), 69; contracts, 203; Employees State Insurance Act (1948), 69; Equal Remuneration Act (1976), 69; IDA of 1947, 203; Industrial Disputes Act (1947), 69, 203; Maternity Benefit Act (1961), 69; Payment of Gratuity Act (1972), 69; self-certification system, 204; Shops and Commercial Establishments Act, 69; Shops and Establishment Acts, 203; Workmen's Compensation Act (1923), 69
industry legislation, 109–10
labour legislation, 110–12

Philippines, *see also* legal and regulatory framework, Philippine BPOs; industry legislation, 109–10; labour legislation, 110–12; Philippine Labour Code, 203–4
Union Network International's Call Centre Charter, 30
United States; 'right-to-know' legislation, 39
US legislation (1996), 27
see also individual countries; regulations
'legitimate strategy' (Dossani and Kenney), 11
Leka, S., 239, 242–3
Levaggi, A., 178
level 4 eSourcing Capability Model for Services Provider (eSCM-SP), 172
Levina, N., 8
Lewin, A.Y., 168–9
Lewis, C., 201
liberalization
financial and exchange rate, 139
trade, 27–8, 60, 109, 175–6
'lift and shift', 26
linguistic/cultural compatibility, 23–5
'hyperglobalizers', 25
IBM's Greenock operation, 24
importance of sophisticated language skills, 24
Lloyds/TSB, 45, 48
López, A., 12–14, 162–95, 198, 201–2, 206, 215–16, 220, 223, 227–8, 230
'lousy boss syndrome', 207

Magitbay-Ramos, N., 13
Mahesh, V.S., 61
management practices, 49, 61, 239–40
abusive/poor, 207–8
Manning, S., 6
Marinho-Silva, A., 153
Marques, F., 171
Marshall, J.N., 42
'mass production model', 67, 83, 226
Maternity Benefit Act (1961), 69
McCabe, D., 82
McMillin, D., 61, 71, 74, 76, 78–80, 89, 91
Mehta, A., 61
Mehta, N., 61

Memorandum of Understanding
(MoU), 68
Messenger, J.C., 1–16, 196–245
migratory process, 'source' to
'destination', 26
Minevich, M., 1
Minimum Wages Act (1948), 69
Miozzo, M., 25
Mirchandani, K., 61, 71, 78, 89, 91–2
Mitter, S., 61, 74, 92, 201
Monihan, L., 9
Morris, J.A., 207
MoU, *see* Memorandum of
Understanding (MoU)
Mphasis, 20, 36
multinational corporations (MNCs), 12,
16, 18–20, 60, 65, 162–3, 165,
172–4, 186, 190–1, 209, 213, 233
multinational service companies, 19–20
acquisition, 20
customer contact services, 20
data and customer relationship
management, 20
EMEA, 20
specialist voice companies, 20

NAC, *see* National Assessment of
Competence (NAC)
NASSCOM, *see* National Association of
Software and Service Companies
(NASSCOM)
Nasscom–McKinsey, 22, 36, 64, 66, 68
National Assessment of Competence
(NAC), 68, 76
National Association of Software and
Service Companies (NASSCOM), 17,
21–3, 36, 57, 62–70, 94–6, 100
National Consumer Price Index, Brazil,
138
national labour laws, 199, 241
see also labour laws, comparative
analysis
National Telecom Policy (1999), 28
National Training Agreement for SIS
sector, 188
nearshoring, 2, 10, 17, 29, 30–2, 50–2,
54–5, 58, 146
neoIT, 11, 213–14
'new-age sweatshops', 83
Ng, C., 61, 92, 201

night work, 12–13, 111–12, 204, 206–7,
219, 221, 232, 241
Night Work Convention, 1990 (No.
171), ILO, 112, 241
noncodifiable processes, 6
'noncompete clauses', 128
Noronha, E., 12, 14, 60–100, 198, 201,
203–4, 206–7, 209, 213, 215, 223–4,
226, 244

Observatorio Pyme-OPSSI, 187, 190
occupational safety and health (OSH),
224–6
offshore relocation, driving factors, 30–2
offshoring and outsourcing
advances in ICTs, 10
automated call distribution systems, 10
call centres, 9–10; location, 10;
nearshoring, 10; qualified
labour, 10
creation of pinch points, 10
impacts on working and employment
conditions: boundaries, social and
organizational, 8; good working
relationship, 8; manager's task, 8;
problems, 9; regular
communication, 8; 'rule of
organizational gravity', 9
Indian experience, 11
'legitimate strategy' (Dossani and
Kenney), 11
motivating factors, 60
process reengineering movement, 10
'push' factors/'pull' factors, 60
rationales; 'captive' unit or third-party
offshore provider, 6; contractual
issues, 7–8; cost savings and
improved efficiency, 4; criteria for
engagement with third-party
offshore provider, 7; decisions,
organizational results, 5;
determining processes to offshore,
6; goal, 3; in-house offshoring, 7;
matrix of decision making, 7;
mistakes, 4; operational and
structural risk, 6; organization of
work and delivery of value, 4;
theories, RBV/TCE, 4–5; 'vendor
agreements', types, 7

variables, 11–12; BPO locations, 11–12; cost, 11; skilled or trained labour, 11
VOIP, 10
see also impacts of offshoring/outsourcing on working and employment conditions
OFW, *see* overseas Filipino workers (OFW)
Ohmae, K., 19
Oliveira, J. R., 152, 155
Oliveira, S.M., 149–50
Omar, R., 201
onshoring, 30–2
Operational risk
components, 6
metrics, 6; codifiable processes, 6; noncodifiable processes, 6; opaque processes, 6; transparent processes, 6
OSH, *see* occupational safety and health (OSH)
outbound services, 34, 47, 54–5, 64, 79, 119, 208–9
outsourcing, *see* offshoring and outsourcing
overseas Filipino workers (OFW), 102, 104–5
'overseas relocation', 37–8, 45

Pal, M., 61
Pandey, A., 89, 91
Patel, A., 22, 225
Patel, R., 61, 71
Paul, J., 240–1
Payment of Gratuity Act (1972), 69
Payment of Wages Act (1936), 69
Pearce, J., 9, 239
Penfold, D., 89
Penrose, E., 5
performance
appraisal, 84, 116, 119, 130
targets/monitoring, 226–7
Philippines
BPO employers, 105–6; Philippine firms in survey sample, 106
business environment, 102–3

change, work schedule, 118
education, 107–8
employee characteristics, 106–7; average age of employee respondents, 107; jobs held by females, 107
global sourcing, unevenness of, 22
'graveyard shift', 102
growth of firms, 105
health and safety, *see* working and employment conditions, Philippines
hours of work; 'flexitime', 117; working and employment conditions, 112–130; working hours and shift work, 117–119
labour laws: Philippine Labour Code, 203–4
labour market, 104–5
legislation, *see also* legal and regulatory framework, Philippine BPOs; industry legislation, 109–10; labour legislation, 110–12
night shift, 118–119
Philippine Labour Code, 203–4
recruitment and training, 109; guarantors or 'backers', 109; 7-minute interview, 109; recruitment companies, 127; recruitment policies, 113
research methodology, 103–4; employee questionnaire, 103; FGDs and interviews, 103; questionnaire for employers, 103; sampling and data limitations, 104
safety, stress and health, 121–6, 131–2
salary: average monthly pay of BPO employees, 112; college degree for pay of BPO Employees, 114; pay differentials by gender, 113–14; pay differentials by level of education, 114; pay differentials by work experience, 114; typical monthly pay of BPO employees and managers, 113
trade union: Right to Organize and Collective Bargaining, 110

Philippines – *continued*
wages and benefits, 112–13, *see also*
working and employment
conditions, Philippines
work experience, 108–9; males and
females, frequency of changing
companies/jobs, 108–9
working and employment conditions,
112–30, *see also* Philippines
Philippine Labour Code, 111–12, 203–4
pinch points, creation of, 10
'poaching', 128, 218
political economy/global
regulation/governance, 27–9
dissemination of ICTs, 27
EU Data Protection Act, 28
'globalization' White Paper, 28
HIPAA, 29, 38
labour market de-regulation, 29
Poster, W., 61, 71, 75, 89, 91–2, 94
Prahalad, C.K., 4
'proactive attitude' of HR managers, 129
process reengineering movement, 10
Professional Education National Plan for
SIS Workers, Argentina, 188
Program for Unemployed Male and
Female Heads of Households,
Argentina, 175
Proni, M.W., 139
Prudential, 45, 49, 65
'pure plays', 65

Ramesh, B., 61, 71, 73–6, 78, 80, 83, 86,
89, 91–2, 94, 99
Ramos, D., 162–95, 201
RBV, *see* resource-based view (RBV)
recruitment
Argentina, *see* working and
employment conditions,
Argentina
Brazil, *see* working and employment
conditions, Brazil
factor driving and inhibiting offshore
relocation, 31
India, 76–80, *see also* working and
employment conditions, India;
employee-related factors, 76;
qualities expected, 76; union
affiliation, 77

perspectives of managers: on criteria
for employee selection, 77; on
employee selection tools, 78; on
sources, 76
perspectives of managers on
sources of ITES–BPO sector
recruitment, 76
Philippines, *see also* Philippines;
recruitment and training, 109;
recruitment companies, 127;
recruitment policies, 113
training, India: generic and
process-specific modules, 78;
post-training/on-the-job training,
78; types of training given, 79
see also government policies and
company practices, implications
for; training
regulations
Contract Labour (Regulation and
Abolition) Act (1970), 69
government influences on BPO:
deregulation, 13–14
India, labour market: Contract Labour
(Regulation and Abolition) Act
(1970), 69
labour laws, *see* labour laws,
comparative analysis
labour market in Indian BPOs:
Contract Labour (Regulation and
Abolition) Act (1970), 69
political economy/global
regulation/governance, 27–9;
dissemination of ICTs, 27; EU
Data Protection Act, 28;
'globalization' White Paper, 28;
HIPPA, 29, 38; labour market
de-regulation, 29
United States, employment relations:
deregulation of industry, 40
see also legislation
'remote sourcing' strategy, 45, 57
Remote Work and Global Sourcing
Project, ILO, 198, 216
remote work arrangements (RWAs), 1,
15, 16, 196–7, 206, 208–10, 213,
218, 234, 242
analysis of job quality, *see* job quality
in RWAs

categorization of: call/contact centre arrangements, 208–9; domestic-focused outsourcing, 209; international facing outsourcing of BPO, 209; IT-enabled back-office services, 208–9
and global sourcing, definitions related to, 2
see also remote work from perspective of developed economies
remote work from perspective of developed economies
Canada, 51–6, *see also* Canada
dynamics, economic/geographical/ locational, 25–6; distance-shrinking technologies, 25
global 'captive' companies, 20–1; HSBC, 20–1
global service delivery, 18–19; accessing deeper skills at 'higher-end' business, 19; 'hyperglobalists', 19; leveraging low costs at 'low-end' business, 19; multilocational, multisite strategies, 18; scale and volume, 18; transformational offshoring, 18
global sourcing, unevenness of, 22–3; diverse locations, attractiveness of, 22; India/Philippines/South Africa, 22
Indian companies, 21; 'end-to-end customer support', 21; reverse shoring, 21; seamless service, 21
labour, 29–30; 'concession bargaining', 29; global framework agreements (GFAs), 30; global low-cost competition, 29; Union Network International's Call Centre Charter, 30
linguistic/cultural compatibility, 23–5; 'hyperglobalizers', 25; IBM's Greenock operation, 24; importance of sophisticated language skills, 24
multinational service companies, 19–20; acquisition, 20; customer contact services, 20; data and

customer relationship management, 20; EMEA, 20; specialist voice companies, 20
offshoring/nearshoring/onshoring, 30–2; factors driving and inhibiting offshore relocation, 31–2
political economy/global regulation/governance, 27–9; dissemination of ICTs, 27; EU Data Protection Act, 28; 'globalization' White Paper, 28; HIPAA, 29, 38; labour market de-regulation, 29
relocation/rising up value chain, 26–7; build–operate–transfer, 26; 'lift and shift', 26; re-engineering revolution, 26
UK, *see* United Kingdom
US, *see* United States
resource-based view (RBV), 4–5
reverse shoring, 21
Richardson, R., 42
Richter, F.-J., 1
'right-to-know' legislation, 39
Royal and Sun Alliance, 45
'rule of organizational gravity', 9, 238
Russell, B., 76, 78–9, 92, 94–5, 228
RWAs, *see* remote work arrangements (RWAs)
Ryan, G., 133

safety
Argentina, *see* working and employment conditions, Argentina
Brazil, *see* working and employment conditions, Brazil
comparative analysis, 212–13, 219, 221, 224–6
India, 93, 97
occupational health and safety (OSH), 224–6
Philippines, safety and health, *see* working and employment conditions, Philippines; stress and health, 121–6, 131–2
see also health
Sako, M., 4

salary
  Argentina: salaries and employment in
    services export sector, 181
  average in BPO industry by country,
    216
  in BPO industry by country, 216
  Brazil, *see* Brazil
  Canada: pay levels in outsourced
    operations, 56
  factors affecting employment
    conditions/responses: pay and
    career development issues, 240–1
  Incomes Data Services (IDS), 42, 44,
    45, 50
  India: competitive compensation
    packages, 75; deductions on
    disciplinary mechanism, 86, 87,
    88; increments on
    performance-based data, 86;
    monthly salary of employees,
    74–5; overtime rates paid to
    employees, 81; Payment of
    Gratuity Act (1972), 69; Payment
    of Wages Act (1936), 69;
    satisfaction of employees with
    aspects of working life, 74;
    stop-gap arrangement, 75
  Philippines: average monthly pay of
    BPO employees, 112; college
    degree for pay of BPO Employees,
    114; pay differentials by gender,
    113–14; pay differentials by level
    of education, 114–15; pay
    differentials by work experience,
    114; typical monthly pay of BPO
    employees and managers, 113
  see also individual countries; wages
San Jose, W., 132, 139
Sarbanes Oxley Act, 38
scheduling issues in BPO industry,
  categories
  infrequent or irregular rest breaks,
    241–2
  irregular work schedules, 242
  night work, 241
Schultz, C.W., 38
'segmented neocorporatism', 176
  see also working and employment
    conditions, Argentina
self-certification system, India, 204

SEZ, *see* special economic zones (SEZ)
Shops and Commercial Establishments
  Act, India, 69, 203, 204
Sieben, I., 201, 244
Singh, J.V., 4, 6–7
Singh, P., 91
SIS, *see* software and information
  services (SIS)
Skarlicki, D., 54
skill requirements and shortages, job
  stability and staff turnover, 243–4
  call centre training, 243
  social referral network, 244
  unionization, 244
Soete, L., 25
Software and Information Services
  Chamber (CESSI), 171
software and information services (SIS),
  163–4, 170–4, 179
  employment in, 186–93
  Professional Education National Plan
    for SIS Workers, Argentina, 188
  SIS labour demand, 186
  *Strategic Plan for Software and
    Information Services 2004–2014,*
    173
Software Industry Promotion Fund
  (FONSOFT), 173
software technology parks (STP), 64
'solo parents', 107
Soskice, D., 29, 57
'source' to 'destination' (migratory
  process), 26
Special Brazilian Regulation for Call
  Centres (NR 17 Standard), 204
special economic zones (SEZ), 64, 110
SPi, 13
SPSS, *see* Statistical Package for the Social
  Sciences (SPSS)
Statistical Package for the Social Sciences
  (SPSS), 62, 104
Steadman, R., 33
STP, *see* software technology parks (STP)
*Strategic Plan for Software and Information
  Services 2004–2014,* 173
stress
  BOSS, 95, 183, 185, 227
  comparative analysis: changing
    workers' accents, 207; emotional
    stress, 'emotional labour', 207;

from interpersonal relations/specific working conditions, 231; from organizational environment, 231; from organizational environment/workplace changes, 232; sources of, 230; from specific working conditions and gender, 232–3
and health/safety, Philippine BPOs, 121–6, 131–2; causes for stress, 122, 123; Health and Safety Committee, 122; health problems, 122–4; physical symptoms of stress, 122; promotional giveaways, 122; psychosocial symptoms of stress, 122–3; rewards and recognition programmes, 122; top causes, interpersonal relations, 122
performance targets and electronic monitoring, and their effects on, 226–33
reason behind high rotation rates, Argentina, 185
recipe for stress-related hazards, 242
stressors: changing workers' accents, 207; emotional stress, 'emotional labour', 207
structural risks, vendors, 6
'sunrise industry', 110
see also Philippines
'sunshine industry', 126
Sutherland Global Survey on BPO, 38, 55, 197, 198
Sykes, 19, 20, 37–8, 54, 170, 184

Tata Consultancy Services, 21, 172
Tate, W.L., 7
Taylor, P., 10, 12, 15, 17–62, 65–70, 82–3, 99, 198, 226–7, 229
Taylorism, 26–7
TCE, *see* transaction cost economics (TCE)
team leaders (TL), 80, 87, 94, 107, 122, 240
technical support eRepresentatives (TSR or eREP), 107
Teixeira, M., 201
TELEBRAS, 147

see also BPO industry in Brazil
Telecommunications Act (1984), UK, 14, 27
telecommunications industry, 9, 13, 27, 149–50, 198
'telecoms auction', 149
see also Brazil
Telecom Service Centres (TSC), 21
telepathology, 157
Teleperformance, 19–20, 34, 54, 170, 184
Telephone operator call centres, 9–10, 32
scarcity of qualified labour, 10
suburban or more rural locations, 10
Teletech, 34, 38, 39, 54, 170, 184
Televist, 39
'tertiarization', 236
theories, resource-based view (RBV) of firm, 4–5
third party/parties, 36, 46–7
MNCs, 65
offshore provider, criteria for engagement with, 7
determining processes to offshore, 6; practical factors and issues, 6; operational and structural risk, 6
provider, 2, 6–9, 12, 33, 42, 79, 149, 206, 209, 213, 218–19, 234, 238–9
Thite, M., 76, 78–9, 92, 94–5
time zone issue, 12
Todd, P.A., 77
Torre, I., 162–95, 201
trade in services, recent trends in Argentina, 165–72
business services offshoring, 168–70
computer and information services exports by destination, 167
cost-based competitive advantage, 165
determinants for offshoring destination selection, 169
factors behind growth in export of activities, 165
global service location index, 169
International Accounts National Direction, 165
other business services exports by destination, 167

trade in services, recent trends in
    Argentina – *continued*
  public policies for services exports,
      172–4; FONSOFT, benefits, 173;
      Law No. 25.856, 173; Law No.
      25.922, 173; Motorola, investment
      in Córdoba, 173–4; provincial SIS
      promotion policies, 173
  services exports, 166
  SIS, 170–2; CESSI, 171; CMMI 5, 172;
      competitive advantages, 170;
      eSCM-SP, 172; potential
      challenges, 171; SIS sector
      statistics in 'late'-entry countries,
      171; MNCs, 172
training, 31, 40, 47, 207, 211–12, 224,
    232, 240–1, 243–4
  Argentina, 162, 188, 192
  Brazil, 153
  call centre training, 243
  Canada, 54
  grants, 29
  India, 54, 69, 78, 79, 86–8, 92, *see also*
      recruitment; types of training
      given to ITES–BPO employees, 79
  Philippines, 109–10, 119, 121–2, 128;
      inadequate training, 128
  voice and accent training, 207
  see also individual countries
transaction cost economics (TCE), 4–6
transformational offshoring, 18
transparent processes, 6
'T-shaped' human resources, 188
  see also working and employment
      conditions, Argentina

UGC, *see* University Grants Commission
    (UGC)
UKs Telecommunications Act (1984),
    14, 27
Union for ITES Professionals (UNITES
    Professional), 62, 98
union formation, India, 95–9
  motivation for employees to form,
      96–7
  perspectives of managers on
      desirability of unions, 97
  reasons for employees wanting/not
      joining unions, 97–8
  UNITES Professional, 62, 98

Union Network International's Call
    Centre Charter, 30
unionization
  Argentina, 143, 174, 176, 178, 186,
      191–2; activity, software and
      information services sector, 191;
      collective bargaining, 179;
      segmented neocorporatism, 176
  Brazil: collective bargaining between
      employers and trade unions, 143
  Canada, 56
  collective agreement, 39–40, 148–9
  collective bargaining, 40, 48–50,
      110–12, 128–9, 132, 143, 174,
      178–9, 186, 191, 240
  India, 62, 68, *see also* union formation,
      India; reasons for not joining
      union, 98
  Philippines: ILO Conventions on
      freedom of association and
      collective bargaining, 110
  United Kingdom, 50
  see also individual countries
United Kingdom
  demographic profile of BPO workforce,
      44–5; attrition, 45; educational
      levels, 45
  employment profile, 43; Contact
      Centre Association, 43
  employment relations, 49–50; trade
      unions, 50
  integration of telephonic and
      communication technologies, 42
  location by region, 43–4; UK's 'call
      centre capital', 43
  mass production call centre, 42
  offshoring, 45–9; back-office
      offshoring, 48; compulsory
      redundancies, 48; cost-cutting and
      profit-maximization, 49;
      dichotomization in call centres,
      47; domestic outsourcers, 46;
      process reengineering, 47; 'remote
      sourcing' strategy, 45;
      unionization, 48
  sectoral breakdown, 44
  trade union, 50
  UK contact centre industry-agent
      positions and employment, 43
  Union Network International, 49

2005 United Nations Conference on
Trade and Development
(UNCTAD), 1
United States
demographic profile of BPO workforce,
35–6; attrition, 35–6; gender
distribution, 35
economic recession/dot.com crash, 32
employment profile, 33–4; outbound
voice services, 34
employment relations, 40; collective
bargaining coverage, 40; CWA, 40;
deregulation of industry, 40
location by region, 34; four regions
(Contact Babel), 34
'noncore' activities, 33
offshoring, 36–40; approaches for
assessing scale of offshoring, 38;
jobs 'lost', 37; KPO, 37; overseas
relocation, 37–8; relocation of
Spanish-speaking services, 36–7;
'right-to-know' legislation, 39;
1990s 'boom', 36
regulations, employment relations:
deregulation of industry, 40
sectoral breakdown, 35; financial
services/retail and distribution/
telecommunications sector, 35
US agent, positions/agents/contact
centres, numbers of, 33
UNITES Professional, *see* Union for ITES
Professionals (UNITES Professional)
University Grants Commission
(UGC), 68
US–EU Safe Harbour Act, 38
US legislation (1996), 27

Valverde, M., 7, 212
Van Den Broek, D., 82, 229
van der Walk, W., 7
van Jaarsveld, D., 53, 54, 56, 201
variables
considered in offshoring decisions,
11–12; BPO locations, 11–12;
cost, 11; skilled or trained
labour, 11
to differentiate call centres, 49
employment related, 186
indicated in wage regression analysis,
115–17

VDUs, *see* visual display units (VDUs)
Venco, S., 12–14, 135–61, 198, 201–6,
208, 215, 220, 223, 227
vendor agreements, 7, 238
detailed contract, 7
loose or task-based contracts, 7
mixed contracts, 7
standard form, 7
voice and accent training, 207
Viasey, S., 211
visual display units (VDUs), 122, 124
voice-over-internet protocol (VOIP), 10
VOIP, *see* voice-over-internet protocol
(VOIP)

Wagar, T., 92
wages
annual wages among BPO and ITO
destination countries, comparison
of, 214–15
Argentina, employment in SIS sector;
high wages, 190
Brazil, *see* labour market, Brazil
India, labour market in; Minimum
Wages Act (1948), 69; Payment of
Wages Act (1936), 69
Philippines, *see also* working and
employment conditions,
Philippines; wages and benefits,
112–13
wage regression analysis, *see* variables
see also salary
Walker, D., 257–8
Wallace, C., 96
Washington Alliance of Technology
Workers (Washtech), 38, 41
WBITSA, *see* West Bengal Information
Technology Services Association
(WBITSA)
weekly hours in BPO industry by gender
and type of RWA, 220
Weekly Rest (Commerce and Offices)
Convention,
1957 (No. 106), ILO, 242
Werle, M.J., 3–4
West Bengal Information Technology
Services Association (WBITSA), 98
WHO, *see* World Health Organization
(WHO)

WHO, four-pronged approach to work
    redesign, 242–3
Willcocks, L.P., 5–7
Williamson, O.E., 4
Wood, S., 45
work card system, Brazil, 142
working and employment conditions,
    Argentina, 174–91
    employment in business services
        export sector, 180–6; availability
        of professionals with skills, 180;
        average workforce in services
        export sector, 182; 'burnout'
        syndrome, 185; high turnover
        rates, 185; knowledge of English
        language, 182; profile of
        employees in the CCC sector,
        184–5; salaries and employment
        in services export sector, 181;
        working conditions, 182–3; 'Y
        generation', 183, 185
    employment in SIS sector, 186–91;
        FOMENI, 188; high wages, 189;
        'Invest in Yourself', 188; 'IT
        Generation', 188; labour shortage,
        186; lack of interest in IT field,
        187; 'predatory' recruiting
        practices, 190; profile of people,
        189; scholarships, 188; SIS labour
        demand, 186; trade union activity,
        191; 'T-shaped' human resources,
        188; worker turnover, 190;
        working conditions, 189
    labour legislation, 178–9; for collective
        bargaining., 178; collective labour
        law, 178; Contract of Employment
        Law, 'professional statute', 178–9;
        fixed-term, seasonal and
        work-team employment contracts,
        178; individual labour law, 178;
        for working accidents, 178
    labour market, 174–8; characteristics,
        1990s to early 2000s, 175;
        collective bargaining, 174;
        employment structure, 177; Heads
        of Household programme, 175;
        informality, 175–6;
        inward-looking development
        strategy, 174; 'job insecurity', 176;
        Program for Unemployed Male

    and Female Heads of Households,
    175; pro-labour policies, 175;
    'segmented neocorporatism', 176;
    socio-economic crisis, mid-1970s,
    175; State's intervention, 174
working and employment conditions,
    Brazil
    business environment for outsourcing,
        137–9
    call centres/customer service centres,
        150–9, *see also* call centres
    'coop' system in Brazil, 202
    customer service centres/call centres,
        conditions in, 152–6
    financial services industry, 147–9
    formal employment, 142
    'happy days', *see* Brazil
    'health risk control', Brazil, 157
    hiring workers through 'consultancy'
        firms, 202
    informal employment, 142
    labour laws, 143–5, *see also* Labour
        laws, comparative analysis
    labour market, 140–2, *see also* labour
        market, Brazil
    legislation, *see* legislation
    'new economy' and 'customer culture',
        148
    overall employment situation,
        140–1
    salary, *see* Brazil; salary
    trade union, *see* unionization
    training, 153
    unemployment and issue of
        informality in employment,
        142
    wages, *see* wages
    work card method, 142
    working hours, *see* hours of work
working and employment conditions,
    India
    attrition, 95–6, *see also* attrition
    24/7 capability and overnight
        turnaround time, 61
    discipline; dismissal, 87–9; manager's
        perspectives on disciplinary
        actions used, 88
    extended work hours, 82
    grievance redressal, 93–4
    health problems, 90

human resources practices, 92–5, *see also* human resource (HR)
job-related discretion, 82–3
labour market, *see* labour market, India
legislation, *see* legislation
odd working hours, 89
performance, 84–7
'push' factors/'pull' factors, 60
recommendations, 100–1
recruitment, *see* recruitment
reverse shoring, 21
safety, 93, 97
salary, *see* salary
satisfaction with working conditions, 93
trade union, *see* India; Unionization
training, *see* training
wages, *see* wages
work-life balance, *see* work-life balance, India
work systems, 80–90, *see also* work systems, Indian ITES-BPO
working and employment conditions, Philippines, 112–30
  attrition and job satisfaction, 126–8; Code of Ethics to prevent poaching, 128; reasons for leaving previous BPO, 127; top reasons for attrition, 126
  employee voice and industrial relations, 128–30; labour laws, 129–30; 'proactive attitude' of HR managers, 129; sources of worry, 128
  pay differentials by education/work experience, 114–15; college degree matters for pay, 114; simple regression analysis, 115; wage regression analysis, 115
  pay differentials by gender, 113–14; pay differentials with their foreign counterparts, 114; productivity incentive scheme, 114; typical monthly pay, 113
  stress, health and safety, 121–6; causes for stress, 122, 123; Health and Safety Committee, 122; health problems, 122–4, 123–4; physical symptoms of stress, 122; promotional giveaways, 122;

psychosocial symptoms of stress, 122, 123; rewards and recognition programmes, 122; top causes, interpersonal relations, 122
  wage regression results, 115–17; most common incentives, 116; nonmonetary incentives, 116; reason for attractiveness, 116
  wages and benefits, 112–13; average monthly pay, 112
  working hours and shift work, 117–19; change, work schedule, 118; clipping about night shift, 118–19; 'flexitime', 117
  work intensity, autonomy and performance, 119–21; 'customer care specialists', 119; degree of freedom, 120; employee autonomy, 121; inbound or outbound calls, 119; measures of performance outcomes, 120; operational performance, 121; technical innovation, 121
  see also Philippines
work-life balance, India
  experience of disruption of non-work due to work, 90
  health problems, 90
  odd working hours, 89
Workmen's Compensation Act (1923), 69
workplace environment in BPO industry, 205–8
  abusive management practices, 207
  back-office and call centre: evaluations, 206; intensive monitoring, 206; night work, 207; rest breaks, 206
  lousy boss syndrome, 207
  managerial skills, lack of, 208
  stressors: changing workers' accents, 207; emotional stress, 'emotional labour', 207
work schedules in BPO industry by gender and type of RWA, 221
work systems, Indian ITES-BPO, 80–90
  discipline, 87–9; dismissal, 87–9; manager's perspectives on disciplinary actions used, 88

work systems, Indian
ITES-BPO – *continued*
job-related discretion, 82–3;
factory-like division of labour, 82;
mass service/engineering model,
82; perspectives of employees and
managers, 83
monitoring and surveillance, 83–4;
means used/opinions, 84;
perspectives of employee and
managers on, 85
performance, 84–7; manager's
perspectives on career
advancement/incentives,
86–7; performance-based
data, 86
work time, 80–2; extended work
hours, 82; overtime rates, 81;
shifts, 80
World Health Organization (WHO),
242
World Information Technology and
Services Alliance (WITSA), 147

'Y generation', 183, 185
Young Professionals Collective
(YPC), 98–9